Lyrical Ballads

Longman Annotated Texts

General Editors:

Charlotte Brewer, Hertford College, Oxford
H.R. Woudhuysen, University College London
Daniel Karlin, University College London

Published Titles:

Michael Mason, *Lyrical Ballads*

Lyrical Ballads

Edited by
Michael Mason

LONGMAN
London and New York

1004528114

Addison Wesley Longman Limited
Edinburgh Gate, Harlow,
Essex CM20 2JE, England
and Associated Companies throughout the world.

Published in the United States of America
by Addison Wesley Longman Publishing, New York

First published 1992
Second impression 1996   1004761140X

British Library Cataloguing-in-Publication Data
Mason, Michael
   Lyrical ballads. – (Longman annotated texts)
   I. Title II. Series
   821

   ISBN 0–582–03302–0
   ISBN 0–582–03303–9 pbk

Library of Congress Cataloging-in-Publication Data
Wordsworth, William, 1770–1850.
   Lyrical ballads / [Wordsworth and Coleridge : edited by] Michael
   Mason.
       p.   cm. —— (Longman annotated texts)
   Includes bibliographical references and index.
   ISBN 0–582–03302–0. —— ISBN 0–582–03303–9 (pbk.)
   I. Coleridge, Samuel Taylor, 1772–1834. II. Mason, Michael, 1941–
   III. Title. IV. Series.
PR5869.L9   1992
821′.7—dc20
                                                      91–3723
                                                        CIP

Data capture by 8FF in 10/11pt Ehrhardt

Transferred to digital print on demand 2001

Printed and bound by Great Britain by Antony Rowe Ltd, Eastbourne

Contents

Arrangements and classifications

Authors' later comment

(arranged alphabetically by title of poem)

Sources

1798 text of 'The Ancient Mariner'

Acknowledgements

I am greatly indebted to Mrs Susan Major, who compiled a basic list of references for me and made many valuable suggestions for the footnotes. Without her help this edition would have been a less good book, and longer in the making.

General Introduction

Lyrical Ballads 1798 to 1805

Lyrical Ballads (*LB*) is a famous work, but not a uniquely famous one. However, it is associated with a date, 1798, which could claim to be uniquely famous, for this is probably the best known publication date in the history of English literature. *LB* has become renowned as an event as well as a text, because it is perceived to be a crucially innovative work from a crucially innovative period of our literature. So the year in which the first edition of the collection came before the public, 1798 – with its suggestive resemblance to the dominating political date of the era, 1789 – has very naturally been given a special status. It is unfortunate that this way of commemorating the novelty of *LB* happens not really to suit the facts. *LB* was not a single phenomenon but a sequence of four editions spread over seven years; its appearance in English literature was not a historical moment but a sequence of moments – 1798, 1800, 1802, 1805.

The collection was first conceived by Coleridge and Wordsworth in the spring of 1798, when Coleridge was twenty-five and Wordsworth just twenty-eight. The two men had been living near each other physically, in Somerset, and in a remarkable personal, artistic and intellectual intimacy for almost a year. Various joint writing and publishing enterprises were attempted by them in this period, but *LB* was the one that came to fruition. It consisted of a few pieces by Coleridge, generally dating from the preceding year (of which one, 'The Ancient Mariner', was in its outlines a joint production), and of poems by Wordsworth that were for the most part very recent. The volume was published by a Bristol bookseller, Joseph Cottle, in October, though within a matter of days he sold his rights and the almost 500 unsold copies to a London firm, J. & A. Arch, which thereafter became the publisher of the first *LB*.

The book retailed at five shillings and did well critically; it received ten reviews, of which only three were hostile in their

general verdict. Where the reviewers did express reservations or
downright dislike, their target was above all 'The Ancient Mariner'.
By contrast, the more ballad-like of Wordsworth's contributions –
'The Idiot Boy' and so forth – were generally well received. The
other poems in the collection, when they were mentioned, were
almost always praised.

In the course of 1800 (when the poets were settled near each
other again in the Lake District, though their intimacy now began
slowly to diminish) a new two-volume edition was planned and the
project sold to Longman, who were to publish this and the
subsequent editions of *LB*. In the end, the entire contents of the
new volume of 1800 were furnished by Wordsworth (Coleridge's
only new contribution being 'Love', which replaced Wordsworth's
'The Convict' in the first volume). The new edition, actually
published in January 1801, was priced at ten shillings; it gathered
only a handful of new reviews but sold quickly. There was room for
a further edition, and Wordsworth worked over the whole collection
to produce the version of 1802, making changes that were extensive
even if generally minor. One of Coleridge's pieces from the first
edition, 'The Dungeon', was now dropped, as was a Wordsworth
item which had been printed in 1800, 'A Character'.

Almost immediately, the most eye-catching critical discussion the
collection had yet received appeared in the newly established
Edinburgh Review in October 1802. It was only obliquely a review of
the latest edition of *LB*, since its author, Francis Jeffrey, was
reviewing Robert Southey's *Thalaba* and cited the collection as a
further example of the pernicious work of the 'Lake School of
Poetry' (Jeffrey's coinage) to which Southey was alleged to belong.
And Jeffrey's lively if facile abuse was really directed at what was by
now an obsolete book, the *LB* of 1798. He made great play with a
phrase about the idiom of the collection, which had not appeared in
print since the Advertisement to that edition ('the language of
conversation in the middle and lower classes of society'), and it is
perhaps to Jeffrey's influence that we can attribute the subsequent
tendency of commentators to conflate this formula with the
Preface's remarks on 'low and rustic' language (see p. 60).

The *Edinburgh Review*'s attack, vehement and subsequently
notorious though it was, does not seem to have disconcerted
Wordsworth, who prepared a final edition of *LB*, again carefully but
not radically revised, for publication in 1805. By this time Coleridge
had left the Lake District. Though Wordsworth was composing new
poetry in these years, the successive editions of *LB* were his only
books of published verse. They tended to differ more from each
other than is normal in successive publishings of collections of verse
under one title, but the effect should not be exaggerated. Basically,

there are two versions of *LB*. There is the first edition of 1798, and there is the greatly enlarged version of this which appeared, with some variation, in the next three editions.

This major divide does bear importantly on the question of the innovativeness of the collection. The most obvious point to make is that the Preface to *LB*, with its famous claims about the idiom, subject matter and function of poetry, did not appear until 1800 (and it was significantly expanded in 1802, and supplemented by an appendix on poetic diction). So, to the extent that *LB* was the vehicle of an explicit new literary–aesthetic programme, 1800 should evidently be celebrated rather than 1798.

It is much harder to be cut and dried about the two versions of the text proper – that is, the poems. The most notorious, to modern taste, of Wordsworth's contributions to *LB* – namely 'The Thorn', 'Goody Blake and Harry Gill', 'Simon Lee' and 'The Idiot Boy' – all appeared in 1798. But modern notoriety should not be confused with historical novelty. Indeed, there are certain respects in which these particular poems seem to have been orthodox in their day, or at least to have resembled a familiar type of contemporary verse (and they were on the whole liked by the reviewers). Moreover, if *LB* really is the momentous text it is taken to be, the contributions of one of its authors cannot all be as enduringly disputed in quality as these four poems have been. The fact is that the uncontroversially great Wordsworth items in *LB*, those poems which are universally recognized to possess an extraordinary quality, almost all appear for the first time in 1800: perhaps only 'Tintern Abbey' from the collection of 1798 has been admired as unreservedly as the Lucy and Matthew poems, the blank verse fragments 'There was a Boy ...' and 'Nutting', and the narrative poems 'Ruth' and 'Michael'. And these poems were utterly novel in their day because they were profoundly idiosyncratic. One could fairly apply to all of them what Coleridge said of ll. 24–5 of 'There was a Boy ...': 'had I met these lines running wild in the deserts of Arabia, I should have instantly screamed out "Wordsworth!" ' (Griggs 1956: 453).

To complicate matters, the first edition of *LB* contained the great Coleridge poem of the collection, 'The Ancient Mariner'. There are readers for whom this fact is sufficient to make 1798 a resonant date – though it may be doubted if in practice the text they have come to admire is usually that of the first edition, with its abundant archaisms of diction and spelling (it is reproduced as an appendix to this edition). All in all, 1798 deserves its celebrity only by a kind of courtesy. One will not find anything significant in the first edition of *LB* which is not retained and perhaps improved in 1800 and later, augmented by Wordsworth's remarkable prose and verse additions. And while the 1798 *LB* has astonishing novelties in it (most

evidently in 'The Ancient Mariner' and the quatrain poems by
Wordsworth on nature subjects and childhood), the version of 1800
is a kind of literary revolution, a moment of discontinuity in English
literary culture.

In the present edition the final variant of this form of the
collection, that of 1805, is used. There was certainly a case for
using the seminal 1800 text itself, even though this would have
meant omitting a major part of the Preface and the appendix on
diction (which is more dispensable). But 1805 has the claim that it
is Wordsworth's and Coleridge's last word on these poems as a
group – not in the sense that it offers a definitive judgement on the
items (one should not fall into the trap of supposing that a poet's
revision to an earlier text necessarily implies a rejection of that text),
but in the sense that the potential of the project formed in the
spring of 1798 was here explored by its creators for the last time.

The Wordsworth–Coleridge collaboration

The 1798 edition of *LB* contained about three thousand lines of
verse, and something approaching a third of this material was by
Coleridge. 'The Ancient Mariner' was not only almost half as long
again as any other poem in the collection, it had pride of place at
the beginning of the volume (followed by another Coleridge item,
'The Foster-mother's Tale', and – after Wordsworth's 'Yew-tree
Lines' – yet another, 'The Nightingale'). In 1800, in what is
essentially the arrangement of the present edition, things were
radically different. The new Volume II was somewhat longer than
the old single-volume edition, and consisted entirely of poems by
Wordsworth, so that Coleridge's contribution now made up only
about a seventh of the collection. 'The Ancient Mariner' was still a
good deal longer than any other piece, but along with the other
Coleridge poems it had lost pole position.

An even greater change in the nature of the two poets'
collaboration is signalled on the title page of 1800. Wordsworth's
name appears as the author of the collection (with the fact of a
different authorship for four of the poems then being dealt with
early in the Preface, and without any mention of Coleridge by
name, though the inclusion of 'Love' would have made his identity
apparent to the well-informed). *LB* in 1798 had been an anonymous
production in which there was a distinct effort to suggest that only
one hand was at work. In the Advertisement 'the author' was
mentioned several times, and this imaginary personage was
associated with individual items by both poets, 'Goody Blake and
Harry Gill' and 'The Ancient Mariner'. We know that Wordsworth
would not have minded if Coleridge had been supposed to be this

single anonymous author of the poems; he wrote to Coleridge in 1799 that such an assumption would be 'the best thing that can befall them' (De Selincourt and Shaver 1967: 281). In some quarters just this assumption was made, because Coleridge was 'confidently' rumoured to be the author of 'The Ancient Mariner' (see *British Critic* XIV, 1799, p. 365 and XVII, 1801, p. 125).

So different is *LB* 1800 that the question of what Coleridge and Wordsworth planned in 1798 is not really relevant here. Readers interested in this topic should be aware, however, that the evidence is all rather late – in the form of reminiscences – and somewhat contradictory. How did the two men see their collaboration on the enlarged edition two years later? Wordsworth had become by far the dominant party in terms of visible contribution to the collection, but it is known that Coleridge was very active in the arrangements for printing, publishing and promoting it. Also, until late in the day there were plans to include substantial additional work by Coleridge, which somehow foundered. Wordsworth is on record as believing that 'The Ancient Mariner' had damaged the sales of the 1798 *LB*, and as wishing to replace it with other poems in the event of a new edition (De Selincourt and Shaver 1967: 264). The 1800 text did contain a note by Wordsworth on 'The Ancient Mariner' (see pp. 39–40) which gives rather more space to its 'great defects' than to its 'several merits'. All this has led commentators to doubt the veracity of Wordsworth's claim here (which is actually the point of the note) that Coleridge was 'very desirous that it should be suppressed' but that he, Wordsworth, had urged its re-publication. In general the consensus about Wordsworth's approach to the partnership in 1800 is probably that he behaved high-handedly, with little responsiveness to Coleridge's feelings and hard work, or to the merits of his poetry.

On the other hand, it is not conceivable that Wordsworth could have printed a note saying that Coleridge wanted to withdraw 'The Ancient Mariner' if this had not been true (and it seems likely that Coleridge saw the text of the note before it went to the printer; Hale White 1897: 25). Wordsworth's sense that the poem had harmed sales in 1798 is supported by – and may simply be derived from – the reviews, which complained more about this item than any other. To have this extremely long piece, with its idiosyncratic archaic idiom (Wordsworth had gathered that the 'old words' had contributed to its unpopularity), at the masthead of the collection could naturally have troubled a co-author. The less archaic version of 1800, in a different place in the collection and looming less large, would have been a very different proposition.

Wordsworth says in his 1800 note that Coleridge, too, had been dismayed by the reviews (again, this can hardly be a fabrication) and was conscious of 'defects' in 'The Ancient Mariner'. There is the plain fact in support of Wordsworth's account that Coleridge did revise the diction of the poem for its second appearance; and at about this time he was at pains to reassure the editor to whom he had submitted another ballad narrative that it was virtually devoid of archaisms (see Coleridge's letter on 'Love', pp. 36–7). In Wordsworth's note, his own list of shortcomings in 'The Ancient Mariner' springs from the question of Coleridge's dissatisfaction, and readers must decide for themselves whether these constitute curmudgeonly resistance to a literary masterpiece or a sensible series of points. 'The Ancient Mariner' *is* a poem which leaves some people cold, though this is heresy to its admirers.

As to the other planned Coleridge contributions of 1800, there is no evidence that these came to naught because Wordsworth shouldered them out. The main case in point is 'Christabel', which Coleridge was working hard on, and hoping to include, until the last moment. Coleridge said (with no rancour) that the main ground for its exclusion was its unsuitability in a collection of poems which was investigating the emotional potential of the everyday, of the 'incidents of common life' (Griggs 1956: 631). In view of the character of 'The Ancient Mariner' this may sound like a rationalization, but it is also known that there was talk of Coleridge providing some 'Poems on the Naming of Places', perhaps as a more 'common life' alternative to 'Christabel' (Wordsworth actually announced them to the printer in October 1800). Recurrent in this history is the brute fact of Coleridge's failure to perform. 'Christabel' was never finished, so Wordsworth cannot be blamed for its omission from the 1800 *LB* unless we imagine that he discouraged Coleridge in his work on it – thus resembling that suspect individual, the 'person from Porlock'. In fact, in a sentence in the Preface which had to be deleted once 'Christabel' was dropped, Wordsworth wrote that he would not have 'ventured to present a second volume to the public' without this 'long and beautiful poem' (Owen and Smyser 1974: I, 118). Of Coleridge's contribution to the 'Poems on the Naming of Places' there is no trace. Coleridge went on the walk described in the fourth of these and recorded its climactic moment in his notebook (Coburn 1957: I, 761), but Wordsworth wrote the poem.

Wordsworth was certainly 'ascendant' in *LB* of 1800 and later (to use the expression of his biographer Stephen Gill), but it does seem that he would have been happy for Coleridge to have had a bigger share in its poetic contents than he achieved. Also, to judge by the fact that he advanced £30 of the £80 he received from Longman in 1801 to a man whose written contributions – only one of them new – amounted to a seventh of the text (De Selincourt and Shaver

1967: 321), Wordsworth was grateful for the hard work and support which had come from Coleridge on the 1800 edition. An unbiased observer might even say that this generous division of the proceeds betokened an affectionate feeling inconsistent with a harsh interpretation of Wordsworth's attitude to 'The Ancient Mariner', for instance. There is no evidence that Coleridge was dissatisfied with Wordsworth's handling of the 1800 edition. All the protests have come from students of Coleridge – and, less defensibly, from students of Wordsworth – who have sought out grounds for offence where none seems to have been felt by the supposedly injured party.

Matters are different where the Preface to *LB* is concerned, however. Here the collaboration of the two men was the subject of not entirely harmonious, or consistent, comment on both sides. In this edition, as is conventional, Wordsworth is generally treated as the author of the first statement of literary–aesthetic intent attached to *LB*, the Advertisement of 1798. In fact, there is no particular reason other than its resemblance to the Preface of 1800 to rule out the possibility that Coleridge was at least the co-author of this document. One of its more memorable phrases, that about the 'gaudiness' of modern literary diction, is echoed both in the letter Coleridge composed for Wilberforce in 1800 (see pp. 45–6) and in *Biographia Literaria*.

The letter to Wilberforce, drafted by Coleridge but sent over Wordsworth's signature with a complimentary copy of the 1800 *LB*, is an intriguing piece of evidence about Coleridge's attitudes at this date. It does not repeat the Preface's high valuation of 'low and rustic life' (and, perhaps, of low and rustic language as a source of poetic idiom) that Coleridge was to attack at length in *Biographia Literaria*, but it does say that poetry should be intelligible to the 'lower classes'. It also implies a standard for poetic idiom which is directly repudiated in *Biographia Literaria*, that of 'the common conversational language of our countrymen' (and its author had contributed a poem to the collection, 'The Nightingale', which he subtitled 'A Conversational Poem'). At least, Coleridge tells Wilberforce that he deplores the 'aversion' to this idiom to be detected in modern writers, while in *Biographia* he argues that even prose 'differs, and ought to differ, from the language of conversation'.

It may be urged that Coleridge was purporting to be Wordsworth in the Wilberforce letter, and hence adopting his views. But even if this were the case (despite Coleridge's saying that this and the Fox letter contained 'a good view of our notions and motives, poetical and political'; Griggs 1956: 665), Coleridge's ability to parrot Wordsworth would still add to the evidence that he was more in agreement with the doctrines of the Preface at the time than he

later acknowledged. For from 1802 onwards, in recording his
disagreement with Wordsworth on these ideas, Coleridge said that
he had not realized what Wordsworth's position amounted to. In
fact this was always an awkward claim: 'we begin to suspect, that
there is, somewhere or other, a *radical* difference in our opinions'
writes Coleridge famously in 1802 – but he is talking here of his
conviction that 'poetry justifies ... some new combinations of
language, and *commands* the omission of many others allowable in
other compositions' (Griggs 1956: 812). How could Coleridge
possibly have failed to see that this is not Wordsworth's point of
view? There was no hidden 'radical difference' to be 'suspected'
and teased out here, but plain disagreement with one of the most
openly stated principles of the Preface, that there is no essential
difference between the language of poetry and the language of
prose.

Matters are made worse by the plentiful evidence of Coleridge's
active participation in the formulation of the Preface's ideas (while
his handwriting appears at least once on the original manuscript;
Hale White 1897: 18–20). Wordsworth said in later life (and hinted
in the Preface itself) that this document was composed in response
to Coleridge's urgings, and in the early planning Coleridge was
actually to have written it. The latter called the Preface, at the time,
an 'invaluable' expression of 'our joint opinions on poetry' and 'half
a child of my own brain'. It arose, Coleridge said, 'out of
conversations, so frequent, that with few exceptions we could
scarcely either of us perhaps positively say, which first started any
particular thought' (and he did, apparently, start to write it, as
planned) (Griggs 1956: 668, 811, 830). If true, all this is fatal to
Coleridge's claim that he recognized only later that he had
disagreed with Wordsworth on the prose–poetry distinction, on
colloquialism in poetic diction, and on the value of rustic life.

Coleridge's diary in the summer of 1800 does contain just one
phrase which crops up also in the Preface: 'poetry ... recalling of
passion in tranquillity'. Is this isolated example a sign that the
interchange of ideas on the Preface was rather sporadic, or is it the
tip of an iceberg of collaboration? Did Coleridge have less to do
with the Preface than he said, or did he undergo a change of
attitude which he sought to disguise? The truth probably lies
between the two. Out of loyalty to Wordsworth, Coleridge could
have exaggerated his involvement with his aesthetic doctrines; while
he could also have liked the anti-elitist feeling of the view that
poetry should resemble bourgeois and even plebeian conversational
usage. Chapters 14 and 17–20 of *Biographia Literaria* are often
applauded as an attack on Wordsworth's Preface; but Coleridge's
admirers should be aware that he had not always subscribed to the

views put here, and around 1800 might have wished to repudiate some of them.

Lyrical Ballads generically considered

The 1805 title, *Lyrical Ballads with Pastoral and other Poems*, has an air of precision, of a wish to specify the contents of the collection with some thoroughness. These are not ballads but 'lyrical' ballads; and there are other kinds of poem also, some of which are 'pastoral'. Versions of the title before 1802 are less precise only by virtue of the omission of this last qualification: *Lyrical Ballads with other Poems* (1800), *Lyrical Ballads with a few other Poems* (1798). In Wordsworth's day writers who favoured a relatively simple style of verse quite often used the word 'ballad' in their titles, but the scholar Robert Mayo, who has traced the affinities between *LB* and this kind of poetry more fully than anyone else, has not found a case where the word appears in the title of a whole collection of poems. 'Ballad' would have had many connotations. As well as the expected ones (narrative mode, simple stanzaic form, possible resemblance to traditional models), an implication of the plebeian may have come more readily into a reader's mind in the 1790s than we would guess: the *Encyclopaedia Britannica* of 1797 defined the ballad as a form 'adapted to the capacity of the lower class of people'.

The term 'lyrical' was probably designed to indicate that some of the formal conventions associated with the ballad had been abandoned or modified. One obvious implication of the term is that these poems would depend less on narrative interest than the ordinary ballad; another is that the versification would not be truly ballad-like. Only one poem of substance in *LB* can be said to have a central, serious narrative interest, namely 'The Ancient Mariner'. This is also the only poem in the collection to use the classic ballad verse, the quatrain of alternating three- and four-stress lines, only two of which rhyme. These facts strongly suggest that the qualifying epithet 'lyrical' was intended to characterize Wordsworth's contributions rather than those of Coleridge. Perhaps Wordsworth devised it. We know that he was under some pressure to change the title in 1800 to avoid a resemblance to the recently published *Lyrical Tales* by the poet Mrs Robinson. Among his reasons for persisting with it may have been a feeling that the word 'lyrical' could not be dispensed with.

The only straightforwardly narrative poem in *LB* apart from 'The Ancient Mariner' is a slight contribution by Wordsworth, 'Ellen Irwin'. Paradoxically, the adoption of a narrative mode here seems to be another token of Wordsworth's wish to distance himself from pure ballad, for in this instance he had a model, a traditional

Scottish ballad (or, rather, its several versions), which was couched
in dramatic rather than narrative form (see the headnote to 'Ellen
Irwin', p. 240). Here the late eighteenth- or early nineteenth-
century poet was encountering one of the paradoxes in the genre,
for traditional ballad had seldom been head-on in its approach to
narrative subjects and was sometimes extremely oblique, while more
recent literary ballads were much more inclined to adopt a simple
narrative approach. Wordsworth altered the mode of the modern
literary ballads of Gottfried Bürger in 'The Idiot Boy' and 'Hart-
leap Well' by introducing narrational, thematic and imagistic
elements which put narrative excitement at a remove, even hold it
up for inspection (and the immediately noticeable pentameters of
the latter poem should stop the reader going up the ballad trail at all
in this instance). But he was forced in the opposite direction by the
precedent of the authentic Scottish ballad, 'Fair Helen'. This is
more than speculation, for Wordsworth himself drew Isabella
Fenwick's attention to certain other devices he adopted in 'Ellen
Irwin' in order to 'preclude all comparison' with the poems in
'simple ballad strain' about Ellen of Kirkonnel:

> accordingly, I chose a construction of stanza quite new in our language;
> in fact, the same as that of Bürger's *Leonora*, except that the first and
> third lines do not, in my stanzas, rhyme. At the outset I threw out a
> classical image to prepare the reader for the style in which I meant to
> treat the story.

He touches here on two questions of form which are important for
the collection generally: versification, and the use of classical
models.

Wordsworth was a fertile, adventurous and even playful experi-
menter with metre and rhyme in his lyrics. This he never ceased to
be, in the sense that novel and complicated stanzaic forms crop up
sporadically until the very end of his career (see, for example, the
eleven-line verses of 'The Cuckoo-clock' of 1845), but his great
period of lyrical experiment was 1802–6, and the results are in the
collected *Poems* of 1807. *LB* is a kind of rehearsal, technically, for
this remarkable group of poems, with fewer experiments propor-
tionally, and with the poet's freedom in experiment controlled
significantly, it seems, by the thought that this was in some sense a
collection of ballads (though even the 'rudest' poems, like 'Goody
Blake and Harry Gill', were required to exhibit a degree of
technical elaboration). The stanza of 'Ellen Irwin' (xAxABBCC) is
exactly representative, in fact, of one tendency in Wordsworth's
formal explorations in *LB*. He has taken an only superficially
complicated stanza – Bürger's mechanically assembled quatrain
and two couplets – and made it more interesting as a hybrid of

rhymed and unrhymed lines, but also in the process turned the first four lines into the classic ballad stanza of 'The Ancient Mariner', while the whole effect continues to fall into fairly short units.

In the 1807 lyrics, and subsequently, Wordsworth shows a considerable interest in forms which Keats would have called 'more interwoven' – in which a rhyme will run over as many as eight lines – but he seldom experiments with mixtures of rhyme and blank verse. In *LB*, by contrast, his inventions do not involve long-sustained patterns of rhyme, but they do tend to be hybrids. Well over half the stanzaic poems in the collection can be called experimental, and about a third of these experiments use unrhymed lines. Once again, the effect is perhaps always to some extent relatable to the classic ballad stanza. Not only in 'Ellen Irwin' does the latter crop up intact but also – at the other end of the stanza – in 'Simon Lee' and (more or less intact) inside the stanza of 'The Last of the Flock'. Wordsworth's comic stanza in 'The Idiot Boy' and 'Andrew Jones' (he used it again for 'Peter Bell') is really the hybrid most tenuously connected with ballad, though obviously these poems are ballad-like to the eye, on the page. The elaborate hybrid stanza of 'The Thorn' (deployed also in 'The Idle Shepherd-Boys' and modulated in the 'Danish boy' fragment) is doubly if not trebly interesting because of the prominence of this poem in the whole collection and the absurd canard about Wordsworth's versification which derives from ll. 33–4 quoted in isolation. The pattern of rhymes is xAxABCDDCEE; lines 4 and 9 have only three stresses. The whole complex result can be seen as opening with a close approximation to the classic ballad stanza, followed by Wordsworth's 'Idiot Boy' stanza (though with the short last line giving a more balladic effect), followed by a rounding-off couplet.

So 'Simon Lee', 'The Last of the Flock' and 'The Thorn' are indeed ballads made 'lyrical' by the freedom of their versification. Another dozen or so of the poems have unusual rhyme schemes which sometimes involve short ballad-like units (see the opening to the stanza in 'The Waterfall and the Eglantine' and 'The Oak and the Broom'), but on other occasions are ballad-like only in scale – and can anticipate Wordsworth's later experiments (the beautiful six-line tail-rhyme stanza of 'Ruth' and other poems has many descendants; see O'Donnell 1989: 127–30). A further dozen are in blank verse, and here we definitely leave the domain of ballad-related writing in the collection.

These are among the 'other' poems in *LB*, and from 1802 some of these were identified as 'pastoral' on the title page. The term was not making its first appearance in the collection; in their individual titles two items had been labelled 'a pastoral poem' ('The Brothers' and 'Michael') and another three 'a pastoral' ('The Oak and the Broom', 'The Idle Shepherd-Boys' and 'The Pet-Lamb'). The second term seems to refer more to matters of form than the first (though 'Michael' does have links with Georgic poetry). 'The Oak and the Broom' and 'The Pet-Lamb' involve poetic utterance by shepherd figures, something in the manner of the lyrical perform-ances that occur in Greek and Latin pastoral verse, and 'The Idle Shepherd-Boys' distinctly recalls the poetry of Theocritus in its festive, quarrelling shepherd lads and their mishap with a lamb. There is one poem which is more unmistakably eclogue-like than any of these – 'The Fountain' – but, curiously, it does not mention its ancestry in the title.

Classical pastoralism evidently plays a rather complicated role in *LB*. When most straightforwardly invoked, by Wordsworth's term 'pastoral' as part of a poem's title, the context is a group of light-hearted and insubstantial poems. On the other hand, the 'pastoral poems' – 'The Brothers' and 'Michael' – are the most solemn and poignant of all the long Wordsworthian items in the collection. And the clearly eclogue-derived 'The Fountain' is not only a demanding poem but also written in a stanza which is actually the closest Wordsworth comes to the traditional ballad stanza of 'The Ancient Mariner'. As in the case of the classical motif that Wordsworth deliberately inserted in 'Ellen Irwin' to 'preclude all comparison' with authentic ballad, Greek and Latin pastoralism can play its part in the process of detaching the stanzaic poems in *LB* from ballads proper. The figure of Ellen, as beautiful 'as a Grecian maid / Adorned with wreaths of myrtle' and provoking intense jealousy in a rejected lover, comes as much from the eclogue as from any classical genre but, again, an explicitly pastoral mode is being deployed in a rather unserious context. The limited function Wordsworth allows classical pastoralism in *LB* may seem surprising in view of his known belief that it was more applicable to modern humanity than other ancient genres, this being in itself a proof of his cherished conviction that rural manners were durable: 'read Theocritus in Ayrshire or Merionethshire and you will find perpetual occasions to recollect what you see daily in Ayrshire or Merionethshire' (De Selincourt and Shaver 1967: 255). But this may be exactly the point; if fourth-century BC Sicily and eighteenth-century Wales and Scotland are really so similar, nothing needs to be borrowed from Theocritus in describing them.

Wordsworth's classicism, which was considerable, is generally not on display in *LB*. Both 'Tintern Abbey' and ' 'Tis said, that some have died for love . . .', for instance, are indebted to the classical ode in their form, but in a completely unobtrusive way. This, together with the absence of any effort to imitate traditional ballad in Coleridge's manner, is surely an aspect of Wordsworth's refusal to give his poetry an extra charge by importing elements that readers would recognize as conventional adjuncts of poetic excitement – a refusal so insisted on in the Preface. For Wordsworth, if the best representation of his subject that a poet could achieve with his own verbal resources did not stir the reader, there was no point in drawing on those of other men; this was to offer a spurious substitute means of excitement. The plainness of idiom Wordsworth announced as his goal in the Preface has several controversial aspects. How original was it? What does it amount to, especially in respect of its social register? How consistently is it employed?

Wordsworth himself mentions in the Preface that 'some of my contemporaries' have tried using touches of 'triviality and meanness, both of thought and language' in their poems, and though he is keen to distance himself from the first kind of deficiency – meagreness of thought – he seems to accept that there is some common ground between him and these contemporaries as far as language is concerned. The problem is to know how close the affinity of style is imagined to be. Unfortunately the fellow poets Wordsworth has in mind here cannot be identified with confidence. Robert Mayo, many years ago, showed the existence of a contemporary school of poetry which espoused simple diction and versification; its productions were outweighed by the large number of poems in a more old-fashioned, literary idiom but still constituted a distinct presence in the periodicals and verse collections of the day. Mayo tended to conclude that the main difference between some, at least, of these poems and *LB* was one of literary quality rather than of style. (He came to an equivalent view about the overlap of subject matter, for these poets shared with Wordsworth an interest in destitute and outcast figures.)

This is in the last resort an imponderable topic; judgements about relative simplicity of style must be somewhat intuitive, and even if they could be made with certainty it is not clear how many poems identical in style to *LB* (and which of *LB*?) would need to be brought in evidence to disprove the hypothesis of Wordsworth's originality. Critics have tended to concentrate on the rhymed poems of 1798 in discussing this question, but Charles James Fox, thanking Wordsworth for his complimentary copy of *LB* 1800, confessed that he was 'no great friend to blank verse for subjects which are to be treated of with simplicity' (Moorman 1957: 505). It may be that the simplicity of idiom of the unrhymed poems was an especially novel effect. Mayo was anyway rather more interested in the thematic aspect of the topic, and does not offer actual quotation from contemporary verse in support of the contention that Wordsworth's simple style was in tune with a current fashion. A recent critic, Heather Glen, has examined the material with stylistic questions more in mind, and offers the following as a parallel to Wordsworth's 'Lines Written in Early Spring' (Glen 1983: 38–9):

> Hark! catch you not their warbling wild,
> That softly flows the leafs among?
> Now loudly shrill – now sweetly mild,
> The descant of their thrilling song.
>
> The earliest primrose of the year,
> Beneath delights its flowers to spread;
> The clustering harebell lingers near
> The cowslip's dew-bespangled bed.
>
> And while the western gales allay
> The fervour of the noontide heat,
> They whisper where retired from day,
> The violet scents her low retreat.
>
> But heedless wanderer, come not here,
> This feast was not prepared for thee,
> Unless thy heart feels nought more dear
> Than *Nature* and *Simplicity*.

The author of this, despite his commitment to 'simplicity', evidently feels no wish to go as far down the road of linguistic purging as Wordsworth. His poem is certainly not ornate writing, but it is still well stocked with inversions, archaisms and specialized poetic usages. In fact, the notion of the plain or simple in poetry, as applied by writers in the late eighteenth century, was by no means uniform. One cannot take the mere deployment of the term 'simplicity' as the token of one and the same aesthetic standard on all occasions. Coleridge's 1797 parody of the simple style, 'To Simplicity' by 'Nehemiah Higginbottom', is sometimes cited as evidence of a kind of subterranean disagreement between the two poets, at this early date, over the principles enunciated in the Preface; but the poem is nothing like any of *LB*.

Available senses of the idea of poetic simplicity were diverse enough to allow one reviewer of the 1798 edition to drive a wedge between virtuous and vicious applications: 'We may distinguish a *simple* style from a style of *simplicity*. By a simple style we may suppose a colloquial diction, debased by inelegance, and gross by familiarity. Simplicity is a manner of expression, facile, pure, and always elegant' (*New London Review* I, 1799, p. 34). He cites ll. 29–32 and 45–8 from 'Goody Blake and Harry Gill' as examples of the 'inartificial and anti-poetical manner'. This reviewer does also say that a 'multitude of rhimers' of the day 'have thought, that rudeness was synonymous to simplicity', but here he seems to be thinking rather of the element of archaism in *LB* (they 'have looked into the earliest efforts of the art, for their models'). It is not clear how much fashionability he would have claimed for a style which is simple by virtue of 'colloquial diction'. This is the really interesting issue about the originality of Wordsworth's idiom, of course, because it is exactly in this way that Wordsworth characterizes the plainness of *LB* in the Advertisement and Preface.

He writes in the Advertisement of employing 'the language of conversation' and in the Preface of working with 'the language really spoken by men'. There may be a shift, between the two documents, away from the idea of speech in its most everyday form, but the claim to be using colloquial English remains intact. The controversial question is what Wordsworth took to be the social foundation of this idiom: where were its users located in the hierarchy of class? The conventional interpretation of Wordsworth's remarks about this was initiated by what is, at best, an approximate quotation of the Preface by Coleridge in Chapter XVII of *Biographia Literaria*; it accuses him, in effect, of a huge inconsistency or an incomprehensible change of attitude.

Socially, according to the Advertisement of 1798, the idiom of *LB* derives from 'the middle and lower classes'. The orthodox reading of the Preface of 1800 and later has it that this idiom is based on the language of 'low and rustic life'. Since the poems of 1798 are almost all included in the later editions, and since these editions are more than twice as long, with many new kinds of poem represented (including 'Michael', whose hero is of the 'middle order' – see Poole letter, p. 48), Wordsworth seems to be guilty of a grotesque self-contradiction, or his sense of his own idiom has undergone a most startling transformation. The only possible route of escape from these conclusions would lie, in fact, in the direction of understanding 'low' not to be synonymous with 'lower'. Wordsworth would not be the first writer to be uncertain in his terminology about class in England, but it is a rather desperate solution to the problem. In the present edition, in the footnote to the relevant section of the Preface (pp. 60–1) it is pointed out that Wordsworth's remarks about 'low and rustic' language in the poems may not refer to their *general style* at all. And the testimony of a well-placed commentator of the day, John Stoddart, is quoted as evidence that Wordsworth was, at most, announcing that a low idiom was deployed in the poems about lower-class life.

Plebeian usage for a plebeian context is easy to pick out in 'The Idiot Boy', for example, and may in fact be more abundant than a modern reader can readily detect – confirming for the reader of the day any apprehensions of the plebeian he or she may have formed on the strength of the collection's title. To say that Betty Foy is 'in a sad quandary' ('The Idiot Boy', ll. 178, 181) may not strike us as a kind of indirect speech using the idiom of her class for her state of mind, but Wordsworth did italicize the word 'quandary' in later editions. The hostile reviewer quoted above seems to be verging on a social characterization of the colloquialism of *LB*, and the lines he quotes from 'Goody Blake and Harry Gill' probably for him contained vulgarities of expression. Crabb Robinson, at any rate, hit on the last sentence ('Sad case it was, as you may think, / For very cold to go to bed; / And then for cold not sleep a wink') as admirable for consisting entirely of 'vulgar everyday expressions'.

Bourgeois idioms are even harder for the modern reader to detect, but to a contemporary may have been just as conspicuous as plebeian usages, with as much power to offend. For Francis Jeffrey, the two social categories in the Advertisement's 'language of conversation in the middle and lower classes of society' did not need to be distinguished; they denoted a single reprehensible project, that of displacing an elite idiom from English poetry. As a consequence, in fact, the modern reader must guess whether Jeffrey's examples of vulgar usage in *LB* would have counted as plebeian or bourgeois. Perhaps 'His cheek is like a cherry' in 'Simon Lee' belonged to the former category, but 'you'll grow double' from 'The Tables Turned' was surely within the ambit of middle-class usage (though this must be a case where the 'conversational' turn in the expression – which will strike even a modern reader – was an important part of the offence against taste). Particularly interesting is the testimony of Wordsworth's brother John as to the 'vulgar' and 'low' character of l. 228 of 'Michael': 'That he could look his trouble in the face'. John Wordsworth's phrasing does, admittedly, suggest the possibility of an overlap in contemporary social classification between 'low' and 'middle', since Wordsworth used the second term about Michael as a person. What is at least clear is that the modern reader should be very cautious in judging where the idiom of these poems is pitched socially.

How far does the style range beyond the colloquial and the bourgeois–plebeian? Wordsworth's statement of aims allows him a freedom of movement here (in the words of the Advertisement, only a 'majority' of the 1798 poems conform to this sociolinguistic specification), and clearly there are poems or parts of poems written in an elevated, non-colloquial idiom. There are even sections of *LB* which violate the taboo – which is not mentioned until the Preface, and which is apparently comprehensive – on 'poetic diction'. The most prominent instance is 'The Female Vagrant'. This poem, which dates from earlier in Wordsworth's career than almost any other in the collection, is full of Miltonisms and other eighteenth-century poetic turns and must be accounted a plain transgressor of the standards proposed in the Preface. Another body of material in *LB* with a distinctively literary idiom can, however, readily coexist with the doctrines of the Preface: the inscription poems so consistently resort to such an idiom that it is clear that Wordsworth used the fiction of an inscribed poem as the occasion for a different kind of utterance.

Special conditions are similarly set up by the narrator's imagining of the 'measured numbers' that Barbara Lewthwaite, heroine of 'The Pet-Lamb', would sing if she could, and in the 'moan' or love complaint reported in ' 'Tis said, that some have died for love . . .'. In both cases the result has literary-sounding elements foreign to the collection as a whole – especially in the use of the second person singular (though this is the rule in Michael's apparently naturalistic speech). The opening lines of 'There was a Boy . . .' are not an inscription, though they are a sort of epitaph; they hover in fact between that kind of utterance and classical pastoral lament, and take on briefly a mannered style of diction. Almost invariably the degree of poeticism in *LB* will be found to be under the author's deliberate and intelligent control. There is an exception in the case of the oddly inversion-rich ll. 117–22 of 'Hart-leap Well', but – leaving aside 'The Female Vagrant' – it would be hard, if not impossible, to find a comparable example in the whole collection.

Finally, Wordsworth's English in *LB* is very similar to ours, but it is none the less the English of two centuries ago and there is a danger of mistaking its occasional obsolete usages for literary ones. Several such cases are identified in the footnotes. Some features of the English Wordsworth was using around the turn of the eighteenth century were actually about to pass out of the standard language, to survive only in literary forms. It was probably in response to the way linguistic change had made his vocabulary more literary than he wished that Wordsworth consistently emended 'sate' to 'sat', for example, in later editions of his poetry; but 'sate' was his regular usage in 1805, and it is retained in this edition. Where spellings were in transition (with no change of pronunciation involved), it has been possible to use the more modern forms Wordsworth later adopted, such as 'basin' for 'bason' and 'ancient' for 'antient'. Wordsworth's situation here is to be contrasted with that of Coleridge, as he progressively eliminated the archaic forms from 'The Ancient Mariner' (see headnote, p. 177). This represented a change of policy on the idiom of a particular poem, which at first, quite deliberately and reasonably, had been cast in a dated language. All archaic forms in 'The Ancient Mariner', including spellings, that Coleridge had not yet eliminated by 1805 (though they did almost all vanish later) are preserved in the present edition.

An infinite complexity of pain and pleasure

In a letter of 1818 John Keats offered a celebrated 'simile of human life'.

> I compare human life to a large mansion of many apartments, two of which I can only describe, the doors of the rest being as yet shut upon me. The first we step into we call the infant or thoughtless chamber, in which we remain as long as we do not think – we remain there a long while, and notwithstanding the doors of the second chamber remain wide open, showing a bright appearance, we care not to hasten to it; but are at length imperceptibly impelled by the awakening of the thinking principle within us – we no sooner get into the second chamber, which I shall call the Chamber of Maiden Thought, than we become intoxicated with the light and the atmosphere, we see nothing but pleasant wonders, and think of delaying there for ever in delight. However among the effects this breathing is father of is that tremendous one of sharpening one's vision into the heart and nature of man – of convincing one's nerves that the world is full of misery and heartbreak, pain, sickness and oppression – whereby this Chamber of Maiden Thought becomes gradually darkened and at the same time on all sides of it many doors are set open – but all dark – all leading to dark passages. We see not the balance of good and evil. We are in a mist. . . . We feel the 'burden of the mystery'. To this point was Wordsworth come, as far as I can conceive, when he wrote 'Tintern Abbey' and it seems to me that his genius is explorative of those dark passages.

It is not clear how many poems in addition to 'Tintern Abbey' Keats was thinking of here, if any, and how firm a sense he would have had of Wordsworth's career, but he is likely to have been aware that 'Tintern Abbey' first appeared in *LB* 1798, and his simile is wonderfully suggestive about this volume and Wordsworth's next published collection, the additional volume of 1800 – in other words, about the poems in the present edition.

Keats has identified the body of motifs which, above all, entitle these poems to be regarded as some of the most significant ever written in English. His imagery is also a convenient point of entry into certain critical problems which attend them. Human suffering, in all the guises listed by Keats and more, is the chief subject of *LB*: roughly half the Wordsworth poems are directly about some condition of this sort, and it makes a notable appearance in a further half-dozen. And in poem after poem this suffering springs from, or is at least linked to, states of intense sensory pleasure. Not surprisingly, Wordsworth's Chamber of Maiden Thought in *LB* is a more elaborated affair than Keats has managed to sketch in a couple of sentences, with some important distinctive elements. Wordsworth's vision of human suffering is even fuller, but its essence is distilled remarkably by Keats, whose image of 'dark passages' conveys the key notions of multiplicity and mystery.

Wordsworthian joy is what a later philosophical idiom would term phenomenologically primitive, or at least it tends to that condition. Its materials are typically light and darkness, colours, linear shapes – the outline of a hill, the curve of a branch – and repetitive sounds, such as birdsong, echoes and running water. The observer of these perceives them in an intensely receptive but passive frame of mind (he may put himself physically in the way to receive them, however); 'idle' is a common Wordsworthian term for his condition. He notes phenomena, as far as is consistent with verbalizing them, in themselves, and not as connected with things outside his immediate sensory field (in an extreme case, Johnny the Idiot Boy describes owl cries and moonlight correctly but misclassifies them: 'The cocks did crow to-whoo, to-whoo, / And the sun did shine so cold'). In particular, the Wordsworthian observer's memory is in abeyance. He experiences the illusion of having had no prior sensations, and then none prior to the unfolding experiential moment; he seems to be at the beginning of all time.

A second distinctive aspect of this condition of joy is that animistic fantasies (that is, fantasies to the effect that in the non-human physical world there are impulses of a human type) accompany the simple experiences. It is appropriate to call these 'fantasies' because no certain claims are made for their truth. Sometimes (as in 'A whirl-blast from behind the hill ...') an animistic perception is presented candidly as an illusion, but even in poems such as 'Expostulation and Reply' and 'Lines Written in Early Spring' the language is of 'deeming' and 'seeming'. For Wordsworth the interest of the feeling that 'there are powers' in the non-human world lies more in what this feeling says about the human mind, or human moods, than in what it might have of truthful content.

Only a handful of poems in *LB* depict this joyful state in an unalloyed form – and even these are greatly outweighed by poems whose subject is undiluted pain. Wordsworthian joy, like Keatsian Maiden Thought, is unstable and highly prone to transformation. This happens in a particularly interesting way in the sequence called 'Poems on the Naming of Places'. The first of these offers as complete a presentation of idle joy as can be found in the collection.

> It was an April morning: fresh and clear
> The rivulet, delighting in its strength,
> Ran with a young man's speed; and yet the voice
> Of waters which the winter had supplied
> Was softened down into a vernal tone.   5
> The spirit of enjoyment and desire,

And hopes and wishes, from all living things
Went circling, like a multitude of sounds.
The budding groves appeared as if in haste
To spur the steps of June; as if their shades   10
Of *various* green were hindrances that stood
Between them and their object; yet, meanwhile,
There was such deep contentment in the air
That every naked ash, and tardy tree
Yet leafless, seemed as though the countenance   15
With which it looked on this delightful day
Were native to the summer. Up the brook
I roamed in the confusion of my heart,
Alive to all things and forgetting all.

The leading elements are all present: raw sensations of sound and
colour emphasized to the point where they are at least as substantial
as anything else in the scene; the observer's amnesia, plus a sense of
universal beginning; impulses of a human type perceived as abroad
in the world. The latter are confidently asserted only to the extent
that the inner life of plants and animals may with some plausibility
be thought to overlap that of humans: 'all living things', perhaps, do
enjoy a 'spirit of enjoyment and desire ... hopes and wishes', but
the idea that budding groves want to spur on the advent of summer
can be only an appearance. These animistic intuitions are in
strikingly close connection with elementary sensations. 'Multitude
of sounds' at l. 8 is technically a simile for the joyful impulses but
strongly suggests birdsong also (later in the poem literal birdsong
'appeared the voice / Of common pleasure', and is then further
transmuted into 'the wild growth / Or ... some natural produce of
the air'). In a remarkable conceit, with a Proustian phenomeno-
logical intensity to it, the green hues of the buds, simply *as* colours,
play their part in a fantasy of desire and obstruction: 'as if their
shades / Of *various* green were hindrances that stood / Between
them and their object'.

This rapturous April morning is put into a very different
perspective as 'Poems on the Naming of Places' unfolds. The fourth
in the series delivers a shocking blow to its vein of animistic conceit,
in particular, when a nature-loving coterie of the poet and his
friends is exposed as affected, smug and even callous. The image of
human pain which brings this about – of an agricultural labourer so
emaciated by disease that he cannot work in the fields, and with no
means of seeking to feed himself other than futile attempts to catch
fish – is one of the most searing depictions of suffering in the
collection. However, the device by which pain is introduced into a
condition of joy here – that of an unexpected encounter with a

human victim – is a rarity, for Wordsworth employs a great variety of techniques to bring about the Keatsian 'effect' of Maiden Thought, the 'convincing one's nerves that the world is full of misery'. In the poem ' 'Tis said, that some have died for love . . .' raw sensation is already horrible, perhaps partly by virtue of the death of a lover but also, it seems, in the way it is for Roquentin, hero of Sartre's *Nausea*. Often, as the link between joy and forgetfulness implies, it is by an act of memory that pleasure becomes embittered, very notably in the second and third Matthew poems. Or the narrator cannot exclude a generalized sense of human cruelty and suffering from his awareness of present beauty (as in 'Lines Written in Early Spring' and 'Tintern Abbey'). In one poem, 'Nutting', the narrator brings the possibility for cruelty with him in his own heart. Yet another device is that whereby the narrator knows of a tragic outcome to another's joy, as in 'There was a Boy . . .'.

Indeed, the variety of Wordsworth's treatment, generally, of a persistent core of motifs is one of the most pressing critical issues concerning *LB*. Coleridge saw it as regrettable 'short tacks, reefing, and hauling and disentangling the ropes', as opposed to the hoped-for steady voyage of *The Recluse* (Griggs 1956: 1013). Keats makes the multiplicity of *LB* sound more respectable, intuitively at least, with his image of 'many doors . . . all leading to dark passages'. But how well does this cope with the undoubted but surprising homology that exists between, say, Betty Foy trying to drum into Johnny – who is 'idle all for very joy' – the crisis of Susan Gale's illness, and the 'still sad music of humanity' impinging on the narrator of 'Tintern Abbey'? Are these two different 'passages' into human pain of which the poet is being 'explorative', or is their odd resemblance just a token of morbidity, of a fixation on pain-in-pleasure about which the poet has little to say but which he cannot shake off? Similar questions can be put about the many appearances of suffering, on its own, as the subject of poems in *LB*. The multiplication of treatments does not necessarily involve a multi-plication of aspects, it may seem: readers of *LB* soon notice how frequently the motif of the deserted and deranged/distraught wife or consort crops up.

A poet does not 'explore' human life in the empirical sense that a sociologist or psychologist does. One aspect of the difference is that the poet is not restricted to literally true data, and Wordsworth seems, indeed, to have been very committed to the fictional and imaginative tendencies of his medium. This important truth can be obscured if certain phrasings in *LB* are interpreted casually (such as the subtitle to 'Goody Blake and Harry Gill': 'A True Story'). As the annotation in this edition shows, Wordsworth is never content just to retell the incident which has prompted a poem (important though he seems to have felt the element of prompting by the real to have been); invariably there are shifts of setting and/or conflations of human models, to such an extent that Wordsworth is obviously seeking to avoid any overlap with the literal. The notes he dictated to Isabella Fenwick in 1843 are often striking in their clear recollection of how real-life materials had contributed up to a certain point, but no further, in the formation of a poem. Wordsworth was quite capable of declining to make use of a story of literal suffering which would have been congenial, when his poetic purposes forbade it; there was such a story in the real-life background to 'The Brothers' (see Coburn 1957, I, 540).

A commitment to the fictitious need not mean that the cause of human truth is being given up, of course. Stripping away local accident may be understood as a means of getting at more durable and representative aspects of human life, and Wordsworth, in the Preface, is quite definite that the object of poetry, in contrast to history and biography, is 'truth, not individual and local, but general, and operative'. Death is certainly one of the most 'general, and operative' truths in our human experience, and it looms large in *LB*, particularly in the second volume. About half the poems in this part of the collection deal with death, and in its opening pages the subject is almost oppressive, monopolising the first nine items and appearing in all the first twelve. Death is much less the explicit topic of the 1798 poems, but it is nearer to the surface than might appear. A recurrent Wordsworthian version of suffering is what I call in the notes, for want of a better word, 'attrition'. Wordsworth is especially preoccupied by suffering that takes the form of the steady deprivation of resources or reduction of powers of an individual, and his attention is usually fixed on the climax of such a process, from which death (as with Simon Lee, or the Indian Woman whose poem first appeared in 1798) may be the next and imminent step.

Does the insight that death and quasi-death are a major occasion of suffering in *LB* help with the problem of the collection's strange way of ringing the changes? On the face of it, the problem is exacerbated. The range of motifs in a sense becomes narrower, with Keats's categories of 'misery and heartbreak, pain, sickness and oppression' tending to collapse into the underlying image of a man or woman at the verge of life: the socially exploited Simon Lee, the grieving Childless Father and the callously betrayed Ruth are one figure in this respect. On the other hand, death comes in an uncountable number of forms, because we all die. It is also perhaps the most baffling evil that befalls us, because it is unique and we have nothing with which to compare it.

To this extent it is possible to argue that the poems in *LB* are puzzlingly diverse although persistent in their treatment of suffering, because of the complexities of the subject. But this reasoning still leaves a good deal unexplained. Of the nine opening poems about death in the second volume, one concerns an animal, two are about plants and yet another ('Ellen Irwin') is a brisk, even cursory rewriting of a Scottish legend. The difficulty is not so much one of subject as of tone. 'Hart-leap Well', 'The Waterfall and the Eglantine' and 'The Oak and the Broom' make their victims anthropomorphic, and the first of them, because it is serious in tone, is not incongruous with, say, 'Michael' at the other end of the volume (while a further subject in 'Hart-leap Well' is that of human cruelty). But the other three poems are all more or less light in tone, so that while 'Ellen Irwin', for example, certainly has continuities of theme with 'We are Seven' and 'The Brothers', it is tempting to say that these continuities are uninteresting.

Matters of tone, if not the whole of the problem about diversity in *LB*, arguably give rise to the most difficult cases. The 'Idiot Boy'–'Tintern Abbey' link mentioned above is a good example. It is primarily tone which makes 'Goody Blake and Harry Gill' and 'The Old Cumberland Beggar' puzzlingly different as studies of savage rural poverty, and the same is true of 'We are Seven' and 'The Two April Mornings' as studies of the death of children, or of 'The Thorn' and the 'Yew-tree Lines' as poems about despairing individuals and the half-wild locations they haunt. These examples have not been chosen deliberately to bring in the question of Wordsworth's narrators. With very few exceptions, any consideration of the tone of one of the poems will quickly lead to consideration of a first-person narrator, because they almost all have such a narrator and he is generally a considerable presence. The contrast between 'The Thorn' and the 'Yew-tree Lines' – one with a fully constructed, obsessive, perhaps deluded narrator, and the other with an authoritative-sounding narrator who might be the poet himself – offers the possibility that the tensions between certain of the poems can be tackled by taking the word of reliable narrators and rejecting that of unreliable ones.

But this project will work to only a limited extent. To start with, Wordsworth's concern to get away from the merely factual almost always has consequences for the autobiographical verisimilitude of his 'I' narrators. In the manuscript note to 'To Joanna' (see 'Poems on the Naming of Places', pp. 324–5) he lets us in on something of the process of building up an imaginary narrator even in a fairly autobiographical context. In the rare case of 'Nutting', where the 'I' does seem to be autobiographical, Wordsworth is interestingly at pains to make his anecdote a hypothetical reconstruction representative of several experiences – in other words, to retain a generality and independence from literal circumstance, such as Aristotle had traditionally required, even in a context of personal reminiscence.

The commentators on *LB* have been strangely reluctant to allow Wordsworth to put distance between himself and his narrating voices. The poem 'Anecdote for Fathers', for example, contains three proper names (Edward, Liswyn, Kilve) which are routinely decoded into three other terms which have a close personal relevance to Wordsworth's life at this period: Basil Montagu, Alfoxden, Racedown. But either Wordsworth had a conversation with Basil about these places such as he describes in the poem, in which case the three disguises are incomprehensible if he means us to take him as the narrator, or he didn't, in which case he can't be the narrator; either way, the 'I' is not Wordsworth. It has even been proposed, in the spirit of autobiographical reading, that the phrase at ll. 67–8 of 'Tintern Abbey' – 'when first / I came among these hills' – refers to an unrecorded visit by Wordsworth to the Wye prior to the visit of 1793 (the latter being recalled in the poem's opening lines). The objection to this is not that Wordsworth may not have paid this earlier visit (though the evidence for it is extremely slight) but rather that 'Tintern Abbey' would be a ridiculously inept poem if Wordsworth had intended us to grasp that the two passages refer to different moments. In fact, quite obviously, Wordsworth has offered us a chronology of two visits separated by five years, and it does not matter in the slightest how many other visits he may in reality have paid to the area. Finally, it is hard to imagine a more unilluminating (not to say improbable) reading of a poem than the comment that in ' 'Tis said, that some have died for love . . .', 'Wordsworth tries to reassure . . . his sister in the event of his dying' (Brett and Jones 1963: 302), but such is the biographical bias of Wordsworthian commentary that this can pass for the main truth about a complex and important poem.

In other words, we cannot assess the reliability of Wordsworth's narrators by measuring how 'close' they are to the poet himself. He simply did not use autobiographical fact in this way; he did not stick to the truth about himself when he wanted an 'I' speaker to be particularly authoritative. On the contrary, Wordsworth drops a perfectly truthful fact about his career into 'The Idiot Boy' (that he has been writing poetry for fourteen years), but it is central to the comic–mystical effect of this poem that its narrator (to his own frustration) supposedly knows no more about Johnny's adventures than does Betty Foy – or Johnny himself. He is in this sense an unreliable narrator, and his kind of unreliability is quite widely shared by the narrators in the collection. Occasionally they admit, like him, to having no more they can tell us (an example is the 'mute' narrator of 'There was a Boy . . .'), but more commonly they break off, whether because they are themselves stalled or because we have been told all we need to know, it is not clear. Such poems in the collection – and they are common – are either enigmas or epiphanies, and they give it a fascinatingly modern flavour.

By contrast, there are distinctly knowledgeable voices, such as the narrator who clearly remembers the architect of the yew-tree seat, and the one who has known the old Cumberland beggar since his childhood. Both these narrators also have a good deal to say about what we should make of the subjects they depict, and it would be perverse, I think, not to accept them as more reliable descriptively and judgementally than certain other speakers. In both these instances there are readily drawn contrasts: with the narrator of 'The Thorn' in the case of the 'Yew-tree Lines', and with the narrator of 'Animal Tranquillity and Decay' in the case of 'The Old Cumberland Beggar'. (The 'Animal Tranquillity and Decay' narrator is one of Wordsworth's stalled or silently illuminated speakers, quite incapable of uttering over a hundred lines beginning 'Statesmen! . . .'.)

If such a hierarchy of reliability existed generally for the poems about suffering and death in *LB* then the remarkable variety of Wordsworth's treatment of these matters would be more orderly, although it would still be problematic; if there *is* an authoritative view, we are entitled to expect it to be offered consistently. Actually, the fullness and decisiveness of 'The Old Cumberland Beggar' does exert an effect on our reading of certain related, more cryptic poems, but there is none sufficiently similar to it that it is thereby rendered redundant. 'Animal Tranquillity and Decay' is not the close parallel it is often claimed to be, even in its basic materials, and the closing lines about the old man's dying son (which appear in this edition's version) introduce an element which would be unthinkable in 'The Old Cumberland Beggar'.

'The Old Cumberland Beggar' is anyway something of a special case. Generally some element of silence or uncertainty characterizes Wordsworth's narrators as they contemplate human suffering. This tends to be assisted by their situation, for often they are pondering not suffering itself but some piece of physical evidence that has a close or even intimate link with suffering – a grave, a pond, a sheepfold, a man's tears, the site of a hermitage, and so forth. They have their counterparts, in fact, in the smaller number of poems which deal with states of joy, especially when it is experienced by children. It is not far-fetched to see the 'Man' that is constructed, and reconstructed, in 'Rural Architecture' as an antithesis to Michael's sheepfold, and even the accounts of their inner states that childish speakers do deliver in 'We are Seven', 'Anecdote for Fathers' and 'The Idiot Boy' impress the narrators in these poems for what they imply rather than for what they say.

What is available for contemplation by a narrator is available to others in the world of the poem, and this possibility is sometimes used by Wordsworth, through the introduction of some kind of communal opinion, to add a further element of uncertainty to the reading of a vestige of suffering or joy. Again, it would be perverse to suggest that such devices put all Wordsworth's narrators on the same footing of unreliability, and an identity of attitude between the narrator and the community (generally rooted in the former's membership of that community over many years) is sometimes used actually to lend weight to the narrator's reading of a vestige. But complications can appear unexpectedly in this area. A careful reading of 'Michael' suggests that Wordsworth intends a divergence between the narrator (together with hypothetical like-minded readers) and the community over the very important question of whether Michael's feelings for Luke sustain him or disable him in the years after his loss. It would be absurd to argue that the narrator here is as unauthoritative as the narrator of 'The Thorn', but we are offered a comparable triangle of elements: narrator, vestige, local opinion. Just to complicate matters, Wordsworth in real life hoped that readers would respond to 'Michael' in a way which might seem more in keeping with the community's 'pity' for the supposedly apathetic old shepherd than with the narrator's conviction of the 'comfort' he receives from his love for Luke – that is, by weeping (see Poole letter, p. 48).

And what, indeed, of *our* reaction to the joy, suffering and suffering-in-joy that are the almost exclusive topics of *LB*? This brings us to the heart of what I take to be Wordsworth's purposes and procedures in the collection. Investigating the strange diversity of these poems has brought out the considerable emphasis that Wordsworth contrives to throw on judgement and response by third parties, whether they be narrators, other observers in the world of the poems, or ourselves when left to our own devices with one of the more taciturn of these texts. It is worth returning to Keats at this point, for I have been a little disingenuous in implying that he takes Wordsworth to be 'explorative' of human suffering in a descriptive or analytical sense. The right reading seems rather to be that Wordsworth, for Keats, is engaged in a metaphysical investigation of suffering, of the 'why' rather than the 'how'; it is metaphysically that suffering is a matter of darkness and mist, because 'we see not the balance of good and evil'. If either poet had brought God into the picture one would say, in fact, that the project Keats attributes to Wordsworth is a theological one – and its concern can certainly be stated in a phrase with theological overtones, namely the problem of pain.

If Keats is right, the stress on death in *LB* becomes particularly intelligible. Death, as Wittgenstein has pointed out, is not a fact of life. As a result, suffering and death are not connected straightforwardly in the way that suffering and dying (Wordsworth's adjacent preoccupation) are. In fact death, in the extra-mortal Wittgensteinian sense, is linked to suffering only by virtue of the attitudes of the living to the loved and lost. Mourning is a profoundly ambiguous thing, and no poem in the language has expressed this better than the second of the Matthew poems, 'The Two April Mornings' (the possibility of a pun in the title must suggest itself). To mourn is to lament and protest, but also to celebrate and express love. We could not feel the evil of deprivation without knowing the good of love. Wordsworth was struck by the 'tranquillity, I might say indifference' with which close-knit Lakeland settlements treated deaths in the community (see p. 231). Matthew, it is suggested at the end of 'The Two April Mornings', is himself mourned by the narrator, and this situation is particularly a feature of the 'sequence' poems concerning Lucy and Matthew (indeed, the only other case is 'There was a Boy ...'). The Lucy poems, if not directly stating the ambiguousness of mourning, are at least surprisingly cryptic about the experience of loss, and 'There was a Boy ...' is utterly reticent. More widely dispersed in the collection is the situation of a narrator, perhaps with other observers, witnessing another's grief: that of Martha Ray, the Childless Father, or Michael (Luke is in effect dead). There are uncertainties about the condition of the mourner, especially as between the narrator and other observers, in each of these cases. In other words, within all these poems, while the 'balance of good and evil' may not be exactly determined, it is indicated that evil may be balanced by good.

The effect cannot be the same, however, when suffering other than grief for the dead (even suffering that brings its victim to the brink of death) is at issue, and in this respect the dead and the quasi-dead in *LB* are very different entities. The Wordsworthian narrator, no longer a mourner or observer of mourning, cannot so readily record a balancing of evil by good. He is starkly confronted by the shocking decrepitude and obsequiousness of Simon Lee, by a man crying his eyes out in public, by an arthritic beggar stirring in the dust with his staff to rake together a couple of coins thrown to him, or by a girl reduced to miserable vagrancy and infantilism, or he *is*, in fact, an Indian Woman left to die by her tribe.

But here the narrator and the reader in *LB* diverge in their experiences. It is open to us as readers to feel more mitigating good when we read about these figures than is available to the first-person speakers. This sounds perverse, but it is a variant of a

familiar truth about literature. Our capacity to find satisfaction in
stories of human degradation and cruelty, when presented in the
form of tragedy, is a well-known paradox. It is obviously less
distressing to read about Simon Lee than actually to see him, and
this too may amount to a more positive response than just being
kept at a remove from disagreeable sensations by the text.
Wordsworth seems to have believed as much, to judge by his very
novel remarks about poetic pleasure in the Preface.

As the annotation in this edition explains, Wordsworth takes a
cliché of neoclassical aesthetics – that pleasure is a distinguishing
feature of poetry – and transforms it from a standard way of
explaining purely decorative aspects of poetry, which he hated
anyway, into an index of a central activity of metrical writing. The
important corollary for the present topic is developed in a passage
from the Preface, here ll. 797–826. It begins with a well-known
description of the process of composition, but this is there only to
prepare for an account of the effects of poetry. According to
Wordsworth, the poet will find pleasure in the act of recreating an
emotion, and this he should seek to pass on to the reader,
producing 'a complex feeling of delight, which is of the most
important use in tempering the painful feeling which will always be
found intermingled with powerful descriptions of the deeper
passions'.

There is a considerable emphasis in this passage on metre as the
channel by which the poet's pleasure translates into reader's
pleasure; it is, indeed, the only aesthetic aspect of poetry specified
by Wordsworth. And a couple of pages earlier in the Preface (here
ll. 726–74), in elaborating on his formula about the purpose of
poetry being 'to produce excitement in co-existence with an
overbalance of pleasure' (a formula, incidentally, which deserves at
least as much attention as the too familiar 'spontaneous overflow of
powerful feelings'), Wordsworth is concerned solely with metre and
rhyme. (He adduces here the example of Shakespeare's 'pathetic
scenes', which indicates that it is right to think of the theory as an
extension of the aesthetics of tragedy.)

This emphasis on metre is interesting in the light of the variety
and adventurousness of the verse forms in *LB* (noted in detail in
this edition), but might help to bolster a kind of incredulity that the
reader may feel when faced with the proposition that in these poems
suffering is mitigated and transformed as it is in the greatest tragic
drama. Wordsworth is right to concentrate on metre in his
statement of aims, it might be said, because that is all there is to
concentrate on in these texts denuded of other aesthetic aspects, but
it is a vain hope to expect that rhythm and rhyme alone can achieve
what is achieved by the panoply of Shakespearean verse. The best

response to this is to urge a return to the poems (as opposed, for example, to allowing the celebrated ll. 33–4 of 'The Thorn' to control one's memory of the whole). And Wordsworth worked to a fine scale when judging and creating poetical effects, perhaps in part because he brought criteria from rhetoric to bear; quite subtle departures from pedestrian usage had great expressive force for him, and he had an abnormal sensitivity to excessive and florid effects. A reader attuned as he was will not find the poems aesthetically bare.

The 'overbalance' of pleasure Wordsworth expects us to feel in reading even the most poignant of the poems has an important bearing on the question of their diversity. Here is a constant, as constant as the fact of metre itself, which links 'Tintern Abbey' and 'The Idiot Boy', 'Goody Blake and Harry Gill' and 'The Old Cumberland Beggar'. But it may be relevant in only a very limited way to \the second of Keats's perceptions about Wordsworth's explorative genius: that he was investigating the problem of pain. Our enjoyment of poems about pain (other than the pain–pleasure of mourning) is certainly a case where the 'balance of good and evil' is favourable, but one so tiny as to be scarcely worth noting. No one would wish to argue that the satisfaction felt by the audience at a tragedy tells us anything about the moral character of the universe. The Wordsworthian 'overbalance' can have significance for the huge world of human pain only if it registers something about the latter, as well as making it less painful in poetic form than it is in reality.

In the Preface Wordsworth does explicitly claim, in fact, that the pleasure-giving function of poetry receives its sanction from aspects of the real human and non-human worlds. 'This necessity of producing immediate pleasure,' says Wordsworth, is far from being 'a degradation of the Poet's art'. On the contrary, a poet's pleasure-giving is both 'an acknowledgement of the beauty of the universe' and 'a homage paid to . . . the grand elementary principle of pleasure, by which [man] knows, and feels, and lives, and moves'. The second part of this rather astounding claim is particularly interesting: that the aesthetic element in literature reflects an inalienable law of the human organism, to the effect that we are always in some sense in a condition of pleasure. Otherwise, Wordsworth implies, we could not be active and sentient beings. His thinking here is indebted to the idiosyncratic English psychologist and theologian David Hartley. In Hartley, psychological speculation and theology flow together in such a way that the predominating influence of pleasure in our neural and mental life is taken to mean that at this level of his being man has not fallen; the resemblance of Wordsworth's preoccupations in *LB* to the problem of pain is thus not accidental.

If poetic pleasure is an echo of something in human nature, it should follow that Wordsworth's narrators are also able to receive a degree of pleasure from the suffering they observe, and Wordsworth does write in the Preface of the poet not only contemplating mankind directly, but also contemplating man as himself 'looking upon this complex scene of ideas and sensations, and finding everywhere objects that immediately excite in him sympathies which, from the necessities of his nature, are accompanied by an overbalance of enjoyment'. On the face of it, the doctrine that it is in the nature of man to contemplate everything, including suffering, with an 'overbalance of enjoyment' could lead to an absurdly and horribly complacent picture, a world in which no one is distressed by another's suffering.

It does appear that Wordsworth felt some anxiety about the way his doctrine of pleasure-taking man might be misinterpreted: 'I would not be misunderstood,' he says, 'but wherever we sympathize with pain it will be found that the sympathy is produced and carried on by subtle combinations with pleasure.' Pleasure, it seems, is at most a cause and not a constituent of our awareness of another's pain in ordinary life. The victims of suffering, however, are also human beings, in whom pleasure – if Wordsworth is consistent on these questions – should be the principle by which they 'know, live, feel, move'. This indeed opens the door to an unwelcome complacency about their plight, and we are likely to rebel against the proposal that the atrocious condition of the dying Simon Lee is somehow acceptable because in reading poetry we are aware how pleasure necessarily predominates over pain in our inner life as human organisms.

Simon does exhibit a capacity for joy which is like our pleasure in metrical language. He 'dearly loves' the 'voices' of the hounds even in his extreme affliction (and compare Ruth's forgiving attitude to natural beauties, the 'engines of her pain'). The poet, as a matter of literal fact, was moved by these words when he heard them uttered by one of the real-life models for Simon. But isn't the pleasure Simon takes in the instruments of his own physical and social destruction actually a token of psychological damage just as telling as his obsequious gratitude at the end of the poem? Surely, to suggest that his power of human enjoyment mitigates his plight is to condone the exploitation of the rural poor by a cruelly unequal social system. A comparable case (though less difficult because of the mourning element), where there is some direct warrant for supposing that Wordsworth intended suffering to be mitigated by the capacity for pleasure, is that of Matthew (himself a kind of poet). Wordsworth's friend John Stoddart, reviewing *LB*, picked out 'The Two April Mornings' and 'The Fountain' as poems where 'a preponderance of pleasure is ultimately produced'; the phrasing is sufficiently like Wordsworth's to suggest that Stoddart had been prompted on these two poems by the author.

Persuasive though expressions of solidarity with Simon Lee may be, it is important to see that they involve us in a contradiction into which Wordsworth's poetry often draws its readers. We speak as if it is we, in our anguished sympathy with the sufferers in these poems, who have a privileged acquaintance with them, while the poet's apparently more cheerful view is unctuous, impertinent and ignorant. The position has only to be stated for its absurdity to appear. It is the poet, with a series of very telling details, who has aroused our indignation about Simon Lee in the first place. As usual Wordsworth, a supremely intelligent poet, is several moves ahead of his readers. He has gone beyond the realm of indignation about human pain into the altogether more difficult territory where it can be asked how this pain counts in the whole life of mankind. We tend to stay halted in front of the wonderful icons of suffering that he has created on route, as if they were our discoveries. In the territory beyond there are certainly dangers of an unacceptable complacency, but we can at least agree with Wordsworth that human life is 'an infinite complexity of pain and pleasure', and that the ultimate verdict on Simon Lee cannot be a wholly black, indignant one, simply because he is a living and conscious man. The rule to be learnt is one that the reader of Wordsworth's poetry can never afford to forget: do not underestimate the challenge it offers.

Note on the Text

The text of the poems, on pages 95–357, is a modernized version of *LB* 1805, as is the text of all the prose matter, in this or other sections, which appeared in that edition. Spellings have not been modernized where a change of pronunciation may be involved or where a spelling was deliberately archaic in 1805. While the use of capitals in the original does not conform to modern practices (in its randomness, among other features), it does have a definitely expressive and systematic character on occasion, and I have retained capitals in many cases on this ground. All occurrences of the word 'nature' have been left in their original capitalized or uncapitalized form. The occasional misprint in 1805 has been silently corrected.

All 1805 poems are by Wordsworth, unless indicated otherwise. Other verse and prose items (with the exception of the transcription of the 1798 text of 'The Ancient Mariner', pp. 389–405) have also been conservatively modernized. Those items for which a source, or an edition of *LB*, is not indicated are based on texts in one of the following: *CPW*, Griggs 1956, *PW*, De Selincourt 1939, De Selincourt and Shaver 1967 (for these and other abbreviations see the Bibliography and suggested reading, pp. 407–14). In annotated publishing details, place of publication is London unless indicated otherwise.

Authors' accompanying statements

In this section are brought together most of the surviving statements made by Coleridge and Wordsworth in the years 1798–1805 which comment on the purpose or character of the collection and specific items in it; a number of shorter and more factual comments which appeared in the 1805 edition itself are reproduced with the texts of individual poems. Some of these statements were published and some not, but they were all designed in some measure to assist a reader or readers of the text involved (in contrast to the manuscript note on 'To Joanna' – see 'Poems on the Naming of Places', pp. 324–5 – whose purpose is uncertain).

Coleridge's lines on 'The Nightingale' (May 1798)

These couplets were sent in a letter to Wordsworth in which Coleridge also forwarded the text of 'The Nightingale'.

In stale blank verse a subject stale
I send *per post* my *Nightingale*:
And like an honest bard, dear Wordsworth,
You'll tell me what you think my Bird's worth.
My opinion's briefly this –   5
His *bill* he opens not amiss;
And when he has sung a stave or so,
His Breast, and some small space below,
So throbs and swells, that you might swear
No vulgar music's working there.   10
So far, so good; but then, 'od rot him!
There's something falls off at his bottom.

Yet, sure, no wonder it should breed,
That my Bird's tail's a tail indeed
And makes its own inglorious harmony   15
Æolio crepitu, non carmine.

16. Latin: 'By farting, not song'.

Advertisement (1798)

Dropped from the 1800 and subsequent editions of *LB* and replaced by the much longer Preface, though partly quarried for that document.

It is the honourable characteristic of Poetry that its materials are to be found in every subject which can interest the human mind. The evidence of this fact is to be sought, not in the writings of critics, but in those of Poets themselves.   5
   The majority of the following Poems are to be considered as experiments. They were written chiefly with a view to ascertain how far the language of conversation in the middle and lower classes of society is adapted to the purposes of poetic pleasure. Readers accustomed to the   10
gaudiness and inane phraseology of many modern writers, if they persist in reading this book to its conclusion, will perhaps frequently have to struggle with feelings of strangeness and awkwardness: they will look round for Poetry, and will be induced to inquire by what species of   15
courtesy these attempts can be permitted to assume that title. It is desirable that such readers, for their own sakes, should not suffer the single word Poetry, a word of very disputed meaning, to stand in the way of their gratification; but that, while they are perusing this book, they should ask   20
themselves if it contains a natural delineation of human passions, human characters, and human incidents; and if the answer be favourable to the author's wishes, that they should consent to be pleased in spite of that most dreadful enemy to our pleasures, our own pre-established codes of   25
decision.
   Readers of superior judgment may disapprove of the style in which many of these pieces are executed: it must be

11. inane: empty (though perhaps already with some sense of stupid, imbecilic).
16. courtesy: favour, indulgence.

expected that many lines and phrases will not exactly suit
their taste. It will perhaps appear to them, that wishing to   30
avoid the prevalent fault of the day, the author has
descended too low, and that many of his expressions are
too familiar, and not of sufficient dignity. It is apprehended
that the more conversant the reader is with our elder
writers, and with those in modern times who have been the   35
most successful in painting manners and passions, the
fewer complaints of this kind will he have to make.

An accurate taste in Poetry and in all the other arts, Sir
Joshua Reynolds has observed, is an acquired talent, which
can only be produced by severe thought and a long-   40
continued intercourse with the best models of composition.
This is mentioned not with so ridiculous a purpose as to
prevent the most inexperienced reader from judging for
himself, but merely to temper the rashness of decision, and
to suggest that if Poetry be a subject on which much time   45
has not been bestowed, the judgment may be erroneous,
and that in many cases it necessarily will be so.

The tale of GOODY BLAKE AND HARRY GILL is founded
on a well-authenticated fact which happened in Warwick-
shire. Of the other poems in the collection it may be proper   50
to say that they are either absolute inventions of the author,
or facts which took place within his personal observation or
that of his friends. The poem of THE THORN, as the reader
will soon discover, is not supposed to be spoken in the
author's own person: the character of the loquacious   55
narrator will sufficiently show itself in the course of the
story. THE RIME OF THE ANCYENT MARINERE was pro-
fessedly written in imitation of the *style* as well as of the
spirit of the elder poets; but with a few exceptions the
author believes that the language adopted in it has been   60
equally intelligible for these three last centuries. The lines
entitled EXPOSTULATION AND REPLY, and those which
follow, arose out of a conversation with a friend who was
somewhat unreasonably attached to modern books of moral
philosophy.   65

36. manners: modes of behaviour.
38–9. Sir . . . observed: for the various remarks by Reynolds Wordsworth
may have in mind, see Owen and Smyser 1974, I, 186.
49. fact: occurrence, event.
51. the author: on the determined fostering of the notion that *LB* 1798 had
a single author, see p. 4 above.
61–5. The lines . . . philosophy: see headnote to 'Expostulation and Reply'
(p. 97).

Argument to 'The Ancient Mariner' (1798)

Replaced in 1800 by a new version.

How a ship having passed the Line was driven by storms to
the cold country towards the South Pole; and how from
thence she made her course to the tropical latitude of the
great Pacific Ocean; and of the strange things that befell;
and in what manner the Ancient Mariner came back to his   5
own country.

1. Line: Equator.

Coleridge's letter on 'Love' (December 1799)

'Love' was first printed in the *Morning Post*, where this letter to the editor
preceded it.

Sir,
    The following poem is the introduction to a somewhat
longer one, for which I shall solicit insertion on your next
open day. The use of the old ballad word, *Ladie*, for Lady,
is the only piece of obsoleteness in it; and as it is
professedly a tale of ancient times, I trust, that 'the   5
affectionate lovers of venerable antiquity' (as Camden says)
will grant me their pardon, and perhaps may be induced to
admit a force and propriety in it. A heavier objection may
be adduced against the author that in these times of fear
and expectation, when novelties *explode* around us in all   10
directions, he should presume to offer to the public a silly
tale of old fashioned love; and, five years ago, I own, I
should have allowed and felt the force of this objection.
But, alas! explosion has succeeded explosion so rapidly,

3–4. The use . . . in it: on the usages that could have been thought obsolete,
see headnote to 'Love', p. 170.
6. as Camden says: the quotation is from William Camden, *Britannia*, trans.
Philemon Holland (1610), p. 753.
10. novelties: this, and the mention of 'revolutions' below, are probably
allusions to the war and political upheaval triggered by Napoleonic France.
Coleridge's awareness of the political background to his activity as a poet
may be compared with Wordsworth's at this date (see p. 64).

that novelty itself ceases to appear new; and it is possible   15
that now, even a simple story, wholly unspiced with politics
or personality, may find some attention amid the hubbub of
revolutions, as to those who have resided a long time by the
falls of Niagara, the lowest whispering becomes distinctly
audible.   20

S.T. Coleridge

17. personality: that is, disparaging allusion to individuals.

Wordsworth's note to 'The Thorn' (1800)

Printed in 1800 and subsequent editions of *LB*.

This Poem ought to have been preceded by an introductory
Poem, which I have been prevented from writing by never
having felt myself in a mood when it was probable that I
should write it well. – The character which I have here
introduced speaking is sufficiently common. The Reader   5
will perhaps have a general notion of it, if he has ever
known a man, a captain of a small trading vessel, for
example, who, being past the middle age of life, had retired
upon an annuity or small independent income to some
village or country town of which he was not a native, or in   10
which he had not been accustomed to live. Such men,
having little to do, become credulous and talkative from
indolence; and from the same cause, and other predisposing
causes by which it is probable that such men may have
been affected, they are prone to superstition. On which   15
account it appeared to me proper to select a character like
this to exhibit some of the general laws by which
superstition acts upon the mind. Superstitious men are
almost always men of slow faculties and deep feelings; their
minds are not loose but adhesive; they have a reasonable   20
share of imagination, by which word I mean the faculty
which produces impressive effects out of simple elements;
but they are utterly destitute of fancy, the power by which
pleasure and surprise are excited by sudden varieties of
situation and by accumulated imagery.   25

    It was my wish in this poem to show the manner in
which such men cleave to the same ideas; and to follow the
turns of passion, always different, yet not palpably
different, by which their conversation is swayed. I had two

objects to attain; first, to represent a picture which should   30
not be unimpressive, yet consistent with the character that
should describe it; secondly, while I adhered to the style in
which such persons describe, to take care that words,
which in their minds are impregnated with passion, should
likewise convey passion to Readers who are not accustomed   35
to sympathize with men feeling in that manner or using
such language. It seemed to me that this might be done by
calling in the assistance of lyrical and rapid metre. It was
necessary that the Poem, to be natural, should in reality
move slowly; yet I hoped, that, by the aid of the metre, to   40
those who should at all enter into the spirit of the Poem, it
would appear to move quickly. The Reader will have the
kindness to excuse this note, as I am sensible that an
introductory Poem is necessary to give this Poem its full
effect.   45

Upon this occasion I will request permission to add a
few words closely connected with THE THORN and many
other Poems in these volumes. There is a numerous class
of readers who imagine that the same words cannot be
repeated without tautology; this is a great error; virtual   50
tautology is much oftener produced by using different
words when the meaning is exactly the same. Words, a
Poet's words more particularly, ought to be weighed in the
balance of feeling, and not measured by the space which
they occupy upon paper. For the Reader cannot be too   55
often reminded that Poetry is passion; it is the history or
science of feelings; now every man must know that an
attempt is rarely made to communicate impassioned
feelings without something of an accompanying conscious-
ness of the inadequateness of our powers, or the   60
deficiencies of language. During such efforts there will be a
craving in the mind, and as long as it is unsatisfied the
speaker will cling to the same words, or words of the same
character. There are also various other reasons why
repetition and apparent tautology are frequently beauties of   65
the highest kind. Among the chief of these reasons is the
interest which the mind attaches to words, not only as
symbols of the passion, but as *things*, active and efficient,
which are of themselves part of the passion. And further,
from a spirit of fondness, exultation, and gratitude, the   70
mind luxuriates in the repetition of words which appear

50. tautology: repetition of sense.
50–1. virtual tautology: what is in effect tautology.
68. efficient: producing effects.

successfully to communicate its feelings. The truth of these remarks might be shown by innumerable passages from the Bible, and from the impassioned Poetry of every nation.

'Awake, awake, Deborah: awake, awake, utter a song: 75
arise, Barak, and lead thy captivity captive, thou son of Abinoam.

At her feet he bowed, he fell, he lay down: at her feet he bowed, he fell; where he bowed, there he fell down dead. Why is his chariot so long in coming? Why tarry the wheels   80
of his chariot?' – *Judges*, chap. 5th, verses 12th, 27th, and part of 28th. See also the whole of that tumultuous and wonderful Poem.

80. chariot: actually, in Authorized Version, 'chariots'. The English version of Robert Lowth's lectures on Old Testament poetry also has 'chariot', due to the way Lowth had rendered the Hebrew in his original Latin translation. And Lowth comments on the 'utmost elegance in the repetitions' in verses 28–30, 'which, notwithstanding their apparent redundancy, are conducted with the most perfect brevity' (Lowth 1787, I, 291–3).

Wordsworth's note to 'The Ancient Mariner' (1800)

This controversial note appeared only in the 1800 edition.

I cannot refuse myself the gratification of informing such Readers as may have been pleased with this Poem, or with any part of it, that they owe their pleasure in some sort to me; as the Author was himself very desirous that it should be suppressed. This wish had arisen from a consciousness   5
of the defects of the Poem, and from a knowledge that many persons had been much displeased with it. The Poem of my Friend has indeed great defects; first, that the principal person has no distinct character, either in his profession of Mariner, or as a human being who having   10
been long under the control of supernatural impressions might be supposed himself to partake of something supernatural: secondly, that he does not act, but is

8–9. the principal ... character: the subtitle furnished for the poem in the edition in which this note was printed – 'A Poet's Reverie' – tends to concede that the narrating voice is not that of an autonomous invented person. It is not known who devised this subtitle.

continually acted upon: thirdly, that the events having no
necessary connection do not produce each other: and lastly, 15
that the imagery is somewhat too laboriously accumulated.
Yet the Poem contains many delicate touches of passion,
and indeed the passion is everywhere true to nature; a
great number of the stanzas present beautiful images, and
are expressed with unusual felicity of language; and the 20
versification, though the metre is itself unfit for long
poems, is harmonious and artfully varied, exhibiting the
utmost powers of that metre, and every variety of which it
is capable. It therefore appeared to me that these several
merits (the first of which, namely that of the passion, is of 25
the highest kind) gave to the Poem a value which is not
often possessed by better Poems. On this account I
requested my Friend to permit me to republish it.

Argument to 'The Ancient Mariner' (1800)

Used only in the edition of 1800.

How a ship, having first sailed to the Equator, was driven
by storms, to the cold country towards the South Pole; how
the Ancient Mariner cruelly, and in contempt of the laws of
hospitality, killed a sea-bird; and how he was followed by
many and strange judgements; and in what manner he 5
came back to his own country.

3–4. *in contempt . . . hospitality*: in the sense that either the albatross or the
Mariner was a guest. See also 1817 gloss (p. 364).

Wordsworth to Charles James Fox
(January 1801)

Of the several letters sent with complimentary copies of the second edition
of *Lyrical Ballads* this is the only one composed by Wordsworth to have
survived.

Sir,
    It is not without much difficulty, that I have summoned
the courage to request your acceptance of these volumes.
Should I express my real feelings, I am sure that I should
seem to make a parade of diffidence and humility.
    Several of the poems contained in these volumes are   5
written upon subjects which are the common property of
all Poets and which, at some period of your life, must have
been interesting to a man of your sensibility, and perhaps
may still continue to be so. It would be highly gratifying to
me to suppose that even in a single instance the manner in   10
which I have treated these general topics should afford you
any pleasure; but such a hope does not influence me upon
the present occasion; in truth I do not feel it. Besides, I am
convinced that there must be many things in this collection
which may impress you with an unfavorable idea of my   15
intellectual powers. I do not say this with a wish to degrade
myself; but I am sensible that this must be the case, from
the different circles in which we have moved, and the
different objects with which we have been conversant.
    Being utterly unknown to you as I am, I am well aware   20
that, if I am justified in writing to you at all, it is necessary
my letter should be short; but I have feelings within me
which I hope will so far show themselves in this letter, as to
excuse the trespass which I am afraid I shall make. In
common with the whole of the English people I have   25
observed in your public character a constant predominance
of sensibility of heart. Necessitated as you have been from
your public situation to have much to do with men in
bodies, and in classes, and accordingly to contemplate
them in that relation, it has been your praise that you have   30
not thereby been prevented from looking upon them as
individuals, and that you have habitually left your heart

26. *your public character*: as a Whig of radical persuasions, generally
commanding a huge popular following, Fox had identified himself with
many egalitarian causes and had been notable for his outspoken sympathy
for revolutionary France right through to 1795. See notes below for more
particular aspects of his policies that Wordsworth may have in mind.

open to be influenced by them in that capacity. This habit
cannot but have made you dear to Poets; and I am sure that
if, since your first entrance into public life, there has been a   35
single true Poet living in England he must have loved you.

But were I assured that I myself had a just claim to the
title of a Poet, all the dignity being attached to the word
which belongs to it, I do not think that I should have
ventured for that reason to offer these volumes to you; at   40
present it is solely on account of two poems in the second
volume, the one entitled 'The Brothers', and the other
'Michael,' that I have been emboldened to take this liberty.

It appears to me that the most calamitous effect which
has followed the measures which have lately been pursued   45
in this country is a rapid decay of the domestic affections
among the lower orders of society. This effect the present
rulers of this country are not conscious of, or they
disregard it. For many years past, the tendency of society
amongst almost all the nations of Europe has been to   50
produce it. But recently by the spreading of manufactures
through every part of the country, by the heavy taxes upon
postage, by workhouses, Houses of Industry, and the
invention of soup-shops &c. &c. superadded to the
increasing disproportion between the price of labour and   55
that of the necessaries of life, the bonds of domestic feeling
among the poor, as far as the influence of these things has
extended, have been weakened, and in innumerable
instances entirely destroyed. The evil would be the less to
be regretted, if these institutions were regarded only as   60
palliatives to a disease; but the vanity and pride of their
promoters are so subtly interwoven with them, that they are
deemed great discoveries and blessings to humanity. In the
meantime parents are separated from their children, and
children from their parents; the wife no longer prepares   65
with her own hands a meal for her husband, the produce of
his labour; there is little doing in his house in which his
affections can be interested, and but little left in it which he
can love. I have two neighbours, a man and his wife, both

46–7. *a rapid . . . society*: in a famous attack on government policy on 24
March 1795 Fox had cited the recent fall in marriage and baptism rates in
Lancashire, but he attributed this to the effects of the war with France.
51. *manufactures*: industrial activity.
53–4. *workhouses . . . soup-shops*: see note on line 172, pp. 315–16.
55–6. *increasing . . . life*: Fox had lamented the inadequacy of wages in
speeches in the Commons in the latter part of 1795.
69. *I have two neighbours*: the letter is written from Grasmere.

upwards of eighty years of age; they live alone; the husband   70
has been confined to his bed many months and has never
had, nor till within these few weeks has ever needed,
anybody to attend to him but his wife. She has recently
been seized with a lameness which has often prevented her
from being able to carry him his food to his bed; the   75
neighbours fetch water for her from the well, and do other
kind offices for them both, but her infirmities increase. She
told my servant two days ago that she was afraid they must
both be boarded out among some other poor of the parish
(they have long been supported by the parish), but she said   80
it was hard, having kept house together so long, to come to
this, and she was sure that 'it would burst her heart.' I
mention this fact to shew how deeply the spirit of
independence is, even yet, rooted in some parts of the
country. These people could not express themselves in this   85
way without an almost sublime conviction of the blessings
of independent domestic life. If it is true, as I believe, that
this spirit is rapidly disappearing, no greater curse can
befall a land.

I earnestly entreat your pardon for having detained you   90
so long. In the two poems, 'The Brothers' and 'Michael' I
have attempted to draw a picture of the domestic affections
as I know they exist amongst a class of men who are now
almost confined to the North of England. They are small
independent *proprietors* of land here called statesmen, men   95
of respectable education who daily labour on their own
little properties. The domestic affections will always be
strong amongst men who live in a country not crowded
with population, if these men are placed above poverty. But
if they are proprietors of small estates, which have   100
descended to them from their ancestors, the power which
these affections will acquire amongst such men is incon-
ceivable by those who have only had an opportunity of
observing hired labourers, farmers, and the manufacturing
poor. Their little tract of land serves as a kind of   105
permanent rallying point for their domestic feelings, as a
tablet upon which they are written which makes them
objects of memory in a thousand instances when they
would otherwise be forgotten. It is a fountain fitted to the
nature of social man, from which supplies of affection, as   110
pure as his heart was intended for, are daily drawn. This
class of men is rapidly disappearing. You, Sir, have a

---

95. statesmen: see also note to line 230, pp. 349–50.

consciousness, upon which every good man will congratulate
you, that the whole of your public conduct has in one way
or other been directed to the preservation of this class of   115
men, and those who hold similar situations. You have felt
that the most sacred of all property is the property of the
poor. The two poems which I have mentioned were written
with a view to show that men who do not wear fine clothes
can feel deeply. 'Pectus enim est quod disertos facit, et vis   120
mentis. Ideoque imperitis quoque, si modo sint aliquo
affectu concitati, verba non desunt.' The poems are faithful
copies from nature; and I hope, whatever effect they may
have upon you, you will at least be able to perceive that
they may excite profitable sympathies in many kind and   125
good hearts, and may in some small degree enlarge our
feelings of reverence for our species, and our knowledge of
human nature, by showing that our best qualities are
possessed by men whom we are too apt to consider, not
with reference to the points in which they resemble us, but   130
to those in which they manifestly differ from us. I thought,
at a time when these feelings are sapped in so many ways,
that the two poems might co-operate, however feebly, with
the illustrious efforts which you have made to stem this and
other evils with which the country is labouring, and it is on   135
this account alone that I have taken the liberty of thus
addressing you.

Wishing earnestly that the time may come when the
country may perceive what it has lost by neglecting your

114–18. the whole . . . poor: part of the sense of 'property' here may be the
wages of the poor, for Wordsworth (like Thomas Paine) applies the term in
this way in his 'Letter to the Bishop of Llandaff' (Owen and Smyser 1974,
I, 43), and Fox had complained about wage levels. But the context makes it
clear that Wordsworth is thinking mainly of land. Fox was egalitarian in his
principles, an advocate of parliamentary reform and an opponent of the
wars with America and France and their economic effects, but it is only in
these indirect ways that he could be regarded as a champion of the landed
poor. Even making allowance for the fact that the economic and social
conditions of the civilian population lay outside the recognized immediate
scope of politics in the period, and for Wordsworth's belief that the wars
were a great social evil, there were enough other causes dear to Fox's heart
(religious toleration and the abolition of slavery, for example) to make
Wordsworth's characterization of his political position lopsided. It is worth
noting that in at least one area (Staveley, near Kendal) Wordsworth
interpreted the historical record to mean that a 'statesmen' system had
come in as the result of seventeenth-century 'Hampdens' resisting
monarchical attempts on their land (Owen and Smyser 1974, II, 264–5).
120–2. 'Pectus . . . desunt': see note to *Motto*, p. 95.

advice, and hoping that your latter days may be attended   140
with health and comfort.

I remain, with the highest respect and admiration,

Your most obedient and humble servt

W. Wordsworth

Coleridge to William Wilberforce (January 1801)

Coleridge composed this and the following letter to Burges although they were sent over Wordsworth's signature. The wording ('gaudy phrases', 'elder poets') sometimes quite closely echoes that of Wordsworth's Advertisement and Preface. For Coleridge's ideas on poetic diction at this point as revealed in the letters, see General Introduction, pp. 7–9.

Sir,

I composed the accompanying poems under the persuasion that all which is usually included under the name of action bears the same proportion (in respect of worth) to the affections, as a language to the thing signified. When the material forms or intellectual ideas which should be   5
employed to represent the internal state of feeling are made to claim attention for their own sake, then commences lip-worship, or superstition, or disputatiousness, in religion; a passion for gaudy ornament and violent stimulants in morals; and in our literature bombast and vicious refine-   10
ments, an aversion to the common conversational language of our countrymen, with an extravagant preference given to *wit* by some, and to outrageous *incident* by others – while the most sacred affections of the human race seem to lay no hold on our sympathies unless we can contemplate them   15
in the train of some circumstances that excite *curiosity*, or unriddle them from some gaudy phrases that are to attract our wonder for themselves.

It was the excellence of our elder Poets to write in such a

Wilberforce: MP, campaigner for the abolition of slavery, and prime mover of the 'Evangelical' religious revival among the upper and middle classes in the early nineteenth century.
2–4. all which . . . signified: the sense here, obscurely put, is that language should be appropriate to its subject in the way that actions should flow from emotions.
16. in the train . . . curiosity: Coleridge seems to be referring to novels with a strong element of narrative suspense.

language as should the *most* rapidly convey their meaning, 20
but the pleasure which I am persuaded the greater number
of Readers receive from our modern writers in verse and
prose arises from the sense of having overcome a difficulty,
of having made a series of lucky guesses, and perhaps, in
some degree, of understanding what they are conscious the 25
lower classes of their countrymen would not be able to
understand. The poems which accompany this letter were
written with no idle expectation of the Author's immediate
fame or their rapid circulation. Had my predominant
influences been either the love of praise or the desire of 30
profit I should have held out to myself other subjects than
the affections which walk 'in silence and in a veil', and
other rules of poetic diction than the determination to
prefer passion to imagery and (except where the contrary
was chosen for dramatic purposes) to express what I meant 35
to express with all possible regard to precision and
propriety, but with very little attention to what is called
dignity.

In thus stating my opinions I state at the same time my
reasons for soliciting your acceptance of these volumes. In 40
your religious treatise these truths are developed, and
applied to the present state of our religion; I have acted on
them in a less awful department, but not I trust with less
serious convictions. Indeed had I not been persuaded
myself that in the composition of them I had been a fellow- 45
labourer with you in the same vineyard – acting under the
perception of some one common truth and attributing to
that truth the same importance and necessity, if I had not
appeared to myself to have discovered (in my intentions at
least) some bond of connection between us, I could not 50
without self-reproof have taken this opportunity of etc etc.

W. Wordsworth

32. *'in silence ... veil'*: it has not been possible to trace this allusion.
40–1. In your ... developed: rather as with Wordsworth's letter to Fox, the
link between author's and recipient's views is fairly tenuous. In his very
important *A Practical View of the Prevailing Religious System of Professed
Christians* (1797) Wilberforce sought to persuade his social peers to
respond emotionally and in their practical lives to a doctrinally aware,
Bible-based Christianity. It is in its urgings about sincerity and authenticity
that Wilberforce's Evangelicalism has some resemblance to the literary
principles enunciated here.
43. awful: awe-inspiring.
45–6. fellow-labourer ... vineyard: a stock image for the active Christian

Coleridge to Sir James Bland Burges (January 1801)

Sir,

I entreat the honour of your acceptance of the accompanying volumes, as an acknowledgment of the pleasure which I have received from your poem. You will permit me to mention, as an excuse of the liberty which I thus take, that I had observed in your poetry, independent 5 of its other merits, a pure and unmixed vein of native English, which induced me to hope that a series of poems written in the spirit of dislike to that diction which proceeds from the individual, not the community, would possess some claim to your attention. The habit of 10 considering the language of our country as a servant and not as a master has infected, with few exceptions, almost all our writers, both in prose and verse, since the death of Dryden and has, I think, co-operated with other causes in some measure to injure the simplicity of our national 15 character, and to weaken our reverence for our ancient institutions and religious offices. Those prepossessions, therefore, which the knowledge of a wise purpose gains in favour of the execution, I rely on from your kindness, and have the honour, 20

Sir, to remain,

Your obedient, humble servant,

William Wordsworth

life, deriving ultimately from *Matthew* 20:1–16 and its application to the disciples. It is not clear if Coleridge is claiming a religious aspect for *LB*, or simply gracefully couching the idea of a similarity of purpose in the language of Wilberforce's Evangelicalism.

Burges: reactionary politician and verbose poet whose social and literary principles seem to have been virtually antithetical to those of Coleridge and Wordsworth. His name, however, chanced to be visible at the time these letters were being sent (see next note) and it was probably plucked out of the air by Coleridge as that of a socially well-connected author whose influence it was worth trying to exploit.

3. your poem: it is most unlikely that Coleridge had done more than hear word of the eighteen-book Spenserian *Richard the First*. It was published in early 1801, and Coleridge dates his letter 14 January 1801. If he had looked into it he would have found a poem which even the *Monthly Mirror* found 'strange' in its diction.

From Wordsworth's letter to Thomas Poole (April 1801)

. . . In the last Poem of my 2nd volume I have attempted to give a picture of a man, of strong mind and lively sensibility, agitated by two of the most powerful affections of the human heart; the parental affection, and the love of property, *landed* property, including the feelings of in-   5
heritance, home, and personal and family independence. This Poem has, I know, drawn tears from the eyes of more than one, persons well acquainted with the manners of the Statesmen, as they are called, of this country; and, moreover, persons who never wept, in reading verse,   10
before. This is a favourable augury for me. But nevertheless I am anxious to know the effect of this Poem upon you, on many accounts; because you are yourself the inheritor of an estate which has long been in possession of your family; and, above all, because you are so well acquainted, nay, so   15
familiarly conversant with the language, manners, and feelings of the middle order of people who dwell in the country. Though from the comparative infrequency of small landed properties in your neighbourhood, your situation has not been altogether so favourable as mine, yet   20
your daily and hourly intercourse with these people must have far more than counterbalanced any disadvantage of this kind; so that, all things considered, perhaps there is not in England a more competent judge than you must be, of the skill or knowledge with which my pictures are drawn.   25
I had a still further wish that this Poem should please you, because in writing it I had your character often before my eyes, and sometimes thought I was delineating such a man as you yourself would have been under the circumstances. . . .

Thomas Poole: a neighbour and friend from Wordsworth's Somerset days.
1. last . . . volume: 'Michael'.
3. agitated: activated.
9. Statesmen: see Wordsworth's letter to Fox, ll. 92–116 (pp. 43–4).
9. country: district.
19. your neighbourhood: west Somerset.

Wordsworth to John Wilson (June 1802)

My dear Sir,

    Had it not been for a very amiable modesty you could not have imagined that your letter could give me any offence. It was on many accounts highly grateful to me. I was pleased to find that I had given so much pleasure to an ingenuous and able mind, and I further considered the enjoyment which you had had from my poems as an earnest that others might be delighted with them in the same or a like manner. It is plain from your letter that the pleasure which I have given you has not been blind or unthinking; you have studied the poems and prove that you have entered into the spirit of them. They have not given you a cheap or vulgar pleasure, therefore I feel that you are entitled to my kindest thanks for having done some violence to your natural diffidence in the communication which you have made to me.

    There is scarcely any part of your letter that does not deserve particular notice, but partly from a weakness in my stomach and digestion and partly from certain habits of mind I do not write any letters unless upon business, not even to my dearest friends. Except during absence from my own family I have not written five letters of friendship during the last five years. I have mentioned this in order that I may retain your good opinion should my letter be less minute than you are entitled to expect. You seem to be desirous of my opinion on the influence of natural objects in forming the character of nations. This cannot be understood without first considering their influence upon men in general first with reference to such subjects as are common to all countries, and next such as belong exclusively to any particular country or in a greater degree to it than to another. Now it is manifest that no human being can be so besotted and debased by oppression, penury or any other evil which unhumanizes man as to be utterly insensible to the colours, forms, or smell of flowers, the voices and motions of birds and beasts, the appearances of the sky and heavenly bodies, the genial warmth of a fine day, the terror and uncomfortableness of a storm, &c &c.

John Wilson: later to become, under the pseudonym Christopher North, a celebrated author and critic in the *Blackwood's* circle, Wilson had written an admiring letter to Wordsworth while still an undergraduate at Glasgow.
3. grateful: pleasing.

How dead soever many full-grown men may outwardly
seem to these things they all are more or less affected by
them, and in childhood, in the first practice and exercise of   40
their senses, they must have been not the nourishers
merely, but often the fathers of their passions. There
cannot be a doubt that in tracts of country where images of
danger, melancholy, grandeur, or loveliness, softness, and
ease prevail, that they will make themselves felt powerfully   45
in forming the characters of the people, so as to produce a
uniformity of national character, where the nation is small
and is not made up of men who, inhabiting different soils,
climates, &c by their civil usages, and relations materially
interfere with each other. It was so formerly, no doubt, in   50
the Highlands of Scotland but we cannot perhaps observe
much of it in our own island at the present day because,
even in the most sequestered places, by manufactures,
traffic, religion, law, interchange of inhabitants &c distinc-
tions are done away which would otherwise have been   55
strong and obvious. This complex state of society does not,
however, prevent the characters of individuals from
frequently receiving a strong bias not merely from the
impressions of general nature, but also from local objects
and images. But it seems that to produce these effects in   60
the degree in which we frequently find them to be
produced there must be a peculiar sensibility of original
organization combining with moral accidents, as is exhibited
in *The Brothers* and in *Ruth* – I mean, to produce this in a
marked degree – not that I believe that any man was ever   65
brought up in the country without loving it, especially in his
better moments, or in a district of particular grandeur or
beauty without feeling some stronger attachment to it on
that account than he would otherwise have felt. I include,
you will observe, in these considerations the influence of   70
climate, changes in the atmosphere and elements, and the
labours and occupations which particular districts require.

You begin what you say upon the Idiot Boy with this
observation, that nothing is a fit subject for poetry which
does not please. But here follows a question, Does not   75
please whom? Some have little knowledge of natural
imagery of any kind and, of course, little relish for it; some
are disgusted with the very mention of the words pastoral
poetry, sheep or shepherds; some cannot tolerate a poem
with a ghost or any supernatural agency in it; others would   80
shrink from an animated description of the pleasures of
love, as from a thing carnal and libidinous; some cannot

bear to see delicate and refined feelings ascribed to men in
low conditions of society, because their vanity and self-love
tell them that these belong only to themselves and men like
themselves in dress, station, and way of life. Others are
disgusted with the naked language of some of the most
interesting passions of men, because either it is indelicate,
or gross, or vulgar; as many fine ladies could not bear
certain expressions in 'The Mad Mother' and 'The
Thorn', and, as in the instance of Adam Smith, who, we
are told, could not endure the Ballad of Clym of the
Clough, because the author had not written like a
gentleman. Then there are professional, local and national
prejudices for, ever more, some take no interest in the
description of a particular passion or quality, as love of
solitariness, we will say, genial activity of fancy, love of
nature, religion, and so forth, because they have little or
nothing of it in themselves, and so on without end. I return
then to the question, please whom? or what? I answer,
human nature, as it has been and ever will be. But where
are we to find the best measure of this? I answer, from
within by stripping our own hearts naked, and by looking
out of ourselves towards men who lead the simplest lives
most according to nature, men who have never known false
refinements, wayward and artificial desires, false criticisms,
effeminate habits of thinking and feeling, or who, having
known these things, have outgrown them. This latter class
is the most to be depended upon, but it is very small in
number. People in our rank in life are perpetually falling
into one sad mistake, namely, that of supposing that human
nature and the persons they associate with are one and the
same thing. Whom do we generally associate with?
Gentlemen, persons of fortune, professional men, ladies –
persons who can afford to buy or can easily procure books
of half a guinea price, hot-pressed, and printed upon
superfine paper. These persons are, it is true, a part of

91–3. Adam Smith ... Clough: refers to the literary opinions of Adam
Smith as reported in *The European Magazine* XX (1791), p. 135. Smith
allegedly said in 1780: 'It is the duty of a poet to write like a gentleman. I
dislike that homely style which some think fit to call the language of nature
and simplicity, and so forth,' mentioning the 'heap of rubbish' in Percy's
Reliques, in particular the traditional ballad 'Adam Bell, Clym of the Clough
and William of Cloudsley'.
116. half a guinea: half a guinea was ten shillings and sixpence. The first
edition of *LB* cost five shillings and the subsequent two-volume editions ten
shillings.

human nature, but we err lamentably if we suppose them to
be fair representatives of the vast mass of human existence.
And yet few ever consider books but with reference to their   120
power of pleasing these persons and men of a higher rank;
few descend lower among cottages and fields and among
children. A man must have done this habitually before his
judgment upon the Idiot Boy would be in any way decisive
with me. I *know* I have done this myself habitually; I wrote   125
the poem with exceeding delight and pleasure, and
whenever I read it I read it with pleasure. You have given
me praise for having reflected faithfully in my poems the
feelings of human nature; I would fain hope that I have
done so. But a great Poet ought to do more than this; he   130
ought to a certain degree to rectify men's feelings, to give
them new compositions of feeling, to render their feelings
more sane, pure and permanent, in short, more consonant
to nature, that is, to eternal nature, and the great moving
spirit of things. He ought to travel before men occasionally   135
as well as at their sides. I may illustrate this by a reference
to natural objects. What false notions have prevailed from
generation to generation as to the true character of the
nightingale. As far as my Friend's Poem in the Lyrical
Ballads is read it will contribute greatly to rectify these.   140
You will recollect a passage in Cowper where, speaking of
rural sounds, he says,

> and *even* the boding Owl
> That hails the rising moon has charms for me.

Cowper was passionately fond of natural objects, yet you   145
see he mentions it as a marvellous thing that he could
connect pleasure with the cry of the owl. In the same poem
he speaks in the same manner of that beautiful plant, the
gorse, making in some degree an amiable boast of his
loving it, '*unsightly* and unsmooth' as it is. There are many   150
aversions of this kind which, though they have some
foundation in nature, have yet so slight a one, that though
they may have prevailed hundreds of years a philosopher
will look upon them as accidents. So with respect to many
moral feelings, either of love or dislike, what excessive   155

139. *my Friend's Poem*: 'The Nightingale' by Coleridge.
143–4. *and even ... me*: The Task (1785), I, 205–6 (Wordsworth's italics).
147–9. *In the same ... gorse*: The Task I, 527–30.
150. '*unsightly and unsmooth*': Paradise Lost IV, 631 (Wordsworth's italics).
154. *accidents*: i.e. not intrinsic to the experience of the plant, animal, etc.
in question.

admiration was paid in former times to personal prowess
and military success (it is so with the latter even at the
present day, but surely not nearly so much as heretofore).
So with regard to birth, and innumerable other modes of
sentiment, civil and religious. But you will be inclined to   160
ask by this time how all this applies to the Idiot Boy. To
this I can only say that the loathing and disgust which many
people have at the sight of an Idiot, is a feeling which,
though having some foundation in human nature, is not
necessarily attached to it in any virtuous degree, but is   165
owing in a great measure to a false delicacy and, if I may
say it without rudeness, a certain want of comprehensive-
ness of thinking and feeling. Persons in the lower classes of
society have little or nothing of this: if an Idiot is born in a
poor man's house it must be taken care of and cannot be   170
boarded out, as it would be by gentlefolks, or sent to a
public or private receptacle for such unfortunate beings.
Poor people, seeing frequently among their neighbours
such objects, easily forget whatever there is of natural
disgust about them, and have therefore a sane state, so that   175
without pain or suffering they perform their duties towards
them. I could with pleasure pursue this subject, but I must
now strictly adopt the plan which I proposed to myself
when I began to write this letter, namely, that of setting
down a few hints or memorandums, which you will think of   180
for my sake.

I have often applied to Idiots, in my own mind, that
sublime expression of scripture that '*their life is hidden with
God.*' They are worshipped, probably from a feeling of this
sort, in several parts of the East. Among the Alps, where   185
they are numerous, they are considered, I believe, as a
blessing to the family to which they belong. I have indeed
often looked upon the conduct of fathers and mothers of
the lower classes of society towards Idiots as the great
triumph of the human heart. It is there that we see the   190
strength, disinterestedness, and grandeur of love, nor have
I ever been able to contemplate an object that calls out so
many excellent and virtuous sentiments without finding it
hallowed thereby, and having something in me which bears
down before it, like a deluge, every feeble sensation of   195
disgust and aversion.

There are in my opinion several important mistakes in

183–4. 'their life ... God': *Colossians* 3:3.

the latter part of your letter which I could have wished to notice; but I find myself much fatigued. These refer both to the Boy and the Mother. I must content myself simply with observing that it is probable that the principal cause of your dislike to this particular poem lies in the *word* 'Idiot'. If there had been any such word in our language, *to which we had attached passion*, as lack-wit, half-wit, witless &c I should have certainly employed it in preference, but there is no such word. Observe (this is entirely in reference to this particular poem), my Idiot is not one of those who cannot articulate and such as are usually disgusting in their persons:

> Whether in cunning or in joy
> And then his words were not a few   &c,

and the last speech at the end of the poem. The Boy whom I had in my mind was by no means disgusting in his appearance – quite the contrary – and I have known several with imperfect faculties who are handsome in their persons and features. There is one, at present, within a mile of my own house remarkably so, though there is something of a stare and vacancy in his countenance. A friend of mine, knowing that some persons had a dislike to the poem such as you have expressed, advised me to add a stanza describing the person of the Boy so as entirely to separate him in the imaginations of my readers from that class of Idiots who are disgusting in their persons; but the narration in the poem is so rapid and impassioned that I could not find a place in which to insert the stanza without checking the progress of it, and so leaving a deadness upon the feeling. This poem has, I know, frequently produced the same effect as it did upon you and your friends, but there are many people also to whom it affords exquisite delight and who, indeed, prefer it to any other of my poems. This proves that the feelings there delineated are such as all men *may* sympathize with. This is enough for my purpose. It is not enough for me as a poet to delineate merely such feelings as all men *do* sympathize with, but it is also highly desirable to add to these others such as all men *may* sympathize with, and such as there is reason to believe they would be better and more moral beings if they did sympathize with.

I conclude with regret, because I have not said one half

216–17. *my own house*: at Grasmere.

of what I intended to say: but I am sure you will deem my 240
excuse sufficient when I inform you that my head aches
violently and I am, in other respects, unwell. I must,
however, again give you my warmest thanks for your kind
letter. I shall be happy to hear from you again, and do not
think it unreasonable that I should request a letter from 245
you when I feel that the answer which I may make to it will
not, perhaps, be above three or four lines. This I mention
to you with frankness, and you will not take it ill after what
I have before said of my remissness in writing letters.

I am, dear Sir 250
With great respect,
Yours sincerely W. Wordsworth

Preface (1802)

The first published version of this celebrated document was attached to the
edition of 1800. It was considerably enlarged in 1802, and in this form was
reprinted in 1805. The Preface has a more complex and ambitious aim than
may at first appear. It falls into two parts, with the first third of the text (to
l. 305) offering a description of what is most distinctive about the poetry of
LB, and the last two-thirds offering a spirited and original defence of the
apparent hybrid that these characteristics have produced. In the descriptive
part it is the naturalism of the poems which is consistently asserted – a
naturalism of content and language (in the second instance, a novel reading
is proposed in this edition for the famous remarks in ll. 119–21, but on any
interpretation Wordsworth's criteria are naturalistic). Wordsworth then
moves to an unexpected but, it could be argued, prophetic issue: how can a
thoroughgoing naturalism of the kind attempted be compatible with the use
of a poetic form? Or, to look at the problem from its opposite ends, why
should a poet be naturalistic? Why should a naturalistic writer choose to
write in verse? In Wordsworth's unabashed defence of both aspects of the
supposed hybrid, naturalistic poetry, he appeals to two kinds of evidence:
first, the reality of past poetry and the poet's situation and powers; second,
the deep human significance of the aesthetic in poetry. He argues that the
naturalistic poet's discourse, compared with other kinds of mimetic
discourse, is by no means in a futile second-best relationship to reality, and
that the proposal that the naturalistic poet should somehow seek to close
the gap by using special verbal substitutes for real-life effects is
unworkable, false to the social and linguistic conditions of poethood, and
refuted by the facts of successful poetic performance. Conversely,
Wordsworth claims that in the pleasure afforded by the aesthetic aspect of
poetry (with a special emphasis here on metre) there is profound fidelity to
the human experience of the world; in other words, something like a lyrical
ballad – an image of ordinary, troubled humanity cast into rhythm and
rhyme – captures the quality of our response to life.

So Parrish (1960) is right to observe that, 'far from leading a . . . revolt . . . against the literary element in poetry . . . Wordsworth offers in his theory of meter a defense of literary art'. The majority of commentators, perhaps, have seen the Preface as an anti-literary document, and a confused and unoriginal one at that. In the footnotes in this edition attention is drawn to the orderliness of the argument at certain points, and the extent of Wordsworth's indebtedness to previous literary theorists is indicated. He was bound to work within an eighteenth-century framework of ideas, but (with the exception of the historical theory offered in the Appendix; see pp. 88–90) antecedents for Wordsworth's main positions simply cannot be discovered (see Stone 1967: 102–3). There is a broader point about his originality which is not illustrated in the notes: the Preface is a uniquely bold conjunction of prescriptive literary theory and poetic practice. Eighteenth-century critics had written treatises, long and short, on literary theory but (although some of these men were also poets) they had not offered original poetry in proof of their views. Poetic prefaces – such as Burns wrote for the 1786 edition of his *Poems* – might touch on Wordsworthian concerns but never in the confident, programmatic spirit of Wordsworth (Burns says he is a plain poet writing about plain people but claims, at least, to be apologetic about this). This aspect of Wordsworth's Preface has a momentous effect on the theory itself: 'after him it becomes awkward to derive criticism from abstract rules whose validity is glibly assumed as axiomatic. In this sense he throws off the classic tradition and introduces into the study of aesthetics a freshness which had been wanting in literary criticism almost without exception since the *Poetics* of Aristotle . . . Wordsworth restores Aristotle's stress upon the importance of practice and makes the rules once more grow out of the usage' (Burgum 1940). The Preface to *LB* is a text appropriate to a dedicated young poet: bursting with convictions about his art forged in the experience of writing, and of reading as a writer. The idiosyncratic and cryptic touches in the expression are due to its being an extremely personal document, and they should be prized accordingly.

The first volume of these Poems has already been submitted to general perusal. It was published as an experiment which, I hoped, might be of some use to ascertain how far, by fitting to metrical arrangement a

---

1. first volume: the first volume of the 1802 edition ends with 'Tintern Abbey' and is virtually the same as the first (1798) single-volume edition. Wordsworth's way of putting things here is slightly misleading about the history of the contents of the first volume, however, since in 1800 two poems from 1798 had been transferred to the second volume of the enlarged edition ('The Complaint of a Forsaken Indian Woman' and 'Lines Written near Richmond'), one had been added (Coleridge's 'Love'), and one had been dropped (Wordsworth's 'The Convict'). One more poem was dropped in 1802 (Coleridge's 'The Dungeon'), along with Wordsworth's 'A Character' from the second volume.

selection of the real language of men in a state of vivid 5
sensation, that sort of pleasure and that quantity of
pleasure may be imparted which a Poet may rationally
endeavour to impart.

I had formed no very inaccurate estimate of the probable
effect of those Poems: I flattered myself that they who 10
should be pleased with them would read them with more
than common pleasure: and, on the other hand, I was well
aware that by those who should dislike them they would be
read with more than common dislike. The result has
differed from my expectation in this only, that I have 15
pleased a greater number than I ventured to hope I should
please.

For the sake of variety, and from a consciousness of my
own weakness, I was induced to request the assistance of a
friend, who furnished me with the Poems of the ANCIENT 20
MARINER, the FOSTER-MOTHER'S TALE, the NIGHTINGALE,
and the Poem entitled LOVE. I should not, however, have
requested this assistance, had I not believed that the Poems
of my friend would in a great measure have the same
tendency as my own, and that, though there would be 25
found a difference, there would be found no discordance in
the colours of our style; as our opinions on the subject of
Poetry do almost entirely coincide.

Several of my friends are anxious for the success of
these Poems from a belief that, if the views with which they 30
were composed were indeed realized, a class of Poetry
would be produced, well adapted to interest mankind
permanently, and not unimportant in the multiplicity and in
the quality of its moral relations: and on this account they
have advised me to prefix a systematic defence of the 35
theory upon which the Poems were written. But I was

5. *language*: this major term in the Preface probably means more than just
vocabulary in most of its occurrences. For an important instance where
'language of men' is used by Wordsworth in connection with the syntax of
one of his poems, see Owen and Smyser 1974, I, 167.
5. *vivid*: lively, vigorous.
27. *colours*: deriving from rhetorical theory, by Wordsworth's day the term
had come to mean any distinctive features of a writer's verbal art.
33–4. *the multiplicity . . . relations*: one of the handful of privileged, repeated
phrases in the Preface; see also ll. 999–1000.
34–5. *they . . . defence*: only Coleridge is mentioned by Wordsworth else-
where as urging him to write the Preface. Wordsworth implies that
Coleridge was thinking of something more elaborate than the document
which resulted.

unwilling to undertake the task, because I knew that on this
occasion the Reader would look coldly upon my arguments,
since I might be suspected of having been principally
influenced by the selfish and foolish hope of *reasoning* him   40
into an approbation of these particular Poems: and I was
still more unwilling to undertake the task because,
adequately to display my opinions, and fully to enforce my
arguments, would require a space wholly disproportionate
to the nature of a preface. For to treat the subject with the   45
clearness and coherence of which I believe it susceptible, it
would be necessary to give a full account of the present
state of the public taste in this country, and to determine
how far this taste is healthy or depraved; which, again,
could not be determined without pointing out in what   50
manner language and the human mind act and re-act on
each other, and without retracing the revolutions, not of
literature alone, but likewise of society itself. I have
therefore altogether declined to enter regularly upon this
defence; yet I am sensible, that there would be some   55
impropriety in abruptly obtruding upon the public, without
a few words of introduction, Poems so materially different
from those upon which general approbation is at present
bestowed.

It is supposed, that by the act of writing in verse an   60
Author makes a formal engagement that he will gratify
certain known habits of association; that he not only thus
apprizes the Reader that certain classes of ideas and
expressions will be found in his book, but that others will
be carefully excluded. This exponent or symbol held forth   65
by metrical language must in different eras of literature
have excited very different expectations: for example, in the

37–8. *on this occasion*: i.e. serving as a preface to his own poems.
52. *revolutions*: profound changes, violent upheavals.
55–7. *there would ... introduction*: not too much should be made of the
corollary, that the poems in *LB* 1798 were not sufficiently unusual to
warrant such an introduction (and in the next paragraph Wordsworth uses
exactly the phrasing of the 1798 Advertisement on 'strangeness and
awkwardness'), but Wordsworth evidently felt that the poems in the second
half of the enlarged collection were at least as likely to cause dismay as
those in the first.
61. *formal*: explicit and definite.
65. *exponent*: the first use in this sense recorded by the *OED* is from
Coleridge, several years later.
67–9. *the age ... Claudian*: that is, republican Rome as opposed to two
phases of imperial culture (Statius in particular was a byword for stylistic

age of Catullus, Terence and Lucretius, and that of Statius
or Claudian; and in our own country, in the age of
Shakespeare and Beaumont and Fletcher, and that of 70
Donne and Cowley, or Dryden, or Pope. I will not take
upon me to determine the exact import of the promise
which by the act of writing in verse an Author, in the
present day, makes to his Reader; but I am certain, it will
appear to many persons that I have not fulfilled the terms 75
of an engagement thus voluntarily contracted. They who
have been accustomed to the gaudiness and inane
phraseology of many modern writers, if they persist in
reading this book to its conclusion, will, no doubt,
frequently have to struggle with feelings of strangeness and 80
awkwardness: they will look round for Poetry, and will be
induced to inquire by what species of courtesy these
attempts can be permitted to assume that title. I hope
therefore the Reader will not censure me, if I attempt to
state what I have proposed to myself to perform, and also 85
(as far as the limits of a preface will permit) to explain
some of the chief reasons which have determined me in the
choice of my purpose: that at least he may be spared any
unpleasant feeling of disappointment, and that I myself
may be protected from the most dishonourable accusation 90
which can be brought against an Author, namely, that of an
indolence which prevents him from endeavouring to
ascertain what is his duty or, when his duty is ascertained,
prevents him from performing it.

The principal object, then, which I proposed to myself in 95
these Poems was to choose incidents and situations from
common life, and to relate or describe them throughout, as
far as was possible, in a selection of language really used by
men; and, at the same time, to throw over them a certain
colouring of imagination, whereby ordinary things should 100
be presented to the mind in an unusual way; and further,

inflatedness). Wordsworth probably thinks of the Metaphysical poets,
Donne and Cowley, and the Augustans, Dryden and Pope, as representing
extremes of artificiality as compared with the writing of Shakespeare,
Beaumont and Fletcher.

77. inane: see note to line 11, p. 34.
82. courtesy: see note to line 16, p. 34.
99–101. to throw ... way: this component of Wordsworth's list of aims is
not taken up again in the Preface (in contrast to the two flanking state-
ments, which are taken up in turn and enlarged on in the next three and a
half paragraphs). Its appearance here may be a vestige of an emphasis on
such effects which arose in the early Wordsworth–Coleridge plans for *LB*

and above all, to make these incidents and situations interesting by tracing in them, truly though not ostentatiously, the primary laws of our nature – chiefly, as far as regards the manner in which we associate ideas in a state of   105
excitement. Low and rustic life was generally chosen, because in that condition the essential passions of the heart find a better soil in which they can attain their maturity, are less under restraint, and speak a plainer and more emphatic language; because in that condition of life our   110
elementary feelings co-exist in a state of greater simplicity and, consequently, may be more accurately contemplated, and more forcibly communicated; because the manners of rural life germinate from those elementary feelings and, from the necessary character of rural occupations, are more   115
easily comprehended, and are more durable; and lastly, because in that condition the passions of men are incorporated with the beautiful and permanent forms of nature. The language, too, of these men is adopted

(see Authors' later comment, pp. 366, 369). This is not to say that it is not an important subsidiary aspect of Wordsworth's programme; see Fenwick note to 'Lucy Gray', p. 376.

106. excitement: emotional arousal.
110. language: in this occurrence, probably in a broader sense than simply verbal language.
110–11. our elementary . . . simplicity: Wordsworth's sense seems to be that the combination and elaboration of basic emotions goes less far among the members of a rural community than elsewhere. The phrasing indicates a transference from the cognitive to the psychological realm (in the same manner as David Hartley; see p. 76) of the tenet of John Locke and the associationists that many of our concepts amount to merely 'co-existing' elementary ideas.
113. manners: customary modes of behaviour.
115. necessary: serving practical needs.
119. The language . . . adopted: usually taken to be a description of the general idiom of the poems, but more naturally interpreted to mean 'the speech, as well as the feelings and behaviour, of rural individuals is presented'. Confusion arises because of the claim in the 1798 Advertisement (there certainly applied to the general idiom) about an experiment with 'the language of conversation in the middle and lower classes of society' (see p. 34). Admittedly Wordsworth drops this sociolinguistic formula when the passage is re-used at the beginning of the Preface, but he cannot have intended the social basis of the style of the 1798 poems to be *narrowed* in the larger collection, if only because no poems of importance are dropped. It should be noticed that Wordsworth is clear (ll. 259–63) that the 'style' of the poems has yet to be discussed (it is derived from 'the language of men'). Wordsworth's ideas were certainly understood, indeed

(purified indeed from what appear to be its real defects, 120
from all lasting and rational causes of dislike or disgust)
because such men hourly communicate with the best
objects from which the best part of language is originally
derived; and because, from their rank in society and the
sameness and narrow circle of their intercourse, being less 125
under the influence of social vanity they convey their
feelings and notions in simple and unelaborated expressions.
Accordingly, such a language, arising out of repeated
experience and regular feelings, is a more permanent, and
a far more philosophical language, than that which is 130
frequently substituted for it by Poets, who think that they
are conferring honour upon themselves and their art, in
proportion as they separate themselves from the sympathies
of men, and indulge in arbitrary and capricious habits of
expression, in order to furnish food for fickle tastes, and 135
fickle appetites, of their own creation.

I cannot, however, be insensible of the present outcry
against the triviality and meanness both of thought and

glossed, in this fashion by his friend John Stoddart in reviewing the
collection: 'where the subjects are supplied by rustic life, the language of
rustics ... is also adopted' (*British Critic* XVII, 1801, p. 127). Bialostosky
(1978) points out that even if the orthodox reading of the passage is correct,
the resulting account of the poet's idiom is not as perverse and/or trivial as
Coleridge argued in *Biographia Literaria*.

119–27. The language ... expressions: the whole passage should be
compared with Lectures 6 and 7 in Lowth (1787), on the role of 'Poetic
Imagery from the Objects of Nature' and 'Poetic Imagery from Common
Life' in the Hebrew poetry of the Old Testament.
130. a far ... language: glossed by Lamb (1982) on the strength of
comparable eighteenth-century usages (including Hartley) as meaning a
more perspicuous language (rather than one better equipped for abstract
argument); in this instance a language 'immediately responsive to the
rhythms and exigencies' of rural life (see also Christie 1983).
130–1. that which ... Poets: in the utterances they invent for characters
from common life.
136. ... their own creation: 'It is worth while here to observe that the
affecting parts of Chaucer are almost always expressed in language pure
and universally intelligible even to this day.' [Wordsworth's note] This
comment on Chaucer's idiom, unless interpreted rather artificially as
referring only to dramatic passages in his poetry, would tend to suggest that
Wordsworth is, after all, characterizing the general idiom of *LB* in the
associated paragraph. But in the original manuscript the note appears to be
written in the hand of Coleridge (Hale White 1897: 19). Peacock (1946)
not only detects Coleridge's hand but argues that he drafted this note.

language, which some of my contemporaries have occasionally introduced into their metrical compositions; and I acknowledge that this defect, where it exists, is more dishonourable to the Writer's own character than false refinement or arbitrary innovation, though I should contend at the same time that it is far less pernicious in the sum of its consequences. From such verses the Poems in these volumes will be found distinguished at least by one mark of difference, that each of them has a worthy *purpose*. Not that I mean to say, that I always began to write with a distinct purpose formally conceived; but I believe that my habits of meditation have so formed my feelings, as that my descriptions of such objects as strongly excite those feelings, will be found to carry along with them a *purpose*. If in this opinion I am mistaken, I can have little right to the name of a Poet. For all good Poetry is the spontaneous overflow of powerful feelings; but though this be true, Poems to which any value can be attached were never produced on any variety of subjects but by a man who, being possessed of more than usual organic sensibility, had also thought long and deeply. For our continued influxes of feeling are modified and directed by our thoughts, which are indeed the representatives of all our past feelings; and, as by contemplating the relation of these general representatives to each other we discover what is really important to men, so, by the repetition and continuance of this act, our feelings will be connected with important subjects, till at length, if we be originally possessed of much sensibility, such habits of mind will be produced that, by obeying blindly and mechanically the impulses of those habits, we shall describe objects, and utter sentiments, of

139. some . . . contemporaries: an allusion which has never been clarified – perhaps other practitioners of simple ballad verse in the periodicals (see General Introduction, pp. 13–14) or members of Wordsworth's circle such as Coleridge, Lamb and Southey who were occasionally trying plain kinds of writing at this date and sometimes being attacked for it (see Barstow 1917: 118–25; Roper 1968: 283–4; Green 1977: 277–91).
142. character: reputation.
145–55. the spontaneous . . . feelings: another of the repeated phrases in the Preface (see ll. 797–8) and a famous one, but it should be noticed that its centrality is immediately qualified: 'though this be true . . .'.
158. organic: pertaining to the organs of sense.
161, 162–3. representatives: Wordsworth's idiosyncratic usage, standing in meaning somewhere between 'representations' and 'tokens'.

such a nature and in such connection with each other, that 170
the understanding of the being to whom we address
ourselves, if he be in a healthful state of association, must
necessarily be in some degree enlightened, and his
affections ameliorated.

I have said that each of these Poems has a purpose. I 175
have also informed my Reader what this purpose will be
found principally to be, namely, to illustrate the manner in
which our feelings and ideas are associated in a state of
excitement. But, speaking in language somewhat more
appropriate, it is to follow the fluxes and refluxes of the 180
mind when agitated by the great and simple affections of
our nature. This object I have endeavoured in these short
essays to attain by various means; by tracing the maternal
passion through many of its more subtle windings, as in the
Poems of the IDIOT BOY and the MAD MOTHER; by 185
accompanying the last struggles of a human being, at the
approach of death, cleaving in solitude to life and society,
as in the Poem of the FORSAKEN INDIAN; by showing, as in
the stanzas entitled WE ARE SEVEN, the perplexity and
obscurity which in childhood attend our notion of death, or 190
rather our utter inability to admit that notion; or by
displaying the strength of fraternal, or to speak more
philosophically, of moral attachment when early associated
with the great and beautiful objects of nature, as in THE
BROTHERS; or, as in the incident of SIMON LEE, by placing 195
my Reader in the way of receiving from ordinary moral
sensations another and more salutary impression than we
are accustomed to receive from them. It has also been part
of my general purpose to attempt to sketch characters
under the influence of less impassioned feelings, as in the 200
TWO APRIL MORNINGS, THE FOUNTAIN, THE OLD MAN
TRAVELLING, THE TWO THIEVES, &c., characters of which
the elements are simple, belonging rather to nature than to
manners, such as exist now, and will probably always exist,
and which from their constitution may be distinctly and 205
profitably contemplated. I will not abuse the indulgence of

181. agitated: strongly moved.
193. moral: pertaining to the moral faculties (in contrast to the instinctual
basis of the maternal attachment mentioned earlier).
195–8. by placing ... from them: in this instance the site of the 'fluxes and
refluxes' explored must be the reader's mind.
204. manners: the social aspect of man.
205. distinctly: separately (an obsolescent sense in Wordsworth's day), on
the assumption that 'their' relates to 'characters'.

my Reader by dwelling longer upon this subject, but it is
proper that I should mention one other circumstance which
distinguishes these Poems from the popular Poetry of the
day; it is this, that the feeling therein developed gives   210
importance to the action and situation, and not the action
and situation to the feeling. My meaning will be rendered
perfectly intelligible by referring my Reader to the Poems
entitled POOR SUSAN and the CHILDLESS FATHER, particu-
larly to the last stanza of the latter Poem.   215
    I will not suffer a sense of false modesty to prevent me
from asserting, that I point my Reader's attention to this
mark of distinction, far less for the sake of these particular
Poems than from the general importance of the subject.
The subject is indeed important! For the human mind is   220
capable of being excited without the application of gross
and violent stimulants; and he must have a very faint
perception of its beauty and dignity who does not know
this, and who does not further know, that one being is
elevated above another in proportion as he possesses this   225
capability. It has therefore appeared to me, that to
endeavour to produce or enlarge this capability is one of
the best services in which, at any period, a Writer can be
engaged; but this service, excellent at all times, is especially
so at the present day. For a multitude of causes, unknown   230
to former times, are now acting with a combined force to
blunt the discriminating powers of the mind and, unfitting
it for all voluntary exertion, to reduce it to a state of almost
savage torpor. The most effective of these causes are the
great national events which are daily taking place, and the   235
increasing accumulation of men in cities, where the
uniformity of their occupations produces a craving for
extraordinary incident, which the rapid communication of
intelligence hourly gratifies. To this tendency of life and
manners the literature and theatrical exhibitions of the   240
country have conformed themselves. The invaluable works
of our elder Writers, I had almost said the works of

221. *excited*: aroused.
224–7. *one being . . . capability*: a view related to the later eighteenth-
century cult of sentiment and sensibility, with its positive valuation of
emotional susceptibility to slight and subtle stimuli.
234. *savage*: primitive, subhuman.
234. *effective*: influential (perhaps somewhat archaic at this date).
235. *great national events*: probably the events of Britain's war with
Napoleonic France.
239. *intelligence*: news.

Shakespeare and Milton, are driven into neglect by frantic novels, sickly and stupid German tragedies, and deluges of idle and extravagant stories in verse. When I think upon 245 this degrading thirst after outrageous stimulation, I am almost ashamed to have spoken of the feeble effort with which I have endeavoured to counteract it; and, reflecting upon the magnitude of the general evil, I should be oppressed with no dishonourable melancholy, had I not a 250 deep impression of certain inherent and indestructible qualities of the human mind, and likewise of certain powers in the great and permanent objects that act upon it, which are equally inherent and indestructible; and did I not further add to this impression a belief that the time is 255 approaching when the evil will be systematically opposed, by men of greater powers, and with far more distinguished success.

Having dwelt thus long on the subjects and aim of these Poems, I shall request the Reader's permission to apprize 260 him of a few circumstances relating to their *style*, in order, among other reasons, that I may not be censured for not having performed what I never attempted. The Reader will find that personifications of abstract ideas rarely occur in these volumes and, I hope, are utterly rejected as an 265 ordinary device to elevate the style, and raise it above Prose. I have proposed to myself to imitate and, as far as is possible, to adopt the very language of men; and assuredly such personifications do not make any natural or regular part of that language. They are, indeed, a figure of speech 270 occasionally prompted by passion, and I have made use of them as such; but I have endeavoured utterly to reject them

---

243–5. frantic . . . verse: it is not possible to identify with confidence the groups of works referred to here apart from the plays of the German Kotzebue, which enjoyed a great success around the turn of the century. Jacobus (1976: 224) argues that among the 'idle and extravagant' verse narratives Wordsworth would have Gottfried Bürger's 'Lenore' in mind.
246. outrageous: excessive, immoderate.
270–5. They are . . . prescription: the idea that the figurative element in language, including the various kinds of personification, is generated by strong emotion is very ancient, and orthodox in the eighteenth century. However, in the complexities of literary theory in the period personification was also often treated as a routine feature of poetry as opposed to prose (see, for example, the first Interlude in Erasmus Darwin's *The Loves of the Plants* (1789) – personification being seen here as an example of poetry's greater concreteness). Wordsworth seems to be original in pressing the logic of the figurative–emotional doctrine to such firm stylistic conclusions.

as a mechanical device of style, or as a family language which Writers in metre seem to lay claim to by prescription. I have wished to keep my Reader in the company of flesh and blood, persuaded that by so doing I shall interest him. I am, however, well aware that others who pursue a different track may interest him likewise; I do not interfere with their claim, I only wish to prefer a different claim of my own. There will also be found in these volumes little of what is usually called poetic diction; I have taken as much pains to avoid it as others ordinarily take to produce it; this I have done for the reason already alleged, to bring my language near to the language of men, and further, because the pleasure which I have proposed to myself to impart is of a kind very different from that which is supposed by many persons to be the proper object of Poetry. I do not know how, without being culpably particular, I can give my Reader a more exact notion of the style in which I wished these Poems to be written, than by informing him that I have at all times endeavoured to look steadily at my subject; consequently I hope that there is in these Poems little falsehood of description, and that my ideas are expressed in language fitted to their respective importance. Something I must have gained by this practice, as it is friendly to one property of all good Poetry, namely good sense; but it has necessarily cut me off from a large portion of phrases and figures of speech which from father to son have long been regarded as the common inheritance of Poets. I have also thought it expedient to restrict myself still further, having abstained from the use of many expressions, in themselves proper and beautiful, but which have been foolishly repeated by bad Poets, till such feelings of disgust are connected with them as it is scarcely possible by any art of association to overpower.

If in a Poem there should be found a series of lines, or even a single line, in which the language, though naturally arranged, and according to the strict laws of metre, does not differ from that of Prose, there is a numerous class of critics, who, when they stumble upon these prosaisms, as they call them, imagine that they have made a notable discovery, and exult over the Poet as over a man ignorant

281. what is ... diction: for contemporary views on the notion of a distinctive poetic idiom, see note to ll. 328–30, p. 67.
304. disgust: distaste.
310. prosaisms: first recorded use of the term in this sense in *OED*.

of his own profession. Now these men would establish a
canon of criticism which the Reader will conclude he must
utterly reject, if he wishes to be pleased with these   315
volumes. And it would be a most easy task to prove to him,
that not only the language of a large portion of every good
Poem, even of the most elevated character, must necessarily,
except with reference to the metre, in no respect differ
from that of good Prose, but likewise that some of the most   320
interesting parts of the best Poems will be found to be
strictly the language of Prose, when Prose is well written.
The truth of this assertion might be demonstrated by
innumerable passages from almost all the poetical writings,
even of Milton himself. I have not space for much   325
quotation; but, to illustrate the subject in a general manner,
I will here adduce a short composition of Gray, who was at
the head of those who, by their reasonings, have attempted
to widen the space of separation betwixt Prose and metrical

327. short ... Gray: the poem is the 'Sonnet on the Death of Richard
West'.
328–30. those who . . . composition: as Wordsworth implies, belief in a
thoroughly distinctive idiom for poetry was only one strand in the
eighteenth-century attitude to this question, and the pattern of opinions is
complicated, not to say contradictory (see Barstow 1917: 53ff). Gray
himself was known as an advocate of the extreme view because of a letter
published in Mason 1775: 138–41, in which he argued that 'the language
of the age is never the language of poetry . . . Our poetry . . . has a language
peculiar to itself', and also because of Johnson's remark in the 'Life' of
Gray that he 'thought his language more poetical as it was more remote
from common use'. All theorists probably agreed with Addison that a
poet could not afford to 'clothe his thoughts in the most plain and natural
expressions' because of the danger of 'meanness' (Cook 1926: 22), but the
nature of the poetic idiom was disputed, and the contending parties
(Spenserians or Miltonians, for example) could on occasion appeal to the
standard of ordinary usage in attacking opponents. Many writers wanted to
put limits on the privileges of this idiom, while accepting it. Examples are
Dennis ('an expression may be too florid or too bold for prose, and yet be
very becoming of verse. . . . But every expression that is false *English* in
prose, is barbarous and absurd in verse' – Hooker 1939, I, 24); Beattie
1776: 267–8 in his qualified admiration for the plain diction of
Shakespeare; and Goldsmith 1812, IV, 22, 407 (poetry is distinguished
from all other discourse by 'a language of its own' but poets are absurd who
think that 'the more their writings are unlike prose, the more they resemble
poetry'). The prose/poetry antithesis naturally makes a frequent appearance
in these discussions, but for some close contemporary parallels to
Wordsworth on this issue, see note to ll. 357–9, pp. 68–9.

composition, and was more than any other man curiously   330
elaborate in the structure of his own poetic diction.

> In vain to me the smiling mornings shine,
> And reddening Phœbus lifts his golden fire:
> The birds in vain their amorous descant join,
> Or cheerful fields resume their green attire.   335
> These ears, alas! for other notes repine;
> *A different object do these eyes require;*
> *My lonely anguish melts no heart but mine;*
> *And in my breast the imperfect joys expire;*
> Yet morning smiles the busy race to cheer,   340
> And new-born pleasure brings to happier men;
> The fields to all their wonted tribute bear;
> To warm their little loves the birds complain.
> *I fruitless mourn to him that cannot hear,*
> *And weep the more because I weep in vain.*   345

It will easily be perceived that the only part of this sonnet
which is of any value is the lines printed in italics; it is
equally obvious that, except in the rhyme, and in the use of
the single word 'fruitless' for fruitlessly, which is so far a
defect, the language of these lines does in no respect differ   350
from that of Prose.

By the foregoing quotation I have shown that the
language of Prose may yet be well adapted to Poetry; and I
have previously asserted that a large portion of the
language of every good Poem can in no respect differ from   355
that of good Prose. I will go further. I do not doubt that it
may be safely affirmed, that there neither is, nor can be,
any essential difference between the language of Prose and

346–7. *the only ... italics*: it should be observed that all the non-italicized
part of the text found objectionable by Wordsworth concerns the poet's
inability to derive a customary pleasure from the beauties of the morning,
and the metaphors here, at once conventional and highly fanciful, may be
intended as rhetorically suitable for this state of mind.
348. *the rhyme*: the fact of rhymed lines.
357–9. *there neither ... composition*: as Mendilow (1957) observes, there
was an enhanced interest at the end of the eighteenth century in the
traditional issue of what distinguishes poetry from prose, and Wordsworth
may have been influenced by some of these discussions in the present
paragraph and the associated footnote. In the footnote he argues that poetry
and metrical composition are not coextensive, and several writers shared
this perception while drawing different conclusions from it. Heron (1793:
2–4) reasons from the thought that 'it is not poetry, but *metre* that is to be
discriminated from prose' to the conservative and very unWordsworthian
view that poetry is distinguished by its 'appropriated words and phrases'.
Darwin (1791, II, 40–2) (despite the mannered diction of his own verse)

metrical composition. We are fond of tracing the resemblance between Poetry and Painting, and, accordingly, we call them sisters; but where shall we find bonds of connection sufficiently strict to typify the affinity betwixt metrical and Prose composition? They both speak by and to the same organs; the bodies in which both of them are clothed may be said to be of the same substance, their affections are kindred, and almost identical, not necessarily differing even in degree; Poetry sheds no tears 'such as Angels weep,' but natural and human tears; she can boast of no celestial ichor that distinguishes her vital juices from those of Prose; the same human blood circulates through the veins of them both.

360

365

370

If it be affirmed that rhyme and metrical arrangement of themselves constitute a distinction which overturns what I have been saying on the strict affinity of metrical language with that of Prose, and paves the way for other artificial distinctions which the mind voluntarily admits, I answer that the language of such Poetry as I am recommending is, as far as is possible, a selection of the language really spoken by men; that this selection, wherever it is made with

375

falls back on the concreteness of poetry rather than its idiom when it is conceded that 'the essential difference between Poetry and Prose' (a phrase that is perhaps remembered by Wordsworth) cannot be metre. Enfield (1796) has a head-on assault on the need for metre, with 'poetry' as the antithesis of 'philosophy'. The last two responses may indicate a certain eclipse of the doctrine of poetic diction at the end of the century, but no one comes near Wordsworth's straight repudiation of it. And Wordsworth, unlike the other theorists, is not at all inclined to play down metre because it is not the defining characteristic of poetry (he will go on to argue that in creating an 'overbalance' of pleasure it assists a central function of poetry).

359–61. We are . . . sisters: a favourite analogy in eighteenth-century aesthetics, deriving ultimately from Horace.
367. Poetry: 'I here use the word "Poetry" (though against my own judgment) as opposed to the word Prose, and synonymous with metrical composition. But much confusion has been introduced into criticism by this contradistinction of Poetry and Prose, instead of the more philosophical one of Poetry and Matter of Fact, or Science. The only strict antithesis to Prose is Metre; nor is this, in truth, a *strict* antithesis; because lines and passages of metre so naturally occur in writing Prose, that it would be scarcely possible to avoid them even were it desirable.' [Wordsworth's note] For the sentence 'lines . . . avoid them', compare Dryden (Ker 1961, I, 6).
367. tears . . . weep: *Paradise Lost* I, 620.
368. ichor: the ethereal fluid which was the equivalent of blood in the gods of Greek mythology.

true taste and feeling, will of itself form a distinction far   380
greater than would at first be imagined, and will entirely
separate the composition from the vulgarity and meanness
of ordinary life; and, if metre be superadded thereto, I
believe that a dissimilitude will be produced altogether
sufficient for the gratification of a rational mind. What   385
other distinction would we have? Whence is it to come?
And where is it to exist? Not, surely, where the Poet speaks
through the mouths of his characters: it cannot be
necessary here, either for elevation of style, or any of its
supposed ornaments. For, if the Poet's subject be   390
judiciously chosen, it will naturally, and upon fit occasion,
lead him to passions the language of which, if selected truly
and judiciously, must necessarily be dignified and variegated,
and alive with metaphors and figures. I forbear to speak of
an incongruity which would shock the intelligent Reader,   395
should the Poet interweave any foreign splendour of his
own with that which the passion naturally suggests: it is
sufficient to say that such addition is unnecessary. And,
surely, it is more probable that those passages, which with
propriety abound with metaphors and figures, will have   400
their due effect, if, upon other occasions where the
passions are of a milder character, the style also be
subdued and temperate.

But, as the pleasure which I hope to give by the Poems I
now present to the Reader must depend entirely on just   405
notions upon this subject, and, as it is in itself of the
highest importance to our taste and moral feelings, I
cannot content myself with these detached remarks. And if,
in what I am about to say, it shall appear to some that my
labour is unnecessary, and that I am like a man fighting a   410
battle without enemies, I would remind such persons, that,
whatever may be the language outwardly holden by men, a
practical faith in the opinions which I am wishing to
establish is almost unknown. If my conclusions are
admitted, and carried as far as they must be carried if   415
admitted at all, our judgments concerning the works of the
greatest Poets both ancient and modern will be far
different from what they are at present, both when we
praise, and when we censure: and our moral feelings
influencing, and influenced by these judgments will, I   420
believe, be corrected and purified.

Taking up the subject, then, upon general grounds, I ask
what is meant by the word Poet? What is a Poet? To whom
does he address himself? And what language is to be

expected from him? He is a man speaking to men: a man, it 425
is true, endued with more lively sensibility, more enthusiasm
and tenderness, who has a greater knowledge of human
nature, and a more comprehensive soul, than are supposed
to be common among mankind; a man pleased with his
own passions and volitions, and who rejoices more than 430
other men in the spirit of life that is in him; delighting to
contemplate similar volitions and passions as manifested in
the goings-on of the universe, and habitually impelled to
create them where he does not find them. To these
qualities he has added a disposition to be affected more 435
than other men by absent things as if they were present, an
ability of conjuring up in himself passions, which are
indeed far from being the same as those produced by real
events, yet (especially in those parts of the general
sympathy which are pleasing and delightful) do more nearly 440
resemble the passions produced by real events, than any
thing which, from the motions of their own minds merely,
other men are accustomed to feel in themselves; whence,
and from practice, he has acquired a greater readiness and
power in expressing what he thinks and feels, and 445
especially those thoughts and feelings which, by his own

423. What is a Poet?: Coleridge was especially struck by the passage which
follows: 'one on the dignity and nature of the office and character of a poet,
that is very grand, and of a sort of Verulamian power and majesty – but it is,
in parts, (and this is the fault, *me judice* [in my opinion], of all the latter
half of that preface) obscure beyond any necessity – and the extreme
elaboration and almost constrainedness of the diction contrasted (to my
feelings) somewhat harshly with the general style of the poems' (Griggs
1956: 830). 'Verulamian' here means 'in the manner of Bacon's prose', a
manner which is well described as 'majestic' but 'constrained'. Coleridge's
dislike for this style in the Preface is not shared by all commentators, but
his observation about the relationship between Wordsworth's prose and
verse styles is acute and has never been taken up by the critics. Given
Wordsworth's emphatic views on the interchangeability of the two modes, it
is very possible that the effect Coleridge has noticed (of elaborateness in
the prose and plainness in the verse) is deliberate.

428. more comprehensive soul: compare Dryden (Ker 1961, I, 79) on
Shakespeare's 'most comprehensive soul'.

435–6. a disposition ... present: recalls Quintilian's account of the
successful orator, who is especially susceptible to experiences 'whereby
things absent are presented to our imagination with such extreme vividness
that they seem actually to be before our very eyes' (*Institutio Oratoria* VI, ii,
29–30). For a link, via Quintilian, with the eloquence of uncultivated
speech, see note to motto, p. 95.

choice, or from the structure of his own mind, arise in him
without immediate external excitement.

But, whatever portion of this faculty we may suppose
even the greatest Poet to possess, there cannot be a doubt   450
but that the language which it will suggest to him must, in
liveliness and truth, fall far short of that which is uttered by
men in real life, under the actual pressure of those
passions, certain shadows of which the Poet thus produces,
or feels to be produced, in himself. However exalted a   455
notion we would wish to cherish of the character of a Poet,
it is obvious that, while he describes and imitates passions,
his situation is altogether slavish and mechanical, compared
with the freedom and power of real and substantial action
and suffering. So that it will be the wish of the Poet to   460
bring his feelings near to those of the persons whose
feelings he describes, nay, for short spaces of time perhaps
to let himself slip into an entire delusion, and even
confound and identify his own feelings with theirs,
modifying only the language which is thus suggested to   465
him, by a consideration that he describes for a particular
purpose, that of giving pleasure. Here, then, he will apply
the principle on which I have so much insisted, namely,
that of selection; on this he will depend for removing what
would otherwise be painful or disgusting in the passion; he   470
will feel that there is no necessity to trick out or to elevate
nature; and, the more industriously he applies this
principle, the deeper will be his faith that no words, which
his fancy or imagination can suggest, will be to be
compared with those which are the emanations of reality   475
and truth.

But it may be said by those who do not object to the
general spirit of these remarks that, as it is impossible for
the Poet to produce upon all occasions language as
exquisitely fitted for the passion as that which the real   480
passion itself suggests, it is proper that he should consider
himself as in the situation of a translator, who deems
himself justified when he substitutes excellences of another
kind for those which are unattainable by him; and
endeavours occasionally to surpass his original, in order to   485
make some amends for the general inferiority to which he
feels that he must submit. But this would be to encourage

---

482. *translator*: Wordsworth may be thinking of the Virgilian translator
Jacques Delille and his remarks on compensating devices in translation (see
Owen and Smyser 1974, I, 179).

idleness and unmanly despair. Further, it is the language of men who speak of what they do not understand; who talk of Poetry as of a matter of amusement and idle pleasure; who will converse with us as gravely about a *taste* for Poetry, as they express it, as if it were a thing as indifferent as a taste for rope-dancing, or Frontiniac or Sherry. Aristotle, I have been told, hath said, that Poetry is the most philosophic of all writing: it is so; its object is truth, not individual and local, but general, and operative; not standing upon external testimony, but carried alive into the heart by passion; truth which is its own testimony, which gives strength and divinity to the tribunal to which it appeals, and receives them from the same tribunal. Poetry is the image of man and nature. The obstacles which stand in the way of the fidelity of the Biographer and Historian, and of their consequent utility, are incalculably greater than those which are to be encountered by the Poet who has an adequate notion of the dignity of his art. The Poet writes under one restriction only, namely, that of the necessity of giving immediate pleasure to a Human Being possessed of that information which may be expected from him, not as a lawyer, a physician, a mariner, an astronomer or a natural philosopher, but as a Man. Except this one restriction, there is no object standing between the Poet and the image of things; between this, and the Biographer and Historian there are a thousand.

Nor let this necessity of producing immediate pleasure be considered as a degradation of the Poet's art. It is far otherwise. It is an acknowledgement of the beauty of the universe, an acknowledgement the more sincere, because it is not formal, but indirect; it is a task light and easy to him who looks at the world in the spirit of love; further, it is a

490

495

500

505

510

515

---

493. *rope-dancing*: acrobatics on a tight-rope.

493. *Frontiniac*: a sweet French wine.

494–5. *Aristotle ... writing*: Wordsworth does not claim to be directly acquainted with the remark in the *Poetics*, and Aristotle's point is slightly different, to the effect that poetry is more philosophic than history; but his reasoning, that poetry possesses permanent and general rather than local truth, is like Wordsworth's (and the latter goes on to draw his comparison with 'the Biographer and Historian').

495–6. *its object ... operative*: 'Truth, narrative, and past, is the Idol of Historians ... and truth operative, and by effects continually alive, is the Mistress of Poets' (Davenant 1971: 10–11).

499. *the tribunal*: the heart.

518. *formal*: explicit, overt.

homage paid to the native and naked dignity of man, to the   520
grand elementary principle of pleasure, by which he knows,
and feels, and lives, and moves. We have no sympathy but

520–2. *the native . . . moves*: 'This is a statement which has great intrinsic
interest, because, if we recognize that it is bold at all, we must also perceive
that it is bold to the point of being shocking' (Trilling 1963). Trilling notes
that it 'controverts' *Acts* 17:28 ('in him [Christ] we live, and move, and have
our being'). See also *Paradise Lost* IV, 289–90: 'with native honour clad / In
naked majesty seemed lords of all'. For Wilkie (1973), the whole statement
from 'The Poet writes . . .', above, to '. . . by pleasure alone', below, is a
'euphoric passage . . . in the spirit of Schiller, Shelley, Whitman, Isadora
Duncan, Apollinaire, Cage, and Allen Ginsberg'. Wordsworth's celebration
of poetic pleasure is the most startling transformation of stock aesthetic and
psychological ideas to be found in the Preface. It was a cliché of
eighteenth-century literary theory that the goal of giving pleasure
distinguished poetry from other kinds of discourse. But (with what Abrams
[1954] calls a 'stubbornly laminating' tendency) this goal was persistently
associated with the ornamental, stylized and fanciful elements in poetry
(e.g. notably in Richard Hurd's very strong statement of the literary
pleasure principle, 'A Dissertation on the Idea of Universal Poetry', 1766),
while imitation was customarily located in the prosaic aspects of poetic
discourse. Wordsworth reverses this scheme boldly, making pleasure not
only mimetic but mimetic of a profound and inalienable part of human
nature (see General Introduction, p. 29). Given his views on poetic diction,
personification, and so forth, it is not surprising that the sources of poetic
pleasure envisaged by Wordsworth are very different from those discussed
by Hurd, and in fact only metre and rhyme (see pp. 79–84) are explicitly
cited in this connection in the Preface. It is a fair assumption, however, that
the whole aesthetic aspect of poetry is intended in the crucial notion of
pleasure: structural, phonetic and verbal (Wordsworth has already denied
that poetry and metrical writing are coextensive, and see p. 70 above on
how a natural poetic language will still be 'dignified and variegated, and
alive with metaphors and figures').
    In linking poetic pleasure to human nature Wordsworth is also boldly
enlarging an orthodox eighteenth-century psychological tenet, in this case
the view that 'self-love' is the foundation of our actions and ethical beliefs
(see Grave 1968). Couched in terms of 'pleasure', the idea appears in
Dennis and Locke ('whatever a Man does . . . Pleasure is, at least, the chief
and the final motive to it' – Hooker 1939, I, 148; 'things then are good or
evil, only in reference to pleasure or pain' – Locke 1690, II, xx), and more
systematically in the idiosyncratic theorizing of Abraham Tucker and the
associationism of Hartley, in the latter case sometimes with imagery
resembling Wordsworth's (see note to line 555, p. 76). Hartley (1749, I,
370) denied that the 'desire of happiness' controls our actions, but he did
believe that our motives are built up from simple sensations that always
have a pleasurable or painful aspect.

what is propagated by pleasure; I would not be misunderstood, but wherever we sympathize with pain it will be found that the sympathy is produced and carried on by 525 subtle combinations with pleasure. We have no knowledge – that is, no general principles drawn from the contemplation of particular facts – but what has been built up by pleasure, and exists in us by pleasure alone. The Man of Science, the Chemist and Mathematician, whatever difficulties and 530 disgusts they may have had to struggle with, know and feel this. However painful may be the objects with which the Anatomist's knowledge is connected, he feels that his knowledge is pleasure; and where he has no pleasure he has no knowledge. What then does the Poet? He considers 535 man and the objects that surround him as acting and re-acting upon each other, so as to produce an infinite complexity of pain and pleasure; he considers man in his own nature and in his ordinary life as contemplating this with a certain quantity of immediate knowledge, with 540 certain convictions, intuitions, and deductions which by habit become of the nature of intuitions; he considers him as looking upon this complex scene of ideas and sensations, and finding everywhere objects that immediately excite in him sympathies which, from the necessities of his nature, 545 are accompanied by an overbalance of enjoyment.

To this knowledge which all men carry about with them, and to these sympathies in which without any other discipline than that of our daily life we are fitted to take

524–6. wherever . . . pleasure: compare Burke 1757, Part I, Sect. 14: 'pity is a passion accompanied with pleasure, because it arises from love and social affection. Whenever we are formed by nature to any active purpose, the passion which animates us to it is attended with delight, or a pleasure of some kind.' Pleasure is given considerable emphasis by Burke in this part of the *Philosophical Enquiry*, though unlike Wordsworth he does not regard it as a continuously active principle.

536–7. acting and re-acting: in context, the phrase acquires connotations of chemistry; the allusions in this and the preceding paragraph to scientific enquiry, and the recognition of its emotional affinity with poetry, may owe something to Humphrey Davy's general introductory lecture to his course on chemistry at the Royal Institution, delivered in January 1802.

538–9. he considers . . . contemplating this: a striking second tier of reference is introduced in the notion of the poet contemplating an individual who is himself pleasurably contemplating the 'infinite complexity of pain and pleasure'. It is consistent with the remarks above on the role of pleasure in sympathy and knowledge, however painful, and evidently has a bearing on Wordsworth's use of a narrator in very many of the poems.

546. overbalance of enjoyment: this interesting formulation appears, with

delight, the Poet principally directs his attention. He 550
considers man and nature as essentially adapted to each
other, and the mind of men as naturally the mirror of the
fairest and most interesting qualities of nature. And thus
the Poet, prompted by this feeling of pleasure which
accompanies him through the whole course of his studies, 555
converses with general nature with affections akin to those,
which, through labour and length of time, the Man of
Science has raised up in himself, by conversing with those
particular parts of nature which are the objects of his
studies. The knowledge both of the Poet and the Man of 560
Science is pleasure; but the knowledge of the one cleaves
to us as a necessary part of our existence, our natural and
unalienable inheritance; the other is a personal and
individual acquisition, slow to come to us, and by no
habitual and direct sympathy connecting us with our 565
fellow-beings. The Man of Science seeks truth as a remote
and unknown benefactor; he cherishes and loves it in his
solitude; the Poet, singing a song in which all human
beings join with him, rejoices in the presence of truth as
our visible friend and hourly companion. Poetry is the 570

slight variations, several times in the Preface and has important roots in the
thought of David Hartley. It owes something to the latter's rather obscure
idea that 'sensible pleasures' are 'more numerous' than 'sensible pains'
(though the latter are 'greater'), leaving a 'remainder' which is 'pure
pleasure' (Hartley 1749, I, 82–3). Hartley makes a deduction from this
capacity of the associationist calculus to yield 'pure pleasure' which is
especially interesting in the light of Wordsworth's echo of *Paradise Lost*
above: 'association . . . has a tendency to reduce the state of those who have
eaten of the Tree of Knowledge of Good and Evil, back again to a
paradisiacal one'. There are in fact closer parallels to Wordsworth in
Hartley's theology (the second part of the *Observations*) than in the better-
known psychological speculations, especially in Proposition 4: 'God is
infinitely benevolent.' Here the venerable issue of God's benevolence is
reduced to the question of 'the balance of happiness, or misery' conferred
on sentient beings, with an 'overbalance of happiness' asserted, and – via a
reiteration of the claim for the 'paradisiacal' tendency of association – the
conclusion is drawn that 'all individuals are actually and always infinitely
happy'. The whole last sentence of Wordsworth's paragraph may be
compared with Hartley's account of his benevolent deity: 'Suppose now a
being of great benevolence, and enlarged intellectual capacities, to look
down upon mankind passing through a mixture of pleasures and pains, in
which, however, there is a balance of pleasure, to a greater balance of
pleasure perpetually, and, at last, to a state of pure and exalted pleasure
made so by association' (Hartley 1749, II, 13–30).

breath and finer spirit of all knowledge; it is the impassioned expression which is in the countenance of all Science. Emphatically may it be said of the Poet, as Shakespeare hath said of man, 'that he looks before and after'. He is the rock of defence of human nature; an 575 upholder and preserver, carrying everywhere with him relationship and love. In spite of difference of soil and climate, of language and manners, of laws and customs, in spite of things silently gone out of mind and things violently destroyed, the Poet binds together by passion and 580 knowledge the vast empire of human society, as it is spread over the whole earth, and over all time. The objects of the Poet's thoughts are everywhere; though the eyes and senses of man are, it is true, his favourite guides, yet he will follow wheresoever he can find an atmosphere of sensation in 585 which to move his wings. Poetry is the first and last of all knowledge – it is as immortal as the heart of man. If the labours of Men of Science should ever create any material revolution, direct or indirect, in our condition, and in the impressions which we habitually receive, the Poet will sleep 590 then no more than at present, but he will be ready to follow the steps of the Man of Science, not only in those general indirect effects, but he will be at his side, carrying sensation into the midst of the objects of the Science itself. The remotest discoveries of the Chemist, the Botanist, or 595 Mineralogist, will be as proper objects of the Poet's art as any upon which it can be employed, if the time should ever come when these things shall be familiar to us, and the relations under which they are contemplated by the followers of these respective Sciences shall be manifestly 600 and palpably material to us as enjoying and suffering beings. If the time should ever come when what is now called Science, thus familiarized to men, shall be ready to put on, as it were, a form of flesh and blood, the Poet will lend his divine spirit to aid the transfiguration, and will 605 welcome the being thus produced, as a dear and genuine inmate of the household of man. It is not, then, to be supposed that anyone, who holds that sublime notion of Poetry which I have attempted to convey, will break in

573–5. *as Shakespeare . . . after*: *Hamlet* IV, iv, 37.
575. *rock of defence*: *Psalms* 31:2.
576. *upholder and preserver*: this phrasing also is perhaps influenced by that of *Psalms*, e.g. *Psalms* 145:14, 20.
586. *first and last*: *Revelation* 1:11.

upon the sanctity and truth of his pictures by transitory and   610
accidental ornaments, and endeavour to excite admiration
of himself by arts, the necessity of which must manifestly
depend upon the assumed meanness of his subject.

What I have thus far said applies to Poetry in general,
but especially to those parts of composition where the Poet   615
speaks through the mouths of his characters; and upon this
point it appears to have such weight that I will conclude,
there are few persons of good sense who would not allow
that the dramatic parts of composition are defective in
proportion as they deviate from the real language of nature,   620
and are coloured by a diction of the Poet's own, either
peculiar to him as an individual Poet, or belonging simply
to Poets in general, to a body of men who, from the
circumstance of their compositions being in metre, it is
expected will employ a particular language.   625

It is not, then, in the dramatic parts of composition that
we look for this distinction of language; but still it may be
proper and necessary where the Poet speaks to us in his
own person and character. To this I answer by referring
my Reader to the description which I have before given of   630
a Poet. Among the qualities which I have enumerated as
principally conducing to form a Poet, is implied nothing
differing in kind from other men, but only in degree. The
sum of what I have there said is, that the Poet is chiefly
distinguished from other men by a greater promptness to   635
think and feel without immediate external excitement, and
a greater power in expressing such thoughts and feelings as
are produced in him in that manner. But these passions
and thoughts and feelings are the general passions and
thoughts and feelings of men. And with what are they   640
connected? Undoubtedly with our moral sentiments and
animal sensations, and with the causes which excite these;
with the operations of the elements and the appearances of
the visible universe; with storm and sunshine, with the

---

614. *What . . . said*: Wordsworth is referring to the discussion of style up to
l. 476. As the rounding-off mention of 'transitory and accidental orna-
ments' in the previous paragraph is designed to indicate, the intervening
discussion (asserting the dignity of the poet as 'translator' of human reality)
has sprung from the proposal about 'excellences of another kind'
(ll. 483–4). Roper (1968: 295) is wrong to see a problem in the
arrangement of the argument here.
642. *animal*: see note to 'Animal Tranquillity and Decay' (title) p. 101
below.

revolutions of the seasons, with cold and heat, with loss of   645
friends and kindred, with injuries and resentments,
gratitude and hope, with fear and sorrow. These, and the
like, are the sensations and objects which the Poet
describes, as they are the sensations of other men, and the
objects which interest them. The Poet thinks and feels in   650
the spirit of the passions of men. How, then, can his
language differ in any material degree from that of all other
men who feel vividly and see clearly? It might be *proved* that
it is impossible. But supposing that this were not the case,
the Poet might then be allowed to use a peculiar language   655
when expressing his feelings for his own gratification, or
that of men like himself. But Poets do not write for Poets
alone, but for men. Unless therefore we are advocates for
that admiration which depends upon ignorance, and that
pleasure which arises from hearing what we do not   660
understand, the Poet must descend from this supposed
height, and, in order to excite rational sympathy, he must
express himself as other men express themselves. To this it
may be added, that while he is only selecting from the real
language of men, or, which amounts to the same thing,   665
composing accurately in the spirit of such selection, he is
treading upon safe ground, and we know what we are to
expect from him. Our feelings are the same with respect to
metre; for, as it may be proper to remind the Reader, the
distinction of metre is regular and uniform, and not like   670
that which is produced by what is usually called poetic
diction, arbitrary, and subject to infinite caprices upon
which no calculation whatever can be made. In the one
case, the Reader is utterly at the mercy of the Poet
respecting what imagery or diction he may choose to   675
connect with the passion, whereas, in the other, the metre
obeys certain laws, to which the Poet and Reader both
willingly submit because they are certain, and because no
interference is made by them with the passion but such as
the concurring testimony of ages has shown to heighten   680
and improve the pleasure which co-exists with it.

It will now be proper to answer an obvious question,
namely: why, professing these opinions, have I written in
verse? To this, in addition to such answer as is included in
what I have already said, I reply in the first place: because,   685
however I may have restricted myself, there is still left open
to me what confessedly constitutes the most valuable object
of all writing, whether in prose or verse, the great and
universal passions of men, the most general and interesting

of their occupations, and the entire world of nature, from 690
which I am at liberty to supply myself with endless
combinations of forms and imagery. Now, supposing for a
moment that whatever is interesting in these objects may be
as vividly described in prose, why am I to be condemned, if
to such description I have endeavoured to superadd the 695
charm which, by the consent of all nations, is acknowledged
to exist in metrical language? To this, by such as are
unconvinced by what I have already said, it may be
answered, that a very small part of the pleasure given by
Poetry depends upon the metre, and that it is injudicious to 700
write in metre, unless it be accompanied with the other
artificial distinctions of style with which metre is usually
accompanied, and that by such deviation more will be lost
from the shock which will be thereby given to the Reader's
associations, than will be counterbalanced by any pleasure 705
which he can derive from the general power of numbers. In
answer to those who still contend for the necessity of
accompanying metre with certain appropriate colours of
style in order to the accomplishment of its appropriate end,
and who also, in my opinion, greatly under-rate the power 710
of metre in itself, it might perhaps, as far as relates to these
Poems, have been almost sufficient to observe, that poems
are extant, written upon more humble subjects, and in a
more naked and simple style than I have aimed at, which
poems have continued to give pleasure from generation to 715
generation. Now, if nakedness and simplicity be a defect,
the fact here mentioned affords a strong presumption that
poems somewhat less naked and simple are capable of
affording pleasure at the present day; and, what I wished
chiefly to attempt, at present, was to justify myself for 720
having written under the impression of this belief.

But I might point out various causes why, when the style
is manly, and the subject of some importance, words
metrically arranged will long continue to impart such a
pleasure to mankind as he who is sensible of the extent of 725
that pleasure will be desirous to impart. The end of Poetry
is to produce excitement in co-existence with an overbalance
of pleasure. Now, by the supposition, excitement is an

708. *colours*: see note to line 27, p. 57.
710–11. *under-rate . . . metre*: Owen (1957: 38–9), assessing the pages
which follow in their historical context, finds that Wordsworth 'probes,
more deeply than any considerable earlier critic, into the psychological
bases of the effect of ordinary metrical patterns'. For a valuable recent
discussion of Wordsworth's theory of metre, see Page 1985.

unusual and irregular state of the mind; ideas and feelings
do not in that state succeed each other in accustomed   730
order. But, if the words by which this excitement is
produced are in themselves powerful, or the images and
feelings have an undue proportion of pain connected with
them, there is some danger that the excitement may be
carried beyond its proper bounds. Now the co-presence of   735
something regular, something to which the mind has been
accustomed in various moods and in a less excited state,
cannot but have great efficacy in tempering and restraining
the passion by an intertexture of ordinary feeling, and of
feeling not strictly and necessarily connected with the   740
passion. This is unquestionably true, and hence, though
the opinion will at first appear paradoxical, from the
tendency of metre to divest language in a certain degree of
its reality, and thus to throw a sort of half consciousness of
unsubstantial existence over the whole composition, there   745
can be little doubt but that more pathetic situations and
sentiments, that is, those which have a greater proportion
of pain connected with them, may be endured in metrical
composition, especially in rhyme, than in prose. The metre
of the old ballads is very artless; yet they contain many   750
passages which would illustrate this opinion, and, I hope, if
the following Poems be attentively perused, similar instances
will be found in them. This opinion may be further
illustrated by appealing to the Reader's own experience of
the reluctance with which he comes to the re-perusal of the 755
distressful parts of *Clarissa Harlowe*, or *The Gamester*. While
Shakespeare's writings, in the most pathetic scenes, never
act upon us as pathetic beyond the bounds of pleasure – an
effect which, in a much greater degree than might at first
be imagined, is to be ascribed to small, but continual and   760
regular impulses of pleasurable surprise from the metrical
arrangement. On the other hand (what it must be allowed
will much more frequently happen) if the Poet's words
should be incommensurate with the passion, and inadequate
to raise the Reader to a height of desirable excitement,   765
then (unless the Poet's choice of his metre has been grossly
injudicious) in the feelings of pleasure which the Reader
has been accustomed to connect with metre in general, and

749. *rhyme*: for Wordsworth's many practical explorations of the possibilities
of rhyme in *LB*, see the headnotes to individual poems in this edition.
756. Clarissa Harlowe: the novel, *Clarissa* (1748), by Samuel Richardson.
756. The Gamester: a successful mid-eighteenth-century prose tragedy by
Edward Moore.

in the feeling, whether cheerful or melancholy, which he
has been accustomed to connect with that particular   770
movement of metre, there will be found something which
will greatly contribute to impart passion to the words, and
to effect the complex end which the Poet proposes to
himself.

If I had undertaken a systematic defence of the theory   775
upon which these Poems are written, it would have been
my duty to develop the various causes upon which the
pleasure received from metrical language depends. Among
the chief of these causes is to be reckoned a principle
which must be well known to those who have made any of   780
the Arts the object of accurate reflection; I mean the
pleasure which the mind derives from the perception of
similitude in dissimilitude. This principle is the great
spring of the activity of our minds, and their chief feeder.
From this principle the direction of the sexual appetite, and   785
all the passions connected with it, take their origin: it is the
life of our ordinary conversation; and upon the accuracy
with which similitude in dissimilitude, and dissimilitude in
similitude are perceived, depend our taste and our moral
feelings. It would not have been a useless employment to   790
have applied this principle to the consideration of metre,
and to have shown that metre is hence enabled to afford
much pleasure, and to have pointed out in what manner
that pleasure is produced. But my limits will not permit me
to enter upon this subject, and I must content myself with a   795
general summary.

I have said that Poetry is the spontaneous overflow of
powerful feelings; it takes its origin from emotion recollected
in tranquillity; the emotion is contemplated till by a species
of reaction the tranquillity gradually disappears, and an   800
emotion, kindred to that which was before the subject of
contemplation, is gradually produced, and does itself
actually exist in the mind. In this mood successful
composition generally begins, and in a mood similar to this
it is carried on; but the emotion, of whatever kind and in   805
whatever degree, from various causes is qualified by
various pleasures, so that in describing any passions
whatsoever, which are voluntarily described, the mind will
upon the whole be in a state of enjoyment. Now, if Nature

---

785. *the direction of the sexual appetite*: 'we ought not to let go unheeded the
explicit connection that Wordsworth makes between poetry and sexuality'
(Trilling 1963).

be thus cautious in preserving in a state of enjoyment a 810
being thus employed, the Poet ought to profit by the lesson
thus held forth to him, and ought especially to take care
that, whatever passions he communicates to his Reader,
those passions, if his Reader's mind be sound and
vigorous, should always be accompanied with an overbalance 815
of pleasure. Now the music of harmonious metrical
language, the sense of difficulty overcome, and the blind
association of pleasure which has been previously received
from works of rhyme or metre of the same or similar
construction, an indistinct perception perpetually renewed 820
of language closely resembling that of real life and yet, in
the circumstance of metre, differing from it so widely, all
these imperceptibly make up a complex feeling of delight,
which is of the most important use in tempering the painful
feeling which will always be found intermingled with 825
powerful descriptions of the deeper passions. This effect is
always produced in pathetic and impassioned Poetry; while,
in lighter compositions, the ease and gracefulness with
which the Poet manages his numbers are themselves
confessedly a principal source of the gratification of the 830
Reader. I might perhaps include all which it is *necessary* to
say upon this subject by affirming, what few persons will
deny, that, of two descriptions, either of passions, manners,
or characters, each of them equally well executed, the one
in prose and the other in verse, the verse will be read a 835
hundred times where the prose is read once. We see that
Pope, by the power of verse alone, has contrived to render
the plainest common sense interesting, and even frequently
to invest it with the appearance of passion. In consequence
of these convictions I related in metre the Tale of GOODY 840
BLAKE AND HARRY GILL, which is one of the rudest of this
collection. I wished to draw attention to the truth, that the
power of the human imagination is sufficient to produce
such changes even in our physical nature as might almost
appear miraculous. The truth is an important one; the fact 845
(for it is a *fact*) is a valuable illustration of it. And I have the
satisfaction of knowing that it has been communicated to
many hundreds of people who would never have heard of

841. rudest: least sophisticated.
845. fact: see note to line 49, p. 35.
847–8. communicated ... people: Wordsworth may have in mind the
reprinting of the poem, shortly after its first publication, in several
periodicals. It achieved considerably more exposure in this way than any
other poem in *LB* (see Bauer 1978).

it, had it not been narrated as a ballad, and in a more impressive metre than is usual in ballads. 850

Having thus explained a few of the reasons why I have written in verse, and why I have chosen subjects from common life, and endeavoured to bring my language near to the real language of men, if I have been too minute in pleading my own cause, I have at the same time been 855 treating a subject of general interest; and it is for this reason that I request the Reader's permission to add a few words with reference solely to these particular Poems, and to some defects which will probably be found in them. I am sensible that my associations must have sometimes been 860 particular instead of general and that, consequently, giving to things a false importance, sometimes from diseased impulses I may have written upon unworthy subjects; but I am less apprehensive on this account, than that my language may frequently have suffered from those arbitrary 865 connections of feelings and ideas with particular words and phrases, from which no man can altogether protect himself. Hence I have no doubt that, in some instances, feelings even of the ludicrous may be given to my Readers by expressions which appeared to me tender and pathetic. 870 Such faulty expressions, were I convinced they were faulty at present, and that they must necessarily continue to be so, I would willingly take all reasonable pains to correct. But it is dangerous to make these alterations on the simple authority of a few individuals, or even of certain classes of 875 men. For where the understanding of an Author is not convinced, or his feelings altered, this cannot be done without great injury to himself: for his own feelings are his stay and support and, if he sets them aside in one instance, he may be induced to repeat this act till his mind loses all 880 confidence in itself, and becomes utterly debilitated. To this it may be added, that the Reader ought never to forget that he is himself exposed to the same errors as the Poet, and perhaps in a much greater degree: for there can be no presumption in saying, that it is not probable he will be so 885 well acquainted with the various stages of meaning through which words have passed, or with the fickleness or stability of the relations of particular ideas to each other – and above all, since he is so much less interested in the subject, he may decide lightly and carelessly. 890

Long as I have detained my Reader, I hope he will permit me to caution him against a mode of false criticism which has been applied to Poetry in which the language

closely resembles that of life and nature. Such verses have
been triumphed over in parodies of which Dr Johnson's   895
stanza is a fair specimen.

> I put my hat upon my head,
> And walked into the Strand,
> And there I met another man
> Whose hat was in his hand.   900

Immediately under these lines I will place one of the most
justly admired stanzas of *The Babes in the Wood.*

> These pretty babes with hand in hand
> Went wandering up and down;
> But never more they saw the man   905
> Approaching from the town.

In both these stanzas the words, and the order of the
words, in no respect differ from the most unimpassioned
conversation. There are words in both, for example 'the
Strand' and 'the town,' connected with none but the most   910
familiar ideas; yet the one stanza we admit as admirable,
and the other as a fair example of the superlatively
contemptible. Whence arises this difference? Not from the
metre, not from the language, not from the order of the
words; but the *matter* expressed in Dr Johnson's stanza is   915
contemptible. The proper method of treating trivial and
simple verses, to which Dr Johnson's stanza would be a fair
parallelism, is not to say, 'This is a bad kind of Poetry,' or
'This is not Poetry' but 'This wants sense; it is neither
interesting in itself, nor can *lead* to anything interesting; the   920
images neither originate in that sane state of feeling which
arises out of thought, nor can excite thought or feeling in
the Reader.' This is the only sensible manner of dealing
with such verses. Why trouble yourself about the species
till you have previously decided upon the genus? Why take   925
pains to prove that an ape is not a Newton, when it is self-
evident that he is not a man?

I have one request to make of my Reader, which is that
in judging these Poems he would decide by his own
feelings genuinely, and not by reflection upon what will   930

---

895. *triumphed over*: their supposed inferiority revelled in.
897–900. *I put . . . hand*: the lines appeared (with slight differences of
phrasing) in the *London Magazine*, April 1785, p. 254.
903–6. *These pretty . . . town*: the particular version Wordsworth quotes
seems to be found only in anthologies by Vicesimus Knox (see Zall 1979).
926. *ape . . . Newton*: compare Pope, *Essay on Man* II, 34.

probably be the judgment of others. How common is it to
hear a person say, 'I myself do not object to this style of
composition, or this or that expression, but to such and
such classes of people it will appear mean or ludicrous.'
This mode of criticism, so destructive of all sound   935
unadulterated judgment, is almost universal: I have
therefore to request, that the Reader would abide
independently by his own feelings, and that if he finds
himself affected he would not suffer such conjectures to
interfere with his pleasure.   940

If an Author by any single composition has impressed us
with respect for his talents, it is useful to consider this as
affording a presumption that on other occasions where we
have been displeased he nevertheless may not have written
ill or absurdly; and, further, to give him so much credit for   945
this one composition as may induce us to review what has
displeased us with more care than we should otherwise
have bestowed upon it. This is not only an act of justice
but, in our decisions upon Poetry especially, may conduce
in a high degree to the improvement of our own taste: for   950
an *accurate* taste in Poetry, and in all the other arts, as Sir
Joshua Reynolds has observed, is an *acquired* talent, which
can only be produced by thought, and a long continued
intercourse with the best models of composition. This is
mentioned, not with so ridiculous a purpose as to prevent   955
the most inexperienced Reader from judging for himself (I
have already said that I wish him to judge for himself), but
merely to temper the rashness of decision, and to suggest
that if Poetry be a subject on which much time has not
been bestowed the judgment may be erroneous and that in   960
many cases it necessarily will be so.

I know that nothing would have so effectually contributed
to further the end which I have in view, as to have shown
of what kind the pleasure is, and how that pleasure is
produced, which is confessedly produced by metrical   965
composition essentially different from that which I have
here endeavoured to recommend: for the Reader will say
that he has been pleased by such composition, and what
can I do more for him? The power of any art is limited;
and he will suspect that, if I propose to furnish him with   970
new friends, it is only upon condition of his abandoning his
old friends. Besides, as I have said, the Reader is himself
conscious of the pleasure which he has received from such

951–2. Sir Joshua Reynolds: see note to ll. 38–9, p. 35.

composition, composition to which he has peculiarly attached the endearing name of Poetry, and all men feel an   975
habitual gratitude, and something of an honourable bigotry for the objects which have long continued to please them; we not only wish to be pleased, but to be pleased in that particular way in which we have been accustomed to be pleased. There is a host of arguments in these feelings; and   980
I should be the less able to combat them successfully, as I am willing to allow that, in order entirely to enjoy the Poetry which I am recommending, it would be necessary to give up much of what is ordinarily enjoyed. But, would my limits have permitted me to point out how this pleasure is   985
produced, I might have removed many obstacles, and assisted my Reader in perceiving that the powers of language are not so limited as he may suppose; and that it is possible that Poetry may give other enjoyments, of a purer, more lasting, and more exquisite nature. This part   990
of my subject I have not altogether neglected; but it has been less my present aim to prove that the interest excited by some other kinds of Poetry is less vivid, and less worthy of the nobler powers of the mind, than to offer reasons for presuming that, if the object which I have proposed to   995
myself were adequately attained, a species of Poetry would be produced, which is genuine Poetry, in its nature well adapted to interest mankind permanently, and likewise important in the multiplicity and quality of its moral relations.   1000

From what has been said, and from a perusal of the Poems, the Reader will be able clearly to perceive the object which I have proposed to myself; he will determine how far I have attained this object; and, what is a much more important question, whether it be worth attaining: 1005
and upon the decision of these two questions will rest my claim to the approbation of the public.

Appendix (1802)

Wordsworth indicates that this end-matter is to be thought of as springing from the phrase 'by what is usually called poetic diction' in the Preface (ll. 671–2 – though the phrase has already appeared to all intents and purposes in l. 281). The Appendix was reprinted in 1805. Significant deleted passages from a now lost manuscript of this document are reproduced in Owen and Smyser 1974, I, 163–5.

As perhaps I have no right to expect from a Reader of an
Introduction to a volume of Poems that attentive perusal
without which it is impossible, imperfectly as I have been
compelled to express my meaning, that what I have said in
the Preface should throughout be fully understood, I am   5
the more anxious to give an exact notion of the sense in
which I use the phrase *poetic diction*; and for this purpose I
will here add a few words concerning the origin of the
phraseology which I have condemned under that name.
The earliest Poets of all nations generally wrote from   10
passion excited by real events; they wrote naturally, and as
men; feeling powerfully as they did, their language was
daring, and figurative. In succeeding times Poets, and men
ambitious of the fame of Poets, perceiving the influence of
such language and, desirous of producing the same effect,   15
without having the same animating passion, set themselves
to a mechanical adoption of those figures of speech, and
made use of them, sometimes with propriety, but much
more frequently applied them to feelings and ideas with
which they had no natural connection whatsoever. A   20
language was thus insensibly produced, differing materially
from the real language of men in *any situation*. The Reader
or Hearer of this distorted language found himself in a
perturbed and unusual state of mind; when affected by the
genuine language of passion he had been in a perturbed   25
and unusual state of mind also; in both cases he was willing
that his common judgment and understanding should be
laid asleep, and he had no instinctive and infallible
perception of the true to make him reject the false; the one
served as a passport for the other. The agitation and   30
confusion of mind were in both cases delightful, and no
wonder if he confounded the one with the other, and
believed them both to be produced by the same, or similar

10–20. The earliest ... whatsoever: the historical explanation for the
distinctive verbal and structural characteristics of poetry proposed here
(that they are a legacy of the aroused emotions experienced by early poets
but not by their successors) is perhaps the most orthodox piece of literary
theory in Wordsworth's apparatus to *LB*. A particularly close parallel will be
found in the first half of Blair's Lecture 38 (Blair 1785, III, 84–99). See
also Lowth 1787, Lectures 14 and 15. Wordsworth goes on to give an
unusually full treatment of the post-primitive history of poetic devices, in
the process perhaps revealing the implausibility of the theory (Blair simply
says that 'in after-ages ... authors began to affect what they did not feel ...
they tried ... to supply the defect of native warmth, by those artificial
ornaments which might give composition a splendid appearance').

causes. Besides, the Poet spake to him in the character of a
man to be looked up to, a man of genius and authority.   35
Thus, and from a variety of other causes, this distorted
language was received with admiration; and Poets, it is
probable, who had before contented themselves for the
most part with misapplying only expressions which at first
had been dictated by real passion, carried the abuse still   40
further, and introduced phrases composed apparently in
the spirit of the original figurative language of passion, yet
altogether of their own invention, and distinguished by
various degrees of wanton deviation from good sense and
nature.   45

It is indeed true that the language of the earliest Poets
was felt to differ materially from ordinary language,
because it was the language of extraordinary occasions, but
it was really spoken by men, language which the Poet
himself had uttered when he had been affected by the   50
events which he described, or which he had heard uttered
by those around him. To this language it is probable that
metre of some sort or other was early superadded. This
separated the genuine language of Poetry still further from
common life, so that whoever read or heard the poems of   55
these earliest Poets felt himself moved in a way in which he
had not been accustomed to be moved in real life, and by
causes manifestly different from those which acted upon
him in real life. This was the great temptation to all the
corruptions which have followed: under the protection of   60
this feeling succeeding Poets constructed a phraseology
which had one thing, it is true, in common with the
genuine language of Poetry, namely, that it was not heard
in ordinary conversation, that it was unusual. But the first
Poets, as I have said, spake a language which, though   65
unusual, was still the language of men. This circumstance,
however, was disregarded by their successors; they found
that they could please by easier means: they became proud
of a language which they themselves had invented, and
which was uttered only by themselves; and, with the spirit   70

52–3. To this language ... superadded: Owen and Smyser (1974, I, 114)
compare Enfield (1796) on metre as an innovation not arising until 'a
period of great refinement', but Wordsworth seems rather to agree with
Blair that metre appeared in primitive poetry. Lowth (1787, I, 55–73) had
brought forward the reasons for thinking that much of the 'poetry' of the
Old Testament was written according to a lost metrical system.
70–1. with the spirit ... own: they monopolized it, in the manner of a
mediaeval guild.

of a fraternity, they arrogated it to themselves as their own.
In process of time metre became a symbol or promise of
this unusual language, and whoever took upon him to write
in metre, according as he possessed more or less of true
poetic genius, introduced less or more of this adulterated   75
phraseology into his compositions, and the true and the
false became so inseparably interwoven that the taste of
men was gradually perverted; and this language was
received as a natural language, and at length, by the
influence of books upon men, did to a certain degree really   80
become so. Abuses of this kind were imported from one
nation to another, and with the progress of refinement this
diction became daily more and more corrupt, thrusting out
of sight the plain humanities of nature by a motley
masquerade of tricks, quaintnesses, hieroglyphics, and   85
enigmas.

It would be highly interesting to point out the causes of
the pleasure given by this extravagant and absurd language,
but this is not the place; it depends upon a great variety of
causes, but upon none perhaps more than its influence in   90
impressing a notion of the peculiarity and exaltation of the
Poet's character, and in flattering the Reader's self-love by
bringing him nearer to a sympathy with that character – an
effect which is accomplished by unsettling ordinary habits
of thinking, and thus assisting the Reader to approach to   95
that perturbed and dizzy state of mind in which if he does
not find himself, he imagines that he is *balked* of a peculiar
enjoyment which Poetry can and ought to bestow.

The sonnet which I have quoted from Gray, in the
Preface, except the lines printed in italics, consists of little 100
else but this diction, though not of the worst kind; and
indeed, if I may be permitted to say so, it is far too
common in the best writers, both ancient and modern.
Perhaps I can in no way, by positive example, more easily
give my Reader a notion of what I mean by the phrase   105
poetic diction than by referring him to a comparison between
the metrical paraphrases which we have of passages in the
old and new Testament, and those passages as they exist in
our common translation. See Pope's 'Messiah' throughout,

---

85. *hieroglyphics*: elements of language with cryptic, oblique meanings.
86. *enigmas*: metaphorical riddles.
99–100. *The sonnet . . . Preface*: see Preface, ll. 332–45.
109. *our common translation*: the Authorized Version.
109. *Pope's 'Messiah'*: 'Messiah a Sacred Eclogue' (1712) is an imitation, in

Prior's 'Did sweeter sounds adorn my flowing tongue,' &c. 110
&c. 'Though I speak with the tongues of men and of
angels,' &c. &c. See *1st Corinthians*, chapter xiiith. By way
of immediate example, take the following of Dr Johnson:

> Turn on the prudent Ant thy heedless eyes,
> Observe her labours, Sluggard, and be wise; 115
> No stern command, no monitory voice,
> Prescribes her duties, or directs her choice;
> Yet, timely provident, she hastes away
> To snatch the blessings of a plenteous day;
> When fruitful Summer loads the teeming plain, 120
> She crops the harvest and she stores the grain.
> How long shall sloth usurp thy useless hours,
> Unnerve thy vigour, and enchain thy powers?
> While artful shades thy downy couch enclose,
> And soft solicitation courts repose, 125
> Amidst the drowsy charms of dull delight,
> Year chases year with unremitted flight,
> Till want now following, fraudulent and slow,
> Shall spring to seize thee, like an ambushed foe.

From this hubbub of words pass to the original. 'Go to the 130
Ant, thou Sluggard, consider her ways, and be wise: which
having no guide, overseer, or ruler, provideth her meat in
the summer, and gathereth her food in the harvest. How
long wilt thou sleep, O Sluggard? When wilt thou arise out
of thy sleep? Yet a little sleep, a little slumber, a little 135
folding of the hands to sleep. So shall thy poverty come as
one that travaileth, and thy want as an armed man.'
Proverbs, chap. vith.

One more quotation and I have done. It is from
Cowper's verses supposed to be written by Alexander 140
Selkirk:

> Religion! what treasure untold
> Resides in that heavenly word!

the manner of Virgil, of certain passages from *Isaiah* (though Pope, as it
happens, uses both the Authorized Version and the Douai Bible as his
originals).

110. 'Did . . . tongue': the first line of Prior's 'Charity' (1712). Wordsworth
then cites the famous Biblical passage Prior is imitating, in its opening
words.
113. the following of Dr Johnson: 'The Ant' (1766).
130. the original: *Proverbs* 6:6–11 in Authorized Version.
139–40. from Cowper's verses: ll. 25–40 of 'Verses supposed to be written by
Alexander Selkirk' (1782).

More precious than silver and gold,
Or all that this earth can afford.   145
But the sound of the church-going bell
These valleys and rocks never heard,
Ne'er sighed at the sound of a knell,
Or smiled when a sabbath appeared.

Ye winds, that have made me your sport,   150
Convey to this desolate shore
Some cordial endearing report
Of a land I must visit no more.
My Friends, do they now and then send
A wish or a thought after me?   155
O tell me I yet have a friend.
Though a friend I am never to see.

I have quoted this passage as an instance of three different
styles of composition. The first four lines are poorly
expressed; some critics would call the language prosaic; the   160
fact is, it would be bad prose, so bad, that it is scarcely
worse in metre. The epithet 'church-going' applied to a
bell, and that by so chaste a writer as Cowper, is an
instance of the strange abuses which Poets have introduced
into their language till they and their Readers take them as   165
matters of course, if they do not single them out expressly
as objects of admiration. The two lines 'Ne'er sigh'd at the
sound,' &c. are, in my opinion, an instance of the language
of passion wrested from its proper use and, from the mere
circumstance of the composition being in metre, applied   170
upon an occasion that does not justify such violent
expressions; and I should condemn the passage, though
perhaps few Readers will agree with me, as vicious poetic
diction. The last stanza is throughout admirably expressed:
it would be equally good whether in prose or verse, except   175
that the Reader has an exquisite pleasure in seeing such
natural language so naturally connected with metre. The
beauty of this stanza tempts me here to add a sentiment
which ought to be the pervading spirit of a system,
detached parts of which have been imperfectly explained in   180
the Preface – namely, that in proportion as ideas and

163–4. an instance . . . abuses: because Cowper's figurative language has led
him into an expression which could mean something ludicrous: that the bell
goes to church. Wordsworth is probably implicitly correcting the epithet in
a line in the Salisbury Plain Mss: 'The church-inviting bell's delightful
chime' (Gill 1975: 73).

feelings are valuable, whether the composition be in prose or in verse, they require and exact one and the same language.

Pectus enim id est quod disertos facit, et vis mentis; ideoque imperitis quoque, si modo sint aliquo affectu concitati, verba non desunt.

Motto. The quotation is slightly adapted from Quintilian, and means: 'For it is feeling and force of imagination that makes us eloquent; it is for this reason that even the uneducated have no difficulty in finding words to express their meaning, if only they are stirred by some strong emotion' (*Institutio Oratoria* X, vii, 15). The context makes 'imagination' an appropriate translation here, for Quintilian alludes to his own earlier account of vivid imaginative powers (a passage known to Wordsworth; see p. 71).

LYRICAL BALLADS

with
PASTORAL
and other poems

BY W. WORDSWORTH

Quam nihil ad genium, Papiniane, tuum!

Epigraph. The point of the epigraph is complex. The quotation is originally from the sixteenth-century Dutch poet Janus Dousa the Elder, but was known to Wordsworth and Coleridge from its citation by the seventeenth-century English jurist John Selden in the introduction to Michael Drayton's *Poly-Olbion* (1613). In that context it may be translated as 'absolutely worthless in comparison with your genius, Papinian!', and is Selden's way of contrasting true/classical with false/mediaeval learning and learned language (Papinian himself was a celebrated jurist of classical Rome). But Wordsworth and his circle (to judge by a use of the quotation in Coleridge's notebook, dated 4 March 1805) took the words, perhaps playfully, in a different sense, as meaning something like 'worthless and insignificant according to your taste, Papinian!'. And Garrod (1923: 152) suggests that there is also here a playful misunderstanding of 'Papinian' to mean 'Popean' (in reference to the poet Alexander Pope).

Expostulation and Reply

Composed late May or early June 1798. The text was not altered. See the Advertisement (p. 35) for Wordsworth's claim that this and the following poem sprang from a conversation with a friend who was too attached to 'modern books of moral philosophy'. In literal fact this friend may have been William Hazlitt, who is known to have got into 'metaphysical argument' with Wordsworth at this date (Howe 1930–4, XVII, 119). But the setting is emphatically Cumbrian (see l. 13) and the 'good friend' the Matthew persona (see p. 288 below). For the significance of the narrator's advocacy of a phenomenologically primitive condition of pure sensation (with a characteristic accompanying personification of the natural world), see General Introduction, p. 19.

'Why, William, on that old grey stone,
Thus for the length of half a day,
Why, William, sit you thus alone,
And dream your time away?

'Where are your books? – that light bequeathed   5
To beings else forlorn and blind!
Up! up! and drink the spirit breathed
From dead men to their kind.

'You look round on your mother earth,
As if she for no purpose bore you;   10
As if you were her first-born birth,
And none had lived before you!'

One morning thus, by Esthwaite Lake,
When life was sweet, I knew not why,
To me my good friend Matthew spake,   15
And thus I made reply:

'The eye it cannot choose but see;
We cannot bid the ear be still;
Our bodies feel, where'er they be,
Against, or with our will.   20

'Nor less I deem that there are powers
Which of themselves our minds impress;
That we can feed this mind of ours
In a wise passiveness.

'Think you, mid all this mighty sum   25
Of things for ever speaking,
That nothing of itself will come,
But we must still be seeking?

28. *still*: always, continually (as often in *LB*).

'– Then ask not wherefore, here, alone,
Conversing as I may,   30
I sit upon this old grey stone,
And dream my time away.'

30. Talking haphazardly, but perhaps, as a result, in a more inspired way.
Wordsworth found it interesting that, as he told Isabella Fenwick, the poem
was 'a favourite among the Quakers'. Quaker worship is notable for its
informal and spontaneous character.

The Tables Turned
An Evening Scene, on the same Subject

Composed late May or early June 1798. Opening stanza rearranged after 1815. Evidently a companion to the previous poem, but the rhetoric of this narrator is not the same as that of 'William' replying earlier to the 'expostulation'; it is both more colloquial and more ambitious in certain phrasings, and (in keeping with the idea of 'tables turned') owes something to the idiom of 'Matthew'.

Up! up! my friend, and clear your looks;
Why all this toil and trouble?
Up! up! my friend, and quit your books,
Or surely you'll grow double.

The sun, above the mountain's head,   5
A freshening lustre mellow
Through all the long green fields has spread,
His first sweet evening yellow.

Books! 'tis a dull and endless strife:
Come, hear the woodland linnet,   10
How sweet his music! On my life
There's more of wisdom in it.

And hark! how blithe the throstle sings!
And he is no mean preacher.
Come forth into the light of things,   15
Let Nature be your teacher.

She has a world of ready wealth,
Our minds and hearts to bless –
Spontaneous wisdom breathed by health,
Truth breathed by cheerfulness.   20

One impulse from a vernal wood
May teach you more of man,
Of moral evil and of good,
Than all the sages can.

4. The line is cited as vulgar in its phrasing by Francis Jeffrey (*Edinburgh Review* I, 1802, p. 68). 'Grow double' means 'become doubled up'.
10. *the woodland linnet*: twitting Wordsworth with the observation that linnets are not woodland birds (e.g. Moorman 1957: 380) may be inappropriate if the vegetation envisaged here is that occupied by linnets in 'Poems on the Naming of Places' I, ll. 31–3 (p. 324). There are literary precedents for the association of linnets and woods in Mark Akenside (*Pleasures of the Imagination*, 1772, II, ll. 176–7) and James Beattie (*The Minstrel*, 1771–4, I, 41–2). 'Linnet of the grove' occurs in Ch. 22 of Samuel Johnson's *Rasselas* (1759) in a passage that may have had a general influence on this poem.

Sweet is the lore which Nature brings;   25
Our meddling intellect
Misshapes the beauteous forms of things;
– We murder to dissect.

Enough of Science and of Art;
Close up these barren leaves;   30
Come forth, and bring with you a heart
That watches and receives.

28. Compare Pope, 'Epistle to Cobham', ll. 29–30.
29. Science . . . Art: probably overlapping rather than antithetical terms, for learning generally.

Animal Tranquillity and Decay
A Sketch

Entitled 'Old Man Travelling' in 1798 (with later title as subtitle). Ll. 1–14 probably written in late 1796/early 1797: ll. 15–20 in 1798. The latter were dropped in all printings after *LB*. Wordsworth told Isabella Fenwick that 'these verses were an overflowing from "The Old Cumberland Beggar",' and this is confirmed by the manuscript evidence (and the manner in which the text starts deliberately suggests a fragment). However, there is no suggestion that the Old Man begs, and he is psychologically and ethically a very different figure from the Beggar: an alternative explanation, so to speak, of the same physical 'expression'. For Wordsworth's classification of this poem in the Preface (under its 1798 title) as a study of a simple, natural, perennial and 'less impassioned' human type, see p. 63.

> The little hedge-row birds
> That peck along the road, regard him not.
> He travels on, and in his face, his step,
> His gait, is one expression; every limb,
> His look and bending figure, all bespeak   5
> A man who does not move with pain, but moves
> With thought. He is insensibly subdued
> To settled quiet: he is one by whom
> All effort seems forgotten; one to whom
> Long patience hath such mild composure given,   10
> That patience now doth seem a thing of which
> He hath no need. He is by nature led
> To peace so perfect, that the young behold
> With envy, what the Old Man hardly feels.

Title. Animal: could bear either of two almost antithetical senses. (1) A specialized meaning already becoming obsolete in Wordsworth's day, but apparently employed by him in the Preface (see Preface, l. 642): 'having to do with mental and nervous function' (on this reading the epithet governs 'tranquillity' only and the whole title means something like 'mental calm and physical deterioration'). (2) 'Pertaining to physical energy and constitution'; on this reading the epithet governs both nouns in the title.

Sketch: for the currency of 'sketch' as a generic term in verse titles of the day, see Mayo 1954.

3. He travels on: the phrase is a repeated one in 'The Old Cumberland Beggar' (pp. 309–16) and slow but unceasing motion is an important point of resemblance between the imagery of the two poems.

11–12. that patience . . . need: compare Lear's prayer (*King Lear* II, iv, 274): 'You Heavens, give me that patience, patience I need!'

I asked him whither he was bound, and what   15
The object of his journey: he replied
That he was going many miles to take
A last leave of his son, a mariner,
Who from a sea-fight had been brought to Falmouth,
And there was dying in an hospital.   20

15–20. These lines have generally been disregarded because they were not part of the poem at the beginning of its life and at the end (see headnote), but this cannot justify ignoring them when they are offered, as here. They create in some measure a different poem, though a characteristic one (see Ryskamp 1965), which chiefly concerns the narrator's changed or even transformed perception of a human being at an extreme of attrition: 'the narrator could hardly have anticipated the "thought" with which the old man moves with such dignity and the feelings which must necessarily accompany such a thought, but the revelation of that thought and those feelings behind the motion which the narrator has so completely misinterpreted cannot but affect him' (Bialostosky 1984: 128). For a stimulating discussion along similar lines, see Pirie 1982: 163–75; Gravil (1982) calls the paragraph a 'curative debunking'. For allusions in contemporary verse to the ill-effects in Britain of the war with France (the obvious candidate if Wordsworth has a literal war in mind) see Jordan 1976: 133–5. A reviewer, Charles Burney, took it that Wordsworth was alluding (disapprovingly) to this campaign (*Monthly Review* XXIX, 1799, p. 209).

Goody Blake and Harry Gill
A True Story

Composed in the first half of 1798. The local references in the fourth stanza deleted in 1837. In the 1845 collected works transferred from 'Poems of the Imagination' to 'Miscellaneous Poems', though Wordsworth had noted as early as the 1815 edition that the original placing was an expedient to 'avoid a needless multiplication of classes', and that 'Goody Blake and Harry Gill' 'refers to' the imagination as opposed to being 'produced by it'. The stanza form is the least adventurous of all Wordsworth's long verse arrangements in the collection, being simply two identical quatrains conjoined (a form frequently to be encountered in traditional and literary ballads published in Wordsworth's day and recognized by him – see p. 84 – as more elaborate than the normal ballad verse). The exclamatory, colloquial effects in the poem, especially in the first and last stanzas, probably owe something to the contemporary German ballad writer Gottfried Bürger (see Jacobus 1976: 239–40). 'The incident' treated by the poem, as Wordsworth mentioned to Isabella Fenwick, is 'from Dr Darwin's *Zoonomia*' (it is reproduced on pp. 385–6). The Advertisement (p. 35) singles out 'Goody Blake and Harry Gill' as the only instance in the collection of a poem based on a non-fictional event which was not witnessed by Wordsworth himself or a friend. For the important remarks on the 'rudeness' of the poem and the sheer effectiveness of versified utterance, see p. 83.

It is clear from these comments that Wordsworth, like Darwin, understood his tale to have an entirely naturalistic explanation, exhibiting what would nowadays be called a psychosomatic phenomenon (the power of a delusion to induce physical symptoms). While he expects his reader to see matters in the same light, his strategy in the text is the characteristic one of an 'I' narrator tracing a story of suffering in a physical vestige, and this narrator does not venture to explain their connection. It is also important to bear in mind that Wordsworth is not telling, and not claiming to tell, the same story as Darwin, but one of his own he has 'founded on' that story; his takes place in Dorsetshire, Darwin's in Warwickshire.

> Oh! what's the matter? what's the matter?
> What is't that ails young Harry Gill?
> That evermore his teeth they chatter,
> Chatter, chatter, chatter still.
> Of waistcoats Harry has no lack,   5
> Good duffle grey, and flannel fine;
> He has a blanket on his back,
> And coats enough to smother nine.

Title. 'Goody' is an abbreviation of 'goodwife', a form of address to a lower-class housewife. The surnames Blake and Gill may be part of the Dorsetshire colouring of the poem (see Moorman 1957: 284).

In March, December, and in July,
'Tis all the same with Harry Gill;   10
The neighbours tell, and tell you truly,
His teeth they chatter, chatter still.
At night, at morning, and at noon,
'Tis all the same with Harry Gill;
Beneath the sun, beneath the moon,   15
His teeth they chatter, chatter still.

Young Harry was a lusty drover,
And who so stout of limb as he?
His cheeks were red as ruddy clover;
His voice was like the voice of three.   20
Old Goody Blake was old and poor;
Ill fed she was, and thinly clad;
And any man who passed her door
Might see how poor a hut she had.

All day she spun in her poor dwelling: 25
And then her three hours' work at night!
Alas! 'twas hardly worth the telling,
It would not pay for candle-light.
This woman dwelt in Dorsetshire,
Her hut was on a cold hill side;   30
And in that country coals are dear,
For they come far by wind and tide.

By the same fire to boil their pottage,
Two poor old dames, as I have known,
Will often live in one small cottage;   35
But she, poor woman! dwelt alone.
'Twas well enough when summer came,
The long, warm, lightsome summer-day;

9, 11. *July, truly*: the traditional pronunciation of the month, with the first
syllable stressed, was still acceptable at this date.
17. *drover*: Harry Gill rears livestock which he drives to market.
25–8. Goody Blake is a victim of the long hours and poor returns of
eighteenth-century cottage industry, in this instance wool spinning.
27. *telling*: plays on the senses of both counting and recounting.
31–2. The coals have to be brought to the region by ship, which raises
their cost. Another touch of Dorsetshire colouring, based on the
Wordsworths' personal knowledge (see Moorman 1957: 284).
31. *country*: district.
33–6. A characteristic image of a human being at an extreme of suffering:
Goody Blake is one stage of deprivation beyond even other very poor rural
folk.
33. *pottage*: see note to 'Michael' l. 102 (p. 346).

Then at her door the *canty* dame
Would sit, as any linnet gay.   40

But when the ice our streams did fetter,
Oh! then how her old bones would shake!
You would have said, if you had met her,
'Twas a hard time for Goody Blake.
Her evenings then were dull and dead;   45
Sad case it was, as you may think,
For very cold to go to bed,
And then for cold not sleep a wink.

Oh joy for her! whene'er in winter
The winds at night had made a rout,   50
And scattered many a lusty splinter
And many a rotten bough about.
Yet never had she, well or sick,
As every man who knew her says,
A pile before hand, wood or stick,   55
Enough to warm her for three days.

Now, when the frost was past enduring,
And made her poor old bones to ache,
Could any thing be more alluring
Than an old hedge to Goody Blake?   60
And, now and then, it must be said,
When her old bones were cold and chill,
She left her fire, or left her bed,
To seek the hedge of Harry Gill.

39. canty: cheerful, healthy. A dialect term but a Northern and Scottish one and hence not part of the Dorsetshire colouring. The italics are perhaps designed to indicate that the word is not part of the narrator's ordinary idiom; there are poetic occurrences in Scottish vernacular verse, including ballads.

41–4. One historian of the period has written that the 'unparalleled series of terrible winters' compounding acute economic distress in the late 1790s is 'the point' of the poem (F.K. Brown, *Fathers of the Victorians*, Cambridge, 1961, p. 125).

46–8. Crabb Robinson praised these lines as 'doubly powerful – doubly poetic' because they consisted entirely of ' "prosaic" . . . vulgar everyday expressions' (Morley 1927: 43).

49–56. According to Crabb Robinson the stanza 'is properly speaking not a purely poetical but a rhetorical description. Poetry as such should awaken no passion, that is the business of rhetoric' (Morley 1927: 46). The remark is especially interesting in the light of Wordsworth's own linking of *LB* with the emotive powers of rhetoric (notably in the motto to the collection, p. 95).

Now Harry he had long suspected   65
This trespass of old Goody Blake;
And vowed that she should be detected,
And he on her would vengeance take.
And oft from his warm fire he'd go,
And to the fields his road would take;   70
And there, at night, in frost and snow,
He watched to seize old Goody Blake.

And once, behind a rick of barley,
Thus looking out did Harry stand:
The moon was full and shining clearly,   75
And crisp with frost the stubble land.
– He hears a noise – he's all awake –
Again? – on tip-toe down the hill
He softly creeps – 'tis Goody Blake,
She's at the hedge of Harry Gill.   80

Right glad was he when he beheld her:
Stick after stick did Goody pull:
He stood behind a bush of elder,
Till she had filled her apron full.
When with her load she turned about,   85
The bye-road back again to take,
He started forward with a shout,
And sprang upon poor Goody Blake.

And fiercely by the arm he took her,
And by the arm he held her fast,   90
And fiercely by the arm he shook her,
And cried, 'I've caught you then at last!'
Then Goody, who had nothing said,
Her bundle from her lap let fall;
And, kneeling on the sticks, she prayed   95
To God that is the judge of all.

---

66. trespass: there was conflict as to whether the collection of easily
gathered wood by the rural poor was a traditional right (as popular opinion
and some local arrangements had it) or a crime (as the law increasingly
tried to insist). On this, with much evidence from Wiltshire, see B.
Bushaway, *By Rite*, 1982, pp. 207–33.
72. watched: kept vigil.
95. Wordsworth retains from Darwin the adaptation of the bundle of sticks
as a hassock, a ritual touch that could be thought to assist the formation of
Harry's delusion.

She prayed, her withered hand uprearing,
While Harry held her by the arm –
'God! who art never out of hearing,
'Oh may he never more be warm!'   100
The cold, cold moon above her head,
Thus on her knees did Goody pray.
Young Harry heard what she had said,
And icy cold he turned away.

He went complaining all the morrow   105
That he was cold and very chill:
His face was gloom, his heart was sorrow,
Alas! that day for Harry Gill!
That day he wore a riding-coat,
But not a whit the warmer he: 110
Another was on Thursday brought,
And ere the Sabbath he had three.

'Twas all in vain, a useless matter,
And blankets were about him pinned;
Yet still his jaws and teeth they clatter,   115
Like a loose casement in the wind.
And Harry's flesh it fell away;
And all who see him say, 'tis plain,
That live as long as live he may,
He never will be warm again.   120

No word to any man he utters,
A-bed or up, to young or old;
But ever to himself he mutters,
'Poor Harry Gill is very cold.'
A-bed or up, by night or day,   125
His teeth they chatter, chatter still.
Now think, ye farmers all, I pray,
Of Goody Blake and Harry Gill.

99–100. Goody's prayer resembles denunciatory prayers in the Old Testament e.g. *Psalms* 145.18–19.
124. Compare *King Lear* III, iv, 152: 'Poor Tom's a-cold.' The adjective so insistently used of Goody Blake is now applied by Harry to himself.

The Last of the Flock

Probably composed in the spring of 1798. The man had ten rather than six children in 1798; minor late changes. The stanza is one of several hybrids of rhymed and unrhymed lines experimented with by Wordsworth in the collection. It may be thought of as a series of four couplets interrupted by two unrhymed lines, and one result is the formation of a ballad-like verse at lines 5 to 8 of the stanza (see General Introduction, p. 11). The shorter eighth line creates something of a break in the stanza before the final couplet. Wordsworth told Isabella Fenwick that 'the incident occurred in the village of Holford, close by Alfoxden', that is, near his residence at the time, but the witness in the episode was not Wordsworth (see note to l. 1).

One of the most epiphanic of all the encounters described in *LB*. It is orthodox to suppose that the poem records the naturalness and healthiness of an attachment to property, and hence is an attack on the proto-Marxist views of William Godwin on this subject. But no particular attachment to his flock is claimed by the weeping man until poverty forces their sale, and then his attitude seems to be an unbalanced response to privation which leads him to value his sheep more than his family (the great unvoiced question of the poem – unvoiced because the shepherd does not ask it – is, what will happen to the children?). The main revelation of the encounter seems to be of the psychic damage that can be caused by hardship, such that the man has an obsession ominously 'more powerful than those ideas which generally interest us most' (for the possible influence of this formula from Erasmus Darwin, see Averill 1980: 157).

> In distant countries I have been,
> And yet I have not often seen
> A healthy Man, a Man full grown,
> Weep in the public roads alone.
> But such a one, on English ground,   5
> And in the broad highway, I met;
> Along the broad highway he came,
> His cheeks with tears were wet.
> Sturdy he seemed, though he was sad;
> And in his arms a Lamb he had.   10
>
> He saw me, and he turned aside,
> As if he wished himself to hide:
> Then with his coat he made essay
> To wipe those briny tears away.

1. I: insofar as the 'I' has a factual origin he is an unknown friend of Wordsworth's (see p. 374). The sense of the narrator's social distance from him felt by the man is made emphatic in the latter's frequent use of 'Sir'.
4. alone: significant, and a sign of a troubling degree of distress (l. 16), because public weeping is almost always communal, as in a funeral procession (see pp. 373–4).

I followed him, and said, 'My friend,   15
'What ails you? wherefore weep you so?'
'Shame on me, Sir! this lusty Lamb,
He makes my tears to flow.
Today I fetched him from the rock;
He is the last of all my flock.   20

'When I was young, a single Man,
And after youthful follies ran,
Though little given to care and thought,
Yet, so it was, a ewe I bought;
And other sheep from her I raised,   25
As healthy sheep as you might see;
And then I married, and was rich
As I could wish to be;
Of sheep I numbered a full score,
And every year increased my store.   30

'Year after year my stock it grew,
And from this one, this single ewe,
Full fifty comely sheep I raised,
As sweet a flock as ever grazed!
Upon the mountain did they feed,   35
They throve, and we at home did thrive.
This lusty Lamb of all my store
Is all that is alive;
And now I care not if we die,
And perish all of poverty.   40

'Six Children, Sir! had I to feed,
Hard labour in a time of need!
My pride was tamed, and in our grief
I of the parish asked relief.
They said I was a wealthy man;   45
My sheep upon the mountain fed,
And it was fit that thence I took
Whereof to buy us bread.
"Do this: how can we give to you,"
They cried, "what to the poor is due?"   50

'I sold a sheep, as they had said,
And bought my little Children bread,
And they were healthy with their food;
For me – it never did me good.
A woeful time it was for me,   55
To see the end of all my gains,

The pretty flock which I had reared
With all my care and pains,
To see it melt like snow away!
For me it was a woeful day.   60

'Another still! and still another!
A little lamb, and then its mother!
It was a vein that never stopped –
Like blood-drops from my heart they dropped.
Till thirty were not left alive   65
They dwindled, dwindled, one by one,
And I may say, that many a time
I wished they all were gone.
They dwindled one by one away;
For me it was a woeful day.   70

'To wicked deeds I was inclined,
And wicked fancies crossed my mind;
And every man I chanced to see,
I thought he knew some ill of me.
No peace, no comfort could I find,   75
No ease, within doors or without,
And crazily, and wearily,
I went my work about.
Oft-times I thought to run away;
For me it was a woeful day.   80

'Sir! 'twas a precious flock to me,
As dear as my own Children be;
For daily with my growing store
I loved my Children more and more.
Alas! it was an evil time;   85
God cursed me in my sore distress;
I prayed, yet every day I thought
I loved my Children less;
And every week, and every day,
My flock, it seemed to melt away.   90

'They dwindled, Sir, sad sight to see!
From ten to five, from five to three,
A lamb, a wether, and a ewe;
And then, at last, from three to two;
And of my fifty, yesterday   95
I had but only one:

93. *wether*: probably in the most customary sense, of a castrated ram.

And here it lies upon my arm,
Alas! and I have none; –
Today I fetched it from the rock;
It is the last of all my flock.'   100

Lines

Left upon a Seat in a YEW-TREE, which stands near the Lake of Esthwaite, on a desolate part of the shore, yet commanding a beautiful prospect

Despite the dating in the long Fenwick note (see p. 374) probably substantially composed in the first half of 1797. Ll. 13–22 were reworked in the successive editions of *LB*; later changes were slight. In the collected works, a 'Poem of Sentiment and Reflection' until 1845. The occasional appearance of a distinctively literary syntax and vocabulary cannot be attributed to the poem's being of a much earlier date than most of *LB*, and these features should be chiefly seen as examples of Wordsworth's inscriptional idiom, which is deployed in several poems in the collection. Inscriptional poetry, especially related to natural features, is a genre with ancient roots that was given a new emphasis and popularity by Akenside and Shenstone in the mid eighteenth century. The whole subject is discussed brilliantly in relation to this poem and Wordsworth generally by Hartman (1965). For some evidence that Coleridge contributed parts (notably ll. 47–9 and 54–8), see Parrish 1973: 66–70.

> Nay, traveller! rest. This lonely yew-tree stands
> Far from all human dwelling: what if here
> No sparkling rivulet spread the verdant herb?
> What if these barren boughs the bee not loves?
> Yet, if the wind breathe soft, the curling waves,   5
> That break against the shore, shall lull thy mind
> By one soft impulse saved from vacancy.
>
>   Who he was
> That piled these stones, and with the mossy sod
> First covered o'er, and taught this aged tree
> With its dark arms to form a circling bower,   10
> I well remember. He was one who owned
> No common soul. In youth by science nursed,

1. traveller! rest: the conventional inscriptional apostrophe to the passer-by is put in the form of the classical epitaph's *Siste viator*. Part of the origins of the Romantic nature inscription lie in classical epitaph, and Wordsworth (who was keenly interested in epitaphs of all kinds) in a sense renews the connection.

1–4. For Sheats (1973: 155–7) these lines are parodically artificial and ostentatious in a manner designed to undermine the reader's conventional attitude to a landscape.

3. herb: in the sense of 'herbage', a poeticism.

7. vacancy: as elsewhere in Wordsworth, mental vacancy. The whole phrase 'saved from vacancy' qualifies 'mind' in the previous line.

8–11. Who he ... remember: there is no uncertainty or epiphanic silence in the interpreting of the vestiges of human tragedy in the case of the yew-tree

And led by nature into a wild scene
Of lofty hopes, he to the world went forth
A favoured being, knowing no desire   15
Which genius did not hallow, 'gainst the taint
Of dissolute tongues, and jealousy, and hate,
And scorn, against all enemies prepared,
All but neglect. The world, for so it thought,
Owed him no service: wherefore he at once   20
With indignation, turned himself away,
And with the food of pride sustained his soul
In solitude. Stranger! these gloomy boughs
Had charms for him; and here he loved to sit,
His only visitants a straggling sheep,   25
The stone-chat, or the glancing sandpiper;
And on these barren rocks, with juniper,
And heath, and thistle, thinly sprinkled o'er,
Fixing his downcast eye, he many an hour
A morbid pleasure nourished, tracing here   30
An emblem of his own unfruitful life:
And lifting up his head, he then would gaze
On the more distant scene – how lovely 'tis
Thou seest – and he would gaze till it became
Far lovelier, and his heart could not sustain   35
The beauty still more beauteous. Nor, that time,
When Nature had subdued him to herself,
Would he forget those beings, to whose minds,
Warm from the labours of benevolence,

seat, and it is appropriate that the 'I' is akin to the poet, a native of the area
who knew this spot well. On the other hand, the sufferer represents a
considerable adaptation of the historical reality. The yew-tree seat (which
was not as remote from human habitation as the narrator makes it) was
erected by the Reverend William Braithwaite, who may have lived a
reclusive life for some years after a not obviously distinguished under-
graduate career, but was active in local affairs from 1787 (with, moreover,
livings in Lincolnshire) and still alive in 1798 (Thompson 1970: 256–65).
There are notable affinities with more obviously fictionalized poems in the
collection – of the seat with the thorn/moss/mound of 'The Thorn', for
example, and of the recluse's experiences with those of the Boy of
Winander (p. 222).
12. science: knowledge.
13. nature: not capitalized here, though it is at ll. 37, 56.
16. taint: carrying some of the force of the obsolete sense, 'false
condemnation'.
26. glancing: darting. A favourite usage of Wordsworth's though one that
was becoming rarer in his day.

The world, and man himself, appeared a scene   40
Of kindred loveliness: then he would sigh
With mournful joy, to think that others felt
What he must never feel: and so, lost man!
On visionary views would fancy feed,
Till his eye streamed with tears. In this deep vale   45
He died – this seat his only monument.

If thou be one whose heart the holy forms
Of young imagination have kept pure,
Stranger! henceforth be warned; and know, that pride,
Howe'er disguised in its own majesty,   50
Is littleness; that he who feels contempt
For any living thing hath faculties
Which he has never used; that thought with him
Is in its infancy. The man whose eye
Is ever on himself doth look on one,   55
The least of Nature's works, one who might move
The wise man to that scorn which wisdom holds
Unlawful, ever. Oh be wiser, thou!
Instructed that true knowledge leads to love,
True dignity abides with him alone   60
Who, in the silent hour of inward thought,
Can still suspect, and still revere himself,
In lowliness of heart.

62. Compare Edward Young, *Night Thoughts* (1742) Night VI, l. 128:
'Revere thyself, and yet thyself despise.'

The Foster-mother's Tale
A narration in dramatic blank verse

By Coleridge. Composed in the summer of 1797 as part of his tragedy *Osorio*, and restored to the play (which was revised and retitled *Remorse*) in some editions – though not in the acted version – as well as continuing to appear as a separate piece. Coleridge judged it 'unfit for the stage' in a comment of 1813 (see Authors' later comment, p. 371). In the first two editions of *LB* it was accompanied by another extract from *Osorio*, 'The Dungeon'. Considerably more of the play text was excerpted to make 'The Foster-mother's Tale' in 1798, with fifteen more lines being included at the beginning of the extract, and the subtitle was 'A Dramatic Fragment'. From 1800 no major changes. The 1800 version brings the project even more into line with Coleridge's stated intention of 1798: 'the extract from my tragedy will have no sort of reference to my tragedy, but is a tale in itself, as the Ancient Mariner' (Griggs 1956: 412). The subject of the tale does not appear elsewhere in the play. Mayo (1954) judges that 'The Foster-mother's Tale' is 'perhaps the most modish poem' in the collection, both because it is a fragment and because of its combination of 'sensibility, sentimental primitivism, and Gothic mystery': it 'conforms strictly to type although it is subtler and more sophisticated than the fragments of the magazines'.

But that entrance, Mother!

Foster-mother
Can no one hear? It is a perilous tale!

Maria

No one.

Foster-mother
My husband's father told it me,

Poor old Leoni! – Angels rest his soul!
He was a woodman, and could fell and saw   5
With lusty arm. You know that huge round beam
Which props the hanging wall of the old chapel;
Beneath that tree, while yet it was a tree,
He found a baby wrapt in mosses lined
With thistle-beards, and such small locks of wool   10
As hang on brambles. Well, he brought him home,
And reared him at the then Lord Velez' cost.
And so the babe grew up a pretty boy,
A pretty boy, but most unteachable –
And never learnt a prayer, nor told a bead,   15

---

1. *entrance*: the 'tale' explains the existence of a dungeon entrance which in the acted version of the play is just assumed to be divulged offstage.
15. *told a bead*: counted a bead on a rosary while praying.

But knew the names of birds, and mocked their notes,
And whistled, as he were a bird himself:
And all the autumn 'twas his only play
To gather seeds of wild flowers, and to plant them
With earth and water on the stumps of trees.   20
A friar, who sought for simples in the wood,
A grey-haired man, he loved this little boy,
The boy loved him – and, when the friar taught him,
He soon could write with the pen, and from that time
Lived chiefly at the convent or the castle.   25
So he became a very learned youth.
But, oh! poor wretch – he read, and read, and read,
Till his brain turned, and ere his twentieth year
He had unlawful thoughts of many things:
And though he prayed, he never loved to pray   30
With holy men, nor in a holy place.
But yet his speech, it was so soft and sweet,
The late Lord Velez ne'er was wearied with him.
And once, as by the north side of the chapel
They stood together, chained in deep discourse,   35
The earth heaved under them with such a groan,
That the wall tottered, and had well-nigh fallen
Right on their heads. My Lord was sorely frightened;
A fever seized him, and he made confession
Of all the heretical and lawless talk   40
Which brought this judgment; so the youth was seized
And cast into that cell. My husband's father
Sobbed like a child – it almost broke his heart.
And once as he was working near the cell
He heard a voice distinctly; 'twas the youth's,   45
Who sang a doleful song about green fields,
How sweet it were on lake or wild savannah
To hunt for food, and be a naked man,
And wander up and down at liberty.
Leoni doted on the youth, and now   50
His love grew desperate; and defying death,
He made that cunning entrance I described,
And the young man escaped.

16. knew the names of birds: Newlyn (1986: 26) notes the similarity to
Adam's naming of the animals in paradise.
   mocked: imitated.
21. simples: medicinal plants. There is a reminiscence of Friar Laurence in
Romeo and Juliet, and of the apothecary in that play who is 'culling of
simples' (II, iii, 1–30; V, i, 40).
48. naked man: a savage.

Maria
    'Tis a sweet tale.
And what became of him?
    Foster-mother
      He went on ship-board,
With those bold voyagers who made discovery   55
Of golden lands. Leoni's younger brother
Went likewise; and when he returned to Spain,
He told Leoni, that the poor mad youth,
Soon after they arrived in that new world,
In spite of his dissuasion, seized a boat,   60
And, all alone, set sail by silent moonlight
Up a great river, great as any sea,
And ne'er was heard of more; but 'tis supposed
He lived and died among the savage men.

---

56. *golden lands*: South and Central America and their riches (*Osorio* is set
in Spain in the sixteenth century). The phrase may be from Abraham
Cowley, 'To Mr Hobbes' (1668), l. 56.

The Thorn

Composed in March/April/May 1798. Changed at several points, mainly from 1815 onwards, and especially in respect of Martha Ray's past as treated in stanzas 10–15. Wordsworth had emphasized that the poem was the utterance of a 'loquacious narrator' in the Advertisement of 1798 (p. 35) and he enlarged on this and other aspects of 'The Thorn' (such as the interplay of metrical and narrative effects, and the use of repetition) in a long note added in all subsequent editions (see pp. 37–9). He foresaw that 'fine ladies' would be offended by some expressions, probably those concerning Martha's pregnancy (see p. 51). The stanza is Wordsworth's most elaborate hybrid of rhyme and blank verse, a complex eleven-line form, sustained throughout, that consists of five lightly rhymed lines followed by six entirely rhymed. Cutting across this pattern is an alternative subdivision of the stanza, by line length (and it tends to be reinforced by the syntax): three-stress lines make two sub-verses out of the otherwise four-stress lines (O'Donnell 1989: 94, 130 calls this 'modified tail-rhyme'). Rhyme and rhythm units finally coincide in the closing couplet of each stanza (so that the emphatic chiming of ll. 32–3, so risible to some readers, is part of a scheme in which rhyming effects ebb and flow). Ker (1966: 229) finds some precedent in the ten-line stanza verse of Thomas Gray.

Several literary precedents may have fed into the stimulus of Wordsworth's fresh sighting of an actual thorn-tree, as recalled in the Fenwick note (p. 380) – which may itself have built on a now lost Lake District anecdote or experience (see Morley 1938: 661). In *The Country Justice* by the Somerset poet John Langhorne a 'solitary thorn' with 'aged limbs' marks the spot where a mother, denied relief by the local Poor Law overseer, dies with her new-born child naked on her breast (Part 2, 1775, pp. 24–5). A ballad by the German poet Gottfried Bürger published in an English version in 1796 as 'The Lass of Fair Wone' (*Monthly Magazine* I, 1796, pp. 223–4) has a jilted unmarried mother slaying and burying her new-born child beside a pond. A passage in *The Pains of Memory* (1796, p. 13) by Robert Merry has a mother and her new-born illegitimate infant dying 'on the chilly grass . . . Beneath that bending solitary thorn'. In many versions of the traditional Scottish ballad 'The Cruel Mother', the labour of the unmarried mother who kills her offspring is associated with a thorn-tree, and one such version was definitely known to Wordsworth by 1800. The details of the thorn as such may be influenced by a passage in Joseph Cottle's 'Malvern Hills' (see Owen 1982).

In all these cases (leaving aside the Cottle lines) the bare incidents of an illegitimate birth and the death of child and/or mother are the whole interest and they are fairly directly treated. Wordsworth believed of Bürger's ballads generally that the only element of human character was the poet's own: 'I do not perceive the presence of character in his personages. I see everywhere the character of Bürger himself' (Griggs 1956: 566), and in 'The Thorn' (in addition to incorporating the powerful new idea of an unmarried mother who frequents her child's grave for more than twenty years) Wordsworth has clearly tried to bring in character of 'personage' to replace character of author, in the form of the loquacious narrator. The significance and success of this device has been the occasion of stark disagreement among critics for at least a century, and is anyway very much a matter of intuitive response (I offer my own comments in the notes which follow). The poem as a whole would be seriously flawed if the narrator's character and mentality were not important, since Wordsworth has evidently striven to establish them. On the other hand, how interesting a poem would 'The Thorn' be if these contributed its *only* interest? If it is just a study of a mendacious or credulous temperament, or even of a poetically imaginative one (to mention some of the accounts that have been offered), can it claim more than passing attention from the modern reader – especially if that reader is being asked to ignore salient themes of madness, death, cruelty and despair? For 'The Thorn' to be a success it must, given its constituent elements, achieve Wordsworth's 'two objects': to create a 'character' and to 'convey passion'. The poem would be consistent with the strategy and content of many other poems in *LB* if it attends to a glimpsed human tragedy, and at the same time to the experience of confronting, understanding and communicating that tragedy; if it is 'a poem not just about suffering, but about the difficulty of comprehending it' (Jacobus 1976: 244).

I

There is a Thorn – it looks so old,
In truth, you'd find it hard to say
How it could ever have been young –
It looks so old and grey.
Not higher than a two years' child   5
It stands erect, this aged Thorn;
No leaves it has, no thorny points;
It is a mass of knotted joints,
A wretched thing forlorn.
It stands erect, and like a stone   10
With lichens it is overgrown.

II

Like rock or stone, it is o'ergrown
With lichens to the very top,
And hung with heavy tufts of moss,
A melancholy crop: 15
Up from the earth these mosses creep,

---

1. Thorn: as if to emphasize the working of the narrator's 'adhesive' attentiveness, Wordsworth capitalized this word and 'Woman' in all appearances of the poem. In the early published versions he used capital letters almost exclusively for the words Hill, Pond, Thorn and Woman in a way that also seems unmistakably significant. In the present edition the 1805 pattern of capitalization for these terms and their synonyms is retained.

And this poor Thorn they clasp it round
So close, you'd say that they were bent
With plain and manifest intent
To drag it to the ground;   20
And all had joined in one endeavour
To bury this poor Thorn for ever.

III

High on a mountain's highest ridge,
Where oft the stormy winter gale
Cuts like a scythe, while through the clouds   25
It sweeps from vale to vale,
Not five yards from the mountain path,
This Thorn you on your left espy;
And to the left, three yards beyond,
You see a little muddy Pond   30
Of water never dry;
I've measured it from side to side:
'Tis three feet long, and two feet wide.

IV

And, close beside this aged Thorn,
There is a fresh and lovely sight,   35
A beauteous heap, a Hill of moss,
Just half a foot in height.

27–31. Though ostensibly a statement of what the imaginary auditor would see, this reads in its preciseness like a disguised report of the narrator's experience (see also stanza IX). The figure of an auditor who shares the narrator's 'tracing' activity is important in the poem if only to indicate the narrator's probable feelings of alienation from the communal local verdict on Martha Ray; it also tends to be used by him as an alter ego on which to project his more alarmed feelings. His temperament is 'superstitious' (see p. 37), but less in what he suspects than in the hold of these suspicions on his mind. For Wordsworth, the superstitious mentality is 'slow' and not more than 'reasonably' imaginative; for this reason (and because of humane feelings for Martha Ray) the narrator is actually wary of leaping to conclusions, at least in his own voice.

32–3. Compare 'The Lass of Fair Wone' (ll. 179–80) on the skull of the gibbeted mother: 'It seems to eye the barren grave / Three spans in length below.' The narrator's pedestrian measuring of the pond in this notorious couplet is consonant with his caution about speculations which he nevertheless cannot shake off. Wordsworth has elected to record it in the two lines that are the most likely to seem pedestrian in an otherwise complicated stanza (see headnote on the rhyme scheme), and though he did alter them some twenty years later this was not necessarily in a spirit of recantation: in 1815 he could still declare stoutly that they 'ought to be liked' (Morley 1938: 166).

All lovely colours there you see,
All colours that were ever seen;
And mossy net-work too is there,   40
As if by hand of lady fair
The work had woven been;
And cups, the darlings of the eye,
So deep is their vermilion dye.

                    V

Ah me! what lovely tints are there!   45
Of olive green and scarlet bright,
In spikes, in branches, and in stars,
Green, red, and pearly white.
This heap of earth o'ergrown with moss,
Which close beside the Thorn you see,   50
So fresh in all its beauteous dyes,
Is like an infant's grave in size,
As like as like can be:
But never, never anywhere,
An infant's grave was half so fair.   55

                    VI

Now would you see this aged Thorn,
This Pond, and beauteous Hill of moss,
You must take care and choose your time
The mountain when to cross.
For oft there sits, between the Heap   60
That's like an infant's grave in size,
And that same Pond of which I spoke,
A Woman in a scarlet cloak,
And to herself she cries,
'Oh misery! oh misery!   65
Oh woe is me! oh misery!'

                    VII

At all times of the day and night
This wretched Woman thither goes;

---

40. net-work: a kind of needlework.
43. cups: refers to blossoms, with perhaps an unspoken link to bleeding, via the medical usage.
63. The familiar symbolism of the 'Scarlet Woman' derives from the whorish 'woman . . . arrayed in purple and scarlet' of *Revelation* 17:4. The narrator's use of this colour imagery is particularly interesting if his description is unsound in the manner mentioned in the note to ll. 98–9.
65–6. The cry the narrator attributes to Martha Ray strongly suggests that compassion for her suffering is his overriding perception of her.

And she is known to every star,
And every wind that blows;   70
And there beside the Thorn she sits
When the blue daylight's in the skies,
And when the whirlwind's on the hill,
Or frosty air is keen and still,
And to herself she cries,   75
'Oh misery! oh misery!
Oh woe is me! oh misery!'

VIII

'Now wherefore, thus, by day and night,
In rain, in tempest, and in snow,
Thus to the dreary mountain-top   80
Does this poor Woman go?
And why sits she beside the Thorn
When the blue daylight's in the sky,
Or when the whirlwind's on the hill,
Or frosty air is keen and still,   85
And wherefore does she cry? –
Oh wherefore? wherefore? tell me why
Does she repeat that doleful cry?'

IX

I cannot tell; I wish I could;
For the true reason no one knows.   90
But if you'd gladly view the spot,
The spot to which she goes;
The Heap that's like an infant's grave,
The Pond – and Thorn, so old and grey;
Pass by her door – 'tis seldom shut –   95
And, if you see her in her hut,
Then to the spot away! –
I never heard of such as dare
Approach the spot when she is there.

91. *if you'd gladly*: a civility to the imaginary auditor ('if it wouldn't inconvenience you'), but intimates the projection of stronger feelings by the narrator.

98–9. Oddities such as this in what is claimed of actual sightings of Martha Ray at the thorn have led critics (especially Parrish, 1957) to argue ingeniously that the unaccompanied narrator's sighting of Martha (stanzas XVIII–XIX) is an optical illusion (and really a sighting of the thorn and its covering of red moss), while the cry he repeatedly hears is an effect of the wind. Relevant to the whole question of the truth of the Martha Ray legend are Wordsworth's wry remarks about his youthful melodramatic imagination in *Prelude* VIII (especially VIII, 533–41 in the 1805 text).

X

'But wherefore to the mountain-top   100
Can this unhappy Woman go,
Whatever star is in the skies,
Whatever wind may blow?'
Nay, rack your brain – 'tis all in vain,
I'll tell you everything I know;   105
But to the Thorn, and to the Pond
Which is a little step beyond,
I wish that you would go:
Perhaps, when you are at the place,
You something of her tale may trace.   110

XI

I'll give you the best help I can:
Before you up the mountain go,
Up to the dreary mountain-top,
I'll tell you all I know.
'Tis now some two-and-twenty years   115
Since she (her name is Martha Ray)
Gave with a maiden's true good will
Her company to Stephen Hill;
And she was blithe and gay,
And she was happy, happy still   120
Whene'er she thought of Stephen Hill.

XII

And they had fix'd the wedding-day,
The morning that must wed them both;
But Stephen to another Maid
Had sworn another oath;   125
And with this other Maid to church
Unthinking Stephen went –
Poor Martha! on that woeful day
A cruel, cruel fire, they say,
Into her bones was sent: 130
It dried her body like a cinder,
And almost turned her brain to tinder.

XIII

They say, full six months after this,
While yet the summer leaves were green,
She to the mountain-top would go,   135
And there was often seen.
'Tis said, a child was in her womb,
As now to any eye was plain;

She was with child, and she was mad;
Yet often she was sober sad   140
From her exceeding pain.
Oh me! ten thousand times I'd rather
That he had died, that cruel father!

XIV

Sad case for such a brain to hold
Communion with a stirring child!   145
Sad case, as you may think, for one
Who had a brain so wild!
Last Christmas when we talked of this,
Old farmer Simpson did maintain,
That in her womb the infant wrought   150
About its mother's heart, and brought
Her senses back again:
And when at last her time drew near,
Her looks were calm, her senses clear.

XV

No more I know, I wish I did,   155
And I would tell it all to you;
For what became of this poor child
There's none that ever knew;
And if a child was born or no,
There's no one that could ever tell;   160
And if 'twas born alive or dead,
There's no one knows, as I have said;
But some remember well,
That Martha Ray about this time
Would up the mountain often climb.   165

XVI

And all that winter, when at night
The wind blew from the mountain-peak,
'Twas worth your while, though in the dark,
The churchyard path to seek:
For many a time and oft were heard   170
Cries coming from the mountain-head:
Some plainly living voices were,
And others, I've heard many swear,
Were voices of the dead:
I cannot think, whate'er they say,   175
They had to do with Martha Ray.

168. 'Twas worth your while: also interpretable as betraying the strength of
the narrator's need to observe Martha Ray.
173–6. The first tokens of an opposition between the narrator's attitude to

XVII

But that she goes to this old Thorn,
The Thorn which I've described to you,
And there sits in a scarlet cloak,
I will be sworn is true.   180
For one day with my telescope,
To view the ocean wide and bright,
When to this country first I came,
Ere I had heard of Martha's name,
I climbed the mountain's height: 185
A storm came on, and I could see
No object higher than my knee.

XVIII

'Twas mist and rain, and storm and rain,
No screen, no fence could I discover,
And then the wind! in faith, it was   190
A wind full ten times over.
I looked around, I thought I saw
A jutting crag, and off I ran,
Head-foremost, through the driving rain,
The shelter of the crag to gain,   195
And, as I am a man,
Instead of jutting crag, I found
A Woman seated on the ground.

XIX

I did not speak – I saw her face,
In truth it was enough for me;   200
I turned about and heard her cry,
'Oh misery! oh misery!'
And there she sits, until the moon
Through half the clear blue sky will go;

Martha and the attitudes of local people (which leads him actually to be less superstitious than they in the content of his beliefs). It is revealed for the first time in the next stanza that the narrator is not a native of the community. 'The superstition of the narrator and the superstition of the village people are biased in utterly opposite directions. The villagers are malevolent.... The narrator brings the poem into a focus of his own choosing by repeatedly driving the reader's attention ... to concentrate on the woman's predicament' (Gérard 1964).

183. *country*: district.
196. *as I am a man*: a Shakespeareanism, e.g. *Tempest* I, ii, 453.
200. *it was enough for me*: This can be read as a record of the narrator's rejection of Martha's suffering or, more plausibly, of his instantaneous conviction that she is to be pitied.

And, when the little breezes make   205
The waters of the Pond to shake,
As all the country know,
She shudders, and you hear her cry,
'Oh misery! oh misery!'

XX

'But what's the Thorn? and what's the Pond?   210
And what's the Hill of moss to her?
And what's the creeping breeze that comes
The little Pond to stir?'
I cannot tell; but some will say
She hanged her baby on the tree;   215
Some say she drowned it in the pond,
Which is a little step beyond:
But all and each agree,
The little babe was buried there,
Beneath that Hill of moss so fair.   220

XXI

I've heard, the moss is spotted red
With drops of that poor infant's blood:
But kill a new-born infant thus
I do not think she could.
Some say, if to the Pond you go,   225
And fix on it a steady view,
The shadow of a babe you trace,
A baby and a baby's face,
And that it looks at you;
Whene'er you look on it, 'tis plain   230
The baby looks at you again.

XXII

And some had sworn an oath that she
Should be to public justice brought;
And for the little infant's bones
With spades they would have sought.   235

208. She shudders: if no one approaches the thorn when Martha is present
(ll. 98–9) the country cannot know with any certainty that she shudders.
215–20. There is possibly a significant withholding of capitals from 'tree'
and 'pond' (the latter consistently capitalized hitherto) in the context of
unfair accusation (according to the narrator) about their murderous use by
Martha. 'Hill', however, is still capitalized, and seems to become the focus
of the narrator's affirmative and compassionate feelings about Martha.
225. you: here generalized, but may none the less again reflect what the 'I'
has done: gazed into the pond and sought to 'trace' the truth of Martha's
tragedy to the point of experiencing a supernatural-seeming hallucination.

But then the beauteous Hill of moss
Before their eyes began to stir;
And for full fifty yards around,
The grass it shook upon the ground;
But all do still aver   240
The little babe is buried there,
Beneath that Hill of moss so fair.

XXIII

I cannot tell how this may be:
But plain it is, the Thorn is bound
With heavy tufts of moss, that strive   245
To drag it to the ground.
And this I know, full many a time,
When she was on the mountain high,
By day, and in the silent night,
When all the stars shone clear and bright,   250
That I have heard her cry,
'Oh misery! oh misery!
'Oh woe is me! oh misery!'

We are Seven

Composed spring 1798. The only notable change is the omission of the second half of l. 1 from 1815, a phrase that had already been troublesome (see note to ll. 1–4). One of the epiphanic encounter poems, tracing in this instance the tokens of an 'overbalance' of happiness, to use the terminology of the Preface. There is no explicit comment on the girl's refusal to subtract her dead brother and sister from the sum of her siblings, but perhaps an implicit comment via the Bible – see note to ll. 18–22. It is likely that any elaboration by Wordsworth on the Preface's gloss ('perplexity and obscurity which in childhood attend our notion of death, or rather our utter inability to admit that notion'; ll. 189–91) would have been complex (as his phrasing here, indeed, suggests). Late in life, in the Fenwick note to the 'Immortality Ode' (see p. 381), Wordsworth cited the first stanza of 'We are Seven' as expressing how 'nothing was more difficult for me in childhood than to admit the notion of death as a state applicable to my own being', a point presumably less relevant to the heroine in the rest of the poem, whose own death is not at issue (on the authorship of the first stanza, see note to ll. 1–4). Wordsworth goes on in this comment to imply that feelings of 'animal vivacity' impel the cottage girl's attitude to death, whereas his own experience had had more to do with 'a sense of the indomitableness of the spirit within me'. But, in a long and important discussion of the general question in the *Essay on Epitaphs* of 1810, Wordsworth's whole emphasis is on the proposal that the 'intimation or assurance within us, that some part of our nature is imperishable', though we feel it from as early as we can remember, is not a component of infantile experience but accompanies the dawning of 'Reason' in a child's mind. It would be a serious error, he claims, to attribute this feeling to 'the same unthinking gaiety or liveliness of animal spirits with which the lamb in the meadow . . . is endowed' or to 'an inability arising from the imperfect state of his [the child's] faculties'. Indeed, in a typically bold speculation Wordsworth associates a child's denial of death with its first conscious speculations about its biological origins (Owen and Smyser 1974, II, 50–1). All this can be harmonized with the 'Immortality Ode' comment if 'animal', in its two occurrences, is taken to have the two meanings given in the title note to 'Animal Tranquillity and Decay' (p. 101); see also footnote to ll. 33–4 below.

> A simple child, dear brother Jim,
> That lightly draws its breath,
> And feels its life in every limb,
> What should it know of death?

1–4. A stanza originally by Coleridge, according to the Fenwick note (see p. 381), though with its 'substance' dictated by Wordsworth. Perhaps the latter point explains the readiness with which Wordsworth treats the stanza as his own utterance, when he cites it as illuminating the 'Immortality Ode' (see headnote). The Fenwick note implies that Wordsworth changed at least one word in Coleridge's stanza – 'Jem' to 'Jim' – because it was 'ludicrous' as a rhyme for 'limb' (and presumably also 'little' to 'simple'). (But was 'Jem' altered at this stage? The associated Jem

I met a little cottage Girl: 5
She was eight years old, she said;
Her hair was thick with many a curl
That clustered round her head.

She had a rustic, woodland air,
And she was wildly clad,   10
Her eyes were fair, and very fair;
Her beauty made me glad.

'Sisters and brothers, little Maid,
How many may you be?'
'How many? Seven in all,' she said,   15
And wondering looked at me.

'And where are they? I pray you tell.'
She answered, 'Seven are we;
And two of us at Conway dwell,
And two are gone to sea.   20

'Two of us in the churchyard lie,
My sister and my brother;
And in the churchyard cottage I,
Dwell near them with my mother.'

'You say that two at Conway dwell,   25
And two are gone to sea,
Yet you are seven; I pray you tell,
Sweet Maid, how this may be?'

Then did the little Maid reply,
'Seven boys and girls are we;   30
Two of us in the churchyard lie,
Beneath the churchyard tree.'

Tobin story would have more point if it were in fact garbled, and Tobin had detected a reference to himself in 'We are Seven'. The story was already being told by Wordsworth in 1812, however; see Morley 1938: 93).
2. *lightly*: as well as shallowly, untroubled by the fears of personal mortality which can assail an adult.

6. *eight years old*: old enough to have reached the age of conscious curiosity about her origins which would carry with it, according to Wordsworth, a conviction of immortality (see headnote).
18–22. In this calculation, the nub of the poem, there is a suggestive echo of *Genesis* 42:13 (also 32), where ten of Joseph's brothers count themselves as twelve: 'the youngest is this day with our father, and one is not'. Nor is this just a matter of Biblical usage; it creates a deliberate dramatic irony, because they are addressing the supposedly dead brother, Joseph.
19. *Conway*: an important market town on the Welsh coast.
31–2. The girl immediately sees what the narrator is driving at.

'You run about, my little Maid,
Your limbs they are alive;
If two are in the churchyard laid,   35
Then ye are only five.'

'Their graves are green, they may be seen,'
The little Maid replied,
'Twelve steps or more from mother's door,
And they are side by side.   40

'My stockings there I often knit,
My kerchief there I hem;
And there upon the ground I sit –
I sit and sing to them.

'And often after sunset, Sir,   45
When it is light and fair,
I take my little porringer,
And eat my supper there.

'The first that died was little Jane;
In bed she moaning lay,   50
Till God released her of her pain;
And then she went away.

'So in the churchyard she was laid;
And all the summer dry,
Together round her grave we played,   55
My brother John and I.

33–4. The narrator, apparently insensitive to the depth of the girl's thinking about our nature, urges her to apply an 'animal' notion of life, the sheer activity of her limbs (in contrast to the intuition of life mediated by those limbs in l. 3). It is significant that the girl does not 'run about' the churchyard, and that there is in fact nothing childish or unreflective in her behaviour at the graves. 'His . . . premise shows a behaviourist interpretation of the concept of life . . . the child, far from clinging irrationally to the idea that her siblings are alive in his terms, admits their deaths, narrates how they died, and denies that those deaths have deprived her of a significant relation to them' (Bialostosky 1984: 116–17).
47. porringer: a small plain bowl.
52–3. Put together with the recognition that Jane 'went away', saying that 'in the churchyard she was laid' does not necessarily denote a belief that Jane is still present in the grave, or no more of a belief to this effect than is implied by many adult practices. Similarly, the girl's saying of John (l. 60) that he 'lies by her side' is simply the idiom of epitaph (as cited, indeed, in 'Ellen Irwin', l. 56, p. 242) and need not be any more the expression of a delusion than Leonard's 'My brother' in 'The Brothers' (l. 407, p. 238). It is as if the girl's function is to remind the narrator of an attitude to death that he has lost sight of but which has come naturally to other men and women.

'And when the ground was white with snow,
And I could run and slide,
My brother John was forced to go,
And he lies by her side.'   60

'How many are you then,' said I,
'If they two are in Heaven?'
The little Maiden did reply,
'Oh master! we are seven.'

'But they are dead: those two are dead!   65
Their spirits are in Heaven!'
'Twas throwing words away: for still
The little Maid would have her will,
And said, 'Nay, we are seven!'

65–9. The last stanza (originally the first to be composed, according to the Fenwick note) is lengthened in the way Coleridge always lengthens his stanza in 'The Ancient Mariner' – from four to five lines with an internal couplet.

Anecdote for Fathers
Showing how the practice of Lying may be taught

Probably composed in April and May 1798. The twelfth stanza was revised significantly on two occasions, and after 1820 the complex mood of the narrator in stanzas 4–6 is rather differently depicted. The subtitle was dropped from 1845 (with a quotation in Latin from Eusebius substituted). It is another epiphanic encounter with the human (but non-suffering) in the form of a child, and clearly a kind of companion to 'We are Seven' (with which it is yoked to some degree in all its published appearances – though see headnote to 'The Idle Shepherd-Boys', p. 262). In the Fenwick note (p. 369), Wordsworth identifies Edward as the five-year-old Basil Montagu, but there is no such warrant for the orthodoxy that Kilve and Liswyn are disguises for Racedown and Alfoxden. Wordsworth explains these names to Isabella Fenwick as if they were intended quite literally. Wordsworth may in fact have visited the real Liswyn with Basil (see Little 1977), but 'Anecdote for Fathers' is probably best regarded as a fiction which makes free use of certain elements in Wordsworth's recent life as its material.

> I have a Boy of five years old;
> His face is fair and fresh to see;
> His limbs are cast in beauty's mould,
> And dearly he loves me.
>
> One morn we strolled on our dry walk, 5
> Our quiet home all full in view,
> And held such intermitted talk
> As we are wont to do.
>
> My thoughts on former pleasures ran:
> I thought of Kilve's delightful shore, 10
> Our pleasant home, when spring began,
> A long, long year before.

3. Compare the Percy *Reliques* version of the Babes in the Wood ballad 'The Children of the Wood', l. 20: 'framed in beautyes mold'.

10. Kilve: see Fenwick note, p. 369.

11–12. The narrator enjoys something of the happy 'idleness' (l. 20) celebrated by the narrator in 'Lines (Written at a small distance from my house)' (pp. 135–6) but not his capacity to start his life afresh at the present springtime. Instead, his pleasure takes the form of reviving and comparing last year's spring, and his response to present experience is in that sense the same as Matthew's in 'The Two April Mornings', pp. 290–2 (or even of the narrator in 'Tintern Abbey').

A day it was when I could bear
To think, and think, and think again;
With so much happiness to spare,   15
I could not feel a pain.

My Boy was by my side, so slim
And graceful in his rustic dress!
And oftentimes I talked to him,
In very idleness.   20

The young lambs ran a pretty race;
The morning sun shone bright and warm;
'Kilve,' said I, 'was a pleasant place;
And so is Liswyn farm.

'My little Boy, which like you more,'   25
I said, and took him by the arm –
'Our home by Kilve's delightful shore,
Or here at Liswyn farm?

'And tell me, had you rather be,'
I said, and held him by the arm,   30
'At Kilve's smooth shore by the green sea,
Or here at Liswyn farm?'

In careless mood he looked at me,
While still I held him by the arm,
And said, 'At Kilve I'd rather be   35
Than here at Liswyn farm.'

'Now, little Edward, say why so;
My little Edward, tell me why.'
'I cannot tell, I do not know.'
'Why, this is strange,' said I.   40

'For, here are woods, and green hills warm:
There surely must some reason be
Why you would change sweet Liswyn farm
For Kilve by the green sea.'

At this, my Boy hung down his head,   45
He blushed with shame, nor made reply;
And five times to the Child I said,
'Why, Edward, tell me why?'

13–16. More explicitly than in 'We are Seven' the normal adult psychological condition is represented as being such that painful ideas are never far away.
24. Liswyn: see Fenwick note, p. 369.

His head he raised – there was in sight,
It caught his eye, he saw it plain –   50
Upon the house-top, glittering bright,
A broad and gilded vane.

Then did the Boy his tongue unlock;
And thus to me he made reply:
'At Kilve there was no weather-cock,   55
And that's the reason why.'

O dearest, dearest Boy! my heart
For better lore would seldom yearn,
Could I but teach the hundredth part
Of what from thee I learn.   60

52. gilded vane: with the imagery of gilding, the echo of 'vain', and the general associations of the weather-cock, there is a considerable accumulation of pejorative suggestion around this element in the tale.

60. what from thee I learn: in a letter conjecturally dated 1826 Wordsworth wrote 'my intention was to point out the injurious effects of putting inconsiderate questions to children, and urging them to give answers upon matters either uninteresting to them, or upon which they had no decided opinion'. The poem's subtitle makes it clear that Edward has lied, and in that sense had received 'injurious' treatment. But Wordsworth apparently intends a lesson more important and more complex than this, or at least an important and complex truth to which this effect simply points. The poem has been concerned mainly to contrast two attitudes to present pleasure, and the lying has arisen from their incompatibility.

Lines

Written at a small distance from my house, and sent by
my little boy to the person to whom they are addressed.

Composed in the first week of March 1798. Not significantly revised. One
of the handful of poems (such as 'Expostulation and Reply', 'The Tables
Turned' and the first of the 'Poems on the Naming of Places') voicing an
unalloyed state of joyful feeling. There is less emphasis than in the other
examples on pure sensation plus animistic fantasy (on the other hand, there
is more glancing over the shoulder to a time when ordinary life, with books,
will be resumed and 'idleness' – a potent but ambiguous concept in *LB* –
finished with). In effect the poem takes the simile of 'Expostulation and
Reply' ll. 11–12, p. 97 (' "As if you were her first-born birth, / And none
had lived before you!" ') and imagines a world which is all beginnings, a
kind of zero point in the month, in the natural world, in the day and, it is
hoped, in the inner lives of the poet and his sister (so that their calendar is
also in a sense at zero; but see note to ll. 19–20). Also, on this bookless day
the very transmission of the text – intimately, over a short distance – is of
the simplest. The linking 'universal' impulse or 'blessed power' that is
common to springtime and humans is love, and this rhetorical situation
therefore brings the trio of poet/little boy/sister into an appropriately close
communion.

It is the first mild day of March:
Each minute sweeter than before,
The redbreast sings from the tall larch
That stands beside our door.

There is a blessing in the air,   5
Which seems a sense of joy to yield
To the bare trees, and mountains bare,
And grass in the green field.

My Sister! ('tis a wish of mine)
Now that our morning meal is done,   10
Make haste, your morning task resign;
Come forth and feel the sun.

Edward will come with you; and pray,
Put on with speed your woodland dress
And bring no book: for this one day   15
We'll give to idleness.

13. *Edward*: see headnote to previous poem and Fenwick note, p. 375.

135

No joyless forms shall regulate
Our living calendar:
We from today, my friend, will date
The opening of the year.   20

Love, now an universal birth,
From heart to heart is stealing,
From earth to man, from man to earth –
It is the hour of feeling.

One moment now may give us more   25
Than fifty years of reason:
Our minds shall drink at every pore
The spirit of the season.

Some silent laws our hearts may make,
Which they shall long obey: 30
We for the year to come may take
Our temper from today.

And from the blessed power that rolls
About, below, above,
We'll frame the measure of our souls: 35
They shall be tuned to love.

Then come, my Sister! come, I pray,
With speed put on your woodland dress –
And bring no book: for this one day
We'll give to idleness.   40

17. forms: rituals or set observances such as punctuate the ordinary calendar.
19–20. This would be to revive, approximately, the practice that obtained almost into Wordsworth's lifetime. Until 1751 and the introduction of the New Style calendar in England, New Year's Day fell on 25 March.
24. hour of feeling: in the sense of both 'the time for feeling' and 'an hour to be devoted to feeling'.
29–30. In the fashion of New Year resolutions.
35. measure: with the sense of a melody, or of a dance. Alexander (1987: 32) finds a musical connotation also in 'temper' (l. 32).

The Female Vagrant

In its first version perhaps composed around 1791, and certainly part of the poem *Salisbury Plain* (written in 1793–4 but never published in its original form in Wordsworth's lifetime). The two projects parted company at some point before the preparation of *LB*, with *Salisbury Plain* remaining a project under revision (perhaps to include a different story about a suffering woman) while 'The Female Vagrant' stanzas were earmarked for *LB* (see Gill 1975: 9–12). The stanza form is that of Spenser's *Faerie Queene*: two quatrains with an additional longer line, or alexandrine, making a couplet at the end of the second. See the various remarks on the poem (Authors' later comment, pp. 370–1). By 1801 Wordsworth was regretting the first *LB* version on the grounds that 'the diction . . . is often vicious, and the descriptions are often false, giving proofs of a mind inattentive to the true nature of the subject on which it was employed' (De Selincourt and Shaver 1967: 328). He changed a good deal to create the version printed here and it seems he felt that these alterations had at least rescued the descriptive element from its falsity. On the other hand, some of these changes were reversed in subsequent editions, and Wordsworth continued to be dissatisfied with 'The Female Vagrant' on other grounds, in particular that there was too much description. The diction and syntax are distinctly more literary than in any other item in *LB*, and there are several obsolete or obsolescent usages. 'The Female Vagrant' seems indeed never to have achieved a form satisfactory to the author, but its concerns are certainly consonant with much else in *LB*, with the process of human attrition to a point of almost complete deprivation being given a particularly elaborate treatment.

'My father was a good and pious man,
An honest man by honest parents bred;
And I believe, that, soon as I began
To lisp, he made me kneel beside my bed,
And in his hearing there my prayers I said.   5
And afterwards, by my good father taught,
I read, and loved the books in which I read;
For books in every neighbouring house I sought,
And nothing to my mind a sweeter pleasure brought.

'The suns of twenty summers danced along –   10
Ah! little marked how fast they rolled away:
Then rose a stately hall our woods among,
And cottage after cottage owned its sway.
No joy to see a neighbouring house, or stray
Through pastures not his own, the master took;   15
My father dared his greedy wish gainsay;
He loved his old hereditary nook,
And ill could I the thought of such sad parting brook.

'But, when he had refused the proffered gold,
To cruel injuries he became a prey,   20
Sore traversed in whate'er he bought and sold:
His troubles grew upon him day by day,
And all his substance fell into decay.
They dealt most hardly with him, and he tried
To move their hearts – but it was vain – for they   25
Seized all he had; and, weeping side by side,
We sought a home where we uninjured might abide.

'It was in truth a lamentable hour,
When, from the last hill-top, my sire surveyed,
Peering above the trees, the steeple tower   30
That on his marriage-day sweet music made.
Till then he hoped his bones might there be laid,
Close by my mother, in their native bowers;
Bidding me trust in God, he stood and prayed –
I could not pray – through tears that fell in showers   35
I saw our own dear home, that was no longer ours.

'There was a youth, whom I had loved so long,
That when I loved him not I cannot say.
'Mid the green mountains many and many a song
We two had sung, like gladsome birds in May.   40
When we began to tire of childish play
We seemed still more and more to prize each other;
We talked of marriage and our marriage day;
And I in truth did love him like a brother;
For never could I hope to meet with such another.   45

'Two years were passed, since to a distant town
He had repaired to ply the artist's trade.
What tears of bitter grief till then unknown!
What tender vows our last sad kiss delayed!
To him we turned – we had no other aid.   50
Like one revived, upon his neck I wept,
And her whom he had loved in joy, he said
He well could love in grief: his faith he kept,
And in a quiet home once more my father slept.

---

21. *traversed*: thwarted.
47. *artist*: skilled manual worker (a sense dying out in Wordsworth's day).
The vagrant's husband seems to have been a handloom weaver (see l. 62).

'We lived in peace and comfort; and were blest   55
With daily bread, by constant toil supplied.
Three lovely infants lay upon my breast;
And often, viewing their sweet smiles, I sighed,
And knew not why. My happy father died
When sad distress reduced the children's meal: 60
Thrice happy! that from him the grave did hide
The empty loom, cold hearth, and silent wheel,
And tears that flowed for ills which patience could not
        heal.

' 'Twas a hard change, an evil time was come;
We had no hope, and no relief could gain.   65
But soon, day after day, the noisy drum
Beat round, to sweep the streets of want and pain.
My husband's arms now only served to strain
Me and his children hungering in his view:
In such dismay my prayers and tears were vain: 70
To join those miserable men he flew:
And now to the sea-coast, with numbers more, we drew.

'There, long were we neglected, and we bore
Much sorrow ere the fleet its anchor weighed;
Green fields before us and our native shore,   75
We breathed a pestilential air that made
Ravage for which no knell was heard. We prayed
For our departure; wished and wished – nor knew
'Mid that long sickness, and those hopes delayed,
That happier days we never more must view.   80
The parting signal streamed, at last the land withdrew.

'But the calm summer season now was past.
On as we drove, the equinoctial deep
Ran mountains-high before the howling blast;
And many perished in the whirlwind's sweep.   85

62. *wheel*: spinning wheel.
65. *no relief*: perhaps, no help under the provisions of the Poor Law.
66–7. Recruiting officers and their men at work, recruiting for the army fighting the American colonists.
68. *strain*: embrace tightly. As applied in this way, obsolete in Wordsworth's day.
77. *no knell was heard*: because the dead were not given church funerals.
81. *The parting signal streamed*: signal flags.
83. *equinoctial deep*: the context suggests that 'equinoctial' refers to the traditionally stormy autumn equinox, though on its own the phrase would more naturally mean the equatorial ocean. In the American Revolution the south was a theatre of war as well as the north.

We gazed with terror on their gloomy sleep,
Untaught that soon such anguish must ensue,
Our hopes such harvest of affliction reap,
That we the mercy of the waves should rue.
We reached the western world, a poor, devoted crew.   90

'The pains and plagues that on our heads came down,
Disease and famine, agony and fear,
In wood or wilderness, in camp or town,
It would thy brain unsettle, even to hear.
All perished – all, in one remorseless year,   95
Husband and children! one by one, by sword
And ravenous plague, all perished: every tear
Dried up, despairing, desolate, on board
A British ship I waked, as from a trance restored.

'Peaceful as some immeasurable plain   100
By the first beams of dawning light impressed,
In the calm sunshine slept the glittering main.
The very ocean has its hour of rest.
I too was calm, though heavily distressed!
Oh me, how quiet sky and ocean were!   105
My heart was healed within me, I was blessed,
And looked, and looked along the silent air,
Until it seemed to bring a joy to my despair.

'Ah! how unlike those late terrific sleeps!
And groans, that rage of racking famine spoke!   110
The unburied dead that lay in festering heaps!
The breathing pestilence that rose like smoke!
The shriek that from the distant battle broke!
The mine's dire earthquake, and the pallid host
Driven by the bomb's incessant thunder-stroke   115
To loathsome vaults, where heart-sick anguish tossed,
Hope died, and fear itself in agony was lost!

90. *western world*: America. Though it is no part of the explicit content of the poem, it is made clear in the Advertisement of 1842 (see p. 370) that Wordsworth linked this account of Britain's campaign in America with her later adventures against revolutionary France. Given Wordsworth's deep revulsion against the latter offensive, it is fair to deduce that in his view the suffering and moral damage (see ll. 223–8) sustained by the vagrant from l. 66 are brought about by a government prosecuting an unjust war.
    devoted: doomed.
94. *thy*: in the original *Salisbury Plain* context, this refers to the vagrant's auditor.
101. *impressed*: a distinctive use, deriving from *Paradise Lost* IV, 150.
109. *terrific*: terrifying.

'At midnight once the storming army came,
Yet do I see the miserable sight,
The bayonet, the soldier, and the flame   120
That followed us and faced us in our flight;
When Rape and Murder by the ghastly light
Seized their joint prey, the mother and the child!
But I must leave these thoughts. From night to night,
From day to day, the air breathed soft and mild: 125
And on the gliding vessel heaven and ocean smiled.

'Some mighty gulf of separation past,
I seemed transported to another world –
A thought resigned with pain, when from the mast
The impatient mariner the sail unfurled,   130
And, whistling, called the wind that hardly curled
The silent sea. From the sweet thoughts of home
And from all hope I was for ever hurled.
For me – farthest from earthly port to roam
Was best, could I but shun the spot where man might   135
    come.

'And oft I thought (my fancy was so strong)
That I at last a resting-place had found;
"Here will I dwell," said I, "my whole life long,
Roaming the illimitable waters round:
Here will I live – of every friend disowned,   140
Here will I roam about the ocean flood." –
To break my dream the vessel reached its bound:
And homeless near a thousand homes I stood,
And near a thousand tables pined, and wanted food.

'By grief enfeebled was I turned adrift,   145
Helpless as sailor cast on desert rock;
Nor morsel to my mouth that day did lift,
Nor dared my hand at any door to knock.
I lay where, with his drowsy mates, the cock
From the cross timber of an outhouse hung;   150
Dismally tolled, that night, the city clock!
At morn my sick heart hunger scarcely stung,
Nor to the beggar's language could I frame my tongue.

114–21. There were several episodes in the American Revolution in which cities held by British troops were besieged and overrun by the American forces.

114. mine: siege tunnel in which an explosive charge is detonated.

122. Rape, Murder: the only occurrence in *LB* of a kind of personification particularly favoured by some eighteenth-century writers, involving the embodiment of general categories of human action or motivation.

144. wanted: lacked.

'So passed another day, and so the third;
Then did I try in vain the crowd's resort.   155
In deep despair by frightful wishes stirred,
Near the sea-side I reached a ruined fort:
There, pains which nature could no more support,
With blindness linked, did on my vitals fall,
And I had many interruptions short   160
Of hideous sense. I sank, nor step could crawl,
And thence was carried to a neighbouring hospital.

'Recovery came with food: but still, my brain
Was weak, nor of the past had memory.
I heard my neighbours, in their beds, complain   165
Of many things which never troubled me;
Of feet still bustling round with busy glee;
Of looks where common kindness had no part;
Of service done with careless cruelty,
Fretting the fever round the languid heart;   170
And groans, which, as they said, would make a dead
    man start.

'These things just served to stir the torpid sense,
Nor pain nor pity in my bosom raised.
My memory and my strength returned; and thence
Dismissed, again on open day I gazed,   175
At houses, men, and common light, amazed.
The lanes I sought, and, as the sun retired,
Came where beneath the trees a faggot blazed;
The travellers saw me weep, my fate inquired,
And gave me food – and rest, more welcome, more   180
    desired.

'My heart is touched to think that men like these,
Wild houseless wanderers, were my first relief:
How kindly did they paint their vagrant ease,
And their long holiday that feared not grief!
For all belonged to all, and each was chief.   185

---

155. *crowd's resort*: either 'the place where the crowd resorts' or 'resort to
the crowd'; on either reading, a strained locution.
160–1. *interruptions ... sense*: atrocious physical pain interrupted by brief
periods of unconsciousness.
179. *travellers*: gypsies.
182. *houseless wanderers*: 'houseless' is apparently something of a standard
epithet in the poetry of destitution; compare Robert Anderson, 'The
Soldier', l. 72 (*Poems on Various Subjects*, 1798) and John Langhorne, *The
Country Justice*, 1774, Part I, p. 17. Ancestral to all these occurrences is
presumably *King Lear* III, iv, 30.

No plough their sinews strained; on grating road
No wain they drove; and yet the yellow sheaf
In every vale for their delight was stowed;
In every field, with milk their dairy overflowed.

'They with their panniered asses semblance made   190
Of potters wandering on from door to door,
But life of happier sort to me portrayed,
And other joys my fancy to allure;
The bag-pipe dinning on the midnight moor
In barn uplighted, and companions boon   195
Well met from far with revelry secure,
Among the forest glades, when jocund June
Rolled fast along the sky his warm and genial moon.

'But ill they suited me; those journeys dark
O'er moor and mountain, midnight theft to hatch!   200
To charm the surly house-dog's faithful bark,
Or hang on tiptoe at the lifted latch;
The gloomy lantern, and the dim blue match,
The black disguise, the warning whistle shrill,
And ear still busy on its nightly watch,   205
Were not for me, brought up in nothing ill.
Besides, on griefs so fresh my thoughts were brooding
     still.

'What could I do, unaided and unblest?
My father! gone was every friend of thine;
And kindred of dead husband are at best   210
Small help; and, after marriage such as mine,
With little kindness would to me incline.
Ill was I then for toil or service fit:
With tears whose course no effort could confine,
By the road-side forgetful would I sit   215
Whole hours, my idle arms in moping sorrow knit.

'I led a wandering life among the fields;
Contentedly, yet sometimes self-accused,
I lived upon what casual bounty yields,
Now coldly given, now utterly refused.   220

187–9. *and yet ... overflowed*: the gypsies steal sheaves of harvested crops
and milk cows in their pastures.
195. *uplighted*: lit up. Probably Wordsworth's coinage; the word is perhaps
an inversion that has turned into a compound.

The ground I for my bed have often used:
But, what afflicts my peace with keenest ruth
Is, that I have my inner self abused,
Foregone the home delight of constant truth,
And clear and open soul, so prized in fearless youth.   225

'Three years thus wandering, often have I viewed,
In tears, the sun towards that country tend
Where my poor heart lost all its fortitude:
And now across this moor my steps I bend –
Oh! tell me whither – for no earthly friend   230
Have I.' – She ceased, and weeping turned away,
As if because her tale was at an end
She wept – because she had no more to say
Of that perpetual weight which on her spirit lay.

229. *this moor*: in the original context, Salisbury Plain.
232–4. She weeps, it seems, because telling of her despair has not
adequately expressed or relieved it, and never will.

Lines Written in Early Spring

Probably composed in April 1798. In 1820 ll. 20–1 changed to: 'If this belief from heaven be sent, / If such be Nature's holy plan'. Combines in a small compass, and indeed represents as coexisting, two phases of feeling which in *LB* are normally experienced separately: the phase of pleasurable primitive sensation ('a thousand blended notes') plus animistic fantasy, and the phase of gnawing, inescapable consciousness of human pain.

I heard a thousand blended notes,
While in a grove I sate reclined,
In that sweet mood when pleasant thoughts
Bring sad thoughts to the mind.

To her fair works did Nature link   5
The human soul that through me ran;
And much it grieved my heart to think
What man has made of man.

Through primrose tufts, in that sweet bower,
The periwinkle trailed its wreaths;   10
And 'tis my faith that every flower
Enjoys the air it breathes.

The birds around me hopped and played:
Their thoughts I cannot measure –
But the least motion which they made,   15
It seemed a thrill of pleasure.

The budding twigs spread out their fan,
To catch the breezy air;
And I must think, do all I can,
That there was pleasure there.   20

If I these thoughts may not prevent,
If such be of my creed the plan,
Have I not reason to lament
What man has made of man?

1/3. notes/thoughts: true rhymes, because of Wordsworth's Cumbrian accent.
8. There is a reminiscence in this refrain of Burns's 'Man's inhumanity to Man' ('Man was Made to Mourn, a Dirge', 1786, l. 55).
9–12. Glen (1983: 40) finds the lines significantly different from magazine poetry they may seem to resemble (see p. 14): 'He is not merely failing to offer the expected graceful clichés. With awkward, naive-seeming honesty he is exposing the complexity of that which such clichés obscure.'
13–20. Ker (1966: 229–30) notes how the rhythm in these two stanzas changes to Common Metre (alternating four- and three-stress lines).
20. Raine (1968) cites Thomas Taylor's translation of Plotinus, 'On

Felicity' (*Five Books of Plotinus*, 1794, pp. 1–54). There are similarities (e.g. 'perhaps, someone may allow felicity to plants, since life is present in these') but they are broad. Similarly, there seems at most to be only a general debt to Erasmus Darwin's *The Loves of the Plants* (1789), a poeticization of the Linnean system in which plants are classified by sexual structure.

Simon Lee
The Old Huntsman
with an incident in which he was concerned

Probably composed in the spring of 1798. It was the subject of constant revisions, chiefly by way of the reordering of stanzas and parts of stanzas. See the suggestive allusion to the poem in the Preface (ll. 195–8). The stanza is a more interesting eight-line verse than that of 'Goody Blake and Harry Gill' since the unrhymed fifth and seventh lines break the pattern of doubled identical quatrains (as well as building a ballad stanza into the scheme – see General Introduction, p. 11). The poem is an epiphanic encounter with human suffering and degradation in the sense that the last four lines tell us that Simon's thanks are to be lamented but do not say any more (for confirmation that this is the correct reading, see note to l. 103). On the other hand, it is very clear what makes Simon's gratitude deplorable – namely, the fact of his shocking dependence – so that a very small action by the narrator can be the difference for Simon between starving and keeping alive. This dependence – crippled legs and all – is the direct result of Simon's having spent about half his adult life devotedly helping the local aristocracy in the pursuit of one of their recreations. 'The strongest emotion in this stanza is indignation, that a man has been brought to the point where a neighbourly offer of help can reduce him to tears . . . it is the *occasion* of the gratitude that leaves us mourning, and this occasion reflects on social injustice' (Storch 1971). The effect is enhanced in the 1805 arrangement of the poems by the immediately preceding 'What man has made of man' in 'Lines Written in Early Spring'. In fact, in every printing of 'Simon Lee' it is adjacent either to this poem or to the thematically related 'Lines (Written at a small distance from my house)' (pp. 135–6) (joining both after 1815 as a Poem of Sentiment and Reflection).

In the sweet shire of Cardigan,
Not far from pleasant Ivor Hall,
An Old Man dwells, a little man,
I've heard he once was tall.
Of years he has upon his back,   5
No doubt, a burthen weighty;
He says he is three score and ten,
But others say he's eighty.

A long blue livery-coat has he,
That's fair behind, and fair before;   10
Yet, meet him where you will, you see
At once that he is poor.

---

2. *Ivor Hall*: an imaginary aristocratic dwelling. See note to ll. 21–2.
9. *livery-coat*: servant's uniform specific to the employer's family.

Full five-and-twenty years he lived
A running huntsman merry;
And, though he has but one eye left,   15
His cheek is like a cherry.

No man like him the horn could sound,
And no man was so full of glee;
To say the least, four counties round
Had heard of Simon Lee;   20
His master's dead, and no one now
Dwells in the hall of Ivor;
Men, dogs, and horses, all are dead;
He is the sole survivor.

And he is lean and he is sick,   25
His dwindled body's half awry;
His ankles they are swoln and thick;
His legs are thin and dry.
When he was young he little knew
Of husbandry or tillage;   30
And now he's forced to work, though weak –
The weakest in the village.

14. running huntsman: as the factual origins of the poem were in Somerset (see Fenwick note, p. 379), and Wordsworth has made Cardigan in Wales the setting, there is unlikely to be any close reference to actual hunting practices in a particular locality (though see the Fenwick note to 'The Childless Father', p. 370, for a local tradition that was perhaps partly drawn on by Wordsworth). There is nevertheless a mode of hunting – authentic or not – clearly envisaged in the poem: hunting by dog pack, with the gentry following on horseback and the huntsman running on foot (ll. 23, 34). Given the pace at which such a hunt could go and the distances covered (implied by Simon's fame in 'four counties', l. 19), it is not surprising that the narrator should attribute shocking injury (loss of an eye at ll. 41–2 and crippled limbs at ll. 27–8, 43) to Simon's employment.
16. Cited by Francis Jeffrey as a vulgarism (*Edinburgh Review* I, 1802, p. 68).
21–2. For the possible origins of the image of a deserted Welsh 'Ivor Hall' in the poetry of Evan Evans, see Bement 1982.
29–30. Even if his work had not crippled him, it would have made survival in old age arduous for Simon because it prevented his acquiring normal countryman's skills.

He all the country could outrun,
Could leave both man and horse behind;
And often, ere the race was done,   35
He reeled and was stone-blind.
And still there's something in the world
At which his heart rejoices;
For when the chiming hounds are out,
He dearly loves their voices!   40

His hunting feats have him bereft
Of his right eye, as you may see:
And then, what limbs those feats have left
To poor old Simon Lee!
He has no son, he has no child,   45
His wife, an aged woman,
Lives with him, near the waterfall,
Upon the village common.

Old Ruth works out of doors with him,
And does what Simon cannot do;   50
For she, not over stout of limb,
Is stouter of the two.
And, though you with your utmost skill
From labour could not wean them,
Alas! 'tis very little, all   55
Which they can do between them.

Beside their moss-grown hut of clay,
Not twenty paces from the door,
A scrap of land they have, but they
Are poorest of the poor.   60
This scrap of land he from the heath
Enclosed when he was stronger;
But what avails the land to them,
Which they can till no longer?

33–6. Simon evidently outran the rest of the hunt because of his dedication, not because of his physical capacities; indeed, he vastly exceeded these (there is a subtle reinforcing of this point in the idea that Simon could bring himself to a grotesque stage of exhaustion even *before* the hunt was finished).
51. stout: strong.
58–9. twenty paces, scrap of land: bitter touches in view of the scale of Simon's exploits as a huntsman.

Few months of life has he in store,   65
As he to you will tell,
For still, the more he works, the more
His poor old ankles swell.
My gentle reader, I perceive
How patiently you've waited,   70
And I'm afraid that you expect
Some tale will be related.

O reader! had you in your mind
Such stores as silent thought can bring,
O gentle reader! you would find   75
A tale in every thing.
What more I have to say is short,
I hope you'll kindly take it.
It is no tale; but, should you think,
Perhaps a tale you'll make it.   80

One summer-day I chanced to see
This Old Man doing all he could
About the root of an old tree,
A stump of rotten wood.
The mattock tottered in his hand;   85
So vain was his endeavour
That at the root of the old tree
He might have worked for ever.

'You're overtasked, good Simon Lee,
Give me your tool,' to him I said;   90
And at the word right gladly he
Received my proffered aid.
I struck, and with a single blow
The tangled root I severed,
At which the poor Old Man so long   95
And vainly had endeavoured.

---

65. That the process of attrition is almost at its end in Simon's case is
made particularly explicit.
69. *gentle reader*: the familiar courteous epithet with which an author
addresses his reader is here tinged with the sense of gentle as 'well-born'.
72–80. The lines contain four uses of the word 'tale', in which the sense of
'memorable relation' is played against that of 'entertaining story'.

The tears into his eyes were brought,
And thanks and praises seemed to run
So fast out of his heart, I thought
They never would have done.   100
I've heard of hearts unkind, kind deeds
With coldness still returning.
Alas! the gratitude of men
Has oftener left me mourning.

98–9. thanks . . . fast: there is perhaps a sardonic implication in the conceit that Simon's thanks and praises (especially the latter) 'run . . . fast' like Simon himself in his prime. Certainly his demeanour here is consistent with what can be gathered of his demeanour towards his former masters, and thus may be an additional reason for 'mourning' his gratitude.
101–4. The closing lines enact very clearly the intention stated in the Preface (ll. 195–8), of offering 'another and more salutary impression' than is customary.
103–4. 'Mourning' for or by 'Man' forms the refrain to the verses of Burns's 'Man was Made to Mourn, a Dirge' (1786), a poem with a considerable element of social indignation.
103. The line is quoted by Dorothy in her journal in 1801 (De Selincourt 1941, I, 83) when a poor neighbour mistakenly reciprocated a gift of goose with a gift of honey and 'a thousand thanks'; Dorothy had to 'set her right about this'. This seems to confirm that Wordsworth's 'Alas!' relates to the frequency of obsequious gratitude like Simon's and not (as some critics have argued) to the poet's failure to value such gratitude in the past.

The Nightingale
Written in April, 1798

By Coleridge. Composed April and May 1798. Subtitled 'A Conversational Poem' in 1798 and 'A Conversation Poem' in printings from 1828. There were no major revisions other than the dropping in 1800 of five lines at l. 64, restored in 1817. The facetious, indecent lines Coleridge wrote when sending the poem to Wordsworth (see Authors' accompanying statements, pp. 33–4) would seem to record his belief that the poem loses quality as it progresses, though it is not clear where Coleridge locates the stages of this deterioration. The poem's air of 'conversational informality and freedom from artificiality or affectation' would, according to Mayo (1954), have put it in a well-known and approved category of verse of the day, though House (1953: 73) stresses how much Coleridge deepens and complicates the conversational idiom of Cowper. And in asserting the Nightingale's passionate joyfulness Coleridge is probably offering a correction to a whole tradition of melancholy verse deriving from Milton's 'Il Penseroso' (see Hopkins 1968). The poem's relationship to Milton's verse in general is complex, however (see Randel 1982).

> No cloud, no relic of the sunken day
> Distinguishes the West, no long thin slip
> Of sullen light, no obscure trembling hues.
> Come, we will rest on this old mossy bridge!
> You see the glimmer of the stream beneath,   5
> But hear no murmuring; it flows silently
> O'er its soft bed of verdure. All is still,
> A balmy night! and though the stars be dim,
> Yet let us think upon the vernal showers
> That gladden the green earth, and we shall find   10
> A pleasure in the dimness of the stars.
> And hark! the Nightingale begins its song,
> 'Most musical, most melancholy' bird!

2. Distinguishes: marks out as the place where the sun has set.

3. sullen: dim.

7. All is still: compare, in the light of the context and further echoes, Milton, 'Sonnet I', ll. 1–2: 'O Nightingale, that on yon bloomy spray / Warblest at eve, when all the woods are still'.

10–11. we shall . . . stars: because the cloud cover (the cause of the uniform dimness described at the outset) denotes rain.

13. 'Most musical, most melancholy': 'This passage in Milton possesses an excellence far superior to that of mere description: it is spoken in the character of the melancholy man, and has therefore a *dramatic* propriety. The Author makes this remark, to rescue himself from the charge of having

A melancholy bird? O idle thought!
In nature there is nothing melancholy. –   15
But some night-wandering man, whose heart was
      pierced
With the remembrance of a grievous wrong,
Or slow distemper, or neglected love,
(And so, poor wretch! filled all things with himself,
And made all gentle sounds tell back the tale   20
Of his own sorrows) he and such as he
First named these notes a melancholy strain:
And many a poet echoes the conceit;
Poet, who hath been building up the rhyme
When he had better far have stretched his limbs   25
Beside a brook in mossy forest-dell
By sun- or moon-light, to the influxes
Of shapes and sounds and shifting elements
Surrendering his whole spirit, of his song
And of his fame forgetful! so his fame   30
Should share in nature's immortality,
A venerable thing! and so his song
Should make all nature lovelier, and itself
Be loved, like nature! – But 'twill not be so;
And youths and maidens most poetical   35
Who lose the deep'ning twilights of the spring
In ball-rooms and hot theatres, they still
Full of meek sympathy must heave their sighs
O'er Philomela's pity-pleading strains.
My friend, and my friend's sister! we have learnt   40
A different lore: we may not thus profane

---

alluded with levity to a line in Milton: a charge than which none could be
more painful to him, except, perhaps, that of having ridiculed his Bible'
(Coleridge's note). Milton's phrase is at l. 62 of 'Il Penseroso', the
imagined utterance of 'the melancholy man'.

18. distemper: depression, disturbance of mind.
23. conceit: fanciful notion.
24. building up the rhyme: see Milton, *Lycidas*, l. 11.
25–6. stretched his limbs / Beside a brook: compare Thomas Gray, 'Elegy
written in a Country Churchyard', ll. 103–4.
35. poetical: that is, influenced by poetic cliché.
39. Philomela: poets built on the Latin version of the Greek legend of
Philomela – whereby the raped and mutilated princess is turned into a
nightingale – with the fancy that the nightingale's song is a lament for her
cruel plight.
40. My friend . . . sister: William and Dorothy Wordsworth.

Nature's sweet voices always full of love
And joyance! 'Tis the merry Nightingale
That crowds, and hurries, and precipitates
With fast thick warble his delicious notes,   45
As he were fearful that an April night
Would be too short for him to utter forth
His love-chant, and disburthen his full soul
Of all its music! And I know a grove
Of large extent, hard by a castle huge   50
Which the great lord inhabits not: and so
This grove is wild with tangling underwood,
And the trim walks are broken up, and grass,
Thin grass and king-cups grow within the paths.
But never elsewhere in one place I knew   55
So many Nightingales: and far and near
In wood and thicket over the wide grove
They answer and provoke each other's songs –
With skirmish and capricious passagings,
And murmurs musical and swift jug jug   60
And one low piping sound more sweet than all –
Stirring the air with such an harmony,
That, should you close your eyes, you might almost
Forget it was not day.

43. joyance: Watson (1966: 72) speculates that the word was 'reintroduced into English poetry' by Coleridge, following *Faerie Queene* III, xii, 18, but *OED* does have some out-of-the-way citations in the interval.
44. precipitates: hastens.
45. his: Coleridge's singing nightingale is not a lamenting female but a male (which is accurate ornithologically) uttering an urgent song of courtship.
52. underwood: Mrs Radcliffe uses this term for woody undergrowth in describing the scene outside a castle (*The Mysteries of Udolpho*, 1794, IV, Ch. 6), and critics have noticed the 'Gothic' character of Coleridge's setting here. The castle, the 'great lord' and the 'gentle maid' in this section have not been reliably identified and may well be fictitious.
58–9. The notion that nightingales engage in musical contest derives from a tradition about the bird alternative to the Philomela one, first found in Pliny's *Natural History* X, 43.
59. passagings: passages of arms (this occurrence cited by *OED* as the first use of 'passage' as a verb in this sense). But 'passage' could probably also at this date still mean an ornamental run of short musical notes.
60. jug jug: the nightingale's traditional note, mentioned as early as Skelton but most familiar in John Lyly, *Campaspe*, 1584, V, i, 34.

A most gentle maid
Who dwelleth in her hospitable home   65
Hard by the castle, and at latest eve
(Even like a lady vowed and dedicate
To something more than nature in the grove)
Glides through the pathways; she knows all their notes,
That gentle maid! and oft, a moment's space,   70
What time the moon was lost behind a cloud,
Hath heard a pause of silence: till the moon
Emerging, hath awakened earth and sky
With one sensation, and those wakeful birds
Have all burst forth with choral minstrelsy,   75
As if one quick and sudden gale had swept
An hundred airy harps! And she hath watched
Many a Nightingale perch giddily
On blosmy twig still swinging from the breeze,
And to that motion tune his wanton song,   80
Like tipsy Joy that reels with tossing head.

Farewell, O warbler! till to-morrow eve,
And you, my friends! farewell, a short farewell!
We have been loitering long and pleasantly,
And now for our dear homes. – That strain again!   85
Full fain it would delay me! My dear babe,
Who, capable of no articulate sound,
Mars all things with his imitative lisp,
How he would place his hand beside his ear,
His little hand, the small forefinger up,   90
And bid us listen! And I deem it wise
To make him Nature's playmate. He knows well
The evening star; and once when he awoke
In most distressful mood (some inward pain

67–8. The image is of a pagan priestess.
77. *airy harps*: Aeolian harps, designed to resound in response to the passage of air.
79. *blosmy*: blossomy. Occurs several times in Chaucer but not recorded again until 'The Nightingale'.
81. There seems to be a reminiscence of *Comus*, l. 104: 'Tipsy dance and jollity'. The poem's more general resemblances to *Comus* (dark forest, two brothers and a sister, etc.) are developed interestingly by Randel (1982).
85. *That strain again*: see *Twelfth Night* I, i, 14.
86. *My dear babe*: Hartley Coleridge. A similar episode is recorded in Coleridge's notebook, in an entry of unknown date (Coburn 1957, I, 219).
88. *mars*: distorts.

Had made up that strange thing, an infant's dream) 95
I hurried with him to our orchard plot,
And he beholds the moon, and hushed at once
Suspends his sobs, and laughs most silently,
While his fair eyes that swam with undropt tears
Did glitter in the yellow moon-beam! Well – 100
It is a father's tale. But if that Heaven
Should give me life, his childhood shall grow up
Familiar with these songs, that with the night
He may associate joy! Once more farewell,
Sweet Nightingale! once more, my friends! farewell. 105

The Idiot Boy

Composed spring 1798. Many small changes after 1820, of which the chief effect is to reduce the colloquialism, especially in the narration. See the important letter to John Wilson of 1802 (pp. 50–4), and comment in the Preface (ll. 183–5) on the poem as a study of maternal feeling. The stanza, leaving aside the anomalous first and last verses, is another experiment in mixing rhymed and unrhymed lines, with an ABBA quatrain preceded by a single unrhymed line. The result, with this metre, is unique to Wordsworth (O'Donnell 1989: 10, 54). The language of the poem is characterized by a number of words which, if not wholly 'low' and colloquial (in the sense that they are all to be found in standard written English of the period), are on the edge of this category: 'girt', 'fiddle-faddle' (l. 14), 'hurly-burly' (l. 60), 'curr' (l. 114), 'hobnob' (l. 299); and there is a dialectal or wholly colloquial usage in 'cattle' (l. 250). 'The Idiot Boy' is another encounter with human joy as exemplified in the experience of a child (or childlike teenager). In this case epiphany is carried to the point of actual if comic inscrutability in the narrator's claimed ignorance of what happened to Johnny (ll. 322–56), in Johnny's inexpressiveness (which would have made a description of his movements during the night uninformative anyway), and, of course, in the fact that the boy is an 'idiot' with unknown mental powers. It is to be noted that in Johnny's few words about his experience he does 'tell us true' about his sensations; he simply classifies them wrongly. Comparable experiences can be had by the non-idiot mind in a state of primary joyful sensation (see 'Poems on the Naming of Places' I, ll. 25–9, p. 324).

'Tis eight o'clock – a clear March night,
The moon is up – the sky is blue,
The owlet in the moonlight air,
He shouts from nobody knows where;
He lengthens out his lonely shout,   5
Halloo! halloo! a long halloo!

Why bustle thus about your door,
What means this bustle, Betty Foy?
Why are you in this mighty fret?
And why on horseback have you set   10
Him whom you love, your Idiot Boy?

Beneath the moon that shines so bright,
Till she is tired, let Betty Foy
With girt and stirrup fiddle-faddle;

1–6. The moonlight, the 'blue' sky and the cries of 'halloo' are all repeated motifs in Bürger's 'Lenore' (Eng. trans. 1796), a poem concerned mainly with a night ride, though in serious would-be spine-chilling mode. For further possible burlesquing of Bürger, see note to ll. 327–46.
14. girt: girth.
    fiddle-faddle: fiddle, fuss.

But wherefore set upon a saddle   15
Him whom she loves, her Idiot Boy?

There's scarce a soul that's out of bed;
Good Betty, put him down again;
His lips with joy they burr at you;
But, Betty! what has he to do   20
With stirrup, saddle, or with rein?

The world will say 'tis very idle,
Bethink you of the time of night;
There's not a mother, no not one,
But when she hears what you have done,   25
O Betty, she'll be in a fright.

But Betty's bent on her intent;
For her good neighbour, Susan Gale,
Old Susan, she who dwells alone,
Is sick, and makes a piteous moan,   30
As if her very life would fail.

There's not a house within a mile,
No hand to help them in distress:
Old Susan lies a-bed in pain,
And sorely puzzled are the twain,   35
For what she ails they cannot guess.

And Betty's husband's at the wood,
Where by the week he doth abide,
A woodman in the distant vale;
There's none to help poor Susan Gale;   40
What must be done? what will betide?

And Betty from the lane has fetched
Her pony, that is mild and good,
Whether he be in joy or pain,
Feeding at will along the lane,   45
Or bringing faggots from the wood.

And he is all in travelling trim,
And by the moonlight, Betty Foy
Has up upon the saddle set,
The like was never heard of yet,   50
Him whom she loves, her Idiot Boy.

And he must post without delay
Across the bridge that's in the dale,
And by the church, and o'er the down,
To bring a doctor from the town,   55
Or she will die, old Susan Gale.

There is no need of boot or spur,
There is no need of whip or wand,
For Johnny has his holly-bough,
And with a hurly-burly now   60
He shakes the green bough in his hand.

And Betty o'er and o'er has told
The Boy who is her best delight
Both what follow, what to shun,
What do, and what to leave undone,   65
How turn to left, and how to right.

And Betty's most especial charge,
Was, 'Johnny! Johnny! mind that you
Come home again, nor stop at all,
Come home again, whate'er befall,   70
My Johnny, do, I pray you do.'

To this did Johnny answer make,
Both with his head, and with his hand,
And proudly shook the bridle too,
And then! his words were not a few,   75
Which Betty well could understand.

And now that Johnny is just going,
Though Betty's in a mighty flurry,
She gently pats the pony's side,
On which her Idiot Boy must ride,   80
And seems no longer in a hurry.

But when the pony moved his legs,
Oh! then for the poor Idiot Boy!
For joy he cannot hold the bridle,
For joy his head and heels are idle,   85
He's idle all for very joy.

And while the pony moves his legs,
In Johnny's left hand you may see
The green bough's motionless and dead:
The moon that shines above his head   90
Is not more still and mute than he.

His heart it was so full of glee,
That till full fifty yards were gone,

---

60. *hurly-burly*: loud cacophonous noise.
84–6. The situation at this point, with Johnny's 'idle' joy impervious to Betty's attempts to impress on him the fact of Susan's suffering, is recognizably Wordsworthian and, in a comic mode, one of many depictions in *LB* of sorrow importuning joy.

He quite forgot his holly whip
And all his skill in horsemanship,   95
Oh! happy, happy, happy John.

And Betty's standing at the door,
And Betty's face with joy o'erflows,
Proud of herself, and proud of him,
She sees him in his travelling trim;   100
How quietly her Johnny goes.

The silence of her Idiot Boy,
What hopes it sends to Betty's heart!
He's at the guide-post – he turns right,
She watches till he's out of sight,   105
And Betty will not then depart.

Burr, burr – now Johnny's lips they burr,
As loud as any mill, or near it;
Meek as a lamb the pony moves,
And Johnny makes the noise he loves,   110
And Betty listens, glad to hear it.

Away she hies to Susan Gale:
And Johnny's in a merry tune,
The owlets hoot, the owlets curr,
And Johnny's lips they burr, burr, burr,   115
And on he goes beneath the moon.

His steed and he right well agree,
For of this pony there's a rumour,
That should he lose his eyes and ears,
And should he live a thousand years,   120
He never will be out of humour.

But then he is a horse that thinks!
And when he thinks his pace is slack,
Now, though he knows poor Johnny well,
Yet for his life he cannot tell   125
What he has got upon his back.

So through the moonlight lanes they go,
And far into the moonlight dale,
And by the church, and o'er the down,
To bring a doctor from the town,   130
To comfort poor old Susan Gale.

---

113. tune: frame of mind.
125–6. Compare Cowper, *John Gilpin* (1782) ll. 95–6: 'What thing upon his back had got / Did wonder more and more'.

And Betty, now at Susan's side,
Is in the middle of her story,
What comfort Johnny soon will bring,
With many a most diverting thing,   135
Of Johnny's wit and Johnny's glory.

And Betty's still at Susan's side:
By this time she's not quite so flurried:
Demure with porringer and plate
She sits, as if in Susan's fate   140
Her life and soul were buried.

But Betty, poor good woman! she,
You plainly in her face may read it,
Could lend out of that moment's store
Five years of happiness or more   145
To any that might need it.

But yet I guess that now and then
With Betty all was not so well,
And to the road she turns her ears,
And thence full many a sound she hears,   150
Which she to Susan will not tell.

Poor Susan moans, poor Susan groans;
'As sure as there's a moon in heaven,'
Cries Betty, 'he'll be back again;
They'll both be here – 'tis almost ten –   155
They'll both be here before eleven.'

Poor Susan moans, poor Susan groans;
The clock gives warning for eleven;
'Tis on the stroke – 'If Johnny's near,'
Quoth Betty, 'he will soon be here,   160
As sure as there's a moon in heaven.'

The clock is on the stroke of twelve,
And Johnny is not yet in sight –
The moon's in heaven, as Betty sees,
But Betty is not quite at ease;   165
And Susan has a dreadful night.

And Betty, half an hour ago,
On Johnny vile reflections cast:
'A little idle sauntering thing!'
With other names, an endless string,   170
But now that time is gone and past.

And Betty's drooping at the heart,
That happy time all past and gone,

'How can it be he is so late?
The doctor he has made him wait,   175
Susan! they'll both be here anon.'

And Susan's growing worse and worse,
And Betty's in a sad quandary;
And then there's nobody to say
If she must go or she must stay!   180
– She's in a sad quandary.

The clock is on the stroke of one;
But neither doctor nor his guide
Appear along the moonlight road;
There's neither horse nor man abroad,   185
And Betty's still at Susan's side.

And Susan she begins to fear
Of sad mischances not a few,
That Johnny may perhaps be drowned,
Or lost, perhaps, and never found;   190
Which they must both for ever rue.

She prefaced half a hint of this
With, 'God forbid it should be true!'
At the first word that Susan said
Cried Betty, rising from the bed,   195
'Susan, I'd gladly stay with you.

'I must be gone, I must away,
Consider, Johnny's but half-wise;
Susan, we must take care of him,
If he is hurt in life or limb' –   200
'Oh God forbid!' poor Susan cries.

'What can I do?' says Betty, going,
'What can I do to ease your pain?
Good Susan tell me, and I'll stay;
I fear you're in a dreadful way,   205
But I shall soon be back again.'

'Nay, Betty, go! good Betty, go!
There's nothing that can ease my pain.'
Then off she hies, but with a prayer
That God poor Susan's life would spare,   210
Till she comes back again.

So, through the moonlight lane she goes,
And far into the moonlight dale;

---

178. quandary: see General Introduction, p. 16.

And how she ran, and how she walked,
And all that to herself she talked, 215
Would surely be a tedious tale.

In high and low, above, below,
In great and small, in round and square,
In tree and tower was Johnny seen,
In bush and brake, in black and green, 220
'Twas Johnny, Johnny everywhere.

She's past the bridge that's in the dale,
And now the thought torments her sore,
Johnny perhaps his horse forsook,
To hunt the moon that's in the brook, 225
And never will be heard of more.

And now she's high upon the down,
Alone amid a prospect wide;
There's neither Johnny nor his horse
Among the fern or in the gorse; 230
There's neither doctor nor his guide.

'Oh saints! what is become of him?
Perhaps he's climbed into an oak,
Where he will stay till he is dead;
Or, sadly he has been misled, 235
And joined the wandering gipsy-folk.

'Or him that wicked pony's carried
To the dark cave, the goblin's hall;
Or in the castle he's pursuing,
Among the ghosts his own undoing; 240
Or playing with the waterfall.'

At poor old Susan then she railed,
While to the town she posts away;
'If Susan had not been so ill,
Alas! I should have had him still, 245
My Johnny, till my dying day.'

Poor Betty! in this sad distemper,
The doctor's self would hardly spare,
Unworthy things she talked and wild;
Even he, of cattle the most mild, 250
The pony had his share.

---

250. cattle: dialectal or colloquial – horses.

And now she's got into the town,
And to the doctor's door she hies;
'Tis silence all on every side;
The town so long, the town so wide,   255
Is silent as the skies.

And now she's at the doctor's door,
She lifts the knocker, rap, rap, rap;
The doctor at the casement shows
His glimmering eyes that peep and doze;   260
And one hand rubs his old night-cap.

'Oh doctor! doctor! where's my Johnny?'
'I'm here, what is't you want with me?'
'Oh sir! you know I'm Betty Foy,
And I have lost my poor dear boy,   265
You know him – him you often see;

'He's not so wise as some folks be.'
'The devil take his wisdom!' said
The doctor, looking somewhat grim,
'What, woman! should I know of him?'   270
And, grumbling, he went back to bed.

'Oh woe is me! oh woe is me!
Here will I die; here will I die;
I thought to find my Johnny here,
But he is neither far nor near,   275
Oh! what a wretched mother I!'

She stops, she stands, she looks about,
Which way to turn she cannot tell.
Poor Betty! it would ease her pain
If she had heart to knock again;   280
The clock strikes three – a dismal knell!

Then up along the town she hies;
No wonder if her senses fail,
This piteous news so much it shocked her,
She quite forgot to send the doctor,   285
To comfort poor old Susan Gale.

And now she's high upon the down,
And she can see a mile of road;
'Oh cruel! I'm almost threescore;
Such night as this was ne'er before,   290
There's not a single soul abroad.'

She listens, but she cannot hear
The foot of horse, the voice of man;

The streams with softest sounds are flowing,
The grass you almost hear it growing,   295
You hear it now if e'er you can.

The owlets through the long blue night
Are shouting to each other still:
Fond lovers! yet not quite hob nob,
They lengthen out the tremulous sob,   300
That echoes far from hill to hill.

Poor Betty now has lost all hope,
Her thoughts are bent on deadly sin:
A green-grown pond she just has passed,
And from the brink she hurries fast,   305
Lest she should drown herself therein.

And now she sits her down and weeps;
Such tears she never shed before;
'Oh dear, dear pony! my sweet joy!
Oh carry back my Idiot Boy!   310
And we will ne'er o'erload thee more.'

A thought is come into her head:
'The pony he is mild and good,
And we have always used him well;
Perhaps he's gone along the dell,   315
And carried Johnny to the wood.'

Then up she springs, as if on wings;
She thinks no more of deadly sin;
If Betty fifty ponds should see,
The last of all her thoughts would be,   320
To drown herself therein.

O reader! now that I might tell
What Johnny and his horse are doing!
What they've been doing all this time,
Oh could I put it into rhyme,   325
A most delightful tale pursuing!

---

299. *hob nob*: in cheerful fellowship.
327–46. The four activities that Johnny could 'perhaps' be engaged in, any
of which the narrator would describe if the Muses permitted, are all to
some extent based on popular or literary stereotypes, though of a
miscellaneous sort: the folk motif of the pocketed star, stories of a ghost (as
in Bürger's 'Lenore') or the devil on horseback, and Don Quixote fighting
sheep. Primeau (1983) cites also Bürger's 'Der Walde Jäger', which
Wordsworth was to adapt in 'Hart-leap Well'. In contrast to the
predominantly non-literary feeling of these stanzas, Durrant (1963) detects

Perhaps, and no unlikely thought!
He with his pony now doth roam
The cliffs and peaks so high that are,
To lay his hands upon a star,   330
And in his pocket bring it home.

Perhaps he's turned himself about,
His face unto his horse's tail,
And still and mute, in wonder lost,
All like a silent horseman-ghost,   335
He travels on along the vale.

And now, perhaps, he's hunting sheep,
A fierce and dreadful hunter he;
Yon valley, that's so trim and green,
In five months' time, should he be seen,   340
A desert wilderness will be.

Perhaps, with head and heels on fire,
And like the very soul of evil,
He's galloping away, away,
And so he'll gallop on for aye,   345
The bane of all that dread the devil.

I to the Muses have been bound
These fourteen years, by strong indentures:
O gentle Muses! let me tell
But half of what to him befell,   350
He surely met with strange adventures.

O gentle Muses! is this kind?
Why will ye thus my suit repel?
Why of your further aid bereave me?
And can ye thus unfriendly leave me;   355
Ye Muses! whom I love so well.

Who's yon, that, near the waterfall,
Which thunders down with headlong force,
Beneath the moon, yet shining fair,
As careless as if nothing were,   360
Sits upright on a feeding horse?

two serious analogues to Johnny's ride in Virgilian journeys to the
underworld.

347–8. Biographically accurate for Wordsworth, whose first poetry
probably dates from 1784.
348. indentures: agreement binding an apprentice to a trade.

Unto his horse, that's feeding free,
He seems, I think, the rein to give;
Of moon and stars he takes no heed;
Of such we in romances read –   365
'Tis Johnny! Johnny! as I live.

And that's the very pony too.
Where is she, where is Betty Foy?
She hardly can sustain her fears;
The roaring waterfall she hears,   370
And cannot find her Idiot Boy.

Your pony's worth his weight in gold,
Then calm your terrors, Betty Foy!
She's coming from among the trees,
And now all full in view she sees   375
Him whom she loves, her Idiot Boy.

And Betty sees the pony too:
Why stand you thus, good Betty Foy?
It is no goblin, 'tis no ghost,
'Tis he whom you so long have lost,   380
Him whom you love, your Idiot Boy.

She looks again – her arms are up –
She screams – she cannot move for joy;
She darts, as with a torrent's force,
She almost has o'erturned the horse,   385
And fast she holds her Idiot Boy.

And Johnny burrs, and laughs aloud,
Whether in cunning or in joy
I cannot tell; but while he laughs,
Betty a drunken pleasure quaffs,   390
To hear again her Idiot Boy.

And now she's at the pony's tail,
And now she's at the pony's head,
On that side now, and now on this,
And almost stifled with her bliss,   395
A few sad tears does Betty shed.

365. The narrator, although not allowed to attribute to Johnny the more
lively adventures he hankered after, is resourceful enough, when he does
see the more subdued reality of the quietly grazing pony and its rider, to
compare them to a Spenserian knight and his steed.

She kisses o'er and o'er again,
Him whom she loves, her Idiot Boy.
She's happy here, she's happy there,
She is uneasy everywhere;   400
Her limbs are all alive with joy.

She pats the pony, where or when
She knows not, happy Betty Foy!
The little pony glad may be,
But he is milder far than she,   405
You hardly can perceive his joy.

'Oh! Johnny, never mind the doctor;
You've done your best, and that is all.'
She took the reins, when this was said,
And gently turned the pony's head   410
From the loud waterfall.

By this the stars were almost gone,
The moon was setting on the hill,
So pale you scarcely looked at her:
The little birds began to stir,   415
Though yet their tongues were still.

The pony, Betty, and her Boy,
Wind slowly through the woody dale;
And who is she, betimes abroad,
That hobbles up the steep rough road?   420
Who is it, but old Susan Gale?

Long Susan lay deep lost in thought,
And many dreadful fears beset her,
Both for her messenger and nurse;
And as her mind grew worse and worse,   425
Her body it grew better.

She turned, she tossed herself in bed,
On all sides doubts and terrors met her;
Point after point did she discuss;
And while her mind was fighting thus,   430
Her body still grew better.

'Alas! what is become of them?
These fears can never be endured,
I'll to the wood.' – The word scarce said,
Did Susan rise up from her bed,   435
As if by magic cured.

Away she posts up hill and down,
And to the wood at length is come;
She spies her friends, she shouts a greeting;
Oh me! it is a merry meeting, 440
As ever was in Christendom.

The owls have hardly sung their last,
While our four travellers homeward wend;
The owls have hooted all night long,
And with the owls began my song, 445
And with the owls must end.

For, while they all were travelling home,
Cried Betty, 'Tell us, Johnny, do,
Where all this long night you have been,
What you have heard, what you have seen, 450
And, Johnny, mind you tell us true.'

Now Johnny all night long had heard
The owls in tuneful concert strive;
No doubt too he the moon had seen;
For in the moonlight he had been 455
From eight o'clock till five.

And thus, to Betty's question, he
Made answer, like a traveller bold
(His very words I give to you),
'The cocks did crow to-whoo, to-whoo, 460
And the sun did shine so cold.' –
Thus answered Johnny in his glory,
And that was all his travel's story.

458. like a traveller bold: perhaps because travellers' tales are full of marvels.
460–1. See Fenwick note, p. 372, on the special importance of this utterance.

Love

By Coleridge. Probably composed late 1799. It did not appear in *LB* until 1800 but had been published over Coleridge's name in December 1799 in the *Morning Post*. In that version it was entitled 'Introduction to the Tale of the Dark Ladie' and had several additional stanzas: four at the beginning, one at l. 44, another at l. 80, and three at the end. The text was only lightly revised in later printings. The opening and closing extra stanzas in 1799 announce an intention to tell 'what cruel wrong / Befel the Dark Ladie', but it does not seem that the episode related in 'Love' was supposed to have any link with this projected tale, or was ever other than a parenthetical 'sister tale' (unless the obscure thirteenth stanza of 'Love', ll. 49–52, relates to the Dark Ladie). The Dark Ladie poem, which was planned for inclusion in *LB* (see p. 367), is another of Coleridge's unachieved projects; it may have reached an extent of 190 lines, of which some 60 survive (*CPW* I, 293–5). Coleridge's claim about the limited anachronism of the original diction in 'Love' (see p. 36) rather understates the facts, though by 1805 there has been a definite modernization, at least of spellings. 'Faultering' (l. 67), and 'ladie' itself, are modernized; the obsolete 'lovely' in the sense of 'loving' (l. 42) and the (by this period) poetic 'darksome' (l. 46) remain.

> All thoughts, all passions, all delights,
> Whatever stirs this mortal frame,
> All are but ministers of Love,
> And feed his sacred flame.
>
> Oft in my waking dreams do I   5
> Live o'er again that happy hour,
> When midway on the mount I lay
> Beside the ruined tower.
>
> The moonshine stealing o'er the scene
> Had blended with the lights of eve;   10
> And she was there, my hope, my joy,
> My own dear Genevieve!
>
> She leaned against the armed man,
> The statue of the armed Knight:
> She stood and listened to my harp   15
> Amid the ling'ring light.
>
> Few sorrows hath she of her own,
> My hope, my joy, my Genevieve!
> She loves me best, whene'er I sing
> The songs, that make her grieve.   20
>
> I played a soft and doleful air,
> I sang an old and moving story –
> An old rude song that fitted well
> The ruin wild and hoary.

24. hoary: ancient.

She listened with a flitting blush, 25
With downcast eyes and modest grace;
For well she knew, I could not choose
But gaze upon her face.

I told her of the Knight, that wore
Upon his shield a burning brand; 30
And that for ten long years he wooed
The Lady of the Land.

I told her, how he pined: and, ah!
The low, the deep, the pleading tone,
With which I sang another's love, 35
Interpreted my own.

She listened with a flitting blush,
With downcast eyes and modest grace;
And she forgave me, that I gazed
Too fondly on her face! 40

But when I told the cruel scorn
Which crazed this bold and lovely Knight,
And that he crossed the mountain woods
Nor rested day nor night;

That sometimes from the savage den, 45
And sometimes from the darksome shade,
And sometimes starting up at once
In green and sunny glade,

There came, and looked him in the face,
An angel beautiful and bright; 50
And that he knew, it was a fiend,
This miserable Knight!

And how, unknowing what he did,
He leapt amid a murd'rous band,
And saved from outrage worse than death 55
The Lady of the Land;

And how she wept and clasped his knees,
And how she tended him in vain –
And ever strove to expiate
The scorn, that crazed his brain: 60

And that she nursed him in a cave;
And how his madness went away
When on the yellow forest leaves
A dying man he lay;

30. *brand*: sword.
42. *lovely*: loving.

His dying words – but when I reached   65
That tenderest strain of all the ditty,
My falt'ring voice and pausing harp
Disturbed her soul with pity!

All impulses of soul and sense
Had thrilled my guileless Genevieve,   70
The music, and the doleful tale,
The rich and balmy eve;

And hopes and fears that kindle hope,
An undistinguishable throng!
And gentle wishes long subdued,   75
Subdued and cherished long!

She wept with pity and delight,
She blushed with love and maiden shame;
And, like the murmur of a dream,
I heard her breathe my name.   80

Her bosom heaved – she stepped aside;
As conscious of my look, she stepped –
Then suddenly with timorous eye
She fled to me and wept.

She half inclosed me with her arms,   85
She pressed me with a meek embrace;
And bending back her head looked up,
And gazed upon my face.

'Twas partly love, and partly fear,
And partly 'twas a bashful art   90
That I might rather feel than see
The swelling of her heart.

I calmed her fears; and she was calm,
And told her love with virgin pride.
And so I won my Genevieve,   95
My bright and beauteous bride!

The Mad Mother

Probably composed spring 1798, and virtually unchanged but retitled 'Her Eyes are Wild' from 1815. See remarks in the Preface (ll. 183–5) on the psychological content. Wordsworth expected that 'fine ladies' would be offended by some expressions in the poem – presumably those involving the mother's breast (see p. 51). The verse form is one of Wordsworth's most ambitious explorations of the long wholly rhymed stanza in *LB*. It combines a quatrain with couplets, and has an additional internal rhyme in the penultimate line. Wordsworth used the stanza again, without the internal rhyme, for the related and contemporary 'The Complaint of a Forsaken Indian Woman' (pp. 253–5). According to the Fenwick note, 'the subject was reported to me by a lady of Bristol who had seen the poor creature', but the poem is also unmistakably modelled on a celebrated ballad (see pp. 386–7 for the text of this source). Wordsworth may also be indebted (especially for the theme of woodland dwelling) to another song in this tradition, 'The Mother's Lullaby', printed in Joseph Ritson's *Ancient Songs* (1792, p. 198). The poem is another study of a human being a short step from an extreme of deprivation (see l. 6). Exceptionally, there is no first-person utterance in the narrative part (i.e. the first stanza).

> Her eyes are wild, her head is bare,
> The sun has burnt her coal-black hair,
> Her eye-brows have a rusty stain,
> And she came far from over the main.
> She has a baby on her arm,   5
> Or else she were alone;
> And underneath the hay-stack warm,
> And on the greenwood stone,
> She talked and sung the woods among;
> And it was in the English tongue.   10
>
> 'Sweet Babe! they say that I am mad,
> But nay, my heart is far too glad;
> And I am happy when I sing
> Full many a sad and doleful thing:

8. greenwood: has connotations of outlawry.

9–10. As Wordsworth explained (see p. 376), the mother is supposed to be either a British woman who has returned from America (in the manner of the Female Vagrant, pp. 140–1) or a native of one of the North American colonies (but presumably it is supposed that her exotic appearance makes her English speech unexpected; she is apparently imbued with North American Indian lore, l. 55).

11–12. The poem's *LB* title (though not the revised one – see headnote) suggests that what 'they say' about the mother's mind is authoritative, and her sense of being 'far too glad' is an aspect of her madness.

Then, lovely Babe, do not fear!   15
I pray thee have no fear of me,
But, safe as in a cradle, here,
My lovely Baby! thou shalt be.
To thee I know too much I owe;
I cannot work thee any woe.   20

'A fire was once within my brain;
And in my head a dull, dull pain;
And fiendish faces one, two, three,
Hung at my breasts, and pulled at me.
But then there came a sight of joy;   25
It came at once to do me good;
I waked, and saw my little Boy,
My little Boy of flesh and blood;
Oh joy for me that sight to see!
For he was here, and only he.   30

'Suck, little Babe, oh suck again!
It cools my blood; it cools my brain;
Thy lips I feel them, Baby! they
Draw from my heart the pain away.
Oh! press me with thy little hand;   35
It loosens something at my chest;
About that tight and deadly band
I feel thy little fingers pressed.
The breeze I see is in the tree;
It comes to cool my Babe and me.   40

'Oh! love me, love me, little Boy!
Thou art thy Mother's only joy;
And do not dread the waves below,
When o'er the sea-rock's edge we go;
The high crag cannot work me harm,   45
Nor leaping torrents when they howl;
The Babe I carry on my arm,
He saves for me my precious soul.
Then happy lie, for blest am I;
Without me my sweet Babe would die.   50

21. See 'The Frantic Lady', l. 1: 'I burn, my brain consumes to ashes' (this
seventeenth-century lyric was reprinted in Percy's *Reliques*). It is clearly
something of a cliché of female madness; see also the mad girl in Henry
MacKenzie, *The Man of Feeling*, 1771, Ch. 20: 'my brain is dry; and it
burns, it burns, it burns!'
32. Perhaps influenced by Erasmus Darwin on the psycho-therapeutic
effects of breast-feeding (*Zoonomia*, 1794–6, II, 360), though Darwin's
remarks concern puerperal depression.

'Then do not fear, my Boy! for thee
Bold as a lion I will be;
And I will always be thy guide,
Through hollow snows and rivers wide.
I'll build an Indian bower; I know   55
The leaves that make the softest bed;
And, if from me thou wilt not go,
But still be true till I am dead,
My pretty thing! then thou shalt sing
As merry as the birds in spring.   60

'Thy Father cares not for my breast,
'Tis thine, sweet Baby, there to rest:
'Tis all thine own! and, if its hue
Be changed, that was so fair to view,
'Tis fair enough for thee, my dove!   65
My beauty, little Child, is flown;
But thou wilt live with me in love,
And what if my poor cheek be brown?
'Tis well for me, thou canst not see
How pale and wan it else would be.   70

'Dread not their taunts, my little life!
I am thy Father's wedded Wife;
And underneath the spreading tree
We two will live in honesty.
If his sweet Boy he could forsake,   75
With me he never would have stayed:
From him no harm my Babe can take,
But he, poor Man! is wretched made,
And every day we two will pray
For him that's gone and far away.   80

'I'll teach my Boy the sweetest things;
I'll teach him how the owlet sings.
My little Babe! thy lips are still,
And thou hast almost sucked thy fill –
Where art thou gone, my own dear Child?   85
What wicked looks are those I see?
Alas! alas! that look so wild,
It never, never came from me:
If thou art mad, my pretty lad,
Then I must be for ever sad.   90

54. *hollow*: probably in the sense (becoming obsolete in Wordsworth's day) of not solid.

'Oh! smile on me, my little lamb!
For I thy own dear Mother am.
My love for thee has well been tried:
I've sought thy Father far and wide.
I know the poisons of the shade,   95
I know the earth-nuts fit for food;
Then, pretty dear, be not afraid;
We'll find thy Father in the wood.
Now laugh and be gay, to the woods away!
And there, my Babe, we'll live for aye.'   100

The Ancient Mariner
A Poet's Reverie

Composed in winter and spring 1797–8. Subtitled from 1800 until 1817 'A Poet's Reverie'; the implication of this subtitle is, however, in some measure maintained by the epigraph in later editions (see p. 363). The main text was revised after 1798, notably in respect of the archaisms (see below) and the deletion of ten stanzas that had considerably elaborated on the spirit crew. Approximately the first third was also revised throughout, especially between ll. 179 and 209. The 1798 text is reproduced on pp. 389–405. After 1805 there were only minor alterations. See the two different forms of the Argument that appeared at the head of the poem in the first two editions (Authors' accompanying statements, pp. 36, 40), and also the marginal glosses of 1817 (pp. 364–6), bearing in mind that the latter are historically conceived fictional utterances, by an imaginary learned editor.

The verse form is 'common measure', quatrains composed of alternate four-stress unrhymed and three-stress rhymed lines. This is the predominant stanza in the traditional ballads which acquired classic status in the eighteenth century, such as 'Chevy Chase'. 'The Ancient Mariner' is the only poem in *LB* to employ it throughout. There are precedents in the traditional ballads – or at least in their eighteenth-century printed versions – for Coleridge's frequent expansion of the stanza to five or six lines, but his rhyme schemes here seem to be his own inventions. Coleridge also commonly creates an internal rhyme, usually in the unrhymed (first and third) lines of the stanza.

Metre is not the only respect in which 'The Ancient Mariner' is much more of an imitation of the old ballads than any other poem in *LB*. As the Advertisement (p. 35) observes, it is 'professedly written in imitation of the *style* ... of the elder poets'. The result, in 1798, was not found as 'intelligible' as the Advertisement had claimed it to be, with much criticism of the archaisms being voiced by the reviewers. Coleridge revised the archaic element in the vocabulary for the 1800 and subsequent editions of *LB*, removing the northernisms particularly and shifting the chronological centre of gravity forward somewhat; the result 'gives the impression of a Renaissance idiom, perhaps that of a poet slightly given to archaizing' (Payne 1978). Only a few strictly archaic forms still survive in 1805: 'countree', 'drouth', 'ee', 'nere' and (probably archaic) 'steddies'. Coleridge eventually removed all these except the first, which remained necessary for rhythmical purposes. In fact the imagined date of the story, insofar as it has one, must always have been the late fifteenth or early sixteenth century; the Advertisement speaks of a language 'intelligible for these three last centuries' and, in terms of historical plausibility, the action must be set between the voyages of Columbus (1492) and Magellan (1519).

The broad outlines of the Mariner's experience derive from the story of the Wandering Jew and from one or more versions of the Flying Dutchman legend. The particular cause of his plight was suggested by a source that Wordsworth brought to Coleridge's attention, George Shelvocke's *Voyage round the World* (1726) (the relevant passage is reproduced on p. 383). A tantalizing possible further source for the plot is the traditional poem known as 'A Wonderful Ballad of the Seafaring Men'. There is no known route by which Coleridge could have been acquainted with the Scandinavian version of this ballad which bears such remarkable resemblances to 'The Ancient Mariner' (no English version is known, and the French lacks the crucial bird motif). Not printed until the 1850s, and not in English until 1881 (*Folk-lore Record* III, 1881, pp. 253–7), this Scandinavian form must at present remain a hypothetical source for 'The Ancient Mariner', but it is reproduced on pp. 383–4. A wide range of travel writings from the sixteenth to the eighteenth century also feeds into the poem, possibly together with real-life models for the Mariner himself, such as the Evangelical ex-slaver John Newton. J.L. Lowes' brilliant demonstration, over sixty years ago, of Coleridge's remarkable blending of motifs and phrases from a multitude of writers has made a powerful impression on all later commentators, but it is worth stressing that many of the poem's best images, even in sections where Coleridge is most indebted to these sources, appear to be simply his own inventions, for example: 'like chaff we drove along' (l. 48); the ice desert of ll. 56–8; the whole of the famous stanza ll. 93–8; 'a painted ship / Upon a painted ocean' (ll. 113–14), etc.

The poem has received a great deal of interpretative comment which it is not possible to summarize here; a useful survey of material up until 1970 will be found in Milton 1981: 3–17. Not all critics would even agree that the poem can be decoded for a consistent meaning in the first place, while those who believe it can are fundamentally divided as to whether the world of the poem is benevolent and infused with spirituality, with the Mariner's experience illustrative of this, or whether it is a cruel and capricious one, with the Mariner its victim. The mode of these readings has also varied, with differing emphasis being given, for example, to religious and epistemological elements. For a comment by the poet himself on the question of the 'moral' of 'The Ancient Mariner', see Authors' later comment, p. 367.

I

It is an ancient Mariner,
And he stoppeth one of three:
'By thy long grey beard and thy glittering eye
Now wherefore stoppest me?

'The bridegroom's doors are opened wide,   5
And I am next of kin;
The guests are met, the feast is set –
May'st hear the merry din.'

5–8. There is a general resemblance to a passage in Schiller's novel *Der Geisterseher* (Coleridge's source for his play *Osorio*, though in the latter he omits the episode). See Lowes 1951: 251.

But still he holds the wedding-guest –
'There was a ship,' quoth he –   10
'Nay, if thou'st got a laughsome tale,
Mariner! come with me.'

He holds him with his skinny hand,
Quoth he, 'There was a ship –'
'Now get thee hence, thou grey-beard loon!   15
Or my staff shall make thee skip.'

He holds him with his glittering eye –
The wedding-guest stood still
And listens like a three years' child;
The Mariner hath his will.   20

The wedding-guest sate on a stone,
He cannot choose but hear:
And thus spake on that ancient man,
The bright-eyed Mariner.

'The ship was cheered, the harbour cleared –   25
Merrily did we drop
Below the kirk, below the hill,
Below the lighthouse top.

'The sun came up upon the left,
Out of the sea came he: 30
And he shone bright, and on the right
Went down into the sea.

---

10. With the namelessness of the ship, even in the Mariner's discourse, the absence of proper names of all kinds from the poem becomes emphatic.

11. laughsome: first recorded use in this sense in *OED*.

16. Compare *King Lear* V, iii, 278–9.

17–18. There is probably an influence in these lines from notions of 'animal magnetism', or hypnosis, which were arousing keen interest in the latter years of the eighteenth century. The bright gaze that is simply an impressive aspect of, for example, the Wandering Jew's appearance in G.M. Lewis's *The Monk* becomes by this device an instrument of compulsion, so that a compelled story-teller is matched by a compelled listener.

17–20. Written by Wordsworth, perhaps together with other lines in this part of the poem not identified (see Fenwick note to 'We Are Seven' and Dyce anecdote, pp. 367–8).

29–32. The first of several clues to the position and direction of the vessel, but beyond the fact of a voyage south into the Atlantic and then north into the Pacific, and a return thence, there is no evidence of the Mariner's route; it cannot be assumed that he circumnavigates the globe.

30. See note to l. 244.

'Higher and higher every day,
Till over the mast at noon –'
The wedding-guest here beat his breast,   35
For he heard the loud bassoon.

The bride hath paced into the hall,
Red as a rose is she;
Nodding their heads before her go
The merry minstrelsy.   40

The wedding-guest he beat his breast,
Yet he cannot choose but hear:
And thus spake on that ancient man,
The bright-eyed Mariner:

'But now the north wind came more fierce,   45
There came a tempest strong!
And southward still for days and weeks
Like chaff we drove along.

'And now there came both mist and snow,
And it grew wondrous cold: 50
And ice mast-high came floating by
As green as emerald.

'And through the drifts the snowy clifts
Did send a dismal sheen;
Nor shapes of men nor beasts we ken –   55
The ice was all between.

34. The ship has reached the equator. The punctuation at the end of the
line, and ll. 107–10, indicate that the Mariner's syntax is broken off and
not completed.
39–40. before her . . . minstrelsy: see Chaucer, *The Squire's Tale*, l. 268.
51. ice mast-high: see several allusions in the travel memoirs of Captain
Thomas James, as quoted by Lowes (1951: 141).
52. See references to emerald-coloured ice in the reminiscences of
Frederick Martens and in John Harris's travel anthology of 1744, in Lowes
(1951: 141).
53. drifts: collections of floating material, in this case the ice masses.
    clifts: clefts (packed with unmelted snow). Coleridge had the authority
of at least two travel writers for this phenomenon (see Lowes 1951: 144).
They can be imagined as huge features of a mountainous coastline, visible
between icebergs.
55–6. Compare James Thomson *The Seasons* (1726–46) 'Winter' ll. 856–8.

'The ice was here, the ice was there,
The ice was all around:
It cracked and growled, and roared and howled,
A wild and ceaseless sound.   60

'At length did cross an Albatross,
Thorough the fog it came;
As if it had been a Christian soul,
We hailed it in God's name.

'The mariners gave it biscuit-worms,   65
And round and round it flew:
The ice did split with a thunder-fit;
The helmsman steered us through.

'And a good south wind sprung up behind,
The Albatross did follow;   70
And every day for food or play
Came to the Mariner's hollo!

59–60. The strange noises made by the polar ice were commonly recorded by travellers, and most of the verbs used here by Coleridge are exemplified in travel literature.

61. Albatross: for the albatross anecdote proposed by Wordsworth to Coleridge as the nub of the story, see p. 368. However, this particular spelling of the word is not found until Cook's *Voyages* (1790): Shelvocke has 'albitross' in the original. The whole relationship of the albatross to the crew and the Mariner seems to be indebted to the traveller George Forster's account of the sheltering of a swallow on board ship, and its death (see Bohm 1983). See also the Scandinavian version of 'A Wonderful Ballad of the Seafaring Men', pp. 383–4.

63. a Christian soul: the literal meaning is simply a human being. Relevant to a figurative reading of the expression is the ancient tradition of the soul as a bird, or transformed into a bird. The petrel family, to which the albatross belongs, were, according to folk traditions, variously the embodiment of dead mariners' souls or devil-birds (see Lowes 1951: 529; E.A. Armstrong, *The Folklore of Birds*, 1958, pp. 213–14).

67–8. The release of the boat with a thunderous splitting of the ice seems to have been suggested by a passage in Commodore Phipps's journal (see Lowes 1951: 146–7). There is perhaps also a reminiscence of an episode in Greek mythology, Jason's passage of the Symplegades, the clashing rocks of the Bosphorus.

67. thunder-fit: Coleridge's coinage.

69. good south wind: also l. 85; one of Lowes' more questionable alleged echoes of the seventeenth-century travel anthologist Samuel Purchas (see Lowes 1951: 149).

'In mist or cloud on mast or shroud
It perched for vespers nine,
Whiles all the night through fog-smoke white   75
Glimmered the white moonshine.'

'God save thee, ancient Mariner!
From the fiends that plague thee thus! –
Why look'st thou so?' – 'With my crossbow
I shot the Albatross.'   80

                        II

'The sun now rose upon the right,
Out of the sea came he;
Still hid in mist; and on the left
Went down into the sea.

'And the good south wind still blew behind,   85
But no sweet bird did follow,
Nor any day for food or play
Came to the Mariner's hollo!

'And I had done an hellish thing,
And it would work 'em woe: 90
For all averred, I had killed the bird,
That made the breeze to blow.

'Nor dim nor red, like an angel's head,
The glorious sun uprist:
Then all averred, I had killed the bird   95
That brought the fog and mist.
'Twas right, said they, such birds to slay
That bring the fog and mist.

---

74. vespers nine: literally, for nine evenings, though again there is evidently
an interesting figurative reading available from the liturgical sense of
vespers.

75. fog-smoke: Coleridge's coinage, condensing into a metaphor a simile
found in one of his travel sources (see Lowes 1951: 148).

79–80. With my . . . Albatross: see the 1817 gloss, p. 364. For the possible
senses of 'inhospitably' in this gloss, see p. 40. 'Pious', if it means
'affectionately dutiful', rather implies that the host is the albatross. It is by
no means certain that Coleridge intended the moral code invoked by the
imaginary author of the gloss to be taken seriously; see his comparison with
an *Arabian Nights* tale, p. 367.

81. An effect mentioned with astonishment by Herodotus (*Histories* IV, 42)
as a proof that the Phoenicians had circumnavigated Africa from east to
west, but perhaps made vivid for Coleridge through its citation by the
historical writer Bryan Edwards (see Lowes 1951: 127).

95–8. See the 1817 gloss (p. 364) on the mariners' complicity.

'The breezes flew, the white foam flew,
The furrow followed free: 100
We were the first that ever burst
Into that silent sea.

'Down dropped the breeze, the sails dropped
down,
'Twas sad as sad could be,
And we did speak only to break   105
The silence of the sea.

'All in a hot and copper sky
The bloody sun at noon,
Right up above the mast did stand,
No bigger than the moon.   110

'Day after day, day after day,
We stuck, nor breath nor motion,
As idle as a painted ship
Upon a painted ocean.

'Water, water, everywhere,   115
And all the boards did shrink;
Water, water, everywhere,
Nor any drop to drink.

99. breezes: easterly winds; the term was applied to the south-easterly trade winds of the South Pacific by some of the travel writers (see Lowes 1951: 128–9).

101–2. Lowes' analogues for these powerful lines (1951: 130) are not close.

104. sad: calamitous, dismaying (as in 'a sad state of affairs').

107. copper sky: see *Deuteronomy* 28:23.

108. bloody sun: enough allusions to a blood-coloured sun have been traced (e.g. Lowes 1951: 158–9; Piper 1962: 93–4) to make it clear that the image can easily occur spontaneously to a writer. For the general effect of the stanza, see *Joel* 2:31 ('The sun shall be turned into darkness, and the moon into blood') and the very comparable *Revelation* 6:12.

109. The equator has been reached again.

113–14. The most familiar use of the metaphor of 'painted' to denote arrested movement is probably *Hamlet* II, ii, 510.

115–16. See the 1817 gloss (p. 364), which on any reading is presumably not literally true (see note to l. 128).

117–18. As with the torment of Tantalus in Hell (*Odyssey* XI, 583–4).

'The very deeps did rot: O Christ!
That ever this should be!   120
Yea, slimy things did crawl with legs
Upon the slimy sea.

'About, about, in reel and rout
The death-fires danced at night;
The water, like a witch's oils,   125
Burnt green and blue and white.

119. *deeps did rot*: thick or 'slimy' (l. 122), apparently putrescent waters in
equatorial latitudes were noticed in the travel literature, and scientific
authors such as Priestley had explained the phenomenon of the
phosphorescent sea as a side-effect of this rotting. Hence, probably, the
transition to this subject in the next stanza. (The references in Lowes 1951:
80–7 should be supplemented by J.R. Forster, *Observations made during a
Voyage Round the World*, 1778, pp. 66–7, and Erasmus Darwin, 1791, I,
'Additional Note' X).
121–2. Compare from Clarence's dream, *Richard III* I, iv, 30–2. Also
Psalms 104:25, with its echo at ll. 227, 232, 609: 'So is this great and wide
sea, wherein are things creeping innumerable, both small and great beasts.'
This psalm is distinctive for its rhapsodic celebration of God's activity in
nature.
121. Slime-fish are described in Martens' *Voyage*, while fish are commonly
'slimy' in Erasmus Darwin, and propulsion of some sea creatures by their
legs (though not exactly crawling) is mentioned by both these authors (see
Lowes 1951: 88; King-Hele 1986: 106; Darwin, 1791: II, i, 264n), but the
image of a slimy crawler in the ocean – powerfully reinforcing the sense of
water both rotting and viscous – is Coleridge's.
123. *About, about*: used with reference to the witches at *Macbeth* I, iii, 34.
      rout: perhaps an innovative combination of the senses of 'disorderly
throng' and 'party'.
124. *death-fires*: this may be an allusion to St Elmo's Fire, an electrostatic
effect that caused dancing lights or flames on ships' rigging. There is some
evidence that in nautical superstition these were believed to be the souls of
the drowned (Tave 1983: 73); St Elmo's Fire is said to be 'fiery spirits or
devils' signifying 'some mischief or other to come to men' in the Burton
passage cited in the note to l. 128, and is treated as terrifying in Camoëns
Lusiads, Bk V, and *The Tempest* I, ii, 196–215. Alternatively Coleridge is
using a figure of speech for phosphorescence, appropriate if he believed
this to be caused by the putrefaction described in the preceding stanza.
Ll. 125–6, which must be about phosphorescence, do suggest that he
envisaged it as something flame-like, although here he seems to have
moved to a different explanation of the phenomenon suggested by his
reading (Lowes 1951: 83): that it was due to the burning of oily matter in
the sea. See, however, note to l. 126.
125. *witch's oils*: there does not appear to be any traditional association of
witches with oils.
126. Apparently describes the colours of flames or flame-like lights, but

'And some in dreams assured were
Of the Spirit that plagued us so:
Nine fathom deep he had followed us
From the land of mist and snow.   130

'And every tongue through utter drouth
Was withered at the root;
We could not speak no more than if
We had been choked with soot.

the mere bright shining of the phosphorescent sea was sometimes called
'burning' in the travel literature (see Lowes 1951: 83), and the steadily
glowing sea is later said to have 'burnt' at l. 264. On this interpretation the
water presumably is oil-like because it is prismatically coloured.

128. the Spirit: though at this stage not necessarily more than the mariners'
superstition, the Spirit of the polar regions becomes an increasingly definite
presence; see Wordsworth's reminiscence, p. 368. The kind of entity
involved is usually regarded as a 'demon', originally a concept in
neoplatonism that also had a lively existence as adapted by popular
superstition in the Renaissance period. The imaginary editor draws
attention to one of the major authorities in the learned tradition in his 1817
gloss (p. 364): Michael Psellus's *De Operatione Daemonum Dialogus* (1618).
The otherwise puzzling reference to Josephus as another authority on the
subject is almost certainly due to Robert Burton's citation of Josephus on
aerial spirits as harbingers of disaster (*Anatomy of Melancholy*, Pt 1, Sect. 2,
Memb. 1, Subsect 2). This passage in Burton also mentions Psellus and
may be Coleridge's whole information on these authorities, but Tave (1983:
56–62, 83–6) cites Psellus on 'aquatic demons' manifesting themselves as
seabirds and argues that the Albatross is a malevolent demon who later
mutates into the Life-in-Death figure. However, the Spirit is a land-
dweller who 'loved the bird who loved the man' (ll. 398–9). It is in fact only
in the 1817 glosses that the Spirit (and the 'voices' of l. 391) are linked to
neoplatonic demons, and Coleridge (as opposed to the scholarly editor he
has created) may be influenced by a broader, looser tradition of 'genii,
daemons, angel guardians and tutelary spirits' such as he found in Dupuis's
Origine de tous les cultes (1795; see Lowes 1951: 232–3, 236). 'Tutelary
spirits' is Wordsworth's phrase in 1843, and Dupuis has '*tutelaires des zones*'
including the polar zone. It is worth recalling also that the giant Adamaster
or Cape of Storms (Cape of Good Hope), in a celebrated episode in Book
Five of Camoëns' *The Lusiads* (1572), announces vengeance on the
Portuguese for venturing into his realm.
131. drouth: drought. On this archaism, see headnote.
134. Compare *Paradise Lost* X, 570.

'Ah well-a-day! what evil looks   135
Had I from old and young!
Instead of the cross the Albatross
About my neck was hung.

III

'So passed a weary time; each throat
Was parched, and glazed each eye,   140
When, looking westward, I beheld
A something in the sky.

'At first it seemed a little speck,
And then it seemed a mist:
It moved and moved, and took at last   145
A certain shape, I wist.

'A speck, a mist, a shape, I wist!
And still it nered and nered;
And as if it dodged a water-sprite,
It plunged and tacked and veered.   150

'With throat unslaked, with black lips baked
We could not laugh nor wail;
Through utter drouth all dumb we stood
Till I bit my arm and sucked the blood,
And cried, A sail! a sail!   155

137–8. To remove the Mariner's cross was to deprive him of its protective powers as an amulet in popular belief. For an explicit link between the crucifixion and the shooting, see ll. 393–5 and note. According to the 1817 gloss (p. 364), however, it is the Mariner who is the Christ-like scapegoat for general guilt. There may be an echo of the Koran as translated by George Sale in 1734 (see Blackstone 1981).

139. weary time: an unremarkable phrase, but Lowes (1951: 154) may be right to cite its use in the impressive context of an early record of European travellers enduring the polar winter.

141–3. Compare Darwin, 1791, II, iv, 273–4.

146. wist: knew, perceived.

148. nered: on this archaism, see headnote.

149. water-sprite: a petty aquatic demon and part of the system of popular animistic belief illustrated at l. 128. The phrase is normally assumed to be the object of 'dodged' but is just possibly in apposition to 'it'. Burton, in the passage cited in the note to l. 128, says of fire spirits: 'they counterfeit . . . little clouds, *ad motum nescio quem volantes*' (i.e. 'flying with a mysterious motion').

151. Compare *Lamentations* 5:10: 'Our skin was black like an oven because of the terrible famine.'

'With throat unslaked, with black lips baked
Agape they heard me call:
Gramercy! they for joy did grin,
And all at once their breath drew in
As they were drinking all.   160

' "See! See!" (I cried) "she tacks no more!
Hither to work us weal
Without a breeze, without a tide
She steddies with upright keel!"

'The western wave was all a flame.   165
The day was well nigh done!
Almost upon the western wave
Rested the broad bright sun;
When that strange shape drove suddenly
Betwixt us and the sun.   170

'And straight the sun was flecked with bars
(Heaven's mother send us grace!)
As if through a dungeon grate he peered
With broad and burning face.

158. they . . . grin: see Coleridge's later comment (p. 367) on the real-life observation behind this phrasing.
163. The 1817 gloss (p. 365) makes explicit what might escape the ordinary reader: that the movement of the boat without wind or current – being a traditional feature of spectre ships (see Lowes 1951: 275–6) – causes dismay. The preceding line is presumably correctly read as the Mariner's attempt to reassure the crew/conjure away the evil aspect of the boat (see also l. 172).
164. steddies: steadies. Probably an archaic spelling by this date.
165–70. A kind of reversal of the account of dawn and vanishing spectres in Milton's 'On the Morning of Christ's Nativity', ll. 229–36.
168. Compare Chaucer, *The Squire's Tale*, l. 394.
171. flecked with bars: see the Dyce anecdote (p. 367) on the dream of a 'skeleton ship', which seems to be incorporated from this point on. (See also the 1817 gloss, p. 365, on this line.)
172. Heaven's mother: the Virgin Mary.
173. dungeon grate: there have been interesting if slightly unconvincing attempts to show that some of the features of the ghost ship indicate that it is a slaving vessel (see Empson and Pirie 1972: 29; Ware 1961).

'Alas! (thought I, and my heart beat loud)   175
How fast she neres and neres!
Are those *her* sails that glance in the sun
Like restless gossameres?

'Are those *her* ribs, through which the sun
Did peer, as through a grate?   180
And are those two all, all her crew,
That woman, and her mate?

'*His* bones were black with many a crack,
All black and bare, I ween;
Jet-black and bare, save where with rust   185
Of mouldy damps and charnel crust
They were patched with purple and green.

'*Her* lips were red, *her* looks were free,
Her locks were yellow as gold;
Her skin was as white as leprosy,   190
And she was far liker Death than he;
Her flesh made the still air cold.

177–8. The anxious question is presumably provoked by the dismayingly impalpable appearance of the ghost ship's sails (the exclamation in l. 155 means no more than 'a vessel in sight!').

177. sails . . . sun: compare William Gilbert, *The Hurricane* (Lowes 1951: 202).

178. gossameres: the only previous plural use noted by *OED* is *Romeo and Juliet* II, vi, 18 (though with a singular verb). Compare Erasmus Darwin, 1791: I, iii, 86, for ships 'harnessed with gossamer'.

179. her ribs: several elements create a kind of fusion of the vessel and its occupants: the italicised occurrences of 'her' apply at first to the boat and later to the female figure, while the ambiguity of 'ribs' anticipates the appearance of the male figure, or 'Death' (see also note to l. 171). The 1817 gloss to ll. 188–9 is 'Like vessel, like crew!'

182. mate: in two senses, sexual and nautical.

184. ween: perceive.

188–92. For Robert Graves this description (especially in respect of 'the leprously white skin') 'is as faithful a record of the White Goddess as exists' (Graves 1948: 380–1).

188. free: immodest, unrestrained. Though the 1817 gloss (p. 365) identifies this figure as 'Life-in-Death', the text itself until that date seems rather to describe a sexually depraved creature.

191–2. If the male figure is Death it would be hard for the reader of this whole stanza before 1817 not to conclude that the female figure is Sin, because of their well-known joint appearance in *Paradise Lost*. Sin is more deadly ('far liker Death') both morally and medically, 'leprosy' standing for both venereal disease and moral corruption (the latter association being something of a commonplace).

'The naked hulk alongside came
And the twain were playing dice;
"The game is done! I've won, I've won!"   195
Quoth she, and whistled thrice.

'A gust of wind sterte up behind
And whistled through his bones;
Through the hole of his eyes and the hole of his mouth
Half-whistles and half-groans.   200

'With never a whisper in the sea
Off darts the spectre-ship;
While clombe above the eastern bar
The horned moon, with one bright star
Almost between the tips.   205

'One after one by the horned moon
(Listen, O stranger! to me)
Each turned his face with a ghastly pang
And cursed me with his ee.

194. For the folk tale of the Dutch murderer Falkenberg, who wanders the sea forever on a vessel with a black and a white spectre dicing for his soul, see Lowes 1951: 277. Coleridge's acquaintance with this tale (which was apparently circulating only orally at this date) may be implied in Southey's calling the poem 'a Dutch attempt at German sublimity' (*Critical Review* XXIV, 1798, p. 200). The Falkenberg story is, however, a particular (German) version of the widespread Flying Dutchman theme, and the basic form of this has the captain perpetually roaming the seas round the Cape of Good Hope.
195. The 1817 gloss (p. 365), if reliable, provides essential information.
196–7. For a Somerset tradition of a malevolent female apparition which whistles up storms, see John Dunton, *Athenianism*, 1710, pp. 353–4. For beliefs in the power of the devil, witches and wizards to conjure up winds (with an associated prohibition on whistling on board ship), see *Gentleman's Magazine*, 1763, pp. 12–15.
197. sterte: started.
198. Taken from Wordsworth's early poem 'The Vale of Esthwaite', ll. 338–9.
203. clombe: becoming an archaic and dialectal usage in Coleridge's day, but not to the extent that may be supposed. Johnson's *Dictionary* has 'clomb' as the preferred form of the past tense. Compare Milton, *Paradise Lost*, IV, 192.
     bar: presumably in the sense of horizon; apparently Coleridge's coinage.
204–5. According to Coleridge, in a manuscript note on a copy of *LB*, a star close to the moon was a bad omen in seamen's lore. For reports that were probably influential on Coleridge of a star seeming to appear in the dark part of the moon, see Lowes 1951: 180.
209. ee: eye. On this archaism, see headnote.

'Four times fifty living men,   210
With never a sigh or groan,
With heavy thump, a lifeless lump
They dropped down one by one.

'Their souls did from their bodies fly –
They fled to bliss or woe;   215
And every soul it passed me by,
Like the whiz of my crossbow.'

                              IV
'I fear thee, ancient Mariner!
I fear thy skinny hand;
And thou art long and lank and brown   220
As is the ribbed sea-sand.

'I fear thee and thy glittering eye
And thy skinny hand so brown' –
'Fear not, fear not, thou wedding-guest!
This body dropped not down.   225

'Alone, alone, all all alone,
Alone on the wide wide sea;
And Christ would take no pity on
My soul in agony.

'The many men so beautiful,   230
And they all dead did lie!
And a million million slimy things
Lived on – and so did I.

'I looked upon the rotting sea,
And drew my eyes away;   235
I looked upon the ghastly deck,
And there the dead men lay.

'I looked to Heaven, and tried to pray;
But or ever a prayer had gushed,

---

215. *bliss or woe*: a Miltonic pairing, and Miltonic terms for Heaven and
Hell.
214–17. See the 1817 gloss (p. 365).
220–1. See Coleridge's 1817 note on Wordsworth's authorship of these
lines, and Wordsworth's supporting recollection (pp. 366–7).
225. If the Mariner had died all aspects of his physical presence would be
alarming, but perhaps especially the touch of his 'skinny hand' and the
activity of his 'glittering eye'. See the 1817 gloss (p. 365).
227, 232. Compare *Psalms* 104:25.
239. *or ever a*: before a single . . .

A wicked whisper came and made   240
My heart as dry as dust.

'I closed my lids and kept them close,
Till the balls like pulses beat;
For the sky and the sea, and the sea and the sky
Lay like a load on my weary eye,   245
And the dead were at my feet.

'The cold sweat melted from their limbs,
Nor rot nor reek did they;
The look with which they looked on me,
Had never passed away.   250

'An orphan's curse would drag to Hell
A spirit from on high:
But oh! more horrible than that
Is the curse in a dead man's eye!
Seven days, seven nights I saw that curse,   255
And yet I could not die.

'The moving moon went up the sky
And nowhere did abide:
Softly she was going up
And a star or two beside –   260

'Her beams bemocked the sultry main
Like April hoar-frost spread;
But where the ship's huge shadow lay,
The charmed water burnt alway
A still and awful red.   265

240–1. A cryptic pair of lines. To judge by the 1817 gloss (p. 365), the 'whisper' is of hatred for the sea creatures because two hundred men are dead. Among the literary antecedents for the Mariner's experience are Claudius's vain prayer in *Hamlet* III, iv, 97–8 and Charles Lloyd's ninth sonnet (see Fruman 1972: 505).
244. See *Aeneid* III, 193: 'caelum undique et undique pontus', itself from *Odyssey* XII, 403–4. See, too, Lucretius, *De Rerum Natura* IV, 434, in a passage that may also be remembered at l. 30.
248. The motif of undecaying bodies accompanying a solitary survivor is traced by Lowes (1951: 292) to an account of a South American journey collected by Purchas.
257–60. See the unusually long gloss of 1817 on this stanza (p. 365) and its intended psychological force.
264. charmed: dead calm, as in Milton's 'charmed wave' ('Ode on the Morning of Christ's Nativity', l. 68).
   burnt: see note to l. 126.

'Beyond the shadow of the ship
I watched the water-snakes:
They moved in tracks of shining white;
And when they reared, the elfish light
Fell off in hoary flakes. 270

'Within the shadow of the ship
I watched their rich attire:
Blue, glossy green, and velvet black
They coiled and swam; and every track
Was a flash of golden fire. 275

'O happy living things! no tongue
Their beauty might declare:
A spring of love gushed from my heart,
And I blessed them unaware!
Sure my kind saint took pity on me, 280
And I blessed them unaware.

'The selfsame moment I could pray;
And from my neck so free
The Albatross fell off, and sank
Like lead into the sea. 285

266–75. The important vision of the water-snakes in these two stanzas amounts to a rewriting of ll. 121–6, with the earlier slimy crawling creatures now perceived as jumping and coiling water-snakes, and the phosphorescence (more accurately, as it happens) as bright components of the water or as colouration in the snakes themselves, rather than putrescence or burning oils. The rich body of previous descriptions Coleridge draws on here is cited in Lowes 1951: 45–52 (one of the *tours de force* of the book). To be added to these is a passage from Forster's *Voyage round the World*, 1777 (see Bohm 1983). The brilliant but colourless spectacle 'Beyond the shadow of the ship' (first stanza) is carefully discriminated from that 'Within the shadow' (second stanza) which is more subdued but coloured.

276–7. Bartram (1792), one of Coleridge's most important sources, provides a notable prompting in the passage (pp. 164–6) where Bartram finds the complex movements of innumerable brightly coloured fish to be like a 'representation of the peaceable and happy state of nature which existed before the fall'. See also Forster in Bohm 1983.

278. Compare Erasmus Darwin, 1791, II, i, 130: 'And life and love gushed mingled from his heart.'

279. The notion of the 'unaware' blessing has been much discussed. It certainly implies that the Mariner has retrospectively conferred a religious aspect on his experience, appropriately or not. The 1817 gloss (p. 365) agrees that he has tacitly blessed the creatures.

280. See the 1817 gloss to ll. 341–7 (p. 365) for the imaginary editor's agreement on the activity of the 'kind saint'.

283–5. Compare the episode in *Pilgrim's Progress* where Christian's burden falls from his back and tumbles into the sepulchre 'just as Christian came up with the Cross' on the highway.

V

'O sleep, it is a gentle thing
Beloved from pole to pole!
To Mary-queen the praise be given,
She sent the gentle sleep from Heaven
That slid into my soul.   290

'The silly buckets on the deck
That had so long remained,
I dreamt that they were filled with dew,
And when I awoke it rained.

'My lips were wet, my throat was cold,   295
My garments all were dank;
Sure I had drunken in my dreams,
And still my body drank.

'I moved and could not feel my limbs,
I was so light, almost   300
I thought that I had died in sleep,
And was a blessed ghost.

'And soon I heard a roaring wind,
It did not come anear;
But with its sound it shook the sails   305
That were so thin and sere.

'The upper air burst into life,
And a hundred fire-flags sheen;
To and fro they were hurried about,
And to and fro, and in and out   310
The wan stars danced between.

---

286. Compare *2 Henry IV* III, i, 5: 'O sleep, O gentle sleep'; but in Shakespeare sleep and sleeplessness are connected memorably on many occasions with guilt/innocence. There is surely also a reminiscence of *Macbeth* II, ii, 36–40.

288. Mary-queen: the Virgin Mary.

289–290. Compare *Aeneid* II, 268–9, and Spenser, *Visions of Bellay*, ll. 1–2: 'rest, soft sliding down / From Heaven's height'.

289. Echoes another famous Shakespearean moment, *Merchant of Venice* IV, i, 185: 'It droppeth as the gentle rain from heaven.'

291. silly: ordinary, homely.

306. sere: worn or thin.

307–11. See the 1817 gloss for ll. 303–6 (p. 365). The whole effect is to suggest a host of beings high in the air.

308. sheen: an adjective, glowing.

311. The 'wan stars' are probably a reminiscence of Erasmus Darwin, 1791, I, i, 134. See also *Much Ado About Nothing* II, i, 349.

'And the coming wind did roar more loud;
And the sails did sigh like sedge:
And the rain poured down from one black cloud,
The moon was at its edge.   315

'The thick black cloud was cleft, and still
The moon was at its side:
Like waters shot from some high crag,
The lightning fell with never a jag
A river steep and wide.   320

'The loud wind never reached the ship,
Yet now the ship moved on!
Beneath the lightning and the moon
The dead men gave a groan.

'They groaned, they stirred, they all uprose,   325
Nor spake, nor moved their eyes:
It had been strange, even in a dream
To have seen those dead men rise.

'The helmsman steered, the ship moved on;
Yet never a breeze up-blew;   330
The mariners all 'gan work the ropes,
Where they were wont to do;
They raised their limbs like lifeless tools –
We were a ghastly crew.

'The body of my brother's son   335
Stood by me knee to knee:
The body and I pulled at one rope,
But he said nought to me.'

316–20. Clearly indebted to Bartram, and possibly other travel literature
(see Lowes 1951: 186–7). To Coleridge, however, is due the image of a
single cloud, actively attended by the moon perhaps, from which the rain
and lightning proceed.
325. Perhaps to be linked to Galvani's recently published research
describing muscular movements induced by electricity (for which lightning
was one of his sources; see Piper 1955: 20). The Mariner and the 1817
gloss to ll. 341–7 (p. 365) favour a quite different explanation. For
Wordsworth's contribution at this point, see p. 368. For the source of the
whole episode, including some features of the arrival of the boat at the
shore, in an AD fourth-century Latin text, see Lowes 1951: 283–5.

'I fear thee, ancient Mariner!'
'Be calm, thou wedding-guest!   340
'Twas not those souls, that fled in pain,
Which to their corses came again,
But a troop of spirits blest:

'For when it dawned – they dropped their arms,
And clustered round the mast: 345
Sweet sounds rose slowly through their mouths,
And from their bodies passed.

'Around, around, flew each sweet sound,
Then darted to the sun:
Slowly the sounds came back again,   350
Now mixed, now one by one.

'Sometimes a-dropping from the sky
I heard the skylark sing;
Sometimes all little birds that are
How they seemed to fill the sea and air   355
With their sweet jargoning!

'And now 'twas like all instruments,
Now like a lonely flute:
And now it is an angel's song
That makes the heavens be mute.   360

'It ceased: yet still the sails made on
A pleasant noise till noon,
A noise like of a hidden brook
In the leafy month of June,
That to the sleeping woods all night   365
Singeth a quiet tune.

341. fled in pain: on the face of it, not consistent with l. 215 above, and more like the classical idea of the separation of soul and body (as at *Aeneid* XII, 952).
342. corses: corpses.
343. The language and the context are perhaps indebted to Milton, *Lycidas*, ll. 177–80.
346–7. See Tave 1983: 103 for confirmation from the harmonious music that these are good spirits rather than demons (though the latter hypothesis is found only in the 1817 gloss to ll. 341–7).
352–5. Perhaps echoes a passage in Bartram 1792: 284.
356. jargoning: a Chaucerian word for birdsong, probably remembered especially from his translation of *Romaunt de la Rose*, l. 716.
359–60. Compare *Merchant of Venice* V, i, 61–3 (a passage that also asserts the connection of harmony and blessedness).

'Till noon we silently sailed on,
Yet never a breeze did breathe:
Slowly and smoothly went the ship
Moved onward from beneath.   370

'Under the keel nine fathom deep
From the land of mist and snow
The Spirit slid: and it was he
That made the ship to go.
The sails at noon left off their tune,   375
And the ship stood still also.

'The sun right up above the mast
Had fixed her to the ocean:
But in a minute she 'gan stir
With a short uneasy motion –   380
Backwards and forwards half her length,
With a short uneasy motion.

'Then, like a pawing horse let go,
She made a sudden bound:
It flung the blood into my head,   385
And I fell into a swound.

'How long in that same fit I lay,
I have not to declare;
But ere my living life returned,
I heard and in my soul discerned   390
Two voices in the air.

' "Is it he?" quoth one, "Is this the man?
By him who died on cross,
With his cruel bow he laid full low
The harmless Albatross.   395

377–8. The Mariner has returned to the equator either by his outward
route or westward into the Atlantic round the Cape of Good Hope (see also
the 1817 gloss to ll. 371–6, p. 365). Lowes (1951: 501) emphasizes how the
sun seems to immobilize the vessel here, and perhaps therefore at
ll. 111–12 also, and links this to various legends of 'stuck' ships.
380–2. The three lines recoil upon themselves appropriately.
383–6. For both the image of the boat as bounding horse, and the
Mariner's unconscious state, see the account of Odysseus's final sea
journey back to Ithaca (*Odyssey* XIII, 78–85).
386. swound: swoon.
388. I have not: I am unable.
391. See the 1817 gloss (p. 365) for the later explanation of these voices in
terms of the machinery of demons.
393–5. The Wandering Jew, it will be remembered, has been punished for
his part in Christ's passion.

' "The Spirit who bideth by himself
In the land of mist and snow,
He loved the bird that loved the man
Who shot him with his bow."

'The other was a softer voice,   400
As soft as honey-dew:
Quoth he, "The man hath penance done,
And penance more will do."

VI
First Voice
' "But tell me, tell me! speak again,
Thy soft response renewing –   405
What makes that ship drive on so fast?
What is the ocean doing?"

Second Voice
' "Still as a slave before his lord,
The ocean hath no blast:
His great bright eye most silently   410
Up to the moon is cast –

' "If he may know which way to go,
For she guides him smooth or grim.
See, brother, see! how graciously
She looketh down on him."   415

First Voice
' "But why drives on that ship so fast
Without or wave or wind?"

Second Voice
"The air is cut away before,
And closes from behind.

' "Fly, brother, fly! more high, more high,   420
Or we shall be belated:
For slow and slow that ship will go,
When the Mariner's trance is abated."

396–8. See note to l. 128 above.
398. the bird . . . man: the first time such feelings are attributed to the
Albatross, and the phrase perhaps reinforces the crucifixion association of
the previous stanza. There is no exact Biblical parallel, but the spirit seems
to be that of several passages in John's Gospel and First Epistle.
410–11. From Sir John Davies, *Orchestra*, 1596, ll. 340–1.
413. I.e. in controlling the tides.
420–3. No commentator has satisfactorily explained why the slowing of the
vessel when the Mariner wakes makes it necessary for the spirits to fly

'I woke, and we were sailing on
As in a gentle weather: 425
'Twas night, calm night, the moon was high;
The dead men stood together.

'All stood together on the deck,
For a charnel-dungeon fitter:
All fixed on me their stony eyes   430
That in the moon did glitter.

'The pang, the curse, with which they died,
Had never passed away;
I could not draw my eyes from theirs,
Nor turn them up to pray.   435

'And now this spell was snapped: once more
I viewed the ocean green,
And looked far forth, yet little saw
Of what had else been seen –

'Like one, that on a lonesome road   440
Doth walk in fear and dread,
And having once turned round, walks on
And turns no more his head;
Because he knows, a frightful fiend
Doth close behind him tread.   445

'But soon there breathed a wind on me,
Nor sound nor motion made:
Its path was not upon the sea
In ripple or in shade.

'It raised my hair, it fanned my cheek,   450
Like a meadow-gale of spring –
It mingled strangely with my fears,
Yet it felt like a welcoming.

'Swiftly, swiftly flew the ship,
Yet she sailed softly too: 455
Sweetly, sweetly blew the breeze –
On me alone it blew.

'more high' if they are to avoid being 'belated'. 'Belated' is frequently used
of being caught by nightfall, and it is night when the Mariner awakes. It is
possible that Coleridge realizes that at higher altitudes the sun might still
be shining.

429. charnel-dungeon: i.e. a prison containing dead prisoners' remains.
Compare James Beattie, *The Minstrel*, 1771–4, I, 285.
440–5. If there is a literary source it is not (*pace* Lowes) Dante, but either
James Blair, *The Grave*, 1743, ll. 63–9, or a passage in G. Masters, 'On the
Battle of Culloden', 1747 (see Ainsworth 1934).

'Oh dream of joy! is this indeed
The lighthouse top I see?
Is this the hill? Is this the kirk?   460
Is this mine own countree?

'We drifted o'er the harbour-bar,
And I with sobs did pray –
"Oh let me be awake, my God!
Or let me sleep alway."   465

'The harbour-bay was clear as glass,
So smoothly it was strewn!
And on the bay the moonlight lay,
And the shadow of the moon.

'The rock shone bright, the kirk no less   470
That stands above the rock:
The moonlight steeped in silentness
The steady weathercock.

'And the bay was white with silent light,
Till rising from the same   475
Full many shapes, that shadows were,
In crimson colours came.

'A little distance from the prow
Those crimson shadows were:
I turned my eyes upon the deck –   480
O Christ! what saw I there?

'Each corse lay flat, lifeless and flat;
And by the holy rood
A man all light, a seraph-man,
On every corse there stood.   485

'This seraph-band, each waved his hand:
It was a heavenly sight:
They stood as signals to the land,
Each one a lovely light:

---

467. strewn: levelled, calmed.
476–7. The shadows of the 'seraph-band', rising from the deck behind the
Mariner, as cast on the water. The seraphim, the highest order of angels,
were supposed to glow with the ardour of their love for God, and the colour
red was often associated with them as a result. See the 1817 gloss to
ll. 478–9 (p. 366).
483. rood: cross.

'This seraph-band, each waved his hand,   490
No voice did they impart –
No voice; but oh! the silence sank
Like music on my heart.

'But soon I heard the dash of oars,
I heard the pilot's cheer: 495
My head was turned perforce away,
And I saw a boat appear.

'The pilot, and the pilot's boy,
I heard them coming fast:
Dear Lord in Heaven! it was a joy   500
The dead men could not blast.

'I saw a third – I heard his voice:
It is the hermit good!
He singeth loud his godly hymns
That he makes in the wood.   505
He'll shrive my soul, he'll wash away
The Albatross's blood.

VII

'This hermit good lives in that wood
Which slopes down to the sea.
How loudly his sweet voice he rears!   510
He loves to talk with mariners
That come from a far countree.

'He kneels at morn and noon and eve –
He hath a cushion plump:
It is the moss that wholly hides   515
The rotted old oak-stump.

---

491. impart: in this sense, Coleridge's coinage.
503–7. With the mention of the hermit the Mariner's time scheme suddenly becomes puzzling, and it is not clear if he is talking about the present or dramatizing his past feelings with present and future tenses (see also ll. 508–16). L. 503 presumably must be read in the latter fashion, but the rest are so construable only with some awkwardness (compare l. 504 and l. 517). If the whole passage ll. 504–16 is the Mariner speaking of the present, there is no evidence that he knew the hermit before the voyage. But if he is remembering the hermit, or his reputation as he was previously acquainted with it, Coleridge may be preparing a telling contrast between the hermit's usual padre-like relations with returning sailors and his reaction to this homecomer (see note to ll. 566–71).
513. Compare *Psalms* 55:17: 'Evening, and morning, and at noon, will I pray'; also *Daniel* 6:10.
515–16. See note to ll. 527–31 below.

'The skiff-boat nered: I heard them talk,
"Why, this is strange, I trow!
Where are those lights so many and fair
That signal made but now?"   520

' "Strange, by my faith!" the hermit said –
"And they answered not our cheer.
The planks look warped, and see those sails
How thin they are and sere!
I never saw aught like to them   525
Unless perchance it were

' "The skeletons of leaves that lag
My forest brook along:
When the ivy-tod is heavy with snow,
And the owlet whoops to the wolf below   530
That eats the she-wolf's young."

' "Dear Lord! it has a fiendish look"
(The pilot made reply)
"I am a-feared." – "Push on, push on!"
Said the hermit cheerily.   535

'The boat came closer to the ship,
But I nor spake nor stirred:
The boat came close beneath the ship,
And straight a sound was heard.

'Under the water it rumbled on,   540
Still louder and more dread:
It reached the ship, it split the bay;
The ship went down like lead.

527–31. With the notion of the male wolf eating the female wolf's cubs, negative images of nature in this stanza reach a startling climax. Hitherto the features of the homeland (harbour, church, rock, wood) have been reassuring and generally in contrast to the scenery of the voyage. Now some of the most telling images from the latter (skeletons, decaying matter in water, freezing conditions) reappear at the heart of the homeland setting, with the new feature of the callousness of natural creatures in time of dearth. The water-snakes did not offer such deterrents to being loved and blessed, and the hermit's attitude to 'my forest' is worth pondering: ll. 515–16 are particularly ambiguous in this regard.
527. *lag*: move sluggishly.
529. *ivy-tod*: ivy bush. The owlet of the next line is not directly associated with the ivy, but the owl in the ivy bush is a proverbial figure.
540–3. Eighteenth-century descriptions of earthquakes stressing the element of an approaching rumbling sound (as collected by Lowes 1951: 289–91) suggest that Coleridge was influenced by such imagery, but this does not make the phenomenon envisaged here an earthquake. Destruction of ships and whirlpools are not found in these accounts.

'Stunned by that loud and dreadful sound,
Which sky and ocean smote,   545
Like one that hath been seven days drowned
My body lay afloat:
But, swift as dreams, myself I found
Within the pilot's boat.

'Upon the whirl, where sank the ship,   550
The boat spun round and round,
And all was still, save that the hill
Was telling of the sound.

'I moved my lips: the pilot shrieked
And fell down in a fit.   555
The holy hermit raised his eyes
And prayed where he did sit.

'I took the oars: the pilot's boy,
Who now doth crazy go,
Laughed loud and long, and all the while   560
His eyes went to and fro.
"Ha! ha!" quoth he – "full plain I see,
The devil knows how to row."

'And now all in mine own countree
I stood on the firm land!   565
The hermit stepped forth from the boat,
And scarcely he could stand.

' "Oh shrieve me, shrieve me, holy man!"
The hermit crossed his brow.
"Say quick," quoth he, "I bid thee say   570
What manner man art thou?"

552–3. Compare *Aeneid* V, 150.
558–63. Tave (1983: 126–7) takes the stanza very seriously, as evidence of
the Mariner's intermittent possession (with God's permission) by the
demon avenging the Albatross's death: his 'glittering eye' would also be
evidence that he is possessed. There are many difficulties in this account,
but the very disturbing reactions to the Mariner's appearance recorded here
(above all l. 559) clearly go beyond mere shock that he is not dead. And the
hermit, significantly, has been completely shaken (l. 567) out of his earlier
cheerful confidence (ll. 511, 535) by coming face to face with the Mariner.
Against this must be set the fairly definite echoes of Biblical episodes
involving Christ and the disciples noted at ll. 571 and 579.
565. firm land: an anglicization of 'terra firma'.
566–71. The hermit's behaviour is of uncertain meaning. His signing of
the cross could be a prelude to hearing a confession, and his question could
be designed to initiate that confession; interrogation is so bound up with

'Forthwith this frame of mine was wrenched
With a woeful agony,
Which forced me to begin my tale,
And then it left me free.   575

'Since then, at an uncertain hour
That agony returns;
And till my ghastly tale is told
This heart within me burns.

'I pass, like night, from land to land;   580
I have strange power of speech;
The moment that his face I see
I know the man that must hear me;
To him my tale I teach.

'What loud uproar bursts from that door!   585
The wedding-guests are there;
But in the garden-bower the bride
And bride-maids singing are;
And hark the little vesper-bell
Which biddeth me to prayer.   590

'O wedding-guest! this soul hath been
Alone on a wide wide sea:
So lonely 'twas, that God himself
Scarce seemed there to be.

the concept of 'shriving' that the word has an extended sense simply of 'questioning, examining', and the 1817 gloss (p. 366) refers to 'penance', the usual accompaniment of absolution. But the hermit could equally be warding off the Devil by crossing himself, and exhibiting a deep fear in his 'What manner man art thou?' (however, see the important Biblical echo in this line noted below). The penance of 1817 is 'the penance of life', which may denote something that has replaced ordinary penance for the Mariner – perhaps the supernaturally induced illusory life, or Death-in-Life, of his Wandering Jew-like activity. Relevant here is the time scheme at ll. 508–16.
571. Compare the disciples' response to Christ's calming of the storm (*Matthew* 8:27): 'But the men marvelled, saying, What manner of man is this, that even the winds and the sea obey him!'

579. Compare the disciples' unwitting recognition of Christ on the road to Emmaeus (*Luke* 24:32): 'Did not our heart burn within us?'
582–4. Whatever the nature of the Mariner's first telling of his tale – to the hermit – it is clear that the retellings are not religious acts.

'Oh sweeter than the marriage-feast, 595
'Tis sweeter far to me
To walk together to the kirk
With a goodly company –

'To walk together to the kirk
And all together pray, 600
While each to his great Father bends,
Old men, and babes, and loving friends,
And youths, and maidens gay.

'Farewell, farewell! But this I tell
To thee, thou wedding-guest! 605
He prayeth well who loveth well
Both man and bird and beast.

'He prayeth best who loveth best
All things both great and small:
For the dear God, who loveth us, 610
He made and loveth all.'

The Mariner, whose eye is bright,
Whose beard with age is hoar,
Is gone; and now the wedding-guest
Turned from the bridegroom's door. 615

He went, like one that hath been stunned
And is of sense forlorn:
A sadder and a wiser man
He rose the morrow morn.

---

597. the kirk: it is normally assumed that the setting of the whole narrational frame is the coastal town from which the Mariner sailed, so that the 'kirk' is the same building in all its occurrences, but it is quite possible that the Mariner is telling his tale at some other location, perhaps even in a different language (again, the interpretation of ll. 508–16 is important).
597–8. Compare *Psalms* 55:14.
609. Compare *Psalms* 104:25.
612–13. The Mariner is no longer represented as an uncanny presence, but as a bright-eyed, venerable-looking old man – a token that he has once again discharged his mysterious, perhaps evil compulsion.
618. sadder: more serious; cited by *OED* as an example of this sense, but the dismaying nature of the Mariner's experiences (see also l. 104) must be relevant too. The deleted ll. 366–9 of the 1798 version read: 'Never sadder tale was told / To a man of woman born: / Sadder and wiser thou wedding-guest! / Thou'lt rise tomorrow morn.' The Mariner does seem to wish to inculcate a less hedonistic attitude in the wedding-guest (ll. 595–8) – who is said to be a 'gallant' in the very first 1817 gloss (p. 364).

Lines
Written a few miles above TINTERN ABBEY, on revisiting the banks of the WYE during a tour. July 13 1798

Composed in the second week of July 1798; scarcely any alterations. The Fenwick note on the circumstances of composition (p. 374) makes it clear that the writing situation proposed in the poem's title and first paragraph is a rhetorical device. The poem was not written confronting the scene it describes, or even 'composed' there (to use the term Wordsworth later substituted for 'written' in the title). The date furnished in the title confirms the Fenwick note, as this was the day on which Wordsworth returned with Dorothy from his walking tour of the summer of 1798 (see McNulty 1945).

The form is blank verse but with affinities to the 'greater' or Pindaric ode. In a note attached to the 1800, 1802 and 1805 editions of *LB* Wordsworth commented, 'I have not ventured to call this Poem an Ode; but it was written with a hope that in the transitions, and the impassioned music of the versification, would be found the principal requisites of that species of composition.' (For a very elaborate subdividing of the poem which starts from this note, see Johnson 1982: 57–65.) The ode-like 'transitions' in the poem are not all equal in scale; there is, in fact, a hierarchy of such changes of mood and subject. The grandest occurs at l. 112, the hinge line of the whole text and the point where it turns from the first to the second of its basic topics (Curran 1986: 77 sees it as the start of the 'epode', that is, the distinct closing section of the classical ode). The new topic (the poet's sister) is introduced with a backward- and forward-looking formula that makes explicit the whole structure of argument in the poem.

> Nor, perchance,
> If I were not thus taught, should I the more
> Suffer my genial spirits to decay:
> For thou art with me
>
> (112–15)

'Thus' here picks up the immediately preceding clause in ll. 108–12 about what the poet is 'well pleased' to recognize in 'nature and the language of the sense'. And this formula itself is a distillation of most of the text hitherto – of the analysis of what an intense sensory encounter with a wild environment five years ago has yielded in the way of delayed effects (this occupies ll. 23–58), and the analysis in ll. 89–103 of what it yields when repeated in the present (though it has emerged that for the second encounter, 'language of the sense' has to be taken with an enlarged meaning, to include what the senses 'half create').

The transitional lines 112–15 mention that this newly learnt lesson has averted a 'decay' of 'genial spirits'. And this turns out to be the key to the shift involved here – the element which links the two grand phases of the poem. The poet's sister, it is proposed, may have no less power to avert a decay of spirits than the positive valuation of 'nature and the language of the sense'. What is chiefly a source of pleasure here is the possibility that this beloved relation, being like the poet's young self, will repeat the process of partly unconscious psychological enrichment from phenomenologically stark encounters with nature that the poet has experienced between his two visits to the Wye; for there is some doubt as to whether such an enrichment can occur for him a second time (ll. 64–7). The threat of a loss of vitality and happiness is thus the groundwork of 'Tintern Abbey' from which the two unequal parts of its double structure both spring by way of antidotes. Such a threat must inform, if almost imperceptibly, the mood of the great opening paragraph.

The two countervailing, curative experiences offered in the poem both depend more than might be expected, and more than some commentators have recognized, on avid and purely physical engagements with the natural world such as Wordsworth attributes to himself at ll. 68–86 and prospectively to Dorothy at ll. 118–19 and 135–8. This is surprising because the description here is couched in a 'picturesque' mode (see note to ll. 77–84), an aesthetic fashion Wordsworth is known to have disliked. Indeed, the vocabulary of ll. 68–86 ('haunted', 'aching', 'dizzy') is sometimes deliberately suggestive of a morbid frame of mind. Part of the explanation can be found in the opening lines of the poem, where with great subtlety typical elements of the panorama-minded discourse of the picturesque literature (such as wildness, connectedness and the sense of the hidden) are brought forward and modified to suggest the potential for continuity between this approach to landscape and the pantheistic intuition of ll. 94–103. For William Gilpin (see note to l. 18) the charcoal smoke on the hills just physically 'unites them with the sky'. For the speaker at ll. 7–8 the cliffs 'connect / The landscape with the quiet of the sky', and this prepares for the sense of 'something' which 'rolls through all things' at ll. 97–103 (picking up also the 'rolling' Wye of l. 3).

The speaker at the opening of 'Tintern Abbey' is not, of course, meant to be the Wordsworth of 1793, whom the poet depicts as imbued with picturesque tastes, but nor is he supposed to be exactly the Wordsworth of 1798, though that may sound paradoxical. It is the tendency of Romantic odes (compare those of Keats) to dramatize a change in the state of mind of the speaker, and 'Tintern Abbey', given its large scale and evident 'transitions', can do this more readily than most, with the 'I' of the opening lines reincarnating in some measure the 'I' of five years earlier whom he recalls. The fact of process within the poem is relevant to a second point about the privileged status of the picturesque or quasi-picturesque: Wordsworth shows himself to be by no means unperturbed by his debt to the experience of environments such as the Wye, and his coming to terms with this debt, as its extent unfolds itself, is part of the action of the text. There is an element of 'sad perplexity' in the recalling of his inexpressible 'haunted' mood of 1793 (it is perhaps called forth from a kind of mental 'seclusion'). Even when the enormous psychological and moral significance of 'nature and the language of the sense' is granted (or granted with some qualifications), it is a matter of the poet being 'well pleased to recognize' this truth.

In other words, there survives in 'Tintern Abbey' a distinct implication that the poet would have been no less pleased to find his 'anchor . . . guide . . . guardian . . . and soul' in the 'intercourse of daily life' among socially congregated human beings. The qualities which rule out this possibility (exemplified at ll. 53–4, 129–31) are perhaps intrinsic to urban life, but this is not presented as a truth to be known *a priori*. The poet is *not* a hermit or man of the woods but someone who has learnt about the anxieties, hypocrisies and cruelties of town life by direct experience. His sojourn in the town is presumably one reason why his response to nature is now crucially enlarged with a sense of 'humanity' and the 'mind of man'. Both the visits to the Wye valley recorded in the poem are flights as well as quests, however subtle the balance (see note to ll. 68–73). Certainly neither is an uncomplicated return to a known good. 'Tintern Abbey' shows how the difficult price that a love of nature exacts, in terms of the giving up of urban human community, may be cheerfully paid.

> Five years have passed; five summers, with the length
> Of five long winters! and again I hear
> These waters, rolling from their mountain-springs
> With a sweet inland murmur. – Once again
> Do I behold these steep and lofty cliffs,   5
> Which on a wild secluded scene impress
> Thoughts of more deep seclusion; and connect

1–2. Five years . . . winters!: Wordsworth had previously visited the Wye in August 1793 (he includes the summer of 1798 in his arithmetic). Enumerating the seasons in this way indicates that it is the length of the interval upon which the exclamation mark comments.

4. inland murmur: 'The river is not affected by the tides a few miles above Tintern' (Wordsworth's note). This detail has the effect of reinforcing what has already been mentioned in the title: that the poem's setting is *not* the celebrated ruined monastic buildings at Tintern.

5–7. cliffs . . . seclusion: 'The cliffs "impress thoughts on . . ." with something of the immediacy and literalness of a craftsman impressing a pattern on wax. And it is almost as though the impressing goes on without the intervention of the observing mind. . . . The formula "Thoughts of . . ." is ambiguous . . . the thoughts are not only *about* deep seclusion, they are themselves deep and secluded' (Clarke 1962: 44–5). Since Clarke, such observations have been repeated and enlarged by several commentators.

7–8. connect . . . sky: Benziger (1950), astutely noting how 'connectedness' of several sorts (including, importantly, connectedness with quiet) characterizes both the description of the landscape and the more abstract speculations which are to come (ll. 97–103), calls this opening scene a '*paysage moralisé*' (on connectedness see also Danby 1954). But this is to put the linkages in too mechanical a light. It is more appropriate to think of connectedness and, just as important, the several kinds of 'seclusion' as significant but unconscious tendencies in the narrator's perception of the landscape which show his mind bridging from one kind of thinking about the human and natural worlds to another (see headnote).

The landscape with the quiet of the sky.
The day is come when I again repose
Here, under this dark sycamore, and view   10
These plots of cottage-ground, these orchard-tufts,
Which, at this season, with their unripe fruits,
Are clad in one green hue, and lose themselves
Among the woods and copses, nor disturb
The wild green landscape. Once again I see   15
These hedgerows, hardly hedgerows, little lines
Of sportive wood run wild; these pastoral farms
Green to the very door; and wreaths of smoke
Sent up, in silence, from among the trees,
With some uncertain notice, as might seem,   20
Of vagrant dwellers in the houseless woods,
Or of some hermit's cave, where by his fire
The hermit sits alone.
                              Though absent long,
These forms of beauty have not been to me
As is a landscape to a blind man's eye: 25
But oft, in lonely rooms, and mid the din
Of towns and cities, I have owed to them,

11. *tufts*: groups of trees.
14. *disturb*: the paradox that cultivated trees might be the disturbing element among wild species is rhetorically effective for the celebration of the interfusion of plant life observed. When (in a characteristic repetition of vocabulary) the word 'disturb' reappears in l. 95 it is again tellingly paradoxical.
17. *pastoral*: among other meanings, with land that is not cultivated but grazed. See William Gilpin, *Observations on the River Wye*, 1782, pp. 29–30: 'The banks of the Wye consist, almost entirely either of wood, or of pasturage: which I mention as a circumstance of peculiar value in landscape. . . . The painter never desires the hand of art to touch his grounds. – But if art *must* . . . mark out the limits of property . . . he wishes, that these limits may be as much concealed as possible; and that the lands they circumscribe, may approach, as nearly as may be, to nature – that is, that they may be pasturage.' It has been suggested that Wordsworth had Gilpin's book (which is very much directed at the amateur painter or pictorially minded tourist) with him on his 1798 visit.
18. *smoke*: perhaps from charcoal-making operations in the woods, as recorded by Gilpin, *op. cit.*, p. 12.
21. *houseless*: see note to 'The Female Vagrant', l. 182 (p. 142).
24–5. Camp (1971) correctly observes that the formulation is puzzling and suggests on the strength of a passage in the 1815 'Essay, Supplementary to the Preface' that the blind man is supposed to have been able to acquire a 'knowledge of outward forms, with perhaps a general intimation as to colour'.

In hours of weariness, sensations sweet,
Felt in the blood, and felt along the heart,
And passing even into my purer mind,   30
With tranquil restoration – feelings too
Of unremembered pleasure: such, perhaps,
As may have had no trivial influence
On that best portion of a good man's life,
His little, nameless, unremembered acts   35
Of kindness and of love. Nor less, I trust,
To them I may have owed another gift,
Of aspect more sublime; that blessed mood,
In which the burthen of the mystery,
In which the heavy and the weary weight   40
Of all this unintelligible world
Is lightened – that serene and blessed mood,
In which the affections gently lead us on,
Until, the breath of this corporeal frame
And even the motion of our human blood   45
Almost suspended, we are laid asleep
In body, and become a living soul:
While with an eye made quiet by the power
Of harmony, and the deep power of joy,
We see into the life of things.

29. 'The expected placing would give: "Felt in the heart and felt along the blood" ... deploying them this way round ... enables Wordsworth to challenge the presupposition that the heart is simply a place and the blood simply diffused' (Ricks 1984: 121). Armstrong (1978) also comments on 'the unobtrusive but astonishing inversion of the expected prepositions'. Wilson (1983), however, draws attention to how 'the works of eighteenth-century physiologists are ... full of attempts to define the processes by which the length of the heart is changed during the muscular impulses of its beat'.
30. As Wilson (1983) points out, Wordsworth's image for these memories that are both physical and intellectual in their impact derives from the traditional notion in Galenic–Arabian medicine (which was by no means extinct in the eighteenth century) that the most purified substance in the blood – the 'animal spirits' – rise into the brain.
31–2. feelings ... pleasure: pleasurable feelings not consciously associated with these past experiences.
34. Recalls Milton's 'Preface' to *The Judgement of Martin Bucer, concerning Divorce* (*Works*, New York 1931–8, IV, 18, ll. 9–10).
39. burthen: burden. Not yet archaic.
46–7. laid asleep / In body: cf. 'the body is laid asleep, before the spirit can converse with God' (William Gilbert, *The Hurricane* (1796), p. 80).

                                    If this   50
Be but a vain belief, yet, oh! how oft,
In darkness, and amid the many shapes
Of joyless daylight, when the fretful stir
Unprofitable, and the fever of the world,
Have hung upon the beatings of my heart,   55
How oft, in spirit, have I turned to thee,
O sylvan Wye! Thou wanderer through the woods,
How often has my spirit turned to thee!

And now, with gleams of half-extinguished thought,
With many recognitions dim and faint,   60
And somewhat of a sad perplexity,
The picture of the mind revives again:
While here I stand, not only with the sense
Of present pleasure, but with pleasing thoughts
That in this moment there is life and food   65
For future years. And so I dare to hope
Though changed, no doubt, from what I was, when first
I came among these hills; when like a roe
I bounded o'er the mountains, by the sides
Of the deep rivers, and the lonely streams,   70
Wherever nature led: more like a man
Flying from something that he dreads, than one

50. *this*: commentators have discussed the referent here. In the light of
what follows, Nabholtz (1974) seems right to urge that it is the belief that
the 'mood' of l. 38 is owed to the experiences of 1793.
53–4. Aspects of the wording are picked up from *Macbeth* III, ii, 23 and
Hamlet I, ii, 133–4.
55. Perhaps, continuing the image of a fever, with the sense of a weakened
pulse.
62. *the picture of the mind*: probably 'my mental picture in 1793' (compare
'The language of my former heart', l. 118) rather than 'the depiction of my
mind in 1793', which l. 76 says the poet 'cannot paint'. Something of the
'reviving' of this picture may be expressed in the vocabulary of the poem's
opening paragraph. See also headnote.
66–7. *And so . . . I was*: i.e. his present state may not hold the possibility of
feeding the future to the extent that his state of five years earlier did.
67–8. *when first . . . hills*: McNulty (1981) argues on slight evidence that
Wordsworth's first visit to the Wye was in 1791, and therefore that
ll. 67–84 do not refer to the visit recalled in the opening lines. But however
many times Wordsworth had seen the Wye, it is clear that in this text he is
setting up a model, for the reader, of two visits separated by five years.
68–73. *like a roe . . . he loved*: the ambiguous and interacting similes in
these lines leave the question of the balance between frightened flight and
loving quest, in the Wordsworth of 1793, intriguingly uncertain. If the 'like'

Who sought the thing he loved. For nature then
(The coarser pleasures of my boyish days,
And their glad animal movements all gone by)   75
To me was all in all – I cannot paint
What then I was. The sounding cataract
Haunted me like a passion: the tall rock,
The mountain, and the deep and gloomy wood,
Their colours and their forms, were then to me   80
An appetite: a feeling and a love,
That had no need of a remoter charm,
By thought supplied, or any interest
Unborrowed from the eye. That time is past,
And all its aching joys are now no more,   85
And all its dizzy raptures. Not for this
Faint I, nor mourn nor murmur; other gifts
Have followed, for such loss, I would believe,

of 'more like a man' has the sense which the 'like' of 'like a roe' at first seems to have – the sense of 'with the appearance of' – then we have a purely exterior picture of Wordsworth's state in 1793. But the second 'like' is perhaps better read as meaning 'in the condition of', and however we take it the image of a fleeing man modifies the bounding roe image significantly through the suggestion of a deer hunt. In 'Hart-leap Well' (pp. 215–21) Wordsworth tells the story of a hunted stag which is in flight *and* seeking to return to a beloved spot.

74–5. The close juxtaposition of the 'glad animal movements' with the roe image has left countless hasty readers with the idea that ll. 68–70 refer to Wordsworth's boyhood, though this is explicitly said not to be the case in this pair of lines.
75. animal: clearly in the second sense mentioned in the note to 'Animal Tranquillity and Decay' on p. 101 rather than the neural sense. Confusingly, Erasmus Darwin has an important chapter in *Zoonomia* (1794–6, I, iii, 1) arguing that sense impressions are 'animal motions' or 'animal movements', also in this second sense.
77–84. The sounding ... the eye: evidently an intensely sensory phase of feeling and an example of Wordsworth's interest in phenomenologically primitive states of mind, but the commentators are right to say that in its emphasis on visual qualities the passage alludes particularly to the cult of the picturesque. Compare Gilpin, *op. cit.*, p. 13 on 'the rock' in the Wye valley: 'Tint it with mosses, and lichens of various hues, and you give it a degree of beauty. Adorn it with shrubs, and hanging herbage, and you still make it more picturesque. Connect it with wood, and water, and broken ground; and you make it in the highest degree interesting. Its colours, and its form are so accommodating, that it generally blends into one of the most beautiful appendages of landscape.'

Abundant recompense. For I have learned
To look on nature, not as in the hour   90
Of thoughtless youth, but hearing oftentimes
The still, sad music of humanity,
Nor harsh nor grating, though of ample power
To chasten and subdue. And I have felt
A presence that disturbs me with the joy   95
Of elevated thoughts; a sense sublime
Of something far more deeply interfused,
Whose dwelling is the light of setting suns,
And the round ocean and the living air,
And the blue sky, and in the mind of man,   100
A motion and a spirit, that impels
All thinking things, all objects of all thought,
And rolls through all things. Therefore am I still
A lover of the meadows and the woods,

89–103. For a famous dissatisfied setting out of the grammatical
ambiguities in this passage, see Empson 1961: 151–4. And for a series of
responses to one of Empson's complaints ('what is *more deeply interfused*
than what?'), see *Explicator* XIV, 1956, items 31, 61, and XVI, 1958, item
36. Maniquis (1969) points out that there are no less than ten 'uncompleted
comparisons' in 'Tintern Abbey' and explores the positive aspects of the
device.

92. Elijah's vision and the 'still, small voice' of God (1 *Kings* 19:12) is
probably invoked.

96–103. a sense ... all things: indebted to *Aeneid* VI, 724–7: '*caelum ac
terram camposque liquentes / Lucentemque globum lunae Titaniaque astra /
Spiritus intus alit, totamque infusa per artus / Mens agitat molem et magno se
corpore miscet*' ('an inner spirit sustains the sky and the earth and the watery
plains, the bright globe of the moon, the sun and the stars, and mind
activates the whole frame, pervading all its members, and blends with the
great body'). Subsidiary influences may be *Georgics* IV, 221–2, a passage
from the dialogue *Octavius* by the early Christian Latin author Minucius
Felix (see Hill 1974), and *Wisdom* 12:1. Armstrong (1978) stresses the
replacement of the *Aeneid*'s 'infusa' by 'interfused' (in this particular use
allegedly 'a new word, suggesting a mutuality of blending which is not
present in "infused" '), though both 'interfused' and 'roll through' in this
sort of context seem due to Coleridge, *Religious Musings*, 1796, ll. 405–6:
'And ye of plastic power, that interfused / Roll through the grosser and
material mass'. These sources, all definite about the presence of a deity,
make Wordsworth's 'sense of something' even more strikingly tentative.

101–2. Durrant (1970: 95) reads the lines as reversed parallels, so that
'motion' belongs with 'objects' (and refers to Newtonian gravity, propagated
in the ether) and 'spirit' with 'thinking things' (also, Newton suggested,
dependent on the ether). Durrant links 'Tintern Abbey' with the post-
Newtonian vein of cosmology-minded religious verse in the eighteenth
century.

And mountains; and of all that we behold 105
From this green earth; of all the mighty world
Of eye and ear, both what they half create
And what perceive; well pleased to recognize
In nature and the language of the sense,
The anchor of my purest thoughts, the nurse, 110
The guide, the guardian of my heart, and soul
Of all my moral being.
             Nor, perchance,
If I were not thus taught, should I the more
Suffer my genial spirits to decay:
For thou art with me, here, upon the banks 115
Of this fair river: thou, my dearest friend,
My dear, dear friend, and in thy voice I catch
The language of my former heart, and read
My former pleasures in the shooting lights
Of thy wild eyes. Oh! yet a little while 120
May I behold in thee what I was once,
My dear, dear sister! And this prayer I make,
Knowing that Nature never did betray
The heart that loved her; 'tis her privilege,

107. 'This line has a close resemblance to an admirable line of Young, the exact expression of which I cannot recollect' (Wordsworth's note). The line from Young, concerning the 'senses', is 'And half create the wondrous world, they see' (*Night Thoughts*, 1742, Night VI, l. 427). As Abrams (1958: 63) points out, Young at this point is evidently poeticizing Locke's notion of secondary qualities.

109. sense: Empson (1951) identifies this as the first occurrence of a Wordsworthian coinage, with the word being used 'absolutely' to mean more than just 'the senses'.

111. the guide, the guardian: compare Akenside, *Pleasures of the Imagination*, 1744, I, 22.

114. genial spirits: the phrase is from Milton, *Samson Agonistes*, l. 594, where it means (in the context of their 'drooping') something like 'spirits natural to my temperament'. Here, in addition, the word 'genial' has connotations of vitality and cheerfulness.

115. thou art with me: compare *Psalms* 23:4.

116. my dearest friend: the first of several elements in the next twenty-five lines that may be influenced by *Antony and Cleopatra* III, ii, 39–41: 'Farewell, my dearest Sister, fare thee well. / The elements be kind to thee, and make / Thy spirits all of comfort.'

123–4. Knowing ... loved her: compare Samuel Daniel, *The Civil Wars*, 1595, II, 225–6: 'Here have you craggy rocks to take your part; / That never will betray their faith to you.'

123. Nature: the first time nature is capitalized in the poem, but evidently because there is an element of personification.

Through all the years of this our life, to lead   125
From joy to joy; for she can so inform
The mind that is within us, so impress
With quietness and beauty, and so feed
With lofty thoughts, that neither evil tongues,
Rash judgments, nor the sneers of selfish men,   130
Nor greetings where no kindness is, nor all
The dreary intercourse of daily life,
Shall e'er prevail against us, or disturb
Our cheerful faith that all which we behold
Is full of blessings. Therefore let the moon   135
Shine on thee in thy solitary walk;
And let the misty mountain winds be free
To blow against thee: and, in after years,
When these wild ecstasies shall be matured
Into a sober pleasure, when thy mind   140
Shall be a mansion for all lovely forms,
Thy memory be as a dwelling-place
For all sweet sounds and harmonies; oh! then,
If solitude, or fear, or pain, or grief,
Should be thy portion, with what healing thoughts   145
Of tender joy wilt thou remember me,
And these my exhortations! Nor, perchance,
If I should be where I no more can hear
Thy voice, nor catch from thy wild eyes these gleams
Of past existence, wilt thou then forget   150
That on the banks of this delightful stream
We stood together; and that I, so long
A worshipper of Nature, hither came,
Unwearied in that service: rather say
With warmer love, oh! with far deeper zeal   155
Of holier love. Nor wilt thou then forget,
That after many wanderings, many years
Of absence, these steep woods and lofty cliffs,
And this green pastoral landscape, were to me
More dear, both for themselves and for thy sake.   160

---

125. this our life: see *As You Like It* II, i, 15 (and the suggestive context).
129. evil tongues: see *Paradise Lost* VII, 26, in the significant context of Milton's remarks about his audience.
137. mountain . . . free: see *The Tempest* I, ii, 495–6.
141. mansion: residence, place of abode or lodging.

Hart-leap Well

Composed sometime in the first five months of 1800. Numerous small-scale revisions including, from 1840, a change in the height jumped by the stag from nine to four roods. The stanza looks somewhat ballad-like to the eye, but the five-stress lines create the very different effect (immediately felt in the first verse) of 'heroic' or 'elegiac' quatrains. Probably influenced, like some other poems in *LB*, by a work of Gottfried Bürger's, in this instance a poem translated by Walter Scott in 1796 as 'The Wild Huntsman'; it, too, has an anti-hunting theme, with the Earl who cannot give up his cruel chase of a white stag being turned into the perpetually hunted quarry of his own hounds. Interestingly, in Bürger's story there is a considerable emphasis on the damage caused to ordinary countrymen and their livelihood by the hunt, a theme that Wordsworth (despite 'Simon Lee') does not pursue: 'No ballad could be more parallel, and more opposed' (Hartman 1968). For further departures from Bürger, see the footnotes. 'Hart-leap Well' exhibits a new level of complexity in Wordsworth's treatment of an 'I' narrator, a vestige of suffering, and a communal tradition about the latter. One aspect of this is that the main tale is told by the 'I' rather than by the apparently fallible story-teller he has learnt it from.

Hart-Leap Well is a small spring of water, about five miles from Richmond in Yorkshire, and near the side of the road which leads from Richmond to Askrigg. Its name is derived from a remarkable chase, the memory of which is preserved by the monuments spoken of in the second part of the following poem, which monuments do now exist as I have there described them.

(Wordsworth's headnote)

The Knight had ridden down from Wensley moor
With the slow motion of a summer's cloud;
He turned aside towards a vassal's door,
And, 'Bring another horse!' he cried aloud.

'Another horse!' – That shout the vassal heard,   5
And saddled his best steed, a comely grey;
Sir Walter mounted him; he was the third
Which he had mounted on that glorious day.

Joy sparkled in the prancing courser's eyes;
The horse and horseman are a happy pair;   10
But, though Sir Walter like a falcon flies,
There is a doleful silence in the air.

9. *courser*: a fast horse.

A rout this morning left Sir Walter's hall,
That as they galloped made the echoes roar;
But horse and man are vanished, one and all;   15
Such race, I think, was never seen before.

Sir Walter, restless as a veering wind,
Calls to the few tired dogs that yet remain:
Brach, Swift, and Music, noblest of their kind,
Follow, and up the weary mountain strain.   20

The Knight hallooed, he chid and cheered them on
With suppliant gestures and upbraidings stern;
But breath and eyesight fail; and, one by one,
The dogs are stretched among the mountain fern.

Where is the throng, the tumult of the race?   25
The bugles that so joyfully were blown? –
This chase it looks not like an earthly chase;
Sir Walter and the Hart are left alone.

The poor Hart toils along the mountain side;
I will not stop to tell how far he fled,   30
Nor will I mention by what death he died;
But now the Knight beholds him lying dead.

Dismounting then, he leaned against a thorn;
He had no follower, dog, nor man, nor boy.
He neither smacked his whip, nor blew his horn,   35
But gazed upon the spoil with silent joy.

Close to the thorn on which Sir Walter leaned,
Stood his dumb partner in this glorious act;
Weak as a lamb the hour that it is yeaned,
And foaming like a mountain cataract.   40

Upon his side the Hart was lying stretched:
His nose half-touched a spring beneath a hill,
And with the last deep groan his breath had fetched
The waters of the spring were trembling still.

---

13. rout: throng.
15. Compare 'The Wild Huntsman', ll. 145–6: 'And horse and man, and
horn and hound, / And clamour of the chase, was gone.' Primeau (1983)
stresses how Wordsworth's 'completely plausible' naturalistic treatment of
this element contrasts with the supernatural devices in Bürger's text.
25–6. Compare 'The Wild Huntsman', ll. 147–8: 'For hoofs, and howls,
and bugle-sound, / A deadly silence reigned alone.'
37–44. There is probably a general reminiscence of Dryden, *Annus
Mirabilis*, ll. 521–8.
39. yeaned: born.

And now, too happy for repose or rest, 45
(Was never man in such a joyful case!)
Sir Walter walked all round, north, south, and west,
And gazed and gazed upon that darling place.

And climbing up the hill (it was at least
Nine roods of sheer ascent) Sir Walter found 50
Three several hoof-marks which the hunted beast
Had left imprinted on the verdant ground.

Sir Walter wiped his face and cried, 'Till now
Such sight was never seen by living eyes:
Three leaps have borne him from this lofty brow, 55
Down to the very fountain where he lies.

'I'll build a pleasure-house upon this spot,
And a small arbour, made for rural joy;
'Twill be the traveller's shed, the pilgrim's cot,
A place of love for damsels that are coy. 60

'A cunning artist will I have to frame
A basin for that fountain in the dell;
And they who do make mention of the same
From this day forth, shall call it HART-LEAP WELL.

'And, gallant brute! to make thy praises known, 65
Another monument shall here be raised;
Three several pillars, each a rough hewn stone,
And planted where thy hoofs the turf have grazed.

'And in the summer-time when days are long,
I will come hither with my paramour; 70
And with the dancers, and the minstrel's song,
We will make merry in that pleasant bower.

'Till the foundations of the mountains fail
My mansion with its arbour shall endure –
The joy of them who till the fields of Swale, 75
And them who dwell among the woods of Ure!'

Then home he went, and left the Hart, stone-dead,
With breathless nostrils stretched above the spring.
And soon the Knight performed what he had said,
The fame whereof through many a land did ring. 80

---

50. nine roods: about sixty yards.
59. shed: in this general sense of shelter, probably becoming confined to
dialectal use in Wordsworth's day.
61. artist: see note to 'The Female Vagrant', l. 47 (p. 138).

Ere thrice the moon into her port had steered,
A cup of stone received the living well;
Three pillars of rude stone Sir Walter reared,
And built a house of pleasure in the dell.

And near the fountain, flowers of stature tall   85
With trailing plants and trees were intertwined,
Which soon composed a little sylvan hall,
A leafy shelter from the sun and wind.

And thither, when the summer-days were long,
Sir Walter journeyed with his paramour;   90
And with the dancers and the minstrel's song
Made merriment within that pleasant bower.

The Knight, Sir Walter, died in course of time,
And his bones lie in his paternal vale. –
But there is matter for a second rhyme,   95
And I to this would add another tale.

Part Second

The moving accident is not my trade:
To freeze the blood I have no ready arts:
'Tis my delight, alone in summer shade,
To pipe a simple song to thinking hearts.   100

As I from Hawes to Richmond did repair,
It chanced that I saw standing in a dell
Three aspens at three corners of a square,
And one, not four yards distant, near a well.

What this imported I could ill divine: 105
And, pulling now the rein my horse to stop,
I saw three pillars standing in a line,
The last stone pillar on a dark hill-top.

The trees were grey, with neither arms nor head;
Half-wasted the square mound of tawny green;   110
So that you just might say, as then I said,
'Here in old time the hand of man has been.'

I looked upon the hills both far and near,
More doleful place did never eye survey;
It seemed as if the spring-time came not here,   115
And Nature here were willing to decay.

97. moving accident: see *Othello* I, iii, 135.
98. freeze the blood: see *Hamlet* I, v, 16.
101. from Hawes to Richmond: see Wordsworth's headnote.

I stood in various thoughts and fancies lost,
When one, who was in shepherd's garb attired,
Came up the hollow. Him did I accost,
And what this place might be I then inquired.   120

The shepherd stopped, and that same story told
Which in my former rhyme I have rehearsed.
'A jolly place,' said he, 'in times of old!
But something ails it now; the spot is cursed.

'You see these lifeless stumps of aspen wood –   125
Some say that they are beeches, others elms –
These were the bower; and here a mansion stood,
The finest palace of a hundred realms!

'The arbour does its own condition tell;
You see the stones, the fountain, and the stream,   130
But as to the great lodge! you might as well
Hunt half a day for a forgotten dream.

'There's neither dog nor heifer, horse nor sheep,
Will wet his lips within that cup of stone;
And oftentimes, when all are fast asleep,   135
This water doth send forth a dolorous groan.

'Some say that here a murder has been done,
And blood cries out for blood: but, for my part,
I've guessed, when I've been sitting in the sun,
That it was all for that unhappy Hart.   140

'What thoughts must through the creature's brain have
         passed!
From the stone upon the summit of the steep
Are but three bounds – and look, sir, at this last –
O master! it has been a cruel leap.

'For thirteen hours he ran a desperate race;   145
And in my simple mind we cannot tell
What cause the Hart might have to love this place,
And come and make his death-bed near the well.

117–22. There are several unusually conspicuous syntactical inversions in
these lines.
125. aspen: probably an adjective: 'asp like' ('asp' being an alternative name
for the variety of poplar now more commonly called the aspen). The poet
has already perceived them as 'aspens' (l. 103) but their decayed state
(l. 109) is sufficient to make them confusable with other species (l. 126).
135–6. An apparently self-defeating claim to knowledge of a bizarre local
phenomenon, rather like 'The Thorn', ll. 98–9 (p. 122). The shepherd has
already lent himself to a clear exaggeration of the facts at ll. 127–8.
138. blood cries out for blood: compare *Macbeth* III, iv, 122.

'Here on the grass perhaps asleep he sank,
Lulled by this fountain in the summer-tide;   150
This water was perhaps the first he drank
When he had wandered from his mother's side.

'In April here beneath the scented thorn
He heard the birds their morning carols sing;
And he, perhaps, for aught we know, was born   155
Not half a furlong from that self-same spring.

'But now here's neither grass nor pleasant shade;
The sun on drearier hollow never shone.
So will it be, as I have often said,
Till trees, and stones, and fountain all are gone.'   160

'Grey-headed shepherd, thou hast spoken well;
Small difference lies between thy creed and mine.
This beast not unobserved by Nature fell;
His death was mourned by sympathy divine.

'The Being, that is in the clouds and air,   165
That is in the green leaves among the groves,
Maintains a deep and reverential care
For them the quiet creatures whom he loves.

'The pleasure-house is dust – behind, before,
This is no common waste, no common gloom;   170
But Nature, in due course of time, once more
Shall here put on her beauty and her bloom.

162. In view of what follows, perhaps to be read, 'there is a small
difference between our creeds' rather than 'our creeds are very similar'.
The poet goes on to emphasize his conviction that the site will eventually
become normally fertile again, and his acceptance of the shepherd's curse
theory (which has troubled some commentators) is qualified: nature has
imposed a 'slow decay' (l. 173) rather than a permanent blight complete
with groaning wells (l. 136). 'The end of the poem explicitly rejects the
superstition' (Averill 1980: 221). Primeau (1983) sees this as another case
of Wordsworth repudiating Bürger's supernatural mode, the close parallel
being with the blighted setting in the ballad which influenced 'The Thorn',
'The Lass of Fair Wone'.

'She leaves these objects to a slow decay,
That what we are, and have been, may be known;
But, at the coming of the milder day,   175
These monuments shall all be overgrown.

'One lesson, shepherd, let us two divide,
Taught both by what she shows, and what conceals,
Never to blend our pleasure or our pride
With sorrow of the meanest thing that feels.'   180

175. The apocalyptic overtones of the phrasing here are confirmed by its setting in another reference to Hart-leap Well in Wordsworth's 'Home at Grasmere': 'when the trance / Came to us, as we stood by Hart-leap Well – / The intimation of the milder day / Which is to come, the fairer world than this' (see Darlington 1977: 50).
177–80. Despite the divergences of attitude, there is 'one lesson' common to both: the immorality of cruelty to living creatures.

'There was a Boy . . .'

Written mainly in October–November 1798. Ll. 26–7 were created in 1805, the Boy's death having been mentioned more briefly in the last line of earlier versions. No substantial changes thereafter. The lines were written as part of *The Prelude*, where they also appeared with the posthumous publication of this work in 1850 (at V, 364 *et seq.*). See the important excerpt from the Preface of 1815 (p. 379). The poem is as cryptic as 'The Idiot Boy', with a narrator as explicitly 'mute' (l. 34) as the narrator of the latter. Since he is mute at the graveside the poem does not even indicate if it is reticent about the Boy's young joy, or about his death, or both. In other words, the reader must decide if this is a text about pleasure or pain or some strange alloy of the two. Moreover, the Boy's experience is itself shifting, sometimes oxymoronic (l. 19), and capable of a variety of assessments. It is clear (despite the careless responses of some critics) that the closing lines are integral with the rest, since the past tenses at the beginning must look forward to the fact of the Boy's death (see also the notes on these lines and on ll. 19–22). There may be in the whole tale a reminiscence of the legend of Narcissus, who was reflected in water with fatal results and beloved of Echo. Even the 'uncertain heaven' of l. 24 may be seen to take up the themes of death and mourning. All in all, the poem is in no interesting sense 'really' about Wordsworth: he explains in the 1815 comment that he was simply 'guided' by experiences of his own. But the pattern of Wordsworth's young life may be a kind of unstated theme via a characteristic conflation of really existing models: a possible classmate of Wordsworth's who died at about the right time has been identified, while William Raincock (mentioned in the Fenwick note, p. 379, commenting on ll. 7–10) went, like Wordsworth, to St John's College, Cambridge.

> There was a Boy, ye knew him well, ye cliffs
> And islands of Winander! many a time,
> At evening, when the stars had just begun
> To move along the edges of the hills,
> Rising or setting, would he stand alone,   5
> Beneath the trees, or by the glimmering lake;
> And there, with fingers interwoven, both hands

1–2. The idiom and motif here are strikingly literary. The apostrophe to 'Winander' is perhaps designed to suggest the device in pastoral elegy (the founding example being Moschus's *Lament for Bion*) whereby the natural world is called upon to mourn for a dead youth. Among Wordsworth's juvenilia is an adaptation of some lines of Moschus's poem (*PW* I, 286–7), and he refers to the convention in *Excursion* I, 475–8, but here does not carry the imitation any further.

2. Winander: Wordsworth's speculative ancient name for Windermere, the lake being usually called 'Winandermere' until the seventeenth century. The effect of a venerable if unfamiliar British topographical name is reminiscent of the practice of Spenser and Milton.

7–10. See Fenwick note, p. 379.

Pressed closely palm to palm and to his mouth
Uplifted, he, as through an instrument,
Blew mimic hootings to the silent owls   10
That they might answer him. And they would shout
Across the watery vale, and shout again
Responsive to his call, with quivering peals,
And long halloos, and screams, and echoes loud
Redoubled and redoubled; concourse wild   15
Of mirth and jocund din! And, when it chanced
That pauses of deep silence mocked his skill,
Then, sometimes, in that silence, while he hung
Listening, a gentle shock of mild surprise
Has carried far into his heart the voice   20
Of mountain torrents; or the visible scene
Would enter unawares into his mind
With all its solemn imagery, its rocks,
Its woods, and that uncertain heaven, received
Into the bosom of the steady lake.   25

This Boy was taken from his mates, and died
In childhood, ere he was ten years old.
Fair are the woods, and beauteous is the spot,
The vale where he was born: the churchyard hangs
Upon a slope above the village school,   30

16. din: as a term for birdsong, perhaps due to Milton, *L'Allegro*, l. 49.
18. hung: in this transferred sense apparently peculiar to Wordsworth; see
also 'The Female Vagrant', l. 202 (p. 143).
19–22. The poem's magnificent climactic lines are full of complexities: the
oxymorons of 'gentle shock', 'mild surprise' (which raise the question of the
degree of contrast between the two phases of experience described); the
paradox of 'surprise' and 'unawares'; the concomitant suggestion that the
'heart' is perhaps more conscious than the 'mind'. These matters have not
been much commented on; but see Huxley 1932: 156, and Glen 1983: 267
(who makes the interesting suggestion that the 'gentle shock' 'prefigures the
shock of death').
20. far: De Quincey comments perceptively on 'this very expression, "far",
by which space and its infinities are attributed to the human heart, and to
its capacities of re-echoing the sublimities of nature' (*Tait's Magazine*, VI,
1839, p. 94). Wordsworth's 1815 note (p. 379) shows that the effect of a
'transfer of internal feeling' was deliberate.
23–5. rocks . . . lake: the scene is reflected in the lake (though 'received /
Into the bosom' expresses this figuratively in a way that sustains the linkage
of human faculties and the external world).
26. This Boy . . . mates: if this sentence is more than a periphrasis for the
Boy's death it adds an implication of suffering before that death occurred.
28–34. These lines strangely recall the account of the Boy's activity, in an
accumulation of slight echoes: 'woods', 'vale', 'hangs', 'along that bank',
'evening', 'oftentimes', 'mute'.

And there, along that bank, when I have passed
At evening, I believe, that oftentimes
A full half-hour together I have stood
Mute – looking at the grave in which he lies.

The Brothers
A pastoral poem

Composed late 1799 to early 1800. Numerous small-scale changes. After 1815 Leonard goes to sea when he is fifteen, rather than twelve (see l. 38), thus making him older on his return and giving him much more of a life as a young shepherd (see ll. 292–302) than in earlier versions. After 1827 James's parting with his companions takes a slightly different form. See Wordsworth's letter to Fox (p. 42), where he links 'The Brothers' with 'Michael'. The latter is also subtitled 'a pastoral poem', and is sometimes suggested to be one of the associated projects mentioned by Wordsworth in his note to the title (see below). Wordsworth seems to intend the generic term 'pastoral poem' very straightforwardly as denoting a study of shepherd life, in contrast to the more literary–historical connotations of 'pastoral' when used by him as a subtitle (see General Introduction, p. 12) – though the distinction was not so hard and fast that he could not use the second term for 'The Brothers' in the less formal context of the title note. For the situation of the Lake District 'statesmen' such as Leonard's ancestors had been, see 'Michael' and its notes (pp. 341–57). It is known that the Ennerdale shepherd of the Fenwick note (p. 369) was a man called Bowman who walked in his sleep to his death over a precipice, but the whole device of Leonard, tracing and not being able to endure a human tragedy of peculiar poignancy for himself, is Wordsworth's characteristic invention. Unusually there is no 'I' speaker, and the dramatic method is used interestingly to complicate the tracing process, with Leonard (who has experienced hallucinations of his home village while at sea) being uncertain in the case of the graves about his reading of the vestiges he finds on his return, and yet reliable in the case of the surrounding landscape (more so than the vicar, who also mistakes Leonard for a self-indulgently melancholy tourist). A clash between personal and communal memory is set up reminiscent of the situation in 'The Thorn', and the issues of outsiderhood and the communal treatment of suffering are if anything more complicated here. See Glen 1983: 325–7, and the headnote to 'Michael' (pp. 341–2).

> 'These tourists, Heaven preserve us! needs must live
> A profitable life: some glance along,
> Rapid and gay, as if the earth were air,
> And they were butterflies to wheel about
> Long as their summer lasted: some, as wise,   5

Title. 'This poem was intended to be the concluding poem of a series of pastorals, the scene of which was laid among the mountains of Cumberland and Westmoreland. I mention this to apologize for the abruptness with which the poem begins' (Wordsworth's note). On the planned series of pastorals, see Dings 1973: 25–45.
1. tourists: the first occurrence known to the *OED* is 1780 (applied, incidentally, to Lake District visitors).
2. glance: see note to the 'Yew-tree lines', l. 26 (p. 113).

226

The Brothers

Upon the forehead of a jutting crag
Sit perched, with book and pencil on their knee,
And look and scribble, scribble on and look,
Until a man might travel twelve stout miles,
Or reap an acre of his neighbour's corn.   10
But, for that moping son of idleness,
Why can he tarry *yonder?* – In our churchyard
Is neither epitaph nor monument,
Tombstone nor name – only the turf we tread,
And a few natural graves.' To Jane, his wife,   15
Thus spake the homely priest of Ennerdale.
It was a July evening, and he sate
Upon the long stone-seat beneath the eaves
Of his old cottage, as it chanced, that day,
Employed in winter's work. Upon the stone   20
His wife sate near him, teasing matted wool,
While, from the twin cards toothed with glittering wire,
He fed the spindle of his youngest child,
Who turned her large round wheel in the open air
With back and forward steps. Towards the field   25
In which the parish chapel stood alone,
Girt round with a bare ring of mossy wall,
While half an hour went by, the priest had sent
Many a long look of wonder, and at last,
Risen from his seat, beside the snow-white ridge   30
Of carded wool which the old man had piled
He laid his implements with gentle care,
Each in the other locked; and, down the path
Which from his cottage to the churchyard led,
He took his way, impatient to accost   35
The stranger, whom he saw still lingering there.

'Twas one well known to him in former days,
A shepherd-lad, who ere his thirteenth year
Had changed his calling, with the mariners

---

9. *stout miles*: a reference to the old 'long mile' of 2428 yards, a measure that survived in the north of England in the eighteenth century alongside the official mile of 1760 yards.
10. The vicar's obsession with 'profitable' work leads him greatly to exaggerate how much reaping could feasibly be done while the imaginary tourist scribbles in his notebook, unless the latter scribbles through at least two whole days.
15. *natural*: consisting entirely of natural materials.
32–3. *he laid ... locked*: presumably a token of the vicar's prudent, workmanlike character.

A fellow-mariner, and so had fared   40
Through twenty seasons; but he had been reared
Among the mountains, and he in his heart
Was half a shepherd on the stormy seas.
Oft in the piping shrouds had Leonard heard
The tones of waterfalls, and inland sounds   45
Of caves and trees – and, when the regular wind
Between the tropics filled the steady sail,
And blew with the same breath through days and weeks,
Lengthening invisibly its weary line
Along the cloudless main, he, in those hours   50
Of tiresome indolence, would often hang
Over the vessel's side, and gaze and gaze,
And, while the broad green wave and sparkling foam
Flashed round him images and hues, that wrought
In union with the employment of his heart,   55
He, thus by feverish passion overcome,
Even with the organs of his bodily eye,
Below him, in the bosom of the deep,
Saw mountains, saw the forms of sheep that grazed
On verdant hills, with dwellings among trees,   60
And shepherds clad in the same country grey
Which he himself had worn.
                    And now at length
From perils manifold, with some small wealth
Acquired by traffic in the Indian Isles,
To his paternal home he is returned,   65
With a determined purpose to resume
The life which he lived there; both for the sake
Of many darling pleasures, and the love
Which to an only brother he has borne
In all his hardships, since that happy time   70
When, whether it blew foul or fair, they two
Were brother shepherds on their native hills.

44–6. Oft . . . trees: the sense would seem to be that, among the ship's
rigging ('shrouds'), the noises of sea and wind sound to Leonard like
waterfalls, etc. And the noise of the rigging itself probably recalled a sound
especially appropriate for a shepherd, that of piping (for young shepherds in
the Lake District playing pipes, see 'The Idle Shepherd-Boys', l. 16, p. 263).
50–62. 'This description of the Calenture is sketched from an imperfect
recollection of an admirable one in prose, by Mr Gilbert, author of "The
Hurricane" ' (Wordsworth's note). The calenture is a delirious disease
afflicting sailors, characterized by hallucinations of the sort described here.
Gilbert's description seems not to have survived. Perhaps it was among the
papers he left with Southey, who writes in May 1797 of their 'bottomless
profundity' (Cottle 1847: 213).

– They were the last of all their race: and now
When Leonard had approached his home, his heart
Failed in him; and, not venturing to inquire   75
Tidings of one whom he so dearly loved,
Towards the churchyard he had turned aside,
That, as he knew in what particular spot
His family were laid, he thence might learn
If still his brother lived, or to the file   80
Another grave was added. – He had found
Another grave, near which a full half-hour
He had remained; but, as he gazed, there grew
Such a confusion in his memory,
That he began to doubt, and he had hopes   85
That he had seen this heap of turf before,
That it was not another grave, but one
He had forgotten. He had lost his path,
As up the vale he came that afternoon,
Through fields which once had been well known to him.   90
And oh! what joy the recollection now
Sent to his heart! He lifted up his eyes,
And looking round he thought that he perceived
Strange alteration wrought on every side
Among the woods and fields, and that the rocks,   95
And the eternal hills, themselves were changed.

By this the priest, who down the field had come
Unseen by Leonard, at the churchyard gate
Stopped short, and thence, at leisure, limb by limb
He scanned him with a gay complacency.   100
Aye, thought the Vicar, smiling to himself,
'Tis one of those who needs must leave the path
Of the world's business to go wild alone;
His arms have a perpetual holiday;
The happy man will creep about the fields   105
Following his fancies by the hour, to bring
Tears down his cheeks, or solitary smiles
Into his face, until the setting sun
Write Fool upon his forehead. Planted thus
Beneath a shed that overarched the gate   110
Of this rude churchyard, till the stars appeared

73. *race*: family.
102–3. The vicar characteristically thinks of profitable work in terms of a rural task (while Leonard has in fact already made enough money by trade to maintain himself for life).
109–12. *Planted . . . himself*: the vicar is not incapable of wasting valuable time on his own brand of meditation.

The good man might have communed with himself,
But that the stranger, who had left the grave,
Approached; he recognized the priest at once,
And, after greetings interchanged, and given   115
By Leonard to the Vicar as to one
Unknown to him, this dialogue ensued.

Leonard
You live, Sir, in these dales, a quiet life:
Your years make up one peaceful family;
And who would grieve and fret, if, welcome come   120
And welcome gone, they are so like each other,
They cannot be remembered? Scarce a funeral
Comes to this churchyard once in eighteen months;
And yet, some changes must take place among you:
And you, who dwell here, even among these rocks   125
Can trace the finger of mortality,
And see, that with our threescore years and ten
We are not all that perish. – I remember,
For many years ago I passed this road,
There was a footway all along the fields   130
By the brook-side – 'tis gone – and that dark cleft!
To me it does not seem to wear the face
Which then it had.

Priest
                    Why, Sir, for aught I know,
That chasm is much the same –

Leonard
                    But, surely, yonder –

Priest
Aye, there, indeed, your memory is a friend   135
That does not play you false – On that tall pike
(It is the loneliest place of all these hills)
There were two springs which bubbled side by side,

136–43. On that . . . still: the story of the two springs is made unmistakably
emblematic of Leonard and James ('brother fountains . . . one is dead') but
is not functional in the narrative. Perhaps it is thought of as finding its way
into whatever legend of Leonard and James takes root in the community.
138. 'The impressive circumstance here described, actually took place
some years ago in this country, upon an eminence called Kidstow Pike, one
of the highest of the mountains that surround Haweswater. The summit of
the Pike was stricken by lightning; and every trace of one of the fountains
disappeared, while the other continued to flow as before' (Wordsworth's
note).

As if they had been made that they might be
Companions for each other: ten years back,   140
Close to those brother fountains, the huge crag
Was rent by lightning – one is dead and gone,
The other, left behind, is flowing still. –
For accidents and changes such as these,
Why, we have store of them! a water-spout   145
Will bring down half a mountain; what a feast
For folks that wander up and down like you
To see an acre's breadth of that wide cliff
One roaring cataract! – a sharp May storm
Will come with loads of January snow,   150
And in one night send twenty score of sheep
To feed the ravens; or a shepherd dies
By some untoward death among the rocks;
The ice breaks up and sweeps away a bridge –
A wood is felled: – and then for our own homes!   155
A child is born or christened, a field ploughed,
A daughter sent to service, a web spun,
The old house-clock is decked with a new face;
And hence, so far from wanting facts or dates
To chronicle the time, we all have here   160
A pair of diaries, one serving, Sir,
For the whole dale, and one for each fireside –
Yours was a stranger's judgment: for historians,
Commend me to these valleys.

Leonard
                              Yet your churchyard
Seems, if such freedom may be used with you,   165
To say that you are heedless of the past.
An orphan could not find his mother's grave:
Here's neither head- nor foot-stone, plate of brass,
Cross-bones or skull, type of our earthly state
Or emblem of our hopes: the dead man's home   170
Is but a fellow to that pasture-field.

---

157. a web spun: enough wool spun to make one piece of woven work.
163. Yours ... judgment: such is the vicar's animus towards this 'tourist'
that he accuses him of ignorantly making a judgement which the vicar has
actually shown more sign of making (see ll. 133–4) than Leonard (whose
point, at ll. 124–8, is now complacently claimed by the vicar).
168–70. Here's neither ... hopes: the apposition between the grave
decorations and their meanings is presumably to be read in reverse, the
cross-bones or skull being the 'type of our earthly state' and the gravestones
or brass plate carrying references to the afterlife.

Priest

Why, there, Sir, is a thought that's new to me.
The stone-cutters, 'tis true, might beg their bread
If every English churchyard were like ours:
Yet your conclusion wanders from the truth.   175
We have no need of names and epitaphs;
We talk about the dead by our firesides,
And then, for our immortal part! *we* want
No symbols, Sir, to tell us that plain tale;
The thought of death sits easy on the man   180
Who has been born and dies among the mountains.

Leonard

Your dalesmen, then, do in each other's thoughts
Possess a kind of second life: no doubt
You, Sir, could help me to the history
Of half these graves?

Priest

　　　　　　　For eight-score winters past,   185
With what I've witnessed, and with what I've heard,
Perhaps I might; and, on a winter's evening,
If you were seated at my chimney's nook,
By turning o'er these hillocks one by one
We two could travel, Sir, through a strange round,   190
Yet all in the broad highway of the world.
Now there's a grave – your foot is half upon it,
It looks just like the rest; and yet that man
Died broken-hearted.

Leonard

　　　　　　　'Tis a common case.
We'll take another: who is he that lies   195
Beneath yon ridge, the last of those three graves?
It touches on that piece of native rock
Left in the churchyard wall.

---

172. Plainly a piece of mock respectfulness to the 'tourist', in view of ll. 13–15.
180. 'There is not any thing more worthy of remark in the manners of the inhabitants of these mountains, than the tranquillity, I might say indifference, with which they think and talk upon the subject of death. Some of the country churchyards, as here described, do not contain a single tomb-stone, and most of them have a very small number' (Wordsworth's note).
188. chimney's nook: has a Northern and Scottish dialectal flavour.

Priest
                    That's Walter Ewbank.
He had as white a head and fresh a cheek
As ever were produced by youth and age   200
Engendering in the blood of hale fourscore.
For five long generations had the heart
Of Walter's forefathers o'erflowed the bounds
Of their inheritance, that single cottage –
You see it yonder! – and those few green fields.   205
They toiled and wrought, and still, from sire to son,
Each struggled, and each yielded as before
A little – yet a little – and old Walter,
They left to him the family heart, and land
With other burthens than the crop it bore.   210
Year after year the old man still kept up
A cheerful mind, and buffeted with bond,
Interest and mortgages; at last he sank,
And went into his grave before his time.
Poor Walter! whether it was care that spurred him   215
God only knows, but to the very last
He had the lightest foot in Ennerdale:
His pace was never that of an old man:
I almost see him tripping down the path
With his two grandsons after him – but you,   220
Unless our landlord be your host tonight,
Have far to travel, and in these rough paths
Even in the longest day of midsummer –

Leonard
But these two orphans!

Priest
                    Orphans! Such they were –
Yet not while Walter lived – for, though their parents   225
Lay buried side by side as now they lie,
The old man was a father to the boys,
Two fathers in one father: and if tears,
Shed when he talked of them where they were not,
And hauntings from the infirmity of love,   230
Are aught of what makes up a mother's heart,

201. *Engendering*: coupling; probably an obsolescent sense in Wordsworth's day.
209–10. *land . . . burthens*: the land has been used as security for loans.
218. *pace*: probably in the sense of 'gait'.
230. *hauntings*: apprehensions (compare 'The Oak and the Broom', l. 72, p. 251, and *Prelude* V, 56 [1850 text]).

This old man in the day of his old age
Was half a mother to them. – If you weep, Sir,
To hear a stranger talking about strangers,
Heaven bless you when you are among your kindred!   235
Aye. You may turn that way – it is a grave
Which will bear looking at.

                    Leonard
                    These boys – I hope
They loved this good old man? –

                    Priest
                    They did – and truly:
But that was what we almost overlooked,
They were such darlings of each other. For   240
Though from their cradles they had lived with Walter,
The only kinsman near them in the house,
Yet he being old, they had much love to spare,
And it all went into each other's hearts.
Leonard, the elder by just eighteen months,   245
Was two years taller: 'twas a joy to see,
To hear, to meet them! from their house the school
Was distant three short miles – and in the time
Of storm and thaw, when every water-course
And unbridged stream, such as you may have noticed   250
Crossing our roads at every hundred steps,
Was swoln into a noisy rivulet,
Would Leonard then, when elder boys perhaps
Remained at home, go staggering through the fords
Bearing his brother on his back. I've seen him,   255
On windy days, in one of those stray brooks,
Aye, more than once I've seen him mid-leg deep,
Their two books lying both on a dry stone
Upon the hither side: and once I said,
As I remember, looking round these rocks   260
And hills on which we all of us were born,
That God who made the great book of the world
Would bless such piety –

263. piety: affectionate loyalty to kin.

Leonard
It may be then –

Priest
Never did worthier lads break English bread!
The finest Sunday that the autumn saw,   265
With all its mealy clusters of ripe nuts,
Could never keep these boys away from church,
Or tempt them to an hour of sabbath breach.
Leonard and James! I warrant, every corner
Among these rocks, and every hollow place   270
Where foot could come, to one or both of them
Was known as well as to the flowers that grow there.
Like roe-bucks they went bounding o'er the hills:
They played like two young ravens on the crags:
Then they could write, aye and speak too, as well   275
As many of their betters – and for Leonard!
The very night before he went away,
In my own house I put into his hand
A Bible, and I'd wager twenty pounds,
That, if he is alive, he has it yet.   280

Leonard
It seems, these brothers have not lived to be
A comfort to each other –

Priest
                         That they might
Live to that end, is what both old and young
In this our valley all of us have wished,
And what, for my part, I have often prayed: 285
But Leonard –

Leonard
         Then James still is left among you?

Priest
'Tis of the elder brother I am speaking:
They had an uncle, he was at that time
A thriving man, and trafficked on the seas:
And, but for this same uncle, to this hour   290
Leonard had never handled rope or shroud.

266. *mealy*: it is not clear which of several senses is intended here. Perhaps,
given 'Nutting', l. 19 (p. 297), the word has its Northumberland dialect
meaning of meal-coloured, i.e. pale fawn.
279–80. *I'd wager . . . yet*: the wager is not decided, thus leaving a challenge
to the reader to make a choice on the strength of his or her sense of the
characters.

For the boy loved the life which we lead here;
And, though a very stripling, twelve years old,
His soul was knit to this his native soil.
But, as I said, old Walter was too weak   295
To strive with such a torrent; when he died,
The estate and house were sold, and all their sheep,
A pretty flock, and which, for aught I know,
Had clothed the Ewbanks for a thousand years.
Well – all was gone, and they were destitute.   300
And Leonard, chiefly for his brother's sake,
Resolved to try his fortune on the seas.
'Tis now twelve years since we had tidings from him.
If there was one among us who had heard
That Leonard Ewbank was come home again,   305
From the great Gavel, down by Leeza's banks,
And down the Enna, far as Egremont,
The day would be a very festival,
And those two bells of ours, which there you see
Hanging in the open air – but, O good Sir!   310
This is sad talk – they'll never sound for him
Living or dead. – When last we heard of him
He was in slavery among the Moors
Upon the Barbary Coast. – 'Twas not a little
That would bring down his spirit, and, no doubt, 315
Before it ended in his death, the lad
Was sadly crossed – Poor Leonard! when we parted

300. Presumably the proceeds went to pay off the ancestral debts.
303. As one of the memorable coincidences attending the brothers' story, it is also twelve years since James's death (l. 353); but see note to ll. 391–2.
306. 'The Great Gavel, so called, I imagine, from its resemblance to the Gable end of a house, is one of the highest of the Cumberland mountains. It stands at the head of the several vales of Ennerdale, Wastdale, and Borrowdale. The Leeza is a river which flows into the Lake of Ennerdale: on issuing from the lake, it changes its name, and is called the End, Eyne, or Enna. It falls into the sea a little below Egremont' (Wordsworth's note).
314–15. 'Twas not . . . spirit: opens an important theme in the presentation of Leonard, with the suggestion that he has not inherited the 'family heart' which kept his grandfather Walter struggling cheerfully against insurmountable difficulties (ll. 202–13) – though his less ebullient heart has not 'o'erflowed the bounds' of his resources like his ancestors. Leonard has perhaps more in common with the unnamed man of l. 194 who 'died broken-hearted' (he calls it 'a common case'). His emotional distress is too great to allow him to settle in the valley again (ll. 417–22) and it is, indeed, his 'weakness of heart' which has brought about the fundamental rhetorical situation of the poem (ll. 428–9). There are several important points of comparison with 'Michael'. See also Wilson letter, p. 50.

He took me by the hand and said to me,
If ever the day came when he was rich,
He would return, and on his father's land   320
He would grow old among us.

                    Leonard
                        If that day
Should come, 'twould needs be a glad day for him;
He would himself, no doubt, be happy then
As any that should meet him –

                    Priest
                    Happy! Sir –

                    Leonard
You said his kindred all were in their graves,   325
And that he had one brother –

                    Priest
                        That is but
A fellow tale of sorrow. From his youth
James, though not sickly, yet was delicate;
And Leonard being always by his side
Had done so many offices about him,   330
That, though he was not of a timid nature,
Yet still the spirit of a mountain boy
In him was somewhat checked; and, when his brother
Was gone to sea and he was left alone,
The little colour that he had was soon   335
Stolen from his cheek, he drooped, and pined and pined
–

                    Leonard
But these are all the graves of full-grown men!

                    Priest
Aye, Sir, that passed away: we took him to us.
He was the child of all the dale – he lived
Three months with one, and six months with another;   340
And wanted neither food, nor clothes, nor love,
And many, many happy days were his.
But, whether blithe or sad, 'tis my belief
His absent brother still was at his heart.
And, when he lived beneath our roof, we found   345
(A practice till this time unknown to him)
That often, rising from his bed at night,
He in his sleep would walk about, and sleeping
He sought his brother Leonard. – You are moved!
Forgive me, Sir: before I spoke to you,   350
I judged you most unkindly.

> *Leonard*
>> But this youth,
> How did he die at last?

> *Priest*
>> One sweet May morning,
> It will be twelve years since, when spring returns,
> He had gone forth among the new-dropped lambs,
> With two or three companions whom it chanced   355
> Some further business summoned to a house
> Which stands at the dale-head. James, tired perhaps,
> Or from some other cause, remained behind.
> You see yon precipice – it almost looks
> Like some vast building made of many crags;   360
> And in the midst is one particular rock
> That rises like a column from the vale,
> Whence by our shepherds it is called the Pillar.
> James pointed to its summit, over which
> They all had purposed to return together,   365
> And told them that he there would wait for them:
> They parted, and his comrades passed that way
> Some two hours after, but they did not find him
> Upon the Pillar – at the appointed place.
> Of this they took no heed: but one of them,   370
> Going by chance, at night, into the house
> Which at that time was James's home, there learned
> That nobody had seen him all that day:
> The morning came, and still, he was unheard of:
> The neighbours were alarmed, and to the brook   375
> Some went, and some towards the lake: ere noon
> They found him at the foot of that same rock –
> Dead, and with mangled limbs. The third day after
> I buried him, poor lad, and there he lies.

> *Leonard*
> And that then *is* his grave? – Before his death   380
> You said that he saw many happy years?

> *Priest*
> Aye, that he did –

> *Leonard*
>> And all went well with him –

> *Priest*
> If he had one, the lad had twenty homes.

---

378. *third day*: in its echo of Christ's resurrection, part of the priest's 'typological idiom' according to Brantley (1975: 162).

Leonard

And you believe, then, that his mind was easy –

Priest

Yes, long before he died, he found that time   385
Is a true friend to sorrow; and unless
His thoughts were turned on Leonard's luckless
     fortune,
He talked about him with a cheerful love.

Leonard

He could not come to an unhallowed end!

Priest

Nay, God forbid! You recollect I mentioned   390
A habit which disquietude and grief
Had brought upon him; and we all conjectured
That, as the day was warm, he had lain down
Upon the grass, and, waiting for his comrades,
He there had fallen asleep; that in his sleep   395
He to the margin of the precipice
Had walked, and from the summit had fallen headlong.
And so no doubt he perished: at the time,
We guess, that in his hands he must have had
His shepherd's staff; for midway in the cliff   400
It had been caught; and there for many years
It hung – and mouldered there.
                    The priest here ended –
The stranger would have thanked him, but he felt
Tears rushing in. Both left the spot in silence;
And Leonard, when they reached the churchyard gate,   405
As the priest lifted up the latch, turned round,
And, looking at the grave, he said, 'My brother.'
The Vicar did not hear the words: and now,
Pointing towards the cottage, he entreated
That Leonard would partake his homely fare: 410

---

389. *come to an unhallowed end*: commit suicide.
391–2. *A habit . . . upon him*: it is perhaps not consoling to Leonard to hear
that James died as he did, since in his sleepwalking James seeks Leonard
(l. 349), and the news of Leonard's disaster is recent (ll. 303, 313–14).
407. There is a feeling that Leonard's naming of the grave adds to and
perhaps completes the communal knowledge which serves instead of
epitaphs in the village graveyard; the action is not communal, however,
being performed in a privacy that excludes even the local priest (and with a
poignant enforced perfunctoriness).

The other thanked him with a fervent voice,
But added, that, the evening being calm,
He would pursue his journey. So they parted.

It was not long ere Leonard reached a grove
That overhung the road: he there stopped short,   415
And, sitting down beneath the trees, reviewed
All that the priest had said: his early years
Were with him in his heart: his cherished hopes,
And thoughts which had been his an hour before,
All pressed on him with such a weight, that now,   420
This vale, where he had been so happy, seemed
A place in which he could not bear to live:
So he relinquished all his purposes.
He travelled on to Egremont: and thence,
That night, he wrote a letter to the priest   425
Reminding him of what had passed between them,
And adding, with a hope to be forgiven,
That it was from the weakness of his heart
He had not dared to tell him who he was.

This done, he went on shipboard, and is now   430
A seaman, a grey-headed mariner.

Ellen Irwin
or the Braes of Kirtle

Probably composed in the winter of 1798/9, but perhaps as late as the summer of 1800. Minor revisions only, but reclassified in the collected works in 1827: see p. 361. See the Fenwick note (p. 370) on Wordsworth's various devices for avoiding the 'presumptuousness' of treating this subject in traditional ballad fashion. (Wordsworth stressed again the function of the 'classical image' at ll. 3–4 in this respect in his Fenwick note to the later 'Ode to Lycoris': 'in the poem of Ellen Irwin I was desirous of throwing the reader at once out of the old ballad, so as, if possible, to preclude a comparison between that mode of dealing with the subject and the mode I meant to adopt'). Wordsworth is right to say that the insertion of unrhymed lines in the stanza-form of a literary ballad, Bürger's 'Lenore', produces a stanza 'quite new in our language', but the experiment is in keeping with Wordsworth's hybridizing of rhymed and unrhymed forms in several other poems in *Lyrical Ballads* (the closest comparison being 'Simon Lee', pp. 147–51); moreover, while the whole stanza may tend to 'preclude . . . comparison' with the ballad the first four lines form a classic ballad verse. There is a systematic use of di- and even trisyllabic rhymes at lines 2, 4, 7 and 8 of each stanza, part of the debt to Bürger's poem, where Wordsworth had found in the 'concluding double rhymes . . . a delicious and *pathetic* effect' (De Selincourt and Shaver 1967: 234).

Another important aspect of Wordsworth's attempt not to infringe the territory of authentic ballad is that he has, contrary to his usual tendency, pushed his poem towards a narrative mode and away from a dramatic (the typical Wordsworthian situation of an 'I' interpreting the traces of human suffering for an audience is only perfunctorily present in the last stanza). The traditional version of the story, the ballad 'Fair Helen', is imagined as the utterance of Helen's sweetheart, longing to be at her grave. It is so allusive as a result, in fact, that the underlying story cannot be gathered from the ballad alone, and in this sense Wordsworth's source must rather be one of the available prose accounts of Ellen of Kirkonnel's history; the closest in its details (though there are some puzzling differences in the personal names) seems to be that provided in Thomas Pennant, *A Tour in Scotland*, 1790, II, 101, also reprinted in Joseph Ritson, *Scottish Songs*, 1794, I, 145–6.

> Fair Ellen Irwin, when she sate
> Upon the Braes of Kirtle,
> Was lovely as a Grecian maid
> Adorned with wreaths of myrtle.

Title. 'The Kirtle is a river in the southern part of Scotland, on the banks of which the events here related took place' (Wordsworth's note).
4. *wreaths of myrtle*: in classical lore the shrub, sacred to Venus, is associated with the consummation of love by a woman, especially in marriage. Ellen is envisaged as a bride-to-be.

Young Adam Bruce beside her lay; 5
And there did they beguile the day
With love and gentle speeches,
Beneath the budding beeches.

From many knights and many squires
The Bruce had been selected; 10
And Gordon, fairest of them all,
By Ellen was rejected.
Sad tidings to that noble youth!
For it may be proclaimed with truth,
If Bruce had loved sincerely, 15
The Gordon loves as dearly.

But what is Gordon's beauteous face?
And what are Gordon's crosses
To them who sit by Kirtle's Braes
Upon the verdant mosses? 20
Alas that ever he was born!
The Gordon, couched behind a thorn,
Sees them and their caressing,
Beholds them blest and blessing.

Proud Gordon cannot bear the thoughts 25
That through his brain are travelling,
And, starting up, to Bruce's heart
He launched a deadly javelin!
Fair Ellen saw it when it came,
And, stepping forth to meet the same, 30
Did with her body cover
The youth her chosen lover.

And, falling into Bruce's arms,
Thus died the beauteous Ellen,
Thus from the heart of her true-love 35
The mortal spear repelling.
And Bruce, as soon as he had slain
The Gordon, sailed away to Spain;
And fought with rage incessant
Against the Moorish crescent. 40

---

18. crosses: slights which he has endured.
38–40. There is perhaps a reminiscence here, supplementing Pennant, of a
literary ballad on the Irwin theme called 'The Fatal Feud' (ll. 253–6): 'At
last to Spain he bent his course / Where many a gallant Lord, / Against the
Moors employed his force, / And fell beneath the sword' (see John Tait,
Poetical Legends, 1776).

But many days, and many months,
And many years ensuing,
This wretched knight did vainly seek
The death that he was wooing:
And coming back across the wave,   45
Without a groan on Ellen's grave
His body he extended,
And there his sorrow ended.

Now ye, who willingly have heard
The tale I have been telling,   50
May in Kirkonnel churchyard view
The grave of lovely Ellen.
By Ellen's side the Bruce is laid;
And, for the stone upon his head,
May no rude hand deface it,   55
And its forlorn HIC JACET!

56. *HIC JACET*: the formal beginning of Latin epitaphs – 'here lies . . .'.

'Strange fits of passion I have known . . .'

Probably composed in the last months of 1798. Almost unchanged until 1836, when there are several rephrasings. This poem is customarily linked with the two that follow it because of the closeness of date of composition, the reference to 'Lucy' in the first and second poems, the apparent continuation of the subject of her death in the third, and the close similarities of form (including the absence of titles). The death of 'Lucy' is also the subject of a fourth untitled poem in *LB* ('Three years she grew . . .', pp. 299–300), probably composed, however, a few months later and using a different stanza. Interestingly, in the arrangement of his poems that he adopted from 1815 Wordsworth kept the first two of the trio together but placed the third, alongside 'Three years she grew . . .', in a quite separate part of the collection (see p. 362). And the first two were now accompanied by a poem with obvious affinities of form and content – 'I travelled among unknown men . . .' – which Wordsworth had thought of inserting before 'A slumber did my spirit seal . . .' in 1802 (Hale White 1897: 45). All in all the facts suggest that the four *LB* poems are indeed linked but in varying degrees (the case against the well-formed 'Lucy cycle' of traditional criticism is vigorously put by Sykes Davies 1965). This would imply that 'she'/'Lucy' are conceived as the same individual, but whether this individual is real or imaginary, and whether she is the same as certain other 'Lucys' in Wordsworth (the only relevant poem in *LB* is 'Lucy Gray', pp. 256–8), are undecided and probably undecidable questions. No real progress has been made on these matters since Hartman 1934, where various views are conveniently summarized. It may be that in the Lucy figure we are confronted with an idiosyncratically Wordsworthian kind of fluid lyrical characterization, comparable to the appearances of 'Matthew' in several of the *LB* poems (some of which are printed in sequence), or even of 'Emma'. Recurrent features of this strange creation would seem to be that she is both child and woman, and deceased. One may go further, and be impressed by Wordsworth's unusual silence on the poems to Isabella Fenwick, his disinclination to give them titles, and the 'radical ambiguity about the status of the object of poetic representation' in the texts themselves (Ferguson 1973; also Bateson 1953), to the point of doubting whether a human being is in any sense the focus of these lyrics.

> Strange fits of passion I have known:
> And I will dare to tell,
> But in the lover's ear alone,
> What once to me befell.
>
> When she I loved, was strong and gay   5
> And like a rose in June,
> I to her cottage bent my way,
> Beneath the evening moon.
>
> Upon the moon I fixed my eye,
> All over the wide lea: 10
> My horse trudged on – and we drew nigh
> Those paths so dear to me.

243

And now we reached the orchard plot;
And, as we climbed the hill,
Towards the roof of Lucy's cot
The moon descended still.

In one of those sweet dreams I slept,
Kind Nature's gentlest boon!
And, all the while, my eyes I kept
On the descending moon.

My horse moved on; hoof after hoof
He raised, and never stopped:
When down behind the cottage roof
At once the planet dropped.

What fond and wayward thoughts will slide
Into a lover's head –
'Oh mercy!' to myself I cried,
'If Lucy should be dead!'

25. fond: foolish.

'She dwelt among th'untrodden ways . . .'

Probably composed in the last months of 1798; virtually unaltered. For general comment, see headnote to 'Strange fits of passion I have known . . .'.

> She dwelt among th'untrodden ways
> Beside the springs of Dove,
> A maid whom there were none to praise,
> And very few to love.
>
> A violet by a mossy stone   5
> Half-hidden from the eye! –
> Fair as a star, when only one
> Is shining in the sky.
>
> She lived unknown, and few could know
> When Lucy ceased to be;   10
> But she is in her grave, and oh!
> The difference to me.

1–2. 'The plural "springs", together with "ways", makes one feel that Lucy does not live in one place, but is part of a landscape' (Cox 1963).

1–6. Compare William Habington, 'The Description of Castara', 1634, ll. 1–4: 'Like the violet which alone / Prospers in some happy shade: / My Castara lives unknown, / To no looser eye betrayed.' A variant of Burns's 'Oh were my love . . .' has the lines, 'O were my love yon vi'let sweet / That peeps frae 'neath the hawthorn spray' (see Noyes 1944). The unseen flower as the type of uncelebrated worth recalls Gray's 'Elegy written in a Country Churchyard', ll. 55–6.

1. untrodden: seldom frequented (i.e. not marked by foot traffic, rather than never walked on). The familiar metaphor of the 'trodden path' is reversed and its literal content restored to it.

2. Dove: several rivers in northern locations, including Northumberland, bear the name. Harris (1935) even proposes a Welsh allusion here, to the Dovey. For a river Dove treated as the quintessence of rural seclusion see Charles Cotton, 'The Retirement' (1676), l. 34.

3. praise: praise publicly, celebrate the fame of (as in Gray's 'Elegy written in a Country Churchyard', l. 40).

5–8. Several critics have detected a tension between the significance of the violet image and that of the star image; but a star in a twilight sky may also be relatively invisible, or 'half-hidden', and in this sense the two images can reinforce one another.

6. eye!: Helms (1979) compares this use of the exclamation mark in an apparently non-exclamatory context to Wordsworth's sonnet 'Composed upon Westminster Bridge', ll. 11, 13–14: all indicate the hidden 'intensity of an apparent peacefulness'.

7. only one: Hartman (1975b: 159) points out that this implies that the star is Venus, or love's star. In its morning appearance the planet is called 'Lucifer'.

'A slumber did my spirit seal . . .'

Probably composed in the last months of 1798; not altered. See headnote to 'Strange fits of passion I have known . . .'.

> A slumber did my spirit seal;
> I had no human fears:
> She seemed a thing that could not feel
> The touch of earthly years.
>
> No motion has she now, no force;   5
> She neither hears nor sees,
> Rolled round in earth's diurnal course
> With rocks and stones and trees!

1–4. Glen (1983: 287–8) sees the stanza as the lover's awakening to his failure to grasp the fact of the loved one's mortality, 'which has been developing throughout the sequence'. But as Sykes Davies (1965) observes, 'Strange fits of passion . . .' on the face of it embodies exactly the opposite attitude to the one recorded in this stanza.
1. There is 'slumber' which 'seals' in Erasmus Darwin, 1791, II, i, 274, and ii, 286.
3. She: Sykes Davies (1965), following Crawfurd (1896), argues that 'she' refers back to 'my spirit' and that the lyric is not a 'Lucy' poem at all but springs from an experience of Wordsworth's such as recorded at *Prelude* I, 452–89 (1805 text: the skating episode). Significant manuscript evidence has, however, been adduced against this reading, of Wordsworth toying with the idea of placing the poem in the 'Epitaphs and Elegiac Pieces' section of the 1815 *Collected Poems* (Ruoff 1966).
5–8. Durrant (1969), observing that 'Lucy' does not lack motion in a mechanical sense but only the motion of animated existence (which in pre-modern physics was thought to underlie all movement in the universe), judges that the poem 'is also about the difficulty of accepting, in a universe of Newtonian mechanics, the classical doctrine of the immortality of the soul'. 'Motion' and 'force' are essential terms in the vocabulary of Newtonian physics. 'Diurnal' is used on three occasions in *Paradise Lost* to refer to the admittedly hypothetical daily rotation of heavenly bodies about the fixed Earth, such as pre-Copernican cosmology requires; see especially IV, 592–5: 'whether the bright orb, / Incredible how swift, had thither rolled / Diurnal, or this less voluble earth / By shorter flight to the east, had left him'.

The Waterfall and the Eglantine

Probably composed in the first half of 1800. Minor subsequent revisions.
The Fenwick note (p. 380), which needs to be read in conjunction with that
for the following poem, implies the extent of the comic melodrama of the
last verse. In the latter the stanza form itself is comically curtailed, the rest
of the poem being another exploration of the rhymed ten-line stanza, like
'The Mad Mother' (pp. 173–6) but mixing quatrains and couplets in a
different pattern. The survival of the eglantine in reality, as recorded by the
Fenwick note, furnished also the possibility of a traditional tale, of the sort
attributed to Æsop, of arrogance discomfited, and a distinct effect in this
poem is of an Æsopian fable *not* reaching its expected end, while the next
poem, 'The Oak and the Broom', seems to some extent to have used the
same literal materials for just such a shapely fable. See the headnote to
latter on this and on the fable background to both texts. The result is a
poem given over entirely to the kind of animistic fantasy which elsewhere in
LB generally has a subordinate or questionable role, in a playful vein also
new to the collection. Erasmus Darwin's *The Loves of the Plants* (1789) may
have contributed to the apparent eroticism of ll. 3–4 (something of a parody
of 'Ellen Irwin', pp. 240–2) and 25–6. For an elaborate symbolic reading of
the poem, see Murray 1967: 127–8.

> 'Begone, thou fond presumptuous elf,'
> Exclaimed a thundering voice,
> 'Nor dare to thrust thy foolish self
> Between me and my choice!'
> A falling water swoln with snows   5
> Thus spake to a poor briar-rose,
> That, all bespattered with his foam,
> And dancing high, and dancing low,
> Was living, as a child might know,
> In an unhappy home.   10
>
> 'Dost thou presume my course to block?
> Off, off! or, puny thing!
> I'll hurl thee headlong with the rock
> To which thy fibres cling.'
> The flood was tyrannous and strong;   15
> The patient briar suffered long,
> Nor did he utter groan or sigh,
> Hoping the danger would be past;
> But seeing no relief, at last
> He ventured to reply.   20

---

5. water: in its sense here, of a small river, the word was probably already
becoming confined to Northern and Scottish dialectal use in Wordsworth's
day.

'Ah!' said the briar, 'blame me not;
Why should we dwell in strife?
We who in this, our natal spot,
Once lived a happy life!
You stirred me on my rocky bed –   25
What pleasure through my veins you spread!
The summer long from day to day
My leaves you freshened and bedewed;
Nor was it common gratitude
That did your cares repay.   30

'When spring came on with bud and bell,
Among these rocks did I
Before you hang my wreath, to tell
That gentle days were nigh!
And in the sultry summer hours   35
I sheltered you with leaves and flowers;
And in my leaves, now shed and gone,
The linnet lodged, and for us two
Chanted his pretty songs, when you
Had little voice or none.   40

'But now proud thoughts are in your breast –
What grief is mine you see.
Ah! would you think, even yet how blest
Together we might be!
Though of both leaf and flower bereft,   45
Some ornaments to me are left –
Rich store of scarlet hips is mine,
With which I in my humble way
Would deck you many a winter's day,
A happy eglantine!'   50

What more he said I cannot tell.
The stream came thundering down the dell,
And galloped loud and fast;
I listened, nor aught else could hear,
The briar quaked – and much I fear,   55
Those accents were his last.

52–3. Compare La Fontaine, 'Le Torrent et la rivière', ll. 1–4 (also a fable
involving a contrast between a small flow of water and a large impressive
one).
56. *accents*: a poeticism for spoken utterance, comically deployed.

The Oak and the Broom
A Pastoral

Probably composed in the first half of 1800. Numerous small changes for different editions. Evidently a companion to the preceding poem (as the shared stanza form emphasizes). It is identified as a 'pastoral' because the narrator is a shepherd, and the term is probably used with literary–historical connotations (see General Introduction, p. 12). In the Fenwick note (p. 377) Wordsworth does not (in contrast to the Fenwick note for 'The Waterfall and the Eglantine') claim to have observed a particular broom situated as the poem relates; indeed, he told Crabb Robinson in 1816 that the story 'proceeded from his beholding a rose in just such a situation as he described the broom to be in' (Morley 1938: 191). A *rose* and an oak would strongly recall the Æsop-based fable which is the major literary forebear of Wordsworth's poem, and it is likely that Wordsworth adapted the elements of a real experience so that the result would not appear to be a mere imitation of this model. (At the same time, ironically enough, the wild rose or 'eglantine' motif *was* used in the companion fable because of another real-life sighting – if the Fenwick note is accurate.) The elements of the classical tale of the large plant which is blown down while its smaller, more flexible companion survives become standardized in post-classical versions as oak and wild rose, most famously in La Fontaine's treatment. Spenser changes the basic plot of the tale considerably in the February eclogue of *The Shepheardes Calender*, but Wordsworth's 'pastoral' frame, the specification of a month (l. 15) and some details of his text (see footnotes) may be influenced by Spenser. In contrast to the preceding poem, he carries through the Æsopian instructive scheme to its conclusion; De Quincey even judged that the spirit of Wordsworth's fable was much more thoughtful than the mere 'levity' of La Fontaine (Masson 1889–90, III, 89–90). Though many natural elements (including rivers) appear in Æsopian fables in addition to animals, the outstandingly successful eighteenth-century English example of the genre, John Gay's *Fables* (1727, 1738), did not contain plant fables, while the Somerset poet John Langhorne specifically experimented with them (*The Fables of Flora*, 1771), as did Cowper occasionally (e.g. 'The Lily and the Rose'); these recent efforts may have had some influence on Wordsworth.

> His simple truths did Andrew glean
> Beside the babbling rills;
> A careful student he had been
> Among the woods and hills.
> One winter's night, when through the trees   5
> The wind was thundering, on his knees
> His youngest born did Andrew hold:
> And while the rest, a ruddy quire,
> Were seated round their blazing fire,
> This tale the shepherd told.   10

8. *quire*: choir, group.

I saw a crag, a lofty stone
As ever tempest beat!
Out of its head an oak had grown,
A broom out of its feet.
The time was March, a cheerful noon – 15
The thaw-wind with the breath of June
Breathed gently from the warm South-west;
When, in a voice sedate with age,
This oak, half giant and half sage,
His neighbour thus addressed: 20

'Eight weary weeks, through rock and clay,
Along this mountain's edge
The frost hath wrought both night and day,
Wedge driving after wedge.
Look up! and think, above your head 25
What trouble surely will be bred;
Last night I heard a crash – 'tis true,
The splinters took another road –
I see them yonder – what a load
For such a thing as you! 30

'You are preparing as before
To deck your slender shape;
And yet, just three years back – no more –
You had a strange escape.
Down from yon cliff a fragment broke, 35
It came, you know, with fire and smoke
And hitherward it bent its way.
This pond'rous block was caught by me,
And o'er your head, as you may see,
'Tis hanging to this day! 40

'The thing had better been asleep,
Whatever thing it were,
Or breeze, or bird, or dog, or sheep,
That first did plant you there.
For you and your green twigs decoy 45
The little witless shepherd-boy
To come and slumber in your bower;
And, trust me, on some sultry noon,
Both you and he, Heaven knows how soon!
Will perish in one hour. 50

---

11. There is no punctuation indicating Andrew's speech, and he is only very slightly developed as a narratorial figure.
45–7. Compare Spenser, *Shepheardes Calender*, 'February', ll. 119–20.

'From me this friendly warning take' –
The broom began to doze,
And thus to keep herself awake
Did gently interpose:
'My thanks for your discourse are due;   55
That it is true, and more than true,
I know, and I have known it long;
Frail is the bond, by which we hold
Our being, be we young or old,
Wise, foolish, weak or strong.   60

'Disasters, do the best we can,
Will reach both great and small;
And he is oft the wisest man,
Who is not wise at all.
For me, why should I wish to roam?   65
This spot is my paternal home,
It is my pleasant heritage;
My father many a happy year
Here spread his careless blossoms, here
Attained a good old age.   70

'Even such as his may be my lot.
What cause have I to haunt
My heart with terrors? Am I not
In truth a favoured plant!
The spring for me a garland weaves   75
Of yellow flowers and verdant leaves;
And, when the frost is in the sky,
My branches are so fresh and gay
That you might look at me and say,
This plant can never die.   80

'The butterfly, all green and gold,
To me hath often flown,
Here in my blossoms to behold
Wings lovely as his own.
When grass is chill with rain or dew,   85
Beneath my shade the mother ewe
Lies with her infant lamb; I see
The love they to each other make,
And the sweet joy, which they partake,
It is a joy to me.'   90

---

72. *haunt*: this reflexive use of the verb seems to be Wordsworth's coinage.
73–6. Am . . . leaves: compare Spenser, *Shep. Cal.*, 'February', ll. 165–7.

Her voice was blithe, her heart was light;
The broom might have pursued
Her speech, until the stars of night
Their journey had renewed.
But in the branches of the oak   95
Two ravens now began to croak
Their nuptial song, a gladsome air;
And to her own green bower the breeze
That instant brought two stripling bees
To feed and murmur there.   100

One night the wind came from the North
And blew a furious blast;
At break of day I ventured forth,
And near the cliff I passed.
The storm had fallen upon the oak   105
And struck him with a mighty stroke,
And whirled and whirled him far away;
And in one hospitable cleft
The little careless broom was left
To live for many a day.   110

96–7. Two ravens . . . song: the correction of a literary cliché about nature in
the manner of Coleridge's 'The Nightingale' (see pp. 152–6, and
Wordsworth's endorsement, p. 52) is here taken to a comic extreme; the
conventional associations of the raven – as heralds of misfortune – are even
further from happy eroticism than those of the nightingale. By a further
irony, the oak is indeed shortly to be visited by disaster.
101. In La Fontaine's 'La Chêne et le roseau' the wind comes from the
north (as does the wind which later damages the briar in Spenser's variant).

The Complaint of a Forsaken Indian Woman

Probably composed in the spring of 1798, and included in the first edition of *LB*. There were minor alterations at various dates, and the last stanza was dropped in 1815, to be restored in 1836. For the main source (to which Wordsworth draws attention in his headnote), see p. 385. Identical phrasing in Hearne and the headnote makes it virtually certain that Wordsworth had Hearne in front of him, at least when drafting the latter; he told Isabella Fenwick that he 'read Hearne's *Journey* with deep interest' at the time. See also Wordsworth's remarks on the psychological content of the poem in the Preface (ll. 185–8). The unusual stanza is the same as that of 'The Mad Mother' (pp. 173–6), except that there is no internal rhyme in this version, and the two poems are contemporary in their composition. Wordsworth evidently believed the stanza to be unique, since he took another poet's use of it to be a plagiarism (De Selincourt and Shaver 1967: 424–5). The two poems are similar in character (and they are classified together from 1815 – see pp. 361–2), but Wordsworth did not print them next to or even near each other in *LB*, and he claims a different psychological focus, on a different kind of mental 'flux and reflux', for each in the Preface. That the emphasis in 'The Complaint . . .' is on an individual who is deserted and almost dead still 'cleaving to life and society' makes it an especially stark treatment of terminal attrition; no sufferer in Wordsworth is represented as nearer to the end-point than the Indian woman. The poem springs from a vigorous eighteenth-century tradition of poems imitating the utterance, in impassioned situations, of individuals from exotic cultures (there are several other 'dying Indian' poems). But Wordsworth has pressed the genre (to which anyway the key was that 'the unfamiliar predicament serves to underline a recognizable humanity. . . . Humanity is viewed in a new light, but it remains human'; Jacobus 1976: 192–3) as far in the direction of the universal as possible; hence there are few specifically North American physical details and no 'Indian' vocabulary, and the woman's predicament is fundamentally due to causes that operate on all individuals, or in many social systems. Samuel Hearne, in Wordsworth's source (p. 385), stresses the intelligibility of the apparently cruel custom involved, and its compatibility with 'humanity and social feeling'.

When a Northern Indian, from sickness, is unable to continue his journey with his companions, he is left behind, covered over with deer-skins; and is supplied with water, food, and fuel, if the situation of the place will afford it. He is informed of the track which his companions intend to pursue, and if he is unable to follow, or overtake them, he perishes alone in the desert; unless he should have the good fortune to fall in with some other tribes of Indians. The females are equally, or still more, exposed to the same fate. See that very interesting work, Hearne's *Journey from Hudson's Bay to the Northern Ocean*. In the high Northern Latitudes, as the same writer informs us, when the Northern

Lights vary their position in the air, they make a rustling and a crackling noise. This circumstance is alluded to in the first stanza of the following poem.

(Wordsworth's note)

Before I see another day,
Oh let my body die away!
In sleep I heard the northern gleams;
The stars they were among my dreams;
In sleep did I behold the skies,　　　　　　　　　　5
I saw the crackling flashes drive;
And yet they are upon my eyes,
And yet I am alive.
Before I see another day,
Oh let my body die away!　　　　　　　　　　　　10

My fire is dead: it knew no pain;
Yet is it dead, and I remain.
All stiff with ice the ashes lie;
And they are dead, and I will die.
When I was well, I wished to live,　　　　　　　　15
For clothes, for warmth, for food, and fire;
But they to me no joy can give,
No pleasure now, and no desire.
Then here contented will I lie!
Alone I cannot fear to die.　　　　　　　　　　　20

Alas! you might have dragged me on
Another day, a single one!
Too soon despair o'er me prevailed;
Too soon my heartless spirit failed;
When you were gone my limbs were stronger;　　25
And oh how grievously I rue,
That, afterwards, a little longer,
My friends, I did not follow you!
For strong and without pain I lay,
My friends, when you were gone away.　　　　　30

My child! they gave thee to another,
A woman who was not thy mother.
When from my arms my babe they took,
On me how strangely did he look!
Through his whole body something ran,　　　　35

3–6. See Wordsworth's note. He is referring to Hearne (1795: 224).
24. *heartless*: timorous, disheartened.

A most strange something did I see –
As if he strove to be a man,
That he might pull the sledge for me.
And then he stretched his arms, how wild!
Oh mercy! like a little child.   40

My little joy! my little pride!
In two days more I must have died.
Then do not weep and grieve for me;
I feel I must have died with thee.
Oh wind, that o'er my head art flying   45
The way my friends their course did bend,
I should not feel the pain of dying,
Could I with thee a message send!
Too soon, my friends, you went away;
For I had many things to say.   50

I'll follow you across the snow;
You travel heavily and slow.
In spite of all my weary pain,
I'll look upon your tents again.
– My fire is dead, and snowy white   55
The water which beside it stood;
The wolf has come to me tonight,
And he has stolen away my food.
For ever left alone am I,
Then wherefore should I fear to die?   60

My journey will be shortly run,
I shall not see another sun;
I cannot lift my limbs to know
If they have any life or no.
My poor forsaken child! if I   65
For once could have thee close to me,
With happy heart I then should die,
And my last thoughts would happy be.
I feel my body die away,
I shall not see another day.   70

45–9. Probably a reversed echo of Cowper, 'Verses Supposed to be
Written by Alexander Selkirk', ll. 33–6, lines admired by Wordsworth and
quoted in the Appendix to *LB* (see p. 92).

Lucy Gray

Probably written in the winter of 1798–9. A few minor changes, and the introduction of a subtitle, 'Or, solitude', in 1815. See Fenwick note, p. 376, on the poem's origins and technique. Wordsworth is recorded as saying in a conversation in 1816 that 'he removed from his poem all that pertained to art ... it being his object to exhibit poetically entire *solitude*, his child as observing the day-*moon*, which no town or village girl would ever notice' (Morley 1938: 190). The poem may owe something to a popular lyric of 1794, Robert Anderson's 'Lucy Gray of Allendale'; compare in particular Wordsworth's first three stanzas and Anderson's first: 'Say, have you seen the blushing rose, / The blooming pink, or lily pale? / Fairer than any flower that blows, / Was Lucy Gray of Allendale.' 'Lucy Gray' plays with a narrator's and a community's sighting of the victim of a poignant but mysterious tragedy in the manner of 'The Thorn' (pp. 119–27), but more teasingly. In the first stanza the narrator's experience of Lucy Gray seems to be very like the 'Thorn' narrator's of Martha Ray, but as the poem unfolds it is apparent that what he saw may have been a ghost, or other bizarre phenomenon. Ll. 57–60 tend to exclude the possibility (which would be less problematic) that this sighting was of Lucy before her disappearance; on the other hand, the narrator's comment here that only 'some' people believe in the phenomenon sounds as if he has doubts about it (and see also ll. 11–12). The fact that the main victim is a child, almost uniquely in *LB*, helps to create a further ambiguity, whereby what happened to Lucy on the night of her 'death' can become almost as equivocal as the experiences of Johnny the Idiot Boy (see notes to ll. 41–4, 50, 62).

> Oft I had heard of Lucy Gray:
> And, when I crossed the wild,
> I chanced to see at break of day
> The solitary child.
>
> No mate, no comrade Lucy knew;   5
> She dwelt on a wide moor –
> The sweetest thing that ever grew
> Beside a human door!
>
> You yet may spy the fawn at play,
> The hare upon the green;   10
> But the sweet face of Lucy Gray
> Will never more be seen.
>
> 'Tonight will be a stormy night –
> You to the town must go;
> And take a lantern, child, to light   15
> Your mother through the snow.'

3. *break of day*: the hour at which Lucy's parents abandoned hope of seeing the living Lucy (l. 37).

'That, father! will I gladly do;
'Tis scarcely afternoon –
The minster-clock has just struck two,
And yonder is the moon.'   20

At this the father raised his hook
And snapped a faggot-band;
He plied his work, and Lucy took
The lantern in her hand.

Not blither is the mountain roe: 25
With many a wanton stroke
Her feet disperse the powdery snow,
That rises up like smoke.

The storm came on before its time;
She wandered up and down;   30
And many a hill did Lucy climb,
But never reached the town.

The wretched parents all that night
Went shouting far and wide;
But there was neither sound nor sight   35
To serve them for a guide.

At day-break on a hill they stood
That overlooked the moor;
And thence they saw the bridge of wood,
A furlong from their door.   40

And now they homeward turned, and cried
'In Heaven we all shall meet!' –
When in the snow the mother spied
The print of Lucy's feet.

20. See headnote.
21–2. Wordsworth seems to have a specific kind of cottage labour in mind,
though the allusion is now obscure.
26. *wanton*: there was no sense of the adjective available in Wordsworth's
day that was not potentially pejorative, but Wordsworth liked to challenge
the moralism of the word in conjunction with children, e.g. *Prelude* (1850
text), V, 412.
28. *rises up*: Murray (1967: 12) finds symbolic force in the phrase.
30. Compare l. 2 of the stanza of 'The Babes in the Wood' quoted
admiringly by Wordsworth in the Preface (ll. 903–6) and his 1816 remark
to Crabb Robinson about the removal of 'art' from the poem (headnote).
41–4. The poignancy but also the strangeness of Lucy's death so near her
door – a furlong (200 yards) away, l. 40 – is subtly enhanced by the parents'
implied assumption that she could have reached home from this point. The

Then downward from the steep hill's edge 45
They tracked the footmarks small;
And through the broken hawthorn-hedge,
And by the long stone wall.

And then an open field they crossed;
The marks were still the same; 50
They tracked them on, nor ever lost;
And to the bridge they came.

They followed from the snowy bank
The footmarks, one by one,
Into the middle of the plank; 55
And further there was none.

– Yet some maintain that to this day
She is a living child;
That you may see sweet Lucy Gray
Upon the lonesome wild. 60

O'er rough and smooth she trips along,
And never looks behind;
And sings a solitary song
That whistles in the wind.

short distance resonates with the strange phrasing of ll. 6–8 ('She dwelt . . . Beside a human door') to intimate that Lucy is in some sense in her home.

50. There is a hint that Lucy's steps (described variously as wanton l. 26, wandering l. 30, and tripping l. 61) did not falter or grow tired. 'Should the speaker grieve over, or stare in wonder at, the point of her disappearance?' (Toliver 1971: 248).
58. The phrasing implies, in keeping with the hints in the three preceding stanzas, that the apparition of popular superstition may not be a ghost: that Lucy, while no longer part of human life, is not precisely dead.
60. Compare the poem attributed to Burns, 'The Lass of Ballochmyle', l. 20.
62–3. Even if Lucy is observed it does not affect her 'entire solitude'.
64. As in 'The Thorn', a naturalistic explanation of the apparition, or part of one, is offered.

' 'Tis said, that some have died for love . . .'

Probably composed in the first half of 1800; minor late changes. The poem opens with a twelve-line partly unrhymed stanza, original to Wordsworth, which resembles that of 'The Thorn', pp. 119–27 (a stanza to which Wordsworth returns in the next poem). The rest of the text, when it is the utterance of the 'wretched man', consists of eight-line stanzas made of doubled but varying quatrains, also an invention of Wordsworth's, for which the closest precedents are Elizabethan and seventeenth-century forms. It may be that Wordsworth associated the general effect with the love complaint (see O'Donnell 1989: 82). Throughout this section there is a more or less patterned variation of line length, unusual for Wordsworth, which suggests an imitation of the Pindaric ode, rather in the manner of Gray and Collins, and gives the stanza more variety than the otherwise identical stanza of 'Goody Blake and Harry Gill' (pp. 103–7). The whole remarkable structure is rounded off by eight blank-verse lines in the narrator's voice.

The central verses, the lament, are stately in their old-fashioned forms of address, but disconcerting in their import. It is envisaged as nowhere else in *LB* that the most elementary experiences of natural beauty may be thoroughly imbued with feelings of distress, so that there is no interval in which joy is available: the 'shades' have 'weight' (l. 21); the noise of the leaves is 'dying' (l. 22) and that of water intolerable (ll. 31–2); the relation of one form to another (ll. 13–16) or the mere curve of a branch (ll. 42–4) 'disturbs' unbearably. Most tellingly, and indeed shockingly, even in a state of apparently unreflective moment-by-moment sensory response at ll. 17–19 (to be compared with 'Poems on the Naming of Places' I, ll. 18–19, p. 324) the lover finds that unwittingly 'my hand is on my heart'. While there is a general suggestion that the horror of these natural phenomena springs from their links with a lost beloved, this is never stated explicitly (in contrast to 'The Two April Mornings', ll. 21–8, p. 291, for example), and in fact only some of the things the lover finds unendurable are readily interpretable in this way: the cottage, for instance, but not a thrush, or the exact form of an eglantine observed three years after her death. If the predominant effect of the lament is to register a kind of Sartrean disgust, the flanking lines, by the narrator, do tend to make this condition seem pathological, but it is not reprehended (compare 'The Nightingale', ll. 14–22, p. 153) even though it can lead to suicide. And these two verses tend to reinforce the theme of flawed happiness by introducing it at another level: in the mind of a narrator whose day of joy with Emma has nevertheless prompted him to think of the giant crushed by misery.

> 'Tis said, that some have died for love:
> And here and there a churchyard grave is found
> In the cold North's unhallowed ground,

1. Compare *As You Like It* IV, i, 96ff.
2–3. There is a subtle disposition of epithets – 'churchyard . . . cold . . .

259

Because the wretched man himself had slain,
His love was such a grievous pain.   5
And there is one whom I five years have known;
He dwells alone
Upon Helvellyn's side.
He loved – the pretty Barbara died,
And thus he makes his moan: 10
Three years had Barbara in her grave been laid
When thus his moan he made.

'Oh move, thou cottage, from behind that oak!
Or let the aged tree uprooted lie,
That in some other way yon smoke   15
May mount into the sky!
The clouds pass on; they from the heavens depart;
I look – the sky is empty space;
I know not what I trace;
But, when I cease to look, my hand is on my heart.   20

'Oh! what a weight is in these shades! Ye leaves,
When will that dying murmur be suppressed?
Your sound my heart of peace bereaves,
It robs my heart of rest.
Thou thrush, that singest loud and loud and free,   25
Into yon row of willows flit,
Upon that alder sit;
Or sing another song, or choose another tree.

'Roll back, sweet rill! back to thy mountain bounds,
And there for ever be thy waters chained!   30
For thou dost haunt the air with sounds
That cannot be sustained;
If still beneath that pine-tree's ragged bough
Headlong yon waterfall must come,
Oh let it then be dumb! –   35
Be any thing, sweet rill, but that which thou art now.

'Thou eglantine, whose arch so proudly towers,
(Even like the rainbow spanning half the vale)
Thou one fair shrub, oh! shed thy flowers,
And stir not in the gale.   40

unhallowed' – whereby the sanctity of the suicide's grave is suggested, and
the unfeelingness of the opposite view.

25–8. There is perhaps a general reminiscence of Burns's 'The Banks o'
Doon', (third version, 1791), ll. 2–6.

For thus to see thee nodding in the air,
To see thy arch thus stretch and bend,
Thus rise and thus descend,
Disturbs me, till the sight is more than I can bear.'

The man who makes this feverish complaint   45
Is one of giant stature, who could dance
Equipped from head to foot in iron mail.
Ah gentle Love! if ever thought was thine
To store up kindred hours for me, thy face
Turn from me, gentle Love! nor let me walk   50
Within the sound of Emma's voice, or know
Such happiness as I have known today.

---

40. gale: breeze; a poeticism, and in keeping with the oddly dignified verbal surface of the lament.

The Idle Shepherd-Boys
or
Dungeon-Gill Force
A Pastoral

Probably composed in the first half of 1800. Quite extensively revised in various editions, but not so as to effect a substantial change of sense. The stanza is the same elaborate construction of rhymed and unrhymed lines as that of 'The Thorn', with the same counter-movement in the pattern of three- and four-stress lines. Of the three 'pastorals' in *LB* this poem, with its two shepherds and their coronals and music-making, is closest to the classical and English 'eclogue' (see also headnote to 'The Fountain', p. 293). Literally a study of how the 'sad voice' of suffering can penetrate the condition of joy, though conceived in the un-urgent manner of other pastorals rather than in the haunted, relentless manner of 'The Thorn'; the 'plaintive cry' and 'piteous moan' could indicate a human being in distress (ll. 60–2) but turn out to be altogether less serious. The issue of attentiveness to suffering is given a particularly complicated twist through the appearance of the 'poet' or 'bard'. He is like William of 'The Tables Turned' (pp. 99–100) in his distaste for books (ll. 84–5) but reproaches the boys, perhaps too officiously, for being 'idle', or for a behaviour which is also, in fact, William-like. It is noteworthy that the poem always appeared in subsequent printings flanked by 'We are Seven' and 'Anecdote for Fathers' (pp. 128–34), texts which exhibit the superiority of child to adult values; it 'seems to have been meant ... as a confrontation of wise innocence with obtuse, meddling experience' (Dings 1973: 70).

I

The valley rings with mirth and joy;
Among the hills the echoes play
A never never ending song
To welcome in the May.
The magpie chatters with delight;   5
The mountain raven's youngling brood
Have left the mother and the nest;
And they go rambling east and west
In search of their own food;
Or through the glittering vapours dart   10
In very wantonness of heart.

Subtitle. 'Gill in the dialect of Cumberland and Westmoreland is a short, and, for the most part, a steep narrow valley, with a stream running through it. *Force* is the word universally employed in these dialects for Waterfall' (Wordsworth's note).

1–4. As with 'The Oak and the Broom' (pp. 249–52), the use of a particular month as a significant setting may have something to do with the Spenserian eclogues of *The Shepheardes Calender.*

11. wantonness: see note to 'Lucy Gray', l. 26 (p. 257).

II

Beneath a rock, upon the grass,
Two boys are sitting in the sun;
It seems they have no work to do,
Or that their work is done. 15
On pipes of sycamore they play
The fragments of a Christmas hymn;
Or with that plant which in our dale
We call stag-horn, or fox's tail,
Their rusty hats they trim. 20
And thus, as happy as the day,
Those shepherds wear the time away.

III

Along the river's stony marge
The sand-lark chants a joyous song;
The thrush is busy in the wood, 25
And carols loud and strong.
A thousand lambs are on the rocks,
All newly born! both earth and sky
Keep jubilee; and more than all,
Those boys with their green coronal; 30
They never hear the cry,
That plaintive cry! which up the hill
Comes from the depth of Dungeon Gill.

IV

Said Walter, leaping from the ground,
'Down to the stump of yon old yew 35
We'll for our whistles run a race.' –
Away the shepherds flew.
They leapt – they ran – and when they came
Right opposite to Dungeon Gill,
Seeing that he should lose the prize, 40
'Stop!' to his comrade Walter cries –
James stopped with no good will:

18–20. See Fenwick note, pp. 372–3.
18. our dale: the fleeting appearance of a first-person narrator, apparently a knowledgeable native sympathetic to the boys' activities, is enough to create a foil to the strolling poet of stanzas VIII and IX. But, as he seems to recognize here, this narrator does have his feet in two linguistic camps (especially if the note on the subtitle above is thought of as his). At various points the diction of the poem is rather literary.
19. stag-horn, fox's tail: staghorn moss, a club moss.
24. sand-lark: probably the shore-lark.
30. coronal: commonly used in English pastoral verse as a term for a shepherd's garland.

Said Walter then, 'Your task is here,
'Twill keep you working half a year.

V

'Now cross where I shall cross – come on,   45
And follow me where I shall lead' –
The other took him at his word,
But did not like the deed.
It was a spot, which you may see
If ever you to Langdale go: 50
Into a chasm a mighty block
Hath fallen, and made a bridge of rock:
The gulf is deep below,
And in a basin black and small
Receives a lofty waterfall.   55

VI

With staff in hand across the cleft
The challenger began his march;
And now, all eyes and feet, hath gained
The middle of the arch.
When list! he hears a piteous moan –   60
Again! – his heart within him dies –
His pulse is stopped, his breath is lost,
He totters, pale as any ghost,
And, looking down, he spies
A lamb, that in the pool is pent   65
Within that black and frightful rent.

VII

The lamb had slipped into the stream,
And safe without a bruise or wound
The cataract had borne him down
Into the gulf profound.   70
His dam had seen him when he fell,
She saw him down the torrent borne;
And, while with all a mother's love
She from the lofty rocks above
Sent forth a cry forlorn,   75
The lamb, still swimming round and round,
Made answer to that plaintive sound.

VIII

When he had learnt what thing it was,
That sent this rueful cry, I ween,
The boy recovered heart, and told   80
The sight which he had seen.
Both gladly now deferred their task;
Nor was there wanting other aid –
A poet, one who loves the brooks
Far better than the sages' books,   85
By chance had thither strayed;
And there the helpless lamb he found
By those huge rocks encompassed round.

IX

He drew it gently from the pool,
And brought it forth into the light: 90
The shepherds met him with his charge,
An unexpected sight!
Into their arms the lamb they took;
Said they, 'He's neither maimed nor scarred.'
Then up the steep ascent they hied,   95
And placed him at his mother's side;
And gently did the bard
Those idle shepherd-boys upbraid,
And bade them better mind their trade.

79. *rueful*: doleful; a sense probably obsolescent in Wordsworth's day.
99. *their trade*: the boys do not behave at ll. 78–82 as if the lamb and sheep are part of their flock, and hence it is doubtful if they have been negligent at all.

Poor Susan

Unknown date of composition between spring 1797 and summer 1800. The date in the Fenwick note (p. 379) is certainly wrong. There was a small but possibly radical change in l. 2 in 1820 (see note), and in 1800 the following stanza concluded the poem: 'Poor outcast! return – to receive thee once more / The house of thy father will open its door, / And thou once again, in thy plain russet gown, / May'st hear the thrush sing from a tree of its own.' See the observation in the Preface (ll. 210–14) on the relation of feeling and situation in the poem. One of the handful of poems in the collection in anapestic or triple rhythm. It also uses a form of quatrain used in only two other poems in *LB* 1805 (though it was very popular in the period – see O'Donnell 1989: 51–2). These formal aspects, together with a date perhaps as early as the spring of 1797, set the poem somewhat apart; it resembles 'The Brothers', ll. 56–62 (p. 227), in its concerns but is otherwise anomalous in content and strategy also.

> At the corner of Wood Street, when daylight appears,
> There's a thrush that sings loud, it has sung for three
>   years:
> Poor Susan has passed by the spot, and has heard
> In the silence of morning the song of the bird.
>
> 'Tis a note of enchantment; what ails her? She sees   5
> A mountain ascending, a vision of trees;
> Bright volumes of vapour through Lothbury glide,
> And a river flows on through the vale of Cheapside.

1. when daylight appears: at dawn. The Fenwick note (p. 379) speaks of 'the freshness and stillness of the spring morning'.
2. There's a thrush: a puzzling point is involved. Wordsworth in 1820 emended the line to imply that the thrush is in a cage (substituting 'Hangs a thrush'), and in the Fenwick note, he claims, in effect, that this is what is described in all versions of the poem. But at the time of first publication a famous plane tree stood at the corner of Cheapside and Wood Street, and could be assumed to be the perch envisaged by Wordsworth in the earlier version were it not for the last line of the 1800 version (see headnote). This line can be squared with either a caged bird or a bird crowded into an isolated urban tree with other birds, but perhaps fits the first reading better. At all events, with the line dropped, the thrush of 1805 must count as a free denizen of the city.
6. ascending: the modifier has the effect of making the mountain appear to participate in the notably kinetic quality of Susan's vision (see also l. 15).
7–8. Lothbury, Cheapside: Manning (1986) comments on these names, as well as Wood Street (all from the City of London), that they 'would have suggested an entire world of mercantile activity' to Wordsworth's readers. The effect intensifies in a significant way, however: 'Wood' Street, with its plane tree, gives Susan's vision a purchase in reality, but Cheapside is not a 'vale', even historically.

Green pastures she views in the midst of the dale,
Down which she so often has tripped with her pail;   10
And a single small cottage, a nest like a dove's,
The one only dwelling on earth that she loves.

She looks, and her heart is in Heaven; but they fade,
The mist and the river, the hill and the shade;
The stream will not flow, and the hill will not rise,   15
And the colours have all passed away from her eyes.

Inscription
For the Spot where the Hermitage stood on
St Herbert's Island, Derwentwater.

Probably composed in the first half of 1800. Reclassified in the collected works; see p. 362. Ll. 4–8, in particular, underwent progressive revision and expansion, though not in a way to affect the gist of the poem. The stately and sometimes rather archaic phrasing is an example of Wordsworth's special inscriptional idiom (see General Introduction, p. 17). Wordsworth's source is the story of St Cuthbert and St Herbert as related in Bede's *Ecclesiastical History*, Vol. IV, Ch. 29, but he has made several important changes. In Bede, St Herbert does not retire to his island solitude from a life of collaboration with St Cuthbert; he goes on annual visits to the latter from the island where he already dwells, to receive spiritual sustenance. On one of these visits he asks St Cuthbert to pray that their deaths will coincide. Wordsworth's changes enable him to produce a characteristic image of sorrow gnawing at a mood which should be joyful (and in no slight sense: St Herbert is devoting himself to God, but in all *LB* versions of the text his heart is 'sick' with unhappiness, l. 4 – thereafter replaced by 'sink').

> If thou in the dear love of some one friend
> Hast been so happy, that thou know'st what thoughts
> Will, sometimes, in the happiness of love
> Make the heart sick, then wilt thou reverence
> This quiet spot. – St Herbert hither came,   5
> And here, for many seasons, from the world
> Removed, and the affections of the world,
> He dwelt in solitude. – But he had left
> A fellow-labourer, whom the good man loved
> As his own soul. And, when within his cave   10
> Alone he knelt before the crucifix
> While o'er the lake the cataract of Lodore
> Pealed to his orisons, and when he paced
> Along the beach of this small isle and thought
> Of his companion, he would pray that both   15
> Might die in the same moment. Nor in vain
> So prayed he: – as our chronicles report,
> Though here the hermit numbered his last days,
> Far from St Cuthbert his beloved friend,
> Those holy men both died in the same hour.   20

Lines

Written with a pencil upon a stone in the wall of the House (an outhouse) on the Island at Grasmere

Probably composed in the first half of 1800. The chief revisions are those of 1837 to ll. 11–12 (see note), which somewhat alter the points of satirical reference in these lines. It is an imaginary inscription in Wordsworth's inscriptional idiom, which is orthodox in being an impersonal and disembodied utterance without a narrator, or virtually so; hence there is a strong invitation to interpret the 'one poet' as a possible disguised self-description, very much in the manner of the close of Gray's 'Elegy' (for echoes of the poem, see note to ll. 21–2). There is actually more distancing between Gray and his hinted fanciful self-portrait as a half-mad solitary than there is between Wordsworth and the persona created here. Nevertheless, Wordsworth's use of such devices elsewhere (e.g. 'The Idle Shepherd-Boys', pp. 262–5) may suggest that the poet with his 'romantic' pleasures (l. 29) is not precisely Wordsworth, or even precisely the imagined voice of the poem.

> Rude is this edifice, and thou hast seen
> Buildings, albeit rude, that have maintained
> Proportions more harmonious, and approached
> To somewhat of a closer fellowship
> With the ideal grace. Yet as it is   5
> Do take it in good part; for he, the poor
> Vitruvius of our village, had no help
> From the great city; never on the leaves
> Of red Morocco folio saw displayed
> The skeletons and pre-existing ghosts   10

1. Rude: unsophisticated.
5. ideal grace: invokes the vocabulary and concepts of neoclassical aesthetics.
7. Vitruvius of our village: the most famous architectural theorist of classical times. If this Gray-like phrasing (see note to ll. 21–2 below) indicates that the narrator of the poem is to be thought of as the poet of ll. 16–29, then he evidently combines his love of romantic solitude with a rootedness in his local community.
9. red Morocco folio: probably a reference to the 'Red-books' of Humphrey Repton, the leading estate designer of the period, in which he displayed to clients proposals for improvements, sometimes using superimposed illustrations (the books were not, however, of orthodox folio size). 'Morocco' is a kind of leather.
10. To call the plans and pictures of as yet unbuilt structures 'skeletons' and 'ghosts' is wittily to imply that an architect's schemes are already obsolete or will not last long. 'Skeletons' suggests architectural plan drawings, which Repton's books contained together with conjectural

Of beauties yet unborn, the rustic Box,
Snug Cot, with Coach-house, Shed and Hermitage.
It is a homely pile, yet to these walls
The heifer comes in the snow-storm, and here
The new-dropped lamb finds shelter from the wind.   15
And hither does one poet sometimes row
His pinnace, a small vagrant barge, up-piled
With plenteous store of heath and withered fern,
(A lading which he with his sickle cuts
Among the mountains,) and beneath this roof   20
He makes his summer couch, and here at noon
Spreads out his limbs, while, yet unshorn, the sheep
Panting beneath the burthen of their wool
Lie round him, even as if they were a part
Of his own household: nor, while from his bed   25
He through that door-place looks toward the lake
And to the stirring breezes, does he want
Creations lovely as the work of sleep,
Fair sights, and visions of romantic joy.

illustrations. The latter, especially when overlaid on pictures of the existing
site, are a kind of 'ghost' (see Dorothy Stroud, *Humphrey Repton*, 1962,
pp. 32, 36, 57, 102, 141).

11–12. Box, Cot, Coach, Shed and Hermitage: all these architectural concepts
betray either pretentiousness (of an architect-designed shooting-box or
coach-house) or bogusness (of a fake cottage, rural shelter or hermitage).
The 1837 version of these lines suggests that, to add to the absurdity, the
'Coach-house, Shed and Hermitage' are appendages of the 'Snug Cot' –
for there 'verandah ... alcove, / Green-house, shell-grot, and moss-lined
hermitage' are definitely understood in this way.
21–2. here ... limbs: compare Gray's 'Elegy written in a Country
Churchyard', l. 104: 'His listless length at noontide would he stretch.' Gray
is also perhaps echoed at ll. 6–7 in 'the poor / Vitruvius of our village',
which resembles the well-known formulations of stanza 15 of the 'Elegy':
'some village-Hampden', etc.
28. work of sleep: dreams.
29. visions of romantic joy: compare James Beattie, *The Minstrel*, 1771–4, II,
79.

To a Sexton

Probably composed in the winter of 1798–9. The jeering 'old grey-beard' (l. 23) was replaced by 'too heedless' in 1845; no other changes. The versification is the collection's third variant on a rhymed eight-line stanza (to be compared with 'Goody Blake and Harry Gill' and ' 'Tis said, that some have died for love ...', pp. 103–7, 259–61) but the rhythm is generally trochaic, the beat falling mainly on first, third etc. syllables in a manner that suits a vehement expostulation. The narrator is one of Wordsworth's most authoritative and socially integrated, apparently an ordinary villager possessed of a long and intimate acquaintance with the community such that its members are naturally addressed by their Christian names (in contrast to even 'Goody Blake and Harry Gill' and 'Simon Lee').

Let thy wheel-barrow alone.
Wherefore, Sexton, piling still
In thy bone-house bone on bone?
'Tis already like a hill
In a field of battle made,   5
Where three thousand skulls are laid.
– These died in peace each with the other,
Father, sister, friend and brother.

Mark the spot to which I point!
From this platform eight feet square   10
Take not even a finger-joint:
Andrew's whole fireside is there.
Here, alone, before thine eyes,
Simon's sickly daughter lies,
From weakness, now, and pain defended,   15
Whom he twenty winters tended.

Look but at the gardener's pride –
How he glories, when he sees
Roses, lilies, side by side,
Violets in families!   20
By the heart of Man, his tears,
By his hopes and by his fears,
Thou, old grey-beard! art the warden
Of a far superior garden.

1–6. The sexton is removing the skeletons of already buried bodies (to a literal or figurative 'bone-house' or ossuary) to make room for new burials – a practice increasingly resorted to before the Victorian legislation establishing cemeteries separate from churchyards.

Thus then, each to other dear,   25
Let them all in quiet lie,
Andrew there and Susan here,
Neighbours in mortality.
And, should I live through sun and rain
Seven widowed years without my Jane,   30
O Sexton, do not then remove her,
Let one grave hold the loved and lover!

Andrew Jones

Probably composed in the early summer of 1800. Written in the stanza of 'The Idiot Boy' (and that of another poem in comic epic mode, 'Peter Bell', from some abandoned stanzas of which it is adapted). Wordsworth did not think well enough of it to continue printing it in his collected works from 1815.

'I hate that Andrew Jones: he'll breed
His children up to waste and pillage.
I wish the press-gang or the drum
With its tantara sound, would come
And sweep him from the village!'   5

I said not this, because he loves
Through the long day to swear and tipple;
But for the poor dear sake of one
To whom a foul deed he had done,
A friendless man, a travelling cripple.   10

For this poor crawling helpless wretch
Some horseman who was passing by
A penny on the ground had thrown;
But the poor cripple was alone,
And could not stoop – no help was nigh.   15

Inch-thick the dust lay on the ground,
For it had long been droughty weather:
So with his staff the cripple wrought
Among the dust till he had brought
The halfpennies together.   20

1–5. A kind of reversal of John Scott's Ode XIII (1782), an attack on recruitment in which each verse begins: 'I hate that drum's discordant sound.'

3. press-gang or the drum: denoting forced recruitment into the navy or army, a fate wished on Andrew in this serio-comic curse because it will remove him from the community but also, presumably, because the armed forces are regarded as antithetical to humane values. Andrew's offspring are envisaged as following in their father's footsteps.

15. no help was nigh: this is consistent with the original 'Peter Bell' context but not with the *LB* version and its first-person witness/narrator. Perhaps the problem of the narrator's not assisting the cripple was one reason for Wordsworth's discarding the poem.

18–20. Whatever the shortcomings of the poem, Wordsworth's power to devise telling indices of extreme need and decrepitude is well exhibited in this image of the cripple stirring in the dust to bring together two coins which he cannot then pick up.

It chanced that Andrew passed that way
Just at the time; and there he found
The cripple in the midday heat
Standing alone, and at his feet
He saw the penny on the ground.   25

He stooped and took the penny up:
And when the cripple nearer drew,
Quoth Andrew, 'Under half-a-crown,
What a man finds is all his own,
And so, my friend, good day to you.'   30

And *hence* I said, that Andrew's boys
Will all be trained to waste and pillage;
And wished the press-gang, or the drum
With its tantara sound, would come
And sweep him from the village!   35

Ruth

Probably composed in the winter of 1798–9. Apart from 'Goody Blake and Harry Gill', this is the only substantial item in *LB* to be transferred into a new category in the successive versions of Wordsworth's collected works, and, unlike the latter, transferred into an important existing group, 'Poems of the Imagination' (from 'Poems of the Affections' – see p. 362). It is also the most heavily and persistently revised of any of the poems in *LB*. The main body of revisions begins with the addition of six whole stanzas, with associated rearrangement of others, in the second (1802) appearance of the poem – a change which was to remain remarkably troublesome and uncertain in form thereafter. Four of these new stanzas were at l. 54 – in the Youth's history of himself – and into the middle of them were also transferred three crucial existing stanzas from the poet's later analysis of the Youth's moral nature when he deserts Ruth (necessarily recast in the first person). In 1805, however, these three were restored in their old position (appearing at l. 157) and a new stanza created where they had been in 1802 ('It was a fresh . . .'). Then, in 1815, the first two and last of these new stanzas of 1802 were dropped altogether and the remaining one plus the 1805 addition themselves transferred forward to the desertion section (though kept as the Youth's speech). In 1820 the second of the 1802 additions was actually restored at this point ('Sometimes most earnestly . . .'). The material involved in this group of changes also received local revision at all stages.

This very complicated history can be summarized as follows, using the stanza numbers of the 1805 edition (stanza 10 starts at l. 55): *1800* 10, 16–33; *1802* 10–12, 27–9, 14–26, 30–3; *1815* 10, 16–32, 13–14, 33; *1820* 10, 16–32, 12–14, 33. It will be seen that the underlying issue is how much Ruth is apprised by the Youth of the erosion of his moral nature in the New World. The bold 1802 version in which she hears a candid confession from the Youth is backed away from more and more, but then returned to somewhat with the restoration of ll. 67–72 (which are, however, placed after the main wooing section). The rest of the substantial changes to 'Ruth' also bear on the heroine's moral standing. The two other stanzas added in 1802 are ll. 13–18 and 241–6 (which were later revised locally), while Wordsworth retuned ll. 202–10 (Ruth's carousing in prison) interestingly on two occasions.

The six-line stanza (the first experiment with this length of verse in *LB*) uses a 'tail-rhyme' arrangement whereby the shorter, concluding lines of each three-line unit rhyme with each other. This particular form of the tail-rhyme verse is found in a great variety of poems (from Chaucer's 'Sir Thopas' through to Gray's 'Ode on the Death of a Favourite Cat' via Habington's 'Cupio Dissolvi') but has tended to be deployed for comic or light effect: 'he has taken up a tricky form of verse and kept out of the pitfalls' (Ker 1966: 232). In fact Wordsworth took it up in the course of his career more than any other stanza except various kinds of Common Metre – that is, rhymed common measure (see O'Donnell 1989: 15, 127–30).

The brief Fenwick note records that 'Ruth' was 'suggested by an account I had of a wanderer in Somersetshire' but is interestingly supplemented by

De Quincey's recollection of Wordsworth's telling him that the real-life model was 'an American lady' abandoned by her husband on embarkation (Masson 1889–90, II, 294). In other words, the original Ruth seems to have crossed the Atlantic and spent a considerable time in America (compare the exile of the Biblical Ruth). 'Ruth' is Wordsworth's fullest treatment in *LB* of one of the recurrent themes in the collection, the destitute and deranged or distraught consort/wife. While the emphasis of the closing verses is characteristically on the facts of Ruth's eventual condition and the narrator's/community's response to this, for most of its length the poem explores themes of nature and morality, including the sexual, not found elsewhere in *LB*, and to judge from the textual history of the poem the project was difficult (see also the comment on environment and character in the Wilson letter, p. 50, which could be relevant to both the main figures). Consequently, in Ruth's case the process of attrition is an interrupted one by comparison with, say, the Female Vagrant's experience; a long interval elapses between her effective orphaning (ll. 1–2) and the next blow, her husband's desertion (though Wordsworth gives the two episodes a marked degree of symmetry, with the adult Ruth reverting to the behaviour of the 'slighted' seven-year old).

> When Ruth was left half desolate
> Her father took another mate;
> And Ruth, not seven years old,
> A slighted child, at her own will
> Went wandering over dale and hill,   5
> In thoughtless freedom bold.
>
> And she had made a pipe of straw,
> And from that oaten pipe could draw
> All sounds of winds and floods;
> Had built a bower upon the green,   10
> As if she from her birth had been
> An infant of the woods.

1 half desolate: rhetorically effective, in that Ruth's desolateness is made cruelly complete in the next line.

4–6. Ironically, Ruth's first experience of rejection leads to a 'freedom' which lays the foundation for her second tragedy. At ll. 229–32 it is made explicit how damaging is the natural world to which she here becomes attached.

5. For the situation and phrasing, see 'Lucy Gray', ll. 30–1 and note (p. 257).

8–10. oaten pipe, floods, bower: in this phrasing ('oaten pipe' occurs several times in Spenser's pastoral verse and 'floods' is a poeticism for rivers and lakes) Ruth's early experience is given a distinctly literary–pastoral colouring.

Beneath her father's roof, alone
She seemed to live; her thoughts her own;
Herself her own delight;   15
Pleased with herself, nor sad nor gay,
She passed her time; and in this way
Grew up to woman's height.

There came a Youth from Georgia's shore –
A military casque he wore   20
With splendid feathers dressed;
He brought them from the Cherokees;
The feathers nodded in the breeze,
And made a gallant crest.

From Indian blood you deem him sprung;   25
Ah no! he spake the English tongue,
And bore a soldier's name;
And, when America was free
From battle and from jeopardy,
He 'cross the ocean came.   30

With hues of genius on his cheek
In finest tones the Youth could speak.
– While he was yet a boy
The moon, the glory of the sun,
And streams that murmur as they run,   35
Had been his dearest joy.

He was a lovely Youth! I guess
The panther in the wilderness
Was not so fair as he;
And when he chose to sport and play,   40
No dolphin ever was so gay
Upon the tropic sea.

13–18. Stanza added in 1802.
19. Youth: consistently capitalized by Wordsworth; the Youth is never given
a name.
20. casque: helmet.
23–4. See the description in Bartram (1792: 499–500) of the headband
worn by Cherokee and other tribes: 'the front peak of it being embellished
with a high waving plume, of crane or heron feathers'.
26. Compare 'The Mad Mother', l. 10 and note (p. 173). The Youth has
evidently served in the British army against the native Indian population
and in alliance with Indians, and subsequently against the American rebels
in the southern arena of the War of Independence.

Among the Indians he had fought;
And with him many tales he brought
Of pleasure and of fear;   45
Such tales as, told to any maid,
By such a Youth, in the green shade,
Were perilous to hear.

He told of girls, a happy rout!
Who quit their fold with dance and shout,   50
Their pleasant Indian town
To gather strawberries all day long,
Returning with a choral song
When daylight is gone down.

He spake of plants divine and strange   55
That every hour their blossoms change,
Ten thousand lovely hues!
With budding, fading, faded flowers
They stand the wonder of the bowers
From morn to evening dews.   60

Of march and ambush, siege and fight,
Then did he tell; and with delight
The heart of Ruth would ache;
Wild histories they were, and dear:
But 'twas a thing of heaven to hear   65
When of himself he spake!

Sometimes most earnestly he said;
'O Ruth! I have been worse than dead:
False thoughts, thoughts bold and vain,
Encompassed me on every side   70
When I, in confidence and pride,
Had crossed the Atlantic main.

'It was a fresh and glorious world,
A banner bright that was unfurled
Before me suddenly: 75

49–54. For the source of this in Bartram, see pp. 387–8.
55–60. This is based on Bartram's description of a species of North American camellia; see p. 388.
60. Compare *Paradise Lost* I, 742–3.
61–6. Stanza added in 1802, dropped in 1815.
65–6. Compare (in light of the context) *Othello* I, iii, 167–8.
67–72. Stanza added in 1802, dropped in 1815, restored in 1820 in desertion section.
73–8. Stanza added in 1805, transferred in 1815 to desertion section.

I looked upon those hills and plains,
And seemed as if let loose from chains
To live at liberty.

'But wherefore speak of this? for now,
Sweet Ruth! with thee, I know not how,   80
I feel my spirit burn –
Even as the east when day comes forth;
And to the west, and south, and north,
The morning doth return.

'It is a purer, better mind: 85
O maiden innocent and kind,
What sights I might have seen!
Even now upon my eyes they break!' –
And he again began to speak
Of lands where he had been.   90

He told of the Magnolia, spread
High as a cloud, high over head!
The Cypress and her spire –
Of flowers that with one scarlet gleam
Cover a hundred leagues, and seem   95
To set the hills on fire.

The Youth of green savannahs spake,
And many an endless, endless lake,
With all its fairy crowds
Of islands, that together lie   100
As quietly as spots of sky
Among the evening clouds.

76–8. The Youth, as well as sharing Ruth's affinity with the natural world,
has responded to America rather as she responded to being abandoned to
her own devices as a child (ll. 4–6).
79–84. Stanza added in 1802, transferred in 1815 to desertion section.
85–90. Stanza added in 1802, dropped in 1815.
91. *Magnolia*: 'Magnolia grandiflora' (Wordsworth's note). The plant is
described in Bartram 1792: 84.
93. See Bartram 1792: 88–9.
94. *flowers*: 'The splendid appearance of these scarlet flowers, which are
scattered with such profusion over the hills in the southern parts of North
America, is frequently mentioned by Bartram in his Travels' (Wordsworth's
note). The chief description of the azalea that causes this effect is at
Bartram 1792: 321, where he mentions 'the apprehension of the hill being
set on fire'.

And then he said 'How sweet it were
A fisher or a hunter there,
A gardener in the shade,
Still wandering with an easy mind   105
To build a household fire, and find
A home in every glade!

'What days and what sweet years! Ah me!
Our life were life indeed, with thee   110
So passed in quiet bliss,
And all the while,' said he, 'to know
That we were in a world of woe,
On such an earth as this!'

And then he sometimes interwove   115
Dear thoughts about a father's love,
'For there,' said he, 'are spun
Around the heart such tender ties,
That our own children to our eyes
Are dearer than the sun.   120

'Sweet Ruth! and could you go with me
My helpmate in the woods to be,
Our shed at night to rear;
Or run, my own adopted bride,
A sylvan huntress at my side,   125
And drive the flying deer!

'Beloved Ruth!' – No more he said.
Sweet Ruth alone at midnight shed
A solitary tear.
She thought again – and did agree   130
With him to sail across the sea,
And drive the flying deer.

103. *How sweet it were*: the closest of several echoes of Coleridge's rendering of the same theme in 'The Foster-mother's Tale', ll. 45–9 (p. 116).
113. *world of woe*: compare *Paradise Lost* IX, 11. The beautiful and fecund American environment in which the Youth offers Ruth a life of blissful exclusive companionship has already recalled Milton's paradise in a general way.
115–20. The symmetry of Ruth's response to the two great desertions of her life is prepared for in the Youth's vision of an enhanced paternal love; l. 116, indeed, seems to be deliberately ambiguous in this regard.
129. *solitary tear*: her lack of guidance and companionship is recalled at this pivotal moment.

'And now, as fitting is and right,
We in the church our faith will plight,
A husband and a wife.'   135
Even so they did; and I may say
That to sweet Ruth that happy day
Was more than human life.

Through dream and vision did she sink
Delighted all the while to think   140
That, on those lonesome floods,
And green savannahs, she should share
His board with lawful joy, and bear
His name in the wild woods.

But, as you have before been told,   145
This Stripling, sportive, gay, and bold,
And with his dancing crest
So beautiful, through savage lands
Had roamed about with vagrant bands
Of Indians in the West.   150

The wind, the tempest roaring high,
The tumult of a tropic sky,
Might well be dangerous food
For him, a Youth to whom was given
So much of earth so much of Heaven,   155
And such impetuous blood.

Whatever in those climes he found
Irregular in sight or sound
Did to his mind impart
A kindred impulse, seemed allied   160
To his own powers, and justified
The workings of his heart.

Nor less to feed voluptuous thought
The beauteous forms of nature wrought,
Fair trees and lovely flowers;   165
The breezes their own languor lent;
The stars had feelings, which they sent
Into those magic bowers.

157–74. In 1802 these three stanzas were rephrased in the first person and
transferred to the wooing section, l. 73; transferred back to this point in
1805.

Yet, in his worst pursuits, I ween
That sometimes there did intervene   170
Pure hopes of high intent;
For passions linked to forms so fair
And stately needs must have their share
Of noble sentiment.

But ill he lived, much evil saw   175
With men to whom no better law
Nor better life was known;
Deliberately and undeceived
Those wild men's vices he received,
And gave them back his own.   180

His genius and his moral frame
Were thus impaired, and he became
The slave of low desires:
A man who without self-control
Would seek what the degraded soul   185
Unworthily admires.

And yet he with no feigned delight
Had wooed the maiden, day and night
Had loved her, night and morn:
What could he less than love a maid   190
Whose heart with so much nature played?
So kind and so forlorn!

But now the pleasant dream was gone;
No hope, no wish remained, not one,
They stirred him now no more;   195
New objects did new pleasure give,
And once again he wished to live
As lawless as before.

Meanwhile, as thus with him it fared,
They for the voyage were prepared,   200
And went to the sea-shore;
But, when they thither came, the Youth
Deserted his poor bride, and Ruth
Could never find him more.

---

169. ween: believe.
191. with so much nature played: nature could be either the indirect object of
the verb or part of an adverbial phrase.
202–3. Youth, Ruth: the rhyme which has been pending for so long arrives
at a cruelly ironical moment: the Youth has deserted Ruth and will not be
mentioned again in the text.

'God help thee, Ruth!' – Such pains she had 205
That she in half a year was mad
And in a prison housed;
And there, exulting in her wrongs,
Among the music of her songs
She fearfully caroused. 210

Yet sometimes milder hours she knew,
Nor wanted sun, nor rain, nor dew,
Nor pastimes of the May –
They all were with her in her cell;
And a wild brook with cheerful knell 215
Did o'er the pebbles play.

When Ruth three seasons thus had lain
There came a respite to her pain,
She from her prison fled;
But of the vagrant none took thought; 220
And where it liked her best she sought
Her shelter and her bread.

Among the fields she breathed again;
The master-current of her brain
Ran permanent and free; 225
And, coming to the banks of Tone,
There did she rest, and dwell alone
Under the greenwood tree.

The engines of her pain, the tools
That shaped her sorrow, rocks and pools, 230
And airs that gently stir
The vernal leaves, she loved them still,
Nor ever taxed them with the ill
Which had been done to her.

215. *knell*: this rather startling application of the word to denote (presumably on onomatopoeic grounds) the lively sound of a pebbly stream seems to be Wordsworth's wholly idiosyncratic usage, repeated once much later in his career (see 'The Unremitting Voice ...', l. 16). In this occurrence there may also be a covert foreshadowing of l. 268.

226. *banks of Tone*: 'The Tone is a river of Somersetshire at no great distance from the Quantock Hills. These hills, which are alluded to a few stanzas below, are extremely beautiful, and in most places richly covered with coppice woods' (Wordsworth's note). 'Coppice woods' are probably woods managed for timber, hence the woodman of l. 258 (but see Fenwick note to 'Nutting', p. 377, for a possibly different sense).

229–34. Ruth's condition is among the most ambiguous compounds of pleasure and suffering in a natural environment depicted by Wordsworth (matching an equally ambiguous picture of nature as both beautiful and

A barn her *winter* bed supplies;   235
But till the warmth of summer skies
And summer days is gone,
(And all do in this tale agree)
She sleeps beneath the greenwood tree,
And other home hath none.   240

An innocent life, yet far astray!
And Ruth will, long before her day,
Be broken down and old.
Sore aches she needs must have! but less
Of mind, than body's wretchedness,   245
From damp, and rain, and cold.

If she is pressed by want of food,
She from her dwelling in the wood
Repairs to a road-side;
And there she begs at one steep place,   250
Where up and down with easy pace
The horsemen-travellers ride.

That oaten pipe of hers is mute,
Or thrown away; but with a flute
Her loneliness she cheers;   255
This flute, made of a hemlock stalk,
At evening in his homeward walk
The Quantock woodman hears.

I, too, have passed her on the hills
Setting her little water-mills   260
By spouts and fountains wild –
Such small machinery as she turned
Ere she had wept, ere she had mourned,
A young and happy child!

evil). Ruth is living where she feels happiest, but she is appallingly deprived
(ll. 235–46) and in some sense deranged, and not really able to recapture
the happiness of the childish condition to which her derangement has made
her revert (ll. 253–5).

239. greenwood tree: see note to 'The Mad Mother', l. 8 (p. 173).
241–6. Stanza added in 1802.
259. hills: see Wordsworth's note to l. 226.

Farewell! and when thy days are told, 265
Ill-fated Ruth! in hallowed mould
Thy corpse shall buried be;
For thee a funeral bell shall ring,
And all the congregation sing
A Christian psalm for thee. 270

---

265. *Farewell*: not a token of the narrator's departure, or of Ruth's death, but of her effective absence from the human world.
    told: completed.

Lines

Written with a slate-pencil, upon a stone, the largest of a
heap lying near a deserted quarry, upon one of the
islands at Rydale.

Probably composed at various dates in 1800, completed by mid August.
Minor changes.

Stranger! this hillock of misshapen stones
Is not a ruin of the ancient time,
Nor, as perchance thou rashly deem'st, the cairn
Of some old British chief: 'tis nothing more
Than the rude embryo of a little dome   5
Or pleasure-house, once destined to be built
Among the birch-trees of this rocky isle.
But, as it chanced, Sir William having learned
That from the shore a full-grown man might wade,
And make himself a freeman of this spot   10
At any hour he chose, the Knight forthwith
Desisted, and the quarry and the mound
Are monuments of his unfinished task. –
The block on which these lines are traced, perhaps,
Was once selected as the corner-stone   15
Of the intended pile, which would have been
Some quaint odd plaything of elaborate skill,
So that, I guess, the linnet and the thrush,
And other little builders who dwell here,
Had wondered at the work. But blame him not,   20
For old Sir William was a gentle Knight
Bred in this vale, to which he appertained
With all his ancestry. Then peace to him,
And for the outrage which he had devised
Entire forgiveness! – But if thou art one   25
On fire with thy impatience to become
An inmate of these mountains, if, disturbed
By beautiful conceptions, thou hast hewn

5–6. *dome / Or pleasure-house*: compare Coleridge, 'Kubla Khan', l. 2.
8. *Sir William*: Sir William Fleming of Rydal Hall, local magnate in the
early eighteenth century.
10. *freeman*: plays with the ideas of having the freedom of a territory and of
being free from feudal servitude.
21. *gentle Knight*: perhaps a playful echo of Chaucer's 'General Prologue',
l. 73, and *Faerie Queene* I, 1.
28. *conceptions*: plans.

Out of the quiet rock the elements
Of thy trim mansion destined soon to blaze   30
In snow-white glory, think again, and, taught
By old Sir William and his quarry, leave
Thy fragments to the bramble and the rose;
Here let the vernal slow-worm sun himself,
And let the redbreast hop from stone to stone.   35

---

31. snow-white glory: refers to the new fashion of whitewashing (though Wordsworth associates this, in *A Guide through the District of the Lakes*, mainly with 'houses not built of hewn stone or brick'; Owen and Smyser 1974, II, 215).

'If Nature . . .'

Probably composed in the winter of 1798–9. The one change of note is 'dew' for the Biblical 'oil' (l. 24) in 1815. Unlike the Lucy group the following three poems, all explicitly about Matthew (who is a schoolmaster in two of them, a father in two, and aged seventy-two in one), were never separated or rearranged in later editions, and never conjoined with the two other poems in *LB* involving a Matthew ('Expostulation and Reply' and 'The Tables Turned', pp. 97–100). However, it would be unwise to conclude that they represent an individual of fixed identity, let alone a really existing man (Wordsworth goes so far as to speak of the 'untruth' of the poems in this respect in the Fenwick note, p. 373). Elsewhere Wordsworth did use the name Matthew to refer to his headmaster at Hawkshead grammar school (not village school), William Taylor (*PW* IV, 256, 451–5), but Taylor died aged thirty-two when Wordsworth was a teenager. He would fit the Matthew of 'Expostulation and Reply' and 'The Tables Turned' better than the Matthew of the later group (which puts biographically minded commentators in a quandary because they also want to say that the former character represents William Hazlitt). In his later remarks (see also the letter to Reed, p. 373) Wordsworth says clearly that 'several' men lay behind the Matthew figure, and that he was a 'composition' rather than an 'invention'. Three additional models have been convincingly identified (Thompson 1970: 151–90), including John Harrison (master of a small boys' school at Hawkshead, whose main hobby was fishing and who had a daughter Emmy who died aged about eight), and Hugh Cowperthwaite (Hawkshead innkeeper – see the imagery of ll. 19–28 – author of comic verses and locally renowned for his facetious disposition, who died aged seventy-two). It is not certain, either, that the narrator is to be thought of as identical in all his appearances; he could, for example, be much younger (along with Matthew) in 'The Two April Mornings' than he is in 'The Fountain'. The unchanged ordering of the three poems makes sense in several ways, perhaps most notably for the increasingly sombre perception thus developed (with a corresponding erosion of standing for the narrator) of that continually mysterious thing, Matthew's 'glee'.

> In the school of —— is a tablet, on which are inscribed, in gilt letters, the names of the several persons who have been schoolmasters since the foundation of the school, with the time at which they entered upon and quitted their office. Opposite one of those names the Author wrote the following lines.
>
> (Wordsworth's note)

If Nature, for a favourite child
In thee hath tempered so her clay,
That every hour thy heart runs wild,
Yet never once doth go astray,

Read o'er these lines; and then review   5
This tablet, that thus humbly rears
In such diversity of hue
Its history of two hundred years.

– When through this little wreck of fame,
Cypher and syllable! thine eye   10
Has travelled down to Matthew's name,
Pause with no common sympathy.

And, if a sleeping tear should wake,
Then be it neither checked nor stayed:
For Matthew a request I make   15
Which for himself he had not made.

Poor Matthew, all his frolics o'er,
Is silent as a standing pool;
Far from the chimney's merry roar,
And murmur of the village school.   20

The sighs which Matthew heaved were sighs
Of one tired out with fun and madness;
The tears which came to Matthew's eyes
Were tears of light, the oil of gladness.

Yet, sometimes, when the secret cup   25
Of still and serious thought went round,
It seemed as if he drank it up –
He felt with spirit so profound.

– Thou soul of God's best earthly mould!
Thou happy soul! and can it be   30
That these two words of glittering gold
Are all that must remain of thee?

---

7. diversity of hue: different colours of paint.
10. Cypher and syllable: refers to the numbers and words composing the
dated list of schoolmasters, perhaps using schoolroom vocabulary familiar
to the child reader who is notionally addressed.
12. sympathy: because of the harmonizing of wild and non-transgressive
elements in the personalities of Matthew and the child reader (ll. 1–4).
24. oil of gladness: see *Hebrews* 1:9.

The Two April Mornings

Probably composed in the winter of 1798–9; scattered revisions, including 'his' to 'a' in l. 59 from 1827. See the poem's classification in the Preface (ll. 198–201) as a study of 'less impassioned feelings'. It is a text which asserts with peculiar emphasis the possible recrudescence of pain in circumstances of sensory delight (Matthew does not directly remember his daughter's death of thirty-odd years ago, he remembers remembering it on an identically beautiful day; there is possibly a pun on mourning/morning in the poem's title). What the reader takes to be the outcome of the encounter of joy and pain depends, however, on how the very intriguing l. 56 is read. It may be either a shocking record of how the long shadow of grief can cast itself across and vitiate all subsequent pleasure, or alternatively a representation of how the memory of the deceased may be valued as much as the most beautiful things in life – and it should not be overlooked that Matthew's primary response to Emma's death seems to be acquiescence: 'The will of God be done!' (l. 4). On either reading, of course, Matthew's pain survives in some measure, for his 'sigh of pain' (l. 53) does not diminish over the next thirty years (l. 16). The reader's experience of Matthew's multiple mourning must also be influenced by the surprising last stanza, in which the conversation with Matthew turns out to be itself a memory of a dead person, but not in this instance one that disturbs joy. And Matthew is in his grave but simultaneously 'seen' in a way that resonates curiously with the vision of the 'blooming girl' near Emma's grave, so that Matthew on his second April walk with his bough of wilding in his hand (though see note to ll. 59–60) takes on some of the affirmative feeling of that figure. There is even resonance in their descriptions: his hair of 'glittering grey' in the morning mist (l. 6) is echoed in her 'hair . . . wet / With points of morning dew' (ll. 43–4).

We walked along, while bright and red
Uprose the morning sun;
And Matthew stopped, he looked, and said,
'The will of God be done!'

A village schoolmaster was he,   5
With hair of glittering grey;
As blithe a man as you could see
On a spring holiday.

And on that morning, through the grass,
And by the steaming rills,   10
We travelled merrily, to pass
A day among the hills.

'Our work,' said I, 'was well begun;
Then, from thy breast what thought,
Beneath so beautiful a sun,   15
So sad a sigh has brought?'

A second time did Matthew stop;
And fixing still his eye
Upon the eastern mountain-top,
To me he made reply: 20

'Yon cloud with that long purple cleft
Brings fresh into my mind
A day like this which I have left
Full thirty years behind.

'And just above yon slope of corn   25
Such colours, and no other
Were in the sky, that April morn,
Of this the very brother.

'With rod and line my silent sport
I plied by Derwent's wave;   30
And, coming to the church, stopped short
Beside my daughter's grave.

'Nine summers had she scarcely seen,
The pride of all the vale;
And then she sung – she would have been   35
A very nightingale.

'Six feet in earth my Emma lay;
And yet I loved her more,
For so it seemed, than till that day
I e'er had loved before.   40

'And turning from her grave, I met
Beside the churchyard yew
A blooming girl, whose hair was wet
With points of morning dew.

'A basket on her head she bare;   45
Her brow was smooth and white;
To see a child so very fair,
It was a pure delight!

21–4. Probably owes something to the ideas of eighteenth-century associationist psychology, particularly as formulated by Hartley. These theories put great weight on the tendency of feelings and ideas to be linked to particular sensory experiences, and thus to be revived by the repetition of those experiences.
29. my silent sport: because fishing requires silence, but also because it is solitary (and in this sense the phrase becomes additionally poignant when the prominence of Emma's singing in her father's memories of her is revealed, ll. 35–6).

'No fountain from its rocky cave
E'er tripped with foot so free;
She seemed as happy as a wave   50
That dances on the sea.

'There came from me a sigh of pain
Which I could ill confine;
I looked at her and looked again: 55
– And did not wish her mine.'

Matthew is in his grave, yet now
Methinks I see him stand,
As at that moment, with his bough
Of wilding in his hand.   60

51–2. Echoes *The Winter's Tale* IV, iii, 140–1: 'When you do dance, I wish you / A Wave o' the sea', from a context which is suggestive both generally (as an encounter with Perdita, lost daughter) and in detail (e.g. 'Not like a corse; or if – not to be buried, / But quick, and in mine arms', *ibid*. ll. 131–2). See also note to ll. 59–60.

59–60. with his ... hand: many readers have understandably found this image to be among the most haunting in all Wordsworth. The human figure with its single very specific accompaniment feels emblematic or iconographic, but what might it symbolize? 'Wilding' can be used of any undomesticated or freely growing plant, but is also specific to the crab-apple (this seems to some extent to be a Midlands and West Country dialectal usage, and see also Moorman 1957: 101). The use of wild plant strains such as the crab as the stock for the grafting of cultivated types is referred to in the *Winter's Tale* scene mentioned above (ll. 92–3). Matthew is presumably holding the wilding when he pauses on his walk (though 'at that moment' is admittedly ambiguous); he may be carrying it just as a switch, but it could be serving as a staff (or even as a fishing-rod, if the 'moment' is the encounter at the grave). In either of the latter readings, 'bough' would have to be distinctly figurative, giving an inert piece of wood connotations of life and growth through a reference to its original nature. See also the headnote for the structural link between Matthew here and the graveyard girl. It must not be forgotten, however, that between us and this intriguing icon is a Wordsworthian narrator; the main point of Matthew and his bough of wilding may be a baffled feeling of significance experienced by this narrator, which the reader can do no more than participate in and observe.

The Fountain
A Conversation

Probably composed in the winter of 1798–9. A handful of changes, mainly slight (though see note to l. 63). Bracketed with 'The Two April Mornings' for its subject matter in the Preface (ll. 198–201). The ambiguities of the latter are arguably resolved in the third of the Matthew sequence, with its startling exposure of the anguish behind Matthew's 'face of joy' – an anguish, it is implied, intrinsic to human life after a certain point. In particular there is a rejection by Matthew of substitute offspring (ll. 61–4) which is much clearer in its emotional bearings than ll. 55–6 of 'The Two April Mornings'. Curran (1986: 100–1) discusses the affinity of the Matthew poems with the classical and Renaissance eclogue; the resemblances are strongest in 'The Fountain', with its old and young speakers and its music-making.

We talked with open heart, and tongue
Affectionate and true;
A pair of friends, though I was young,
And Matthew seventy-two.

We lay beneath a spreading oak,   5
Beside a mossy seat;
And from the turf a fountain broke,
And gurgled at our feet.

'Now, Matthew! let us try to match
This water's pleasant tune   10
With some old Border song, or catch
That suits a summer's noon.

'Or of the church clock and the chimes
Sing here beneath the shade,
That half-mad thing of witty rhymes   15
Which you last April made!'

In silence Matthew lay, and eyed
The spring beneath the tree;
And thus the dear old man replied,
The grey-haired man of glee: 20

'Down to the vale this water steers,
How merrily it goes!
'Twill murmur on a thousand years,
And flow as now it flows.

'And here, on this delightful day,   25
I cannot choose but think
How oft, a vigorous man, I lay
Beside this fountain's brink.

'My eyes are dim with childish tears,
My heart is idly stirred,   30
For the same sound is in my ears
Which in those days I heard.

'Thus fares it still in our decay:
And yet the wiser mind
Mourns less for what age takes away   35
Than what it leaves behind.

'The blackbird in the summer trees,
The lark upon the hill,
Let loose their carols when they please,
Are quiet when they will.   40

'With Nature never do *they* wage
A foolish strife; they see
A happy youth, and their old age
Is beautiful and free:

'But we are pressed by heavy laws;   45
And often, glad no more,
We wear a face of joy, because
We have been glad of yore.

'If there is one who need bemoan
His kindred laid in earth,   50
The household hearts that were his own,
It is the man of mirth.

'My days, my friend, are almost gone,
My life has been approved,
And many love me; but by none   55
Am I enough beloved.'

'Now both himself and me he wrongs,
The man who thus complains!
I live and sing my idle songs
Upon these happy plains,   60

34–6. Wordsworth's characteristic theme of attrition is given a bitter twist:
Matthew's life is made more painful (even on a 'wise' estimate) by what he
still possesses than by what he has lost.
49–52. The harsh logic is presumably an example of the 'heavy laws'
governing human as opposed to animal life (l. 45): the sources of human joy
are such that the greater our pleasure the greater our eventual pain will be.

'And, Matthew, for thy children dead
I'll be a son to thee!'
At this he grasped his hands, and said
'Alas! that cannot be.'

We rose up from the fountain-side;   65
And down the smooth descent
Of the green sheep-track did we glide;
And through the wood we went;

And, ere we came to Leonard's Rock,
He sang those witty rhymes   70
About the crazy old church clock
And the bewildered chimes.

63. grasped his hands: Matthew's response to the narrator's perhaps rather coarse and self-centred attempts to cheer him up is brilliantly conveyed in this wording: an action in itself poignant (Matthew wringing or clutching his hands) is put in a way that expressively withholds the expected 'grasped my hand'. 'He does not grasp the young man's hands: he grasps his own, in a closing-off from any further attempt at intimacy' (Glen 1983: 300). In 1815 Wordsworth did change the reading here to 'grasped my hand'.
65–8. The phrasing tends to link the two men with the stream that flows 'down to the vale . . . merrily' at ll. 21–2.
69. Leonard's Rock: see 'The Brothers', *passim*.
71–2. None of the several allusions to derangement in connection with Matthew's songs (see also l. 15) involves the thing which is likely to be mad, an old man's mind. There is a strong feeling of displacement in this vocabulary, perhaps reflecting a displacement of his own distracted mood by Matthew in his 'rhymes' (though the occasion for the displacement existed in the historical fact of the irregularity of the Hawkshead church clock – see Thompson 1970: 173–4). Many commentators see an implication here that Matthew has some kind of fun at the expense of human, clock-dependent time in a manner reflecting back on his earlier utterance.

Nutting

Probably composed in the last months of 1798; several changes of phrasing at various dates. Wordsworth is recorded as feeling that this poem and 'To Joanna' (pp. 324–8) were his most inspired achievements ('show the greatest genius') in the second volume of *LB* (Moorman 1957: 506). Another study of pain intruding on a condition of joy, at a much younger age than in any other poem of this type (except, on some accounts, 'There was a Boy . . .', pp. 222–4), and consequently not to an extent that deters the boy from many other such expeditions (see ll. 1–2 and note); the reality of his dismay is anyway in some doubt (ll. 47–8). What distress the boy does feel cannot come from his acquaintance with the human world, but none the less proceeds from his human nature; it is his unmotivated violence in gathering his crop (energized perhaps by a boy's early sexual impulses) which brings in its wake the Wordsworthian 'sense of pain'. The poem is exceptional in *LB* in the straightforwardness of its narrational arrangements; the external evidence is that it is autobiographical and the internal evidence (such as the footnote to l. 4) is that Wordsworth wished the reader to take the 'I' as himself.

> It seems a day,
> (I speak of one from many singled out)
> One of those heavenly days which cannot die,
> When forth I sallied from our cottage-door,
> And with a wallet o'er my shoulder slung,   5
> A nutting crook in hand, I turned my steps
> Towards the distant woods, a figure quaint,
> Tricked out in proud disguise of beggar's weeds
> Put on for the occasion, by advice

1–2. Wordsworth told Isabella Fenwick that he was an 'impassioned' nut-gatherer as a boy and that the poem springs from 'feelings I had often had' (see p. 377). L. 2 affirms the recurrence of the kind of experience reported in the poem, but Wordsworth wants to balance this with specific description and he resorts to the device of putting this particular 'day' on the footing, at first, of a hypothetical reconstruction: 'It seems a day . . .'. The description then proceeds as if it were straightforwardly recollective, but the hypothetical mode is kept in mind and revived at l. 24 ('or . . .') and l. 29 ('Perhaps . . .').

1. The half-line is to indicate that the poem is a fragment, as indeed it probably was in historical fact. The Fenwick note (p. 377) says the larger intended as the conclusion to some other poem, never satisfactorily completed (see *PW* II, 504).

4. 'The house at which I was boarded during the time I was at school' (Wordsworth's note). A unique instance in the collection of Wordsworth affirming his identity with a first-person narrator. The house is Ann Tyson's cottage where Wordsworth lodged while at Hawkshead School.

8. weeds: garments.

And exhortation of my frugal Dame.   10
Motley accoutrement! of power to smile
At thorns, and brakes, and brambles, and, in truth,
More ragged than need was. Among the woods,
And o'er the pathless rocks, I forced my way
Until, at length, I came to one dear nook   15
Unvisited, where not a broken bough
Drooped with its withered leaves, ungracious sign
Of devastation, but the hazels rose
Tall and erect, with milk-white clusters hung,
A virgin scene! – A little while I stood,   20
Breathing with such suppression of the heart
As joy delights in; and with wise restraint
Voluptuous, fearless of a rival, eyed
The banquet, or beneath the trees I sate
Among the flowers, and with the flowers I played;   25
A temper known to those, who, after long
And weary expectation, have been blessed
With sudden happiness beyond all hope.
Perhaps it was a bower beneath whose leaves
The violets of five seasons re-appear   30
And fade, unseen by any human eye;
Where fairy water-breaks do murmur on
For ever, and I saw the sparkling foam,
And with my cheek on one of those green stones
That, fleeced with moss, beneath the shady trees,   35
Lay round me, scattered like a flock of sheep,
I heard the murmur and the murmuring sound,

10. frugal Dame: an identifiable individual, Ann Tyson, Wordsworth's beloved landlady in his schooldays.
11–12. smile / At: not recorded in this precise sense by the *OED* but perhaps influenced by certain occurrences in Shakespeare, e.g. *The Taming of the Shrew* V, ii, 3 and *Macbeth* V, vii, 12.
11. Motley: mixed, diversified. The specialized application of the term to a jester's costume is also evoked in 'smile'.
15. dear: well-loved, Wordsworth's usual (and frequent) sense. The weaker modern meaning of endearingly pretty does not seem to occur and was probably not even available to him. 'Unvisited' in the next line may be construed to mean 'unvisited by other nut-gatherers' – hence the unbroken boughs – rather than 'never visited by myself'.
31. unseen . . . eye: in apparent contradiction of l. 15, but in the hypothetical mode of the poem (see headnote) this is not necessarily the same spot as earlier described. However, as with 'unvisited' in l. 16, the possibility of a commonsense interpretation should not dispel the feeling of paradox.
32. water-breaks: miniature rapids in a stream; Wordsworth's coinage.

In that sweet mood when pleasure loves to pay
Tribute to ease; and, of its joy secure,
The heart luxuriates with indifferent things,   40
Wasting its kindliness on stocks and stones,
And on the vacant air. Then up I rose,
And dragged to earth both branch and bough, with
    crash
And merciless ravage; and the shady nook
Of hazels, and the green and mossy bower,   45
Deformed and sullied, patiently gave up
Their quiet being; and, unless I now
Confound my present feelings with the past,
Even then, when from the bower I turned away
Exulting, rich beyond the wealth of kings,   50
I felt a sense of pain when I beheld
The silent trees and the intruding sky. –

Then, dearest maiden! move along these shades
In gentleness of heart; with gentle hand
Touch – for there is a Spirit in the woods.   55

53. dearest maiden: in associated manuscript lines Wordsworth addresses 'my beloved friend' and 'Lucy' (*PW* II, 504–5).

'Three years she grew . . .'

Probably composed in late February 1799; slight changes before 1805. The stanza is the tail-rhyme construction Wordsworth introduces into the collection with 'Ruth' (see headnote to that poem, p. 275). Mitchell (1974) compares Wordsworth's deployment of it here particularly with mediaeval practice, finding one example (the poem 'Lenten is come with love to town . . .', printed in Ritson's *Ancient Songs*, 1790) which is complex enough to have possibly influenced Wordsworth's sophisticated use of this stanza form. For the first two verses the subject of this poem may seem to be the death of a three-year-old girl in a manner that echoes 'Lucy Gray' (pp. 256–8). Indeed, in the first stanza, where Nature 'takes' the child who is already in 'sun and shower', such a reading is probably the easiest. The impossibility of this interpretation establishes itself slowly, but it is apparent that Lucy grows to maturity and then dies young. The character of Nature's 'taking' remains obscure, however, and strongly associated with the idea of Lucy's death or at least disablement for living. Not only her physical but her moral being seem in some sense to have been captured by Nature (perhaps a comparable phenomenon to the childhood life that is the undoing of Ruth); 'The work was done' (l. 37), which seems at first to be a summary of Nature's formative activity, turns out in the light of the next two lines to mean also, perhaps, that Lucy died as soon as Nature had completed her operations. If this is right, and given that the syntax of l. 37 suggests that Lucy's death follows on Nature's speech (which has been continuous from the first verse) like an action following a command, the natural reading of the opening stanza tends to reinstate itself as correct after all.

> Three years she grew in sun and shower,
> Then Nature said, 'A lovelier flower
> On earth was never sown;
> This child I to myself will take;
> She shall be mine, and I will make   5
> A lady of my own.
>
> 'Myself will to my darling be
> Both law and impulse; and with me
> The girl, in rock and plain,
> In earth and heaven, in glade and bower,   10
> Shall feel an overseeing power
> To kindle or restrain.
>
> 'She shall be sportive as the fawn
> That wild with glee across the lawn
> Or up the mountain springs;   15
> And hers shall be the breathing balm,
> And hers the silence and the calm
> Of mute insensate things.

'The floating clouds their state shall lend
To her; for her the willow bend;   20
Nor shall she fail to see
Even in the motions of the storm
Grace that shall mould the maiden's form
By silent sympathy.

'The stars of midnight shall be dear   25
To her; and she shall lean her ear
In many a secret place
Where rivulets dance their wayward round,
And beauty born of murmuring sound
Shall pass into her face.   30

'And vital feelings of delight
Shall rear her form to stately height,
Her virgin bosom swell;
Such thoughts to Lucy I will give
While she and I together live   35
Here in this happy dell.'

Thus Nature spake – The work was done –
How soon my Lucy's race was run!
She died, and left to me
This heath, this calm, and quiet scene;   40
The memory of what has been,
And never more will be.

The Pet-Lamb
A pastoral

Probably composed in 1800, before mid September. Ll. 58–60 were recast in 1802; otherwise no revisions. The stanza is like that of 'Poor Susan' (pp. 266–7) but the metre is iambic and the lines hexameters. This is in fact Wordsworth's only sustained use of this length of line; he systematically contrasts the rhythmically unbroken last line of each stanza with the first three lines and their mid-pauses (see O'Donnell 1989: 50). The verse form is foregrounded in the fact that most of its 'measured numbers' (l. 19) are an imaginary 'ballad' by the heroine. The Fenwick note (pp. 377–8) on the oblique relationship between the Barbara of the poem and the really existing Barbara Lewthwaite is instructive and to be compared with the use of real persons as models in, for example, the 'Yew-tree Lines', 'There was a Boy . . .' and the Matthew poems (among the connecting themes 'implied' in the note are the girl's beauty, orphanhood and, perhaps, the sister-as-mother). Wordsworth indicates that he has conflated Barbara Lewthwaite with a second real-life model, an unnamed girl 'whom I had seen and overheard' tending her pet lamb. He may also have had in mind his sister-in-law Joanna Hutchinson (see Ketcham 1969: 94). The poem is one of the *LB* studies of the child as experienced by the adult (compare 'We are Seven' and 'Anecdote for Fathers' especially, pp. 128–34) but with an unusual and complex attention to the process of adult articulation of a child's thoughts. The narrator hears Barbara utter four words which 'almost' create a complete identity of feeling with her, and he offers some forty lines of literary verse which are what Barbara 'might sing' if she could, and which are in some sense 'more than half' due to her (l. 66).

> The dew was falling fast, the stars began to blink;
> I heard a voice; it said, 'Drink, pretty creature, drink!'
> And, looking o'er the hedge, before me I espied
> A snow-white mountain Lamb with a maiden at its side.
>
> No other sheep were near, the Lamb was all alone,   5
> And by a slender cord was tethered to a stone;
> With one knee on the grass did the little maiden kneel
> While to that mountain Lamb she gave its evening meal.
>
> The Lamb while from her hand he thus his supper took
> Seemed to feast with head and ears; and his tail with   10
>   pleasure shook.
> 'Drink, pretty creature, drink,' she said in such a tone
> That I almost received her heart into my own.

2. Drink . . . drink: these simple but eloquent words are all that Barbara herself utters, but they are the key element in the narrator's experience of her (see also ll. 11–12).

'Twas little Barbara Lewthwaite, a child of beauty rare!
I watched them with delight, they were a lovely pair.
Now with her empty can the maiden turned away;   15
But ere ten yards were gone her footsteps did she stay.

Towards the Lamb she looked; and from that shady
    place
I unobserved could see the workings of her face:
If Nature to her tongue could measured numbers bring,
Thus, thought I, to her Lamb that little maid might   20
    sing.

'What ails thee, Young One? What? Why pull so at thy
    cord?
Is it not well with thee? Well both for bed and board?
Thy plot of grass is soft, and green as grass can be;
Rest, little Young One, rest; what is't that aileth thee?

'What is it thou wouldst seek? What is wanting to thy   25
    heart?
Thy limbs are they not strong? And beautiful thou art;
This grass is tender grass; these flowers they have no
    peers;
And that green corn all day is rustling in thy ears!

'If the sun be shining hot, do but stretch thy woollen
    chain,
This beech is standing by, its covert thou canst gain;   30
For rain and mountain storms! the like thou need'st not
    fear –
The rain and storm are things which scarcely can come
    here.

'Rest, little Young One, rest; thou hast forgot the day
When my father found thee first in places far away;
Many flocks were on the hills, but thou wert owned by   35
    none;
And thy mother from thy side for evermore was gone.

19–20. The ten stanzas of Barbara's imaginary song which follow are, in
their fairly mannered and literary language, what they are here said to be: a
poet's hypothesis as to what Barbara would have uttered if she were also a
poet. It is not, in fact, the poetic idiom of the narrator in the rest of the
poem.

'He took thee in his arms, and in pity brought thee
    home:
A blessed day for thee! then whither wouldst thou roam?
A faithful nurse thou hast, the dam that did thee yean
Upon the mountain tops no kinder could have been.   40

'Thou know'st that twice a day I have brought thee in
    this can
Fresh water from the brook as clear as ever ran:
And twice in the day when the ground is wet with dew
I bring thee draughts of milk, warm milk it is and new.

'Thy limbs will shortly be twice as stout as they are now,   45
Then I'll yoke thee to my cart like a pony in the plough;
My playmate thou shalt be; and when the wind is cold
Our hearth shall be thy bed, our house shall be thy fold.

'It will not, will not rest! – poor creature, can it be
That 'tis thy mother's heart which is working so in thee?   50
Things that I know not of belike to thee are dear,
And dreams of things which thou canst neither see nor
    hear.

'Alas! the mountain tops that look so green and fair!
I've heard of fearful winds and darkness that come
    there;
The little brooks that seem all pastime and all play,   55
When they are angry, roar like lions for their prey.

'Here thou need'st not dread the raven in the sky;
Night and day thou art safe – our cottage is hard by.
Why bleat so after me? Why pull so at thy chain?
Sleep – and at break of day I will come to thee again!'   60

– As homeward through the lane I went with lazy feet,
This song to myself did I oftentimes repeat;
And it seemed, as I retraced the ballad line by line,
That but half of it was hers, and one half of it was mine.

Again, and once again did I repeat the song;   65
'Nay,' said I, 'more than half to the damsel must belong,
For she looked with such a look, and she spake with
    such a tone,
That I almost received her heart into my own.'

39. yean: give birth to.
61. feet: the idea of metrical feet is in the background.

Written in Germany
on one of the coldest days of the century

Composed in the winter of 1798–9. The main revision is the dropping of the second stanza in 1820. The acutely cold European weather of this winter started at Christmas: Reed (1967: 256) suggests that the 'day' is Christmas Day itself because of Dorothy's assertion that no day in the century had been colder (De Selincourt and Shaver 1967: 243). For evidence of the coldness of the period generally, and of Christmas Day in Germany in particular, see C. Easton, *Les Hivers dans l'Europe occidentale*, Leyden 1928, pp. 141–2, 194. Apart from the slightly variant first two stanzas the verse form is the expanded quatrain of 'The Idiot Boy' and 'Andrew Jones' (and of 'Peter Bell') with varying line lengths and anapestic rhythms enhancing the comic effect that Wordsworth seems to have associated with this stanza. The whole structure is in fact a 'fairly common form in later 18thc. ballad revival' (O'Donnell 1989: 56) and is used by Bürger in 'Des Pfarrers Tochter von Taubenhain'. There is therefore a further comic effect, probably, in the allying of this form to material that is not sensational narrative, but the light tone coexists with some of Wordsworth's most serious preoccupations. 'Written in Germany' was later classified as a 'Poem of Sentiment and Reflection' and not, as might be expected, a 'Poem of the Fancy'. It may seem to be a personifying nature poem of the 'Waterfall and Eglantine'/'Oak and Broom' variety (pp. 247–52 – pieces which did become 'Poems of the Fancy'), but in fact no actions or impulses are attributed to the fly which are not consistent with a very limited estimate of an insect's inner workings, and the poem is a convenient benchmark against which the varying degree of personification in other poems may be set.

I must apprise the Reader that the stoves in North Germany generally have the impression of a galloping horse upon them, this being part of the Brunswick arms.

(Wordsworth's note)

A fig for your languages, German and Norse!
Let me have the song of the kettle;
And the tongs and the poker, instead of that horse
That gallops away with such fury and force
On this dreary dull plate of black metal.   5

Our earth is no doubt made of excellent stuff;
But her pulses beat slower and slower;

1–5. The point of the stanza is to contrast an enclosed German stove with an open hearth.
3. that horse: see Wordsworth's note.

The weather in 'forty was cutting and rough,
And then, as Heaven knows, the glass stood low
    enough;
And *now* it is four degrees lower.   10

Here's a fly, a disconsolate creature, perhaps
A child of the field, or the grove;
And, sorrow for him! this dull treacherous heat
Has seduced the poor fool from his winter retreat,
And he creeps to the edge of my stove.   15

Alas! how he fumbles about the domains
Which this comfortless oven environ!
He cannot find out in what track he must crawl,
Now back to the tiles, and now back to the wall,
And now on the brink of the iron.   20

Stock-still there he stands like a traveller bemazed;
The best of his skill he has tried;
His feelers methinks I can see him put forth
To the East and the West, and the South and the
    North;
But he finds neither guide-post nor guide.   25

See! his spindles sink under him, foot, leg and thigh;
His eyesight and hearing are lost;
Between life and death his blood freezes and thaws;
And his two pretty pinions of blue dusky gauze
Are glued to his sides by the frost.   30

No brother, no friend has he near him – while I
Can draw warmth from the cheek of my love;
As blest and as glad in this desolate gloom,
As if green summer grass were the floor of my room,
And woodbines were hanging above.   35

Yet, God is my witness, thou small helpless thing!
Thy life I would gladly sustain
Till summer comes up from the South, and with crowds
Of thy brethren a march thou shouldst sound through
    the clouds,
And back to the forests again.   40

---

8. weather in 'forty: the winter of 1739–40 as a whole in England was by far the coldest of the eighteenth century, with mean temperatures for December, January and February below freezing.
21. bemazed: bewildered.
26. spindles: skinny legs (in this connection the word is usually in adjectival form).

The Childless Father

Probably composed in 1800, completed by mid September. Clearer phrasings at ll. 9–10 from 1820 the only revisions. The stanza is exactly the same as that of 'Poor Susan' (pp. 266–7), a poem with which Wordsworth links 'The Childless Father' in the Preface (ll. 210–15) on the grounds of their similar handling of situation and feeling. A picture of an individual who as a father has suffered an extreme of deprivation (l. 12), and the place of that individual's suffering in the life of others. The community generally has joined in an intimate traditional funeral rite with Timothy (ll. 9–10) and six months later is thoroughly caught up in the hunt. In the first stanza a voice, perhaps the narrator's but certainly voicing this communal enthusiasm, urges Timothy to join in, which he does at his own slow pace, weeping slightly. The narrator notices this, but Timothy does not articulate to him what he may be thinking about his dead daughter.

'Up, Timothy, up with your staff and away!
Not a soul in the village this morning will stay;
The hare has just started from Hamilton's grounds,
And Skiddaw is glad with the cry of the hounds.'

– Of coats and of jackets grey, scarlet and green,   5
On the slopes of the pastures all colours were seen;
With their comely blue aprons, and caps white as snow,
The girls on the hills made a holiday show.

The basin of box-wood, just six months before,
Had stood on the table at Timothy's door;   10
A coffin through Timothy's threshold had passed;
One child did it bear, and that child was his last.

Now fast up the dell came the noise and the fray,
The horse and the horn, and the hark! hark away!
Old Timothy took up his staff, and he shut   15
With a leisurely motion the door of his hut.

3. *Hamilton's grounds*: the name does not appear to have been explained.
4. *Skiddaw*: one of the highest Lake District peaks.
9. *basin of box-wood*: 'In several parts of the North of England, when a funeral takes place, a basin full of sprigs of box-wood is placed at the door of the house from which the coffin is taken up, and each person who attends the funeral ordinarily takes a sprig of this box-wood, and throws it into the grave of the deceased' (Wordsworth's note).
12. Timothy is 'childless' not just through one death but through the deaths of all his children.
13. *fray*: tumult.

Perhaps to himself at that moment he said,
'The key I must take, for my Ellen is dead.'
But of this in my ears not a word did he speak,
And he went to the chase with a tear on his cheek.   20

17–20. The stanza works in a surprising way, to give a rather pedestrian thought of Timothy's, which he may not even have had, more weight (and, in the reading experience, more poignancy) than a palpable and, conventionally speaking, more expressive token of sorrow, a tear (an effect Wordsworth draws attention to at Preface ll. 214–15). But Timothy's hypothetical thought may be understood as the narrator's speculation about the cause of the tear, which he guesses to be a sudden acute awareness of the fact of Ellen's death cruelly ambushing Timothy in the middle of a banal action six months later – a moment of emotion which would convey much more about the experience of bereavement than the simple outer token of weeping. Even if the narrator is wrong (and it would surely damage the poem's treatment of grief if Timothy were allowed to articulate the hypothetical thought), his guess still stands as a moving act of empathy.

The Old Cumberland Beggar
A description

As a separate poem probably composed in and around February 1798 (see headnote to 'Animal Tranquillity and Decay', p. 101). Scattered revisions, minor apart from the addition of eight lines at l. 79 in 1837. Wordsworth's remarks on the Poor Law in the Fenwick note (p. 377) are elucidated in the notes to ll. 67 and 172. The poem has perhaps aroused more disparate responses than any other in *LB*. Its critics (who have sometimes been severe) have all attacked it as a political or social statement; its admirers (who have sometimes been fervent) have both defended it as such (Brooks 1965; Gill 1969) and denied that politics are relevant (Bloom 1961: 173–8). The enemies of 'The Old Cumberland Beggar' have often mistaken the nature of its political element; apart from the merely negative fact that Wordsworth did not choose, in writing about mendicancy, to compose a poem advocating a redistribution of wealth, there is nothing in 'The Old Cumberland Beggar' which amounts to a condoning of the beggar's poverty – nothing, in other words, to suggest that Wordsworth has moved from the disapproval of a society that produced beggars which he had expressed five years earlier in the 'Letter to the Bishop of Llandaff' (Owen and Smyser 1974, I, p. 43). His taking of mendicancy as a given, in 1798, shows a reduced optimism perhaps, but not less humaneness. One half of Wordsworth's appeal is, in fact, for the more humane treatment of a particular 'class of beggars' – the single, elderly, non-able-bodied rural paupers – in a political and ideological climate in which workhouses (some likely to be repellently regimented, most already depressing) promise to become the main mechanism for poor relief. Wordsworth's recognition in 'Ruth', ll. 242–3 (p. 284), of the life-shortening effects of a vagrant life is a measure of his distrust of the beggar's alternative: on the beggar's boldly portrayed 'real and ordinary suffering' on the road, see also Sampson 1984. It may escape the modern reader that Wordsworth's case here involves a brave attempt to remove the stigma attending begging (very much in the spirit of his defence of minor larceny in 'The Two Thieves', pp. 336–7); the lines added in 1837 at l. 79 (see note) actually call contempt for the beggar a 'sin'. This attempt is undertaken, however, without attributing to the beggar any implausibly ennobling traits; he is as limited physically and mentally as such an individual ever could be in reality.

Wordsworth's second claim is that giving support to a pauper directly, in the form of alms to a beggar, is a more healthy practice for a community than giving support via an institution like the workhouse. His chief point is not the humbugging one satirized by Blake ('Pity would be no more / If we did not make somebody poor') but rather that offering people opportunities to be humane or at least unself-centred can make them more so. This, as Brooks (1965) says, 'has a fine common sense' (the humbug is in the view that only spontaneous kindness is worth anything), and is convincingly grounded in images such as that of the 'sauntering horseman-traveller' who stops in the act of merely throwing his alms in the dust when he sees how 'helpless in appearance' the old man is (ll. 25–9). For another important thematic connection between the descriptive material on the beggar in the early part of the poem and the narrator's later interpretative remarks, see note to ll. 1–21; the absence of such links has often been alleged by commentators.

> The class of Beggars to which the Old Man here described belongs, will probably soon be extinct. It consisted of poor, and, mostly, old and infirm persons, who confined themselves to a stated round in their neighbourhood, and had certain fixed days, on which, at different houses, they regularly received alms, sometimes in money, but mostly in provisions.
>
> (Wordsworth's note)

I saw an aged beggar in my walk,
And he was seated by the highway side
On a low structure of rude masonry
Built at the foot of a huge hill, that they
Who lead their horses down the steep rough road   5
May thence remount at ease. The aged Man
Had placed his staff across the broad smooth stone
That overlays the pile, and from a bag
All white with flour, the dole of village dames,
He drew his scraps and fragments, one by one,   10
And scanned them with a fixed and serious look
Of idle computation. In the sun,

1–21. Dings (1974) finely notes how this opening tableau, in which 'the whole social organism ... is presented as working by a kind of inadvertency', supports the poem's attack on 'the Enlightenment spirit of reform, with its complete trust in the efficacy of rational design in social institutions': 'that mounting block, so blatantly meant for the man rich enough to own a horse, performs an unintended but nonetheless real service for the poor man; and the beggar himself is shown to be charitable in spite of himself'.
2–3. That the built structure immediately associated with the beggar should be to do with travel, rather than habitation, while he is none the less stationary on it, establishes one of the key paradoxes of his nature: 'he is all process ... and yet almost stasis' (Bloom 1961: 175).
6. Man: in this lightly capitalized text, 'Man' as applied to the beggar is conspicuous for being consistently capitalized.
9. flour: the meal which is referred to again at ll. 150–1, presumably made by the beggar into primitive bread.
10–12. He drew ... computation: Brooks (1965), stressing the lack of sentimentality here, observes that 'the beggar becomes a kind of parody of the business man, casting up his accounts, or of the miser fingering his treasures'.

Upon the second step of that small pile,
Surrounded by those wild unpeopled hills,
He sat, and ate his food in solitude: 15
And ever, scattered from his palsied hand,
That, still attempting to prevent the waste,
Was baffled still, the crumbs in little showers
Fell on the ground, and the small mountain birds,
Not venturing yet to peck their destined meal,   20
Approached within the length of half his staff.

Him from my childhood have I known; and then
He was so old, he seems not older now;
He travels on, a solitary Man,
So helpless in appearance, that for him   25
The sauntering horseman-traveller does not throw
With careless hand his alms upon the ground,
But stops, that he may safely lodge the coin
Within the old Man's hat; nor quits him so,
But still when he has given his horse the rein   30
Towards the aged beggar turns a look,
Sidelong and half-reverted. She who tends
The toll-gate, when in summer at her door
She turns her wheel, if on the road she sees

14. *wild unpeopled hills*: one of several allusions to the rarity of human life
in the beggar's territory, so that the road, and travel and communication via
the road, are the chief manifestations of a human population in the poem.
The effect is to impart a feeling of centrality to the beggar's way of life.
16–21. Brooks (1965) notes how Wordsworth emphatically refrains from
representing the beggar as himself dispensing charity, or as other than at
the end of the process of alms-giving: 'he only *seems* to be dispensing his
largesse to the birds. . . . The stress on the bird's caution points up this
fact.' The reality is that the beggar is still the parodic would-be miser of
ll. 10–12, whose physical impairment prevents his husbanding his resources
as he would wish.
25–32. So helpless . . . half-reverted: the contrast between perfunctory,
automatic alms-giving and alms-giving which is conscious and attentive is
in the same vein as Wordsworth's distinction between 'forced' and
'Christian' charity in the Fenwick note (p. 377). Evidently there are for
Wordsworth also qualitative differences within the unforced kind of alms-
giving. The ensuing lines give other examples of consideration for the
beggar intensified by his decrepitude. These vivid pictures of how a direct
encounter with the beggar, and in particular with his infirmity, can modify
conduct are a telling preparation for the later arguments on behalf of
personal alms-giving to the elderly poor.
34. wheel: spinning-wheel.

The aged beggar coming, quits her work,   35
And lifts the latch for him that he may pass.
The post-boy, when his rattling wheels o'ertake
The aged beggar in the woody lane,
Shouts to him from behind, and, if perchance
The old Man does not change his course, the boy   40
Turns with less noisy wheels to the road-side,
And passes gently by, without a curse
Upon his lips, or anger at his heart.
He travels on, a solitary Man,
His age has no companion. On the ground   45
His eyes are turned, and, as he moves along,
They move along the ground; and, evermore,
Instead of common and habitual sight
Of fields with rural works, of hill and dale,
And the blue sky, one little span of earth   50
Is all his prospect. Thus, from day to day,
Bowbent, his eyes for ever on the ground,
He plies his weary journey; seeing still,
And never knowing that he sees, some straw,
Some scattered leaf, or marks which, in one track,   55
The nails of cart or chariot wheel have left
Impressed on the white road, in the same line,
At distance still the same. Poor traveller!
His staff trails with him; scarcely do his feet
Disturb the summer dust; he is so still   60
In look and motion, that the cottage curs,
Ere he have passed the door, will turn away,
Weary of barking at him. Boys and girls,
The vacant and the busy, maids and youths,

37. *post-boy*: see p. 42 (ll. 52–3) for Wordsworth's implicit belief in the right of the poor to a mail service.
52. *Bowbent*: perhaps (given the similarity also to the imagery of Wordsworth's opening lines) from Michael Bruce, 'Lochleven', 1770, ll. 444–6: 'the mendicant, / Bowbent with age, that on the old grey stone, / Sole sitting, suns him in the public way'. But see also Milton, 'At a Vacation Exercise', l. 69: 'A Sibyl old, bow-bent with crooked age'.
57. 'I can scarcely say that I admit any limits to the dislocation of the verse, that is, I know none that may not be justified by some passion or other. . . . The most dislocated line I know in my writing, is this in the Cumberland Beggar, which taken by itself has not the sound of a verse. The words to which the passion is attached are "white road", "same line", and the verse dislocates for the sake of these' (De Selincourt and Shaver 1967: 434). The background metre Wordsworth is departing from is iambic, and it is 'white' and 'same' that receive irregular stresses to make the stressed pairs.

And urchins newly breeched all pass him by: 65
Him even the slow-paced waggon leaves behind.

But deem not this Man useless. – Statesmen! ye
Who are so restless in your wisdom, ye
Who have a broom still ready in your hands
To rid the world of nuisances; ye proud,   70
Heart-swoln, while in your pride ye contemplate
Your talents, power, and wisdom, deem him not
A burthen of the earth. 'Tis Nature's law

61–3. *cottage . . . at him*: as at ll. 19–21 there is no suggestion of the non-human natural world (despite some commentators' application of ll. 73–9) participating in the moral activity surrounding the beggar; the dogs desist because they have barked enough.

61. *cottage curs*: perhaps from James Beattie, *The Minstrel*, 1771–4, I, 343.

64. *vacant*: not occupied.

67. *Statesmen*: the only recent strictly political initiative on poor relief of any significance at this date was Pitt's abortive Bill of 1796, which would have qualified for Wordsworth's disapproval as it provided for an elaboration and extension of all kinds of institutionalized relief (to meet the economic crisis of these years) but with a special emphasis on a new version of the workhouse, the 'School of Industry' (see note to l. 172). The arrogant and sweeping reformism imputed by Wordsworth in the following lines would better fit certain non-political Poor Law innovators of the day, however, especially Benjamin Thompson (Count Rumford) and Jeremy Bentham. Rumford's grandiose workhouse project in Munich (as described for the benefit of English readers in 1796) sprang directly from a strongly expressed disgust for beggars, and had 'No Alms will be Received here' emblazoned over its entrance, while Bentham argued that all beggars should be apprehended. These anti-mendicity programmes were, as Wordsworth observes in the Fenwick note (p. 377), inevitably anti-alms in tendency (in Rumford's case not just 'by implication') and in a way perhaps particularly repugnant to him: voluntary private charity was actively encouraged in both schemes, but their great merit was supposed to be that the targets of charity were selected by an expert bureaucracy who then channelled these donations. All Bentham's abundant Poor Law writings date from the 1790s; they circulated mostly in manuscript form, though one important discussion was published prominently in the *Annals of Agriculture* in 1797–8. Another of the writers whom Wordsworth is right to identify in the Fenwick note as a force behind the 1834 new Poor Law but active as early as the 1790s, was Thomas Malthus, important in the present context because he had already, in the first edition of the *Essay on Population* (1798), forcefully if parenthetically called in question the whole principle of poor relief, private and public. Malthus had been partly anticipated by J. Townsend in 1786. The indispensable survey of this complex topic is J.R. Poynter, *Society and Pauperism*, 1969, pp. 21–185. See also Dings 1974.

That none, the meanest of created things,
Of forms created the most vile and brute,   75
The dullest or most noxious, should exist
Divorced from good – a spirit and pulse of good,
A life and soul to every mode of being
Inseparably linked. While thus he creeps
From door to door, the villagers in him   80
Behold a record which together binds
Past deeds and offices of charity,
Else unremembered, and so keeps alive
The kindly mood in hearts which lapse of years,
And that half-wisdom half-experience gives,   85
Make slow to feel, and by sure steps resign
To selfishness and cold oblivious cares.
Among the farms and solitary huts,
Hamlets and thinly-scattered villages,
Where'er the aged beggar takes his rounds,   90
The mild necessity of use compels
To acts of love; and habit does the work
Of reason; yet prepares that after joy
Which reason cherishes. And thus the soul,
By that sweet taste of pleasure unpursued,   95
Doth find itself insensibly disposed
To virtue and true goodness. Some there are,
By their good works exalted, lofty minds
And meditative, authors of delight
And happiness, which to the end of time   100
Will live, and spread, and kindle; minds like these,
In childhood, from this solitary being,
This helpless wanderer, have perchance received
(A thing more precious far than all that books
Or the solicitudes of love can do!)   105
That first mild touch of sympathy and thought,
In which they found their kindred with a world
Where want and sorrow were. The easy man

74–7. Sheer disgust at beggary, as a sign of depravity, is widespread in the
literature. See also headnote.
79. *linked*: after this word there follows in the 1837 version: 'Then be
assured / That least of all can aught – that ever owned / The heaven-
regarding eye and front sublime / Which man is born to – sink, howe'er
depressed. / So low as to be scorned without a sin; / Without offence to
God cast out of view; / Like the dry remnant of a garden-flower / Whose
seeds are shed, or as an implement / Worn out and worthless.'
107–8. *kindred . . . were*: the phrasing is ambiguous, for the 'world' may be
the world of the poor, or the world of mankind in general, which contains

Who sits at his own door, and, like the pear
Which overhangs his head from the green wall,   110
Feeds in the sunshine; the robust and young,
The prosperous and unthinking, they who live
Sheltered, and flourish in a little grove
Of their own kindred, all behold in him
A silent monitor, which on their minds   115
Must needs impress a transitory thought
Of self-congratulation, to the heart
Of each recalling his peculiar boons,
His charters and exemptions; and, perchance,
Though he to no one give the fortitude   120
And circumspection needful to preserve
His present blessings, and to husband up
The respite of the season, he, at least,
And 'tis no vulgar service, makes them felt.
Yet further. – Many, I believe, there are   125
Who live a life of virtuous decency,
Men who can hear the Decalogue and feel
No self-reproach; who of the moral law
Established in the land where they abide
Are strict observers; and not negligent,   130
Meanwhile, in any tenderness of heart
Or act of love to those with whom they dwell,
Their kindred, and the children of their blood.
Praise be to such, and to their slumbers peace! –
But of the poor man ask, the abject poor,   135
Go and demand of him, if there be here
In this cold abstinence from evil deeds,
And these inevitable charities,

'want and sorrow'. On the first reading the kind of altruistic individual
imagined seems to be a radical or democrat, a man who recognizes the poor
as human rather than repugnant and alien. On the second reading the
altruist is a man who has felt his bond with all human life, including
suffering. The latter may sound rather more like the Poet as characterized
in the Preface (ll. 535–46), and the mention of his childhood awareness of
the beggar (l. 102) echoes the narrator's recollection at l. 22.

108–24. The easy . . . felt: even the most selfishly affluent are made aware
that they are lucky. The striking imagery in this passage – of the stationary,
domestic and sheltered – is in deliberate contrast to that associated with the
beggar.
110. green wall: of foliage.
120. he: the beggar.
123. respite: apparently in the sense of 'surplus'; not recorded in the *OED*.
127. Decalogue: Ten Commandments.

Wherewith to satisfy the human soul?
No – Man is dear to Man; the poorest poor   140
Long for some moments in a weary life
When they can know and feel that they have been
Themselves the fathers and the dealers out
Of some small blessings, have been kind to such
As needed kindness, for this single cause,   145
That we have all of us one human heart. –
Such pleasure is to one kind Being known,
My neighbour, when with punctual care, each week
Duly as Friday comes, though pressed herself
By her own wants, she from her chest of meal   150
Takes one unsparing handful for the scrip
Of this old mendicant, and, from her door
Returning with exhilarated heart,
Sits by her fire and builds her hope in heaven.

Then let him pass, a blessing on his head!   155
And while in that vast solitude to which
The tide of things has led him, he appears
To breathe and live but for himself alone,
Unblamed, uninjured, let him bear about
The good which the benignant law of Heaven   160
Has hung around him; and, while life is his,
Still let him prompt the unlettered villagers
To tender offices and pensive thoughts.
Then let him pass, a blessing on his head!
And, long as he can wander, let him breathe   165
The freshness of the valleys; let his blood
Struggle with frosty air and winter snows;
And let the chartered wind that sweeps the heath
Beat his grey locks against his withered face.
Reverence the hope whose vital anxiousness   170
Gives the last human interest to his heart.
May never HOUSE, misnamed of INDUSTRY!

147–54. This anecdote, standing in contrast to the behaviour of the rich and the spirit of the Decalogue, has affinities of content and doctrine with Christ's parable of the widow's mites (*Mark* 12:41–4).
151. scrip: the beggar's bag, as referred to at l. 8.
154. hope in heaven: Colossians 1:5.
164. let him pass: compare, from a suggestively similar context, *King Lear* V, iii, 315.
168. chartered wind: compare *As You Like It* II, vii, 48. 'Chartered' means free, unrestrained.
172. HOUSE ... INDUSTRY: small, often short-lived establishments in rural and urban parishes in which the poor were supposed to work for their

Make him a captive! for that pent-up din,
Those life-consuming sounds that clog the air,
Be his the natural silence of old age!   175
Let him be free of mountain solitudes;
And have around him, whether heard or not,
The pleasant melody of woodland birds.
Few are his pleasures: if his eyes, which now
Have been so long familiar with the earth,   180
No more behold the horizontal sun
Rising or setting, let the light at least
Find a free entrance to their languid orbs.
And let him, *where* and *when* he will, sit down
Beneath the trees, or by the grassy bank   185
Of highway side, and with the little birds
Share his chance-gathered meal; and, finally,
As in the eye of Nature he has lived,
So in the eye of Nature let him die.

relief, date from the early seventeenth century. Larger and better organized workhouses serving 'unions' of several adjacent parishes (such as Wordsworth later refers to in the Fenwick note, p. 377) were increasingly standard in towns from the end of the seventeenth century and in some country districts (including Lancashire) from the mid eighteenth. There had been many proposals for Poor Law reform which advocated more commercially efficient workhouses (the term 'House of Industry' was increasingly in use from the 1770s) to cut the poor rate, and an enormous emphasis was put on new kinds of super-workhouse in the end-of-century programmes of Rumford and Bentham. Pitt's 1796 Bill envisaged 'Schools of Industry' in which whole families were put to work together. Because Malthus's antagonism to the Poor Law had not reached its full dimensions in the only edition of the *Essay on Population* published before 1800, Wordsworth would have found in him a commentator who regarded the workhouse as the sole legitimate means of poor relief. Neither the older workhouses nor their more efficiency-minded descendants put their inmates to remunerative work effectively. Wordsworth's point in the Fenwick note about the 1834 new Poor Law is that the right quality of alms-giving could never flourish in a system in which the workhouse is an alternative: because the uncharitable cease to give alms (they have contributed as much as they see fit through the poor rate and thence to the workhouse) the charitable feel forced to, so that some paupers will remain unconfined.

174. life-consuming sounds: presumably, sounds which denote the unhealthy labour of the working inmates.

Rural Architecture

Probably composed in 1800, completed by early October (the date of composition given in the Fenwick note, p. 379, being mistaken). In the 1827 collected works, uniquely, the boys' names were omitted. In 1800 there was an additional verse at the end which was restored in 1820: 'Some little I've seen of blind boisterous works / In Paris and London, 'mong Christians or Turks, / Spirits busy to do and undo: / At remembrance whereof my blood sometimes will flag; / Then, light-hearted boys, to the top of the crag; / And I'll build up a giant with you.' (The second line was emended in 1820.) The extra verse brings in a narrator cooperating as a poet with the actions of the children (compare 'The Pet-Lamb', pp. 301–3, which comes next in the arrangement of the collected works). In rhyme and metrical length the poem's stanza is an anapestic version of that of 'Ruth' and 'Three years she grew . . .' (pp. 276–85, 299–300). The poem may be seen as a kind of antithesis to 'Michael' and in general to Wordsworth's poetry of vanishing or ambiguous physical vestiges of suffering. Youthful vitality creates and then renews a testimony of itself (though the Fenwick note implies that the artefact involved was in reality typically constructed by adult shepherds).

> There's George Fisher, Charles Fleming, and Reginald
>   Shore,
> Three rosy-cheeked schoolboys, the highest not more
> Than the height of a counsellor's bag;
> To the top of GREAT HOW did it please them to climb;
> And there they built up, without mortar or lime,   5
> A Man on the peak of the crag.
>
> They built him of stones gathered up as they lay;
> They built him and christened him all in one day,
> An urchin both vigorous and hale;
> And so without scruple they called him Ralph Jones.   10
> Now Ralph is renowned for the length of his bones;
> The Magog of Legberthwaite dale.
>
> Just half a week after, the wind sallied forth,
> And, in anger or merriment, out of the North
> Coming on with a terrible pother,   15
> From the peak of the crag blew the giant away.
> And what did these schoolboys? – The very next day
> They went and they built up another.

3. *counsellor's bag*: the bag in which lawyers carry their robes to court.
4. *GREAT HOW*: 'Great How is a single and conspicuous hill, which rises towards the foot of Thirlmere, on the western side of the beautiful dale of Legberthwaite, along the high road between Keswick and Ambleside' (Wordsworth's note).
9. *urchin*: probably implies that the statue looks hunchbacked or otherwise deformed.
12. *Magog*: a legendary giant.
15. *pother*: commotion, tumult.

317

A Poet's Epitaph

Probably composed in the winter of 1798–9; various minor changes. Loosely based on an actual classical epitaph, Theocritus's Epigram XIX for the tomb of the poet Hipponax. There is also a debt to Burns's 'A Bard's Epitaph' (1786), though in that poem all the various visitors are meant to have an affinity with the now remorseful poet. The language is the slightly poeticized idiom Wordsworth consistently uses in his inscriptional poems (especially in its second-person singular form of address to the readers of the epitaph, though not to the more generalized 'you' of ll. 43–4). The figure of the 'idle' visitor who alone is welcomed to the grave, and the values he stands for (ll. 37–60), are represented as having a definite but not straightforward importance for poethood (it is only implied – ll. 39, 49–50 – that he is a poet). The ordinary epitaphic trope of urging the traveller to pause at the grave is strangely turned in the last stanza into a vehement summons to this figure, as if (perhaps in the manner of the 'idle' poet of 'The Fountain', pp. 293–5) an intimate acquaintance with death will remedy his deficiencies. Conversely, it is the place of death in the various value systems of the other potential visitors, as much as an incapacity to love the dead, which debars them.

Art thou a Statesman, in the van
Of public business trained and bred? –
First learn to love one living man;
Then mayst thou think upon the dead.

A Lawyer art thou? – draw not nigh; 5
Go, carry to some other place
The hardness of thy coward eye,
The falsehood of thy sallow face.

Art thou a man of purple cheer?
A rosy man, right plump to see? 10
Approach; yet, Doctor, not too near;
This grave no cushion is for thee.

Art thou a man of gallant pride,
A Soldier, and no man of chaff?
Welcome! – but lay thy sword aside, 15
And lean upon a peasant's staff.

Physician art thou? One, all eyes,
Philosopher! a fingering slave,
One that would peep and botanize
Upon his mother's grave? 20

11. *Doctor*: Doctor of Divinity, therefore a priest.
18. *Philosopher*: natural philosopher, i.e. a scientist.

Wrapped closely in thy sensual fleece
Oh turn aside, and take, I pray,
That he below may rest in peace,
Thy pinpoint of a soul away!

– A Moralist perchance appears,   25
Led, Heaven knows how! to this poor sod;
And he has neither eyes nor ears;
Himself his world, and his own God;

One to whose smooth-rubbed soul can cling
Nor form, nor feeling, great nor small;   30
A reasoning, self-sufficient thing,
An intellectual All in All!

Shut close the door; press down the latch;
Sleep in thy intellectual crust;
Nor lose ten tickings of thy watch   35
Near this unprofitable dust.

But who is he, with modest looks,
And clad in homely russet brown?
He murmurs near the running brooks
A music sweeter than their own.   40

He is retired as noontide dew,
Or fountain in a noonday grove;
And you must love him, ere to you
He will seem worthy of your love.

21. *sensual*: empirical, materialistic (in a philosophical sense).
25. *Moralist*: a moral philosopher. The term in itself is not necessarily disparaging in Wordsworth's usage, but here he has in mind the exponent of a systematic moral philosophy constructed by general argument rather than from an acquaintance with actual human cases. Several such systems could be in Wordsworth's eye.
38. *russet brown*: the closest echo of James Thomson's description of the Druid bard in *The Castle of Indolence* (1748), a passage which seems to be influential generally on Wordsworth's poem at this point ('his eye was keen, / With sweetness mixed. In russet brown bedight, / As is his sister of the copses green, / He crept along, unpromising of mien. / Gross he who judges so. His soul was fair' – II, 290–3). There is also a broad reminiscence of the 'Youth' described in Gray's 'Elegy written in a Country Churchyard', ll. 101–8, not least in the refraining from explicit identification of the figure as a poet.
40. Compare Pope, *Pastorals* 'Winter', l. 58.

A Poet's Epitaph

The outward shows of sky and earth,⠀⠀⠀⠀⠀⠀45
Of hill and valley, he has viewed;
And impulses of deeper birth
Have come to him in solitude.

In common things that round us lie
Some random truths he can impart –⠀⠀⠀⠀50
The harvest of a quiet eye
That broods and sleeps on his own heart.

But he is weak, both man and boy,
Hath been an idler in the land;
Contented if he might enjoy⠀⠀⠀⠀⠀⠀55
The things which others understand.

– Come hither in thy hour of strength;
Come, weak as is a breaking wave!
Here stretch thy body at full length;
Or build thy house upon this grave.⠀⠀⠀⠀60

57–8. Compare Burns, 'A Bard's Epitaph', ll. 13–17.

A Fragment

Probably composed in the winter of 1798–9. Several minor revisions; in 1800 there was a penultimate verse which was dropped in 1802 and never restored: 'When near this blasted tree you pass, / Two sods are plainly to be seen / Close at its root, and each with grass / Is covered fresh and green. / Like turf upon a new-made grave / These two green sods together lie, / Nor heat, nor cold, nor rain, nor wind / Can these two sods together bind, / Nor sun, nor earth, nor sky, / But side by side the two are laid, / As if just severed by the spade.' The lines seem to relate to some such narrative project as Wordsworth describes in his 1827 note (p. 372). He told Isabella Fenwick that the latter was 'never written', and that this 'prelude' was 'entirely a fancy'. The poem's stanza is a kind of variant on that of 'The Thorn' and 'The Idle Shepherd-Boys' (pp. 119–27, 262–5), with the first four lines made into a wholly rhymed quatrain that goes well with the stress pattern (and the deleted verse of 1800 is particularly 'Thorn'-like in its motifs). As it stands, 'A Fragment' is a poem about a traced tragedy of which the vestige is, unusually, the plain-to-see phantom.

Between two sister moorland rills
There is a spot that seems to lie
Sacred to flowrets of the hills,
And sacred to the sky.
And in this smooth and open dell   5
There is a tempest-stricken tree;
A corner-stone by lightning cut,
The last stone of a cottage hut;
And in this dell you see
A thing no storm can e'er destroy,   10
The shadow of a Danish Boy.

In clouds above, the lark is heard,
He sings his blithest and his best;
But in this lonesome nook the bird
Did never build his nest.   15
No beast, no bird hath here his home;
The bees borne on the breezy air
Pass high above those fragrant bells
To other flowers, to other dells,
Nor ever linger there.   20
The Danish Boy walks here alone:
The lovely dell is all his own.

---

11. *shadow*: phantom.

A spirit of noon-day is he,
He seems a form of flesh and blood;
Nor piping shepherd shall he be,   25
Nor herd-boy of the wood.
A regal vest of fur he wears,
In colour like a raven's wing;
It fears not rain, nor wind, nor dew;
But in the storm 'tis fresh and blue   30
As budding pines in spring;
His helmet has a vernal grace,
Fresh as the bloom upon his face.

A harp is from his shoulder slung;
He rests the harp upon his knee;   35
And there in a forgotten tongue
He warbles melody.
Of flocks upon the neighbouring hills
He is the darling and the joy;
And often, when no cause appears,   40
The mountain ponies prick their ears,
They hear the Danish Boy,
While in the dell he sits alone
Beside the tree and corner-stone.

There sits he: in his face you spy   45
No trace of a ferocious air,
Nor ever was a cloudless sky
So steady or so fair.
The lovely Danish Boy is blest
And happy in his flowery cove;   50
From bloody deeds his thoughts are far,
And yet he warbles songs of war;
They seem like songs of love,
For calm and gentle is his mien;
Like a dead boy he is serene.   55

32. Presumably, his helmet looks newly made.
36–7. For an account prompted by the thought that the Danish Boy is singing ancient northern ballads (of war, l. 52), see Hartman 1975a.
50. *cove*: possibly in the sense, from Cumbrian local usage, of a kind of recess in the mountain, but more plausibly in the literary sense of any kind of nook, which fits the repeated 'dell' of earlier lines.

Poems on the Naming of Places

By persons resident in the country and attached to rural objects, many places will be found unnamed or of unknown names, where little incidents will have occurred, or feelings been experienced, which will have given to such places a private and peculiar interest. From a wish to give some sort of record to such incidents, or renew the gratification of such feelings, names have been given to places by the author and some of his friends, and the following poems written in consequence.

(Wordsworth's advertisement)

I

Probably composed in 1800, completed by mid October; late minor changes. The narrator, exceptionally, is in the position of himself creating a vestige from which others may trace his experience (ll. 44–7), and this is in keeping with the thoroughly prospective, or forward-looking, rhetoric of the description throughout (for the manner in which so much is perceived as being in a condition of beginning, see 'Lines written at a small distance from my house'). It is possible that those who understand the meaning of 'EMMA'S DELL' will be saddened, or at least mute like the narrator at the grave of the Boy of Winander (p. 224), since by this time the narrator and Emma are imagined to be dead. There can be no mistaking the character of the mood recorded by the narrator at the time of his original naming, however: it is a mood of joy, almost uniquely unembittered by the sense of pain, with characteristic Wordsworthian accompaniments of phenomenologically raw sensation plus animistic fantasy given an unusually full and complicated treatment (see General Introduction, pp. 19–20).

> It was an April morning: fresh and clear
> The rivulet, delighting in its strength,
> Ran with a young man's speed; and yet the voice
> Of waters which the winter had supplied
> Was softened down into a vernal tone.   5
> The spirit of enjoyment and desire,
> And hopes and wishes, from all living things
> Went circling, like a multitude of sounds.
> The budding groves appeared as if in haste
> To spur the steps of June; as if their shades   10
> Of *various* green were hindrances that stood
> Between them and their object; yet, meanwhile,

3. *Ran . . . speed*: compare Psalms 19:5.
5. 'What a "vernal tone" is, the reader must infer from his own experience of hearing the sound of water in the spring, or when it is muffled by surrounding growth' (Murray 1967: 14).

There was such deep contentment in the air
That every naked ash, and tardy tree
Yet leafless, seemed as though the countenance   15
With which it looked on this delightful day
Were native to the summer. – Up the brook
I roamed in the confusion of my heart,
Alive to all things and forgetting all.
At length I to a sudden turning came   20
In this continuous glen, where down a rock
The stream, so ardent in its course before,
Sent forth such sallies of glad sound, that all
Which I till then had heard, appeared the voice
Of common pleasure: beast and bird, the lamb,   25
The shepherd's dog, the linnet and the thrush
Vied with this waterfall, and made a song
Which, while I listened, seemed like the wild growth
Or like some natural produce of the air
That could not cease to be. Green leaves were here,   30
But 'twas the foliage of the rocks, the birch,
The yew, the holly, and the bright green thorn,
With hanging islands of resplendent furze:
And on a summit, distant a short space,
By any who should look beyond the dell,   35
A single mountain cottage might be seen.
I gazed and gazed, and to myself I said,
'Our thoughts at least are ours; and this wild nook,
My EMMA, I will dedicate to thee.' –
Soon did the spot become my other home,   40
My dwelling, and my out-of-doors abode.
And, of the shepherds who have seen me there,
To whom I sometimes in our idle talk
Have told this fancy, two or three, perhaps,
Years after we are gone and in our graves,   45
When they have cause to speak of this wild place,
May call it by the name of EMMA'S DELL.

II
To Joanna

Probably composed in the summer of 1800; scattered minor revisions. The following manuscript commentary, illuminating as a description of how Wordsworth went about creating a dramatized narrator in a particular instance, dates from the time of composition (see *PW* II, 487).

The poem supposes that at the rock something had taken place in my mind either then, or afterwards in thinking upon what then took place, which, if related, will cause the vicar to smile. For something like this you are prepared by the phrase 'Now by those dear immunities', etc. I begin to relate the story, meaning in a certain degree to divert or partly play upon the vicar. I begin – my mind partly forgets its purpose, being softened by the images of beauty in the description of the rock, and the delicious morning, and when I come to the two lines 'The rock, like something', etc., I am caught in the trap of my own imagination. I entirely lose sight of my first purpose. I take fire in the lines 'That ancient woman.' I go on in that strain of fancy 'Old Skiddaw' and terminate the description in tumult 'And Kirkstone,' etc., describing what for a moment I believed either actually took place at the time, or when I have been reflecting on what did take place I have had a temporary belief, in some fit of imagination, did really or might have taken place. When the description is closed, or perhaps partly before I waken from the dream and see that the vicar thinks I have been extravagating, as I intended he should, I then tell the story as it happened really; and as the recollection of it exists permanently and regularly in my mind, mingling allusions suffused with humour, partly to the trance in which I have been, and partly to the trick I have been playing on the vicar. The poem then concludes in a strain of deep tenderness.

In this note Wordsworth analyses only the procedure of ll. 18–35; the narrational structure acquires a further level at ll. 1–17.

For Wordsworth's high opinion of 'To Joanna', see the headnote to 'Nutting' (p. 296). The Joanna figure may be based on Wordsworth's sister-in-law but the detail concerning her and the walk is not literally true of this individual. The mode of the first 'Naming of Places' poem is maintained (deep absorption in sheer sensations, personified natural phenomena, a vestige created) but is now curiously if mildly satirical in treatment (both in Joanna's frank laughter at the narrator's 'ravishment' and in the admittedly fantastic treatment of the echoes). In the fourth of the series doubts about a coterie keen on pathetic fallacy – such as Joanna is supposed to entertain at ll. 5–11 – will become much more weighty.

> Amid the smoke of cities did you pass
> Your time of early youth; and there you learned,
> From years of quiet industry, to love
> The living beings by your own fireside,
> With such a strong devotion, that your heart   5
> Is slow towards the sympathies of them
> Who look upon the hills with tenderness,
> And make dear friendships with the streams and groves.
> Yet we, who are transgressors in this kind,
> Dwelling retired in our simplicity   10
> Among the woods and fields, we love you well,
> Joanna! and I guess, since you have been
> So distant from us now for two long years,

That you will gladly listen to discourse
However trivial, if you thence are taught 15
That they, with whom you once were happy, talk
Familiarly of you and of old times.

While I was seated, now some ten days past,
Beneath those lofty firs, that overtop
Their ancient neighbour, the old steeple tower, 20
The vicar from his gloomy house hard by
Came forth to greet me; and when he had asked,
'How fares Joanna, that wild-hearted maid!
And when will she return to us?' he paused;
And, after short exchange of village news, 25
He with grave looks demanded, for what cause,
Reviving obsolete idolatry,
I, like a runic priest, in characters
Of formidable size had chiselled out
Some uncouth name upon the native rock, 30
Above the Rotha, by the forest side. –
Now, by those dear immunities of heart
Engendered betwixt malice and true love,
I was not loth to be so catechized,
And this was my reply: 'As it befell, 35
One summer morning we had walked abroad
At break of day, Joanna and myself.
– 'Twas that delightful season, when the broom,
Full-flowered, and visible on every steep,
Along the copses runs in veins of gold. 40
Our pathway led us on to Rotha's banks;
And when we came in front of that tall rock
Which looks towards the East, I there stopped short,
And traced the lofty barrier with my eye
From base to summit; such delight I found 45
To note in shrub and tree, in stone and flower,
That intermixture of delicious hues,

28. I, like a runic priest: 'In Cumberland and Westmoreland are several inscriptions, upon the native rock, which, from the wasting of time, and the rudeness of the workmanship, had been mistaken for runic. They are without doubt Roman' (Wordsworth's note). Runes are the early alphabet of the Germanic settlers in post-Roman Britain. The vicar shares the popular delusion that the inscriptions are runic; he may also think that runes were used by the druids.
31. Rotha: 'The Rotha, mentioned in this poem, is the river which, flowing through the lakes of Grasmere and Rydale, falls into Wyndermere' (Wordsworth's note).

Along so vast a surface, all at once,
In one impression, by connecting force
Of their own beauty, imaged in the heart. –   50
When I had gazed perhaps two minutes' space,
Joanna, looking in my eyes, beheld
That ravishment of mine, and laughed aloud.
The rock, like something starting from a sleep,
Took up the lady's voice, and laughed again;   55
That ancient woman seated on Helm-crag
Was ready with her cavern; Hammar Scar,
And the tall steep of Silver How sent forth
A noise of laughter; southern Loughrigg heard,
And Fairfield answered with a mountain tone;   60
Helvellyn far into the clear blue sky
Carried the lady's voice – old Skiddaw blew
His speaking-trumpet; – back out of the clouds
Of Glaramara southward came the voice;
And Kirkstone tossed it from his misty head.   65
Now whether, (said I to our cordial friend
Who in the heyday of astonishment
Smiled in my face) this were in simple truth
A work accomplished by the brotherhood
Of ancient mountains, or my ear was touched   70
With dreams and visionary impulses,
Is not for me to tell; but sure I am
That there was a loud uproar in the hills.
And, while we both were listening, to my side
The fair Joanna drew, as if she wished   75
To shelter from some object of her fear. –
And hence, long afterwards, when eighteen moons
Were wasted, as I chanced to walk alone
Beneath this rock, at sunrise, on a calm

---

55. again: in response.
56–65. 'On Helm-Crag, that impressive single mountain at the head of the Vale of Grasmere, is a rock which from most points of view bears a striking resemblance to an old woman cowering. Close by this rock is one of those fissures or caverns, which in the language of the country are called dungeons. Most of the mountains here mentioned immediately surround the Vale of Grasmere; of the others, some are at a considerable distance, but they belong to the same cluster' (Wordsworth's note). The whole passage is a reminiscence of Michael Drayton, *Poly-Olbion*, 1613, Song XXX, ll. 155–64.
71. dreams . . . impulses: the manuscript commentary (see headnote) implies that this refers to the 'trance' of ll. 43–51 (but the poem in its eventual form perhaps departs slightly from this description at ll. 66ff.).

And silent morning, I sat down, and there,   80
In memory of affections old and true,
I chiselled out in those rude characters
Joanna's name upon the living stone.
And I, and all who dwell by my fireside,
Have called the lovely rock, JOANNA'S ROCK.'   85

III

Probably composed in 1800; scarcely changed. The words 'we', 'us' or 'our'
occur some eight times in the poem but the first-person plural is resolved
(with an equivalent profusion of singular pronouns in the last four lines)
into a pair of individuals, and the vitiated coterie of the next poem does not
yet materialize. The sense of a humanized universe is re-grounded in these
lines in feelings between persons (ll. 15–16). At the same time – in the
naming of a particularly 'lonesome' peak after one of the parties in this
'communion' – a gentle jest is made of the habit of treating this non-human
world as other than autonomous; the habit had been bordering on
narcissism in such expressions as 'our hills' (l. 1) and 'we have' (l. 13).

There is an eminence – of these our hills
The last that parleys with the setting sun.
We can behold it from our orchard-seat;
And, when at evening we pursue our walk
Along the public way, this cliff, so high   5
Above us, and so distant in its height,
Is visible, and often seems to send
Its own deep quiet to restore our hearts.
The meteors make of it a favourite haunt:
The star of Jove, so beautiful and large   10
In the mid heavens, is never half so fair
As when he shines above it. 'Tis in truth
The loneliest place we have among the clouds.
And she who dwells with me, whom I have loved
With such communion, that no place on earth   15
Can ever be a solitude to me,
Hath said, this lonesome peak shall bear my name.

83. *living stone*: a phrase for stone in its native site, though Murray (1967:
17) detects an implied reference back to ll. 54–5.

3. The Fenwick note (p. 378) is interestingly definite about the element
of fiction involved in the description.
10. *star of Jove*: Jupiter.
15. *communion*: the *OED* cites this as the first use in the sense of intimate
personal converse.

IV

Probably composed in late summer and autumn 1800. Some subsequent alterations, with a marginally more favourable treatment of the walkers. In the Fenwick note (p. 378) Wordsworth makes an unusual claim for autobiographical veracity. This is the most startling and extreme of all the poems in *LB* in which human tragedy intrudes on joy, both because the mood of joy is depicted and deplored as inherently unresponsive to the suffering of others, and because the condition of the angler is worse even than that of the beggars in 'Andrew Jones' and 'The Old Cumberland Beggar' (pp. 273–4, 309–16). In the whole gamut of individuals terminally suffering in *LB*, only Simon Lee approximates to his atrocious situation.

> A narrow girdle of rough stones and crags,
> A rude and natural causeway, interposed
> Between the water and a winding slope
> Of copse and thicket, leaves the eastern shore
> Of Grasmere safe in its own privacy.   5
> And there, myself and two beloved friends,
> One calm September morning, ere the mist
> Had altogether yielded to the sun,
> Sauntered on this retired and difficult way.
> – Ill suits the road with one in haste, but we   10
> Played with our time; and, as we strolled along,
> It was our occupation to observe
> Such objects as the waves had tossed ashore,
> Feather, or leaf, or weed, or withered bough,
> Each on the other heaped along the line   15
> Of the dry wreck. And, in our vacant mood,
> Not seldom did we stop to watch some tuft
> Of dandelion seed or thistle's beard,

11–12. Played, occupation: prepares for the satire of ll. 56–60.
11–27. One of the most extensive descriptions in all Wordsworth of a natural phenomenon having the appearance of being animated by some kind of soul or feeling, and in this instance heavy with sardonic amusement at the observers who value such effects. Wordsworth seems to have in his sights a kind of irresponsible self-deception about these appearances, a trifling with the thought that the tuft of down has a soul despite a basic certainty that it does not. This is striking in view of the echoes of passages in Wordsworth where such divided states of mind are more indulgently regarded (for example, compare ll. 19–20 and 'Tintern Abbey', ll. 101–3, 107–8 [pp. 212–13]). But it is Coleridge (one of the observers) who in practice falls foul of this kind of accusation most readily (see, for example, 'The Aeolian Harp').
16. wreck: that is, wrack, or debris on the shore; in this variant becoming a Scottish and Northern dialectal form in Wordsworth's day.

Which, seeming lifeless half, and half impelled
By some internal feeling, skimmed along   20
Close to the surface of the lake that lay
Asleep in a dead calm – ran closely on
Along the dead calm lake, now here, now there,
In all its sportive wanderings all the while
Making report of an invisible breeze   25
That was its wings, its chariot, and its horse,
Its very playmate, and its moving soul.
– And often, trifling with a privilege
Alike indulged to all, we paused, one now,
And now the other, to point out, perchance   30
To pluck, some flower or water-weed, too fair
Either to be divided from the place
On which it grew, or to be left alone
To its own beauty. Many such there are,
Fair ferns and flowers, and chiefly that tall fern   35
So stately, of the Queen Osmunda named;
Plant lovelier in its own retired abode
On Grasmere's beach, than Naiad by the side
Of Grecian brook, or Lady of the Mere
Sole-sitting by the shores of old romance.   40
– So fared we that sweet morning: from the fields,
Meanwhile, a noise was heard, the busy mirth
Of reapers, men and women, boys and girls.
Delighted much to listen to those sounds,
And, in the fashion which I have described,   45
Feeding unthinking fancies, we advanced
Along the indented shore; when suddenly,
Through a thin veil of glittering haze, we saw
Before us on a point of jutting land
The tall and upright figure of a man   50
Attired in peasant's garb, who stood alone
Angling beside the margin of the lake.

35–6. *that tall . . . named*: the royal fern, or *Osmunda regalis*. However, no
reference to a Queen Osmunda seems to lie behind the name.
46. *unthinking fancies*: these may be taken to include the whole range of
responses catalogued in ll. 16–44, even if the beauty of the fern and even
the mirth of the reapers is not as fanciful as the inner life of the tuft of
down.
54. *making ready comments*: the angler is treated very much in the manner of
the debris and vegetation the group were pleased to observe and comment
on earlier.

That way we turned our steps; nor was it long
Ere, making ready comments on the sight
Which then we saw, with one and the same voice   55
We all cried out, that he must be indeed
An idle man, who thus could lose a day
Of the mid harvest, when the labourer's hire
Is ample, and some little might be stored
Wherewith to cheer him in the winter time.   60
Thus talking of that peasant we approached
Close to the spot where with his rod and line
He stood alone; whereat he turned his head
To greet us – and we saw a man worn down
By sickness, gaunt and lean, with sunken cheeks   65
And wasted limbs, his legs so long and lean
That for my single self I looked at them,
Forgetful of the body they sustained. –
Too weak to labour in the harvest field,
The man was using his best skill to gain   70
A pittance from the dead unfeeling lake
That knew not of his wants. I will not say
What thoughts immediately were ours, nor how
The happy idleness of that sweet morn,
With all its lovely images, was changed   75
To serious musing and to self-reproach.
Nor did we fail to see within ourselves
What need there is to be reserved in speech,
And temper all our thoughts with charity. –

56–60. Reminiscent of the poet in 'The Idle Shepherd-Boys' (p. 265) who is no less ready to switch from pleasurable rambling to rebuke of rural people for their supposed idleness. The coterie's smugness about meagre agricultural wages (ll. 58–9) makes this a much harsher passage, however. For Wordsworth's indignation at this time over 'the increasing disproportion between the price of labour and that of the necessaries of life', see the letter to Fox, p. 42.

71. dead unfeeling lake: the deadness of the lake has been recognized, indeed stressed, in ll. 22–3 – but in the fossilized metaphor of 'dead calm', and with the suggestion that the lake is asleep rather than dead. Now it is realized that the epithet has an unwelcome truth to it, for the lake is inanimate, and devoid of any affinity with human life.

78–9. 'Clearly the tag is no answer to what has happened. . . . Yet it does manage to supply what nature cannot, a compassionate awareness (limited and partly selfish though it may be) of the man's plight. Just below the surface is the assertion that man can feel if nature cannot' (Garber 1971: 116).

Therefore, unwilling to forget that day,   80
My friend, myself, and she who then received
The same admonishment, have called the place
By a memorial name, uncouth indeed
As e'er by mariner was given to bay
Or foreland on a new-discovered coast,   85
And POINT RASH-JUDGMENT is the name it bears.

V
To M.H.

Composed in the last week of December 1799; not altered. The Fenwick
note reads 'To Mary Hutchinson, two years before our marriage. The pool
alluded to is in Rydal Upper Park', although Wordsworth and Mary were in
fact married in October 1802. Wordsworth later regarded the poem as the
first of several poems chronicling his feelings for Mary Hutchinson; see
Morley 1938: 616. In contrast to the narcissism of the third of the series
and the light-minded pantheism and botanizing of the fourth, the final
poem asserts nature's autonomy and – within limits that do not violate
common sense and science – her power to behave in a quasi-human
fashion, her various elements interacting to create an environment such as
the 'woodman' or 'herdsman' would contrive. It is on these terms that man
should approach the natural world – not looking for a shared psychic life in
natural phenomena but also recognizing that they represent more than a
spray of raw sensations, and have their own self-directed purposes. Man
should, literally, coexist with nature and no more, following his human
routine in her company while she follows her natural one.

Our walk was far among the ancient trees;
There was no road, nor any woodman's path;
But the thick umbrage, checking the wild growth
Of weed and sapling, on the soft green turf
Beneath the branches of itself had made   5
A track, which brought us to a slip of lawn,
And a small bed of water in the woods.
All round this pool both flocks and herds might drink
On its firm margin, even as from a well,
Or some stone basin which the herdsman's hand   10
Had shaped for their refreshment; nor did sun
Or wind from any quarter ever come,
But as a blessing, to this calm recess,
This glade of water and this one green field;

7. *bed of water*: one of two striking phrases in the poem (see also 'glade of
water', l. 14) in which terms for areas of ground are transferred to the pool.
8. *both flocks and herds*: presumably, both tame and wild animals.

The spot was made by Nature for herself;   15
The travellers know it not, and 'twill remain
Unknown to them; but it is beautiful;
And if a man should plant his cottage near,
Should sleep beneath the shelter of its trees,
And blend its waters with his daily meal,   20
He would so love it that in his death hour
Its image would survive among his thoughts:
And therefore, my sweet MARY, this still nook
With all its beeches we have named for you.

16. *travellers*: gypsies.

Lines
Written when sailing in a boat at evening

Composed, probably in early 1797, as part of a single poem consisting of this and the following item, which appeared in the 1798 *LB* as 'Lines written near Richmond, upon the Thames at evening'. Slightly revised. Both poems were transferred from 'Poems of Sentiment and Reflection' to 'Poems written in Youth' in the collected works of 1845. See the Fenwick note (pp. 375–6) for the quite elaborate fictionalizing of a literal experience involved (which becomes even fuller in the second poem). The double-quatrain stanzas making up the 1798 poem are fused into a sixteen-line unit in the first of the 1800 poems but retained in the second. An interesting contrast is implied between the 'bard', who does not foresee suffering and sorrow, and the poet, who knows better. The boat/light/darkness construct acts chiefly as an allegory of life but there is also a suggestion that natural beauty, in a literal sense, will be 'faithless' and a site of 'pain' (again, the 'bard' does not know this but the poet does).

> How rich the wave, in front, impressed
> With evening twilight's summer hues,
> While, facing thus the crimson west,
> The boat her silent course pursues!
> And see how dark the backward stream!　　　　5
> A little moment past, so smiling!
> And still, perhaps, with faithless gleam,
> Some other loiterer beguiling.
> Such views the youthful bard allure;
> But, heedless of the following gloom,　　　　10
> He deems their colours shall endure
> Till peace go with him to the tomb. –
> And let him nurse his fond deceit,
> And what if he must die in sorrow!
> Who would not cherish dreams so sweet,　　　　15
> Though grief and pain may come tomorrow?

1. impressed: see 'The Female Vagrant', l. 101 and note (p. 140).
5. how . . . stream: compare *The Tempest* I, ii, 50: 'the dark backward and abysm of time'.

Remembrance of Collins
Written upon the Thames near Richmond

Probably composed in early 1797; slight revisions. See headnote to previous poem and Fenwick note, pp. 375–6. The verse is that of 'Goody Blake and Harry Gill'.

Glide gently, thus for ever glide,
O Thames! that other bards may see
As lovely visions by thy side
As now, fair river! come to me.
O glide, fair stream! for ever so,   5
Thy quiet soul on all bestowing,
Till all our minds for ever flow
As thy deep waters now are flowing.

Vain thought! ... Yet be as now thou art,
That in thy waters may be seen   10
The image of a poet's heart,
How bright, how solemn, how serene!
Such as did once the poet bless,
Who, pouring here a later ditty,
Could find no refuge from distress   15
But in the milder grief of pity.

Now let us, as we float along,
For *him* suspend the dashing oar;
And pray that never child of song
May know that poet's sorrows more.   20
How calm! how still! the only sound,
The dripping of the oar suspended! –
The evening darkness gathers round
By virtue's holiest powers attended.

Title. Collins: William Collins (1721–59), English poet who became mad and died young. The suffering of which the 'bard' of the previous lines was not conscious is now recalled as endured by a really existing poet.
14. a later ditty: 'Collins's Ode on the death of Thomson, the last written, I believe, of the poems which were published during his lifetime. This Ode is also alluded to in the next stanza' (Wordsworth's note). Wordsworth has evidently read the 'he, whose heart in sorrow bleeds' of Collins' 1749 poem (see 'Ode occasioned by the Death of Mr Thomson', l. 7) as a reference by the poet to his own depression ('pity' for the dead Thomson is mentioned in Collins' next stanza, while Thomson's spirit is called 'soothing' at l. 8). The more affirmative 'image of a poet's heart' which Wordsworth attributes to Collins at an earlier stage in his career is probably an allusion to Collins' 'Ode on the Poetical Character' (*passim* but especially ll. 41–50); this is of uncertain date but definitely earlier than the Thomson ode.
18. A deliberate echo of the Thomson ode, l. 15 (see Wordsworth's note above): 'And oft suspend the dashing oar'. What Collins urges as homage to Thomson is now urged in turn for him.

The Two Thieves
Or the last stage of avarice

Probably composed in the first half of 1800. Various small-scale alterations; through a revision to l. 13 from 1820 the grandson is no longer named. See Wordsworth's classification of the poem in the Preface (ll. 198–202), by which Old Daniel is linked interestingly to the old man of 'Animal Tranquillity and Decay'. The anapestic double-couplet stanza is that of 'Poor Susan' and 'The Childless Father'. As usual, Wordsworth is accurate in the Fenwick note (p. 380) on the biographical background. Models for Old Daniel (a Daniel Mackreth), his grandson and daughter have been convincingly identified from the right period, though Wordsworth may have exaggerated the old man's age slightly (Thompson 1970: 192–3). The intimacy and identity of the narrator's relationship to the community in which the two Daniels live is consistent with this background.

> O now that the genius of Bewick were mine,
> And the skill which he learned on the banks of the
>   Tyne!
> Then the Muses might deal with me just as they chose,
> For I'd take my last leave both of verse and of prose.
>
> What feats would I work with my magical hand!   5
> Book learning and books should be banished the land:
> And for hunger and thirst and such troublesome calls!
> Every ale-house should then have a feast on its walls.
>
> The traveller would hang his wet clothes on a chair;
> Let them smoke, let them burn, not a straw would he   10
>   care;
> For the Prodigal Son, Joseph's Dream and his Sheaves,
> Oh, what would they be to my tale of two thieves?
>
> Little Dan is unbreeched, he is three birthdays old;
> His grandsire that age more than thirty times told;
> There are ninety good seasons of fair and foul weather   15
> Between them, and both go a-stealing together.

1–2. Thomas Bewick is the celebrated Newcastle-born wood engraver of rural subjects.
11–12. Though the narrator would need Bewick's skill to supplant Biblical pictures in public houses with his own depiction of the two thieves, by implication his written version of the story is at least as instructive as the Old Testament stories alluded to here. There is also a suggestion, in the invoking of Bewick's name, that a knowledgeable fidelity to rural life characterizes the narrator's approach.
13. *unbreeched*: not yet in short trousers.

With chips is the carpenter strewing his floor?
Is a cart-load of peats at an old woman's door?
Old Daniel his hand to the treasure will slide;
And his grandson's as busy at work by his side.   20

Old Daniel begins, he stops short – and his eye
Through the lost look of dotage is cunning and sly.
'Tis a look which at this time is hardly his own,
But tells a plain tale of the days that are flown.

Dan once had a heart which was moved by the wires   25
Of manifold pleasures and many desires:
And what if he cherished his purse? 'Twas no more
Than treading a path trod by thousands before.

'Twas a path trod by thousands; but Daniel is one
Who went something further than others have gone,   30
And now with old Daniel you see how it fares;
You see to what end he has brought his grey hairs.

The pair sally forth hand in hand: ere the sun
Has peered o'er the beeches their work is begun:
And yet, into whatever sin they may fall,   35
This child but half knows it, and that not at all.

They hunt through the streets with deliberate tread,
And each in his turn is both leader and led;
And, wherever they carry their plots and their wiles,
Every face in the village is dimpled with smiles.   40

Neither checked by the rich nor the needy they roam;
For grey-headed Dan has a daughter at home,
Who will gladly repair all the damage that's done;
And three, were it asked, would be rendered for one.

Old man! whom so oft I with pity have eyed,   45
I love thee, and love the sweet boy at thy side:
Long yet mayst thou live! for a teacher we see
That lifts up the veil of our nature in thee.

17–18. The only two thefts specified are of fire-making materials, as with
Goody Blake (see pp. 105–6).
36. *This child, that*: old Daniel and young Daniel.
48. In the light of the challenging 'I love thee' (l. 46) the revelation
referred to here is not likely to be the sense of human mutability mentioned
in the Fenwick note, but rather a recognition that an old man's
depredations on the community do not betoken immorality.

'A whirl-blast from behind the hill . . .'

Probably composed in March 1798. L. 11 was dropped in 1820, as were the important ll. 24–7 in 1815 (with changes of wording in ll. 22–3). The form is unparalleled elsewhere in the collection, being couplet verse flanked by a quatrain at each end (though l. 19 is actually unrhymed). The central event of the poem – which is coextensive with the couplet writing, as if to emphasize its separate character – is an episode of animistic fantasy very reminiscent of the fourth 'Naming of Places' poem (pp. 329–32), but one that is much more affirmatively presented. There are nevertheless complications in the treatment. It is made as plain as possible that the leaf-dance is an illusion or 'appearance' (l. 26) – the leaves are dead, 'withered' things, animated by hailstones – so the whole emphasis is thrown on the capacities of the narrator's mind to entertain this illusion ('even' with such unpropitious materials – l. 26). These capacities are positively regarded, but perhaps chiefly because they mean something about his emotional condition, a 'heart at ease' (l. 24) exempt from the familiar Wordsworthian sense of pain.

> A whirl-blast from behind the hill
> Rushed o'er the wood with startling sound:
> Then all at once the air was still,
> And showers of hailstones pattered round.
> Where leafless oaks towered high above,   5
> I sat within an undergrove
> Of tallest hollies, tall and green;
> A fairer bower was never seen.
> From year to year the spacious floor
> With withered leaves is covered o'er,   10
> You could not lay a hair between:
> And all the year the bower is green.
> But see! where'er the hailstones drop
> The withered leaves all skip and hop,
> There's not a breeze – no breath of air –   15
> Yet here, and there, and everywhere
> Along the floor, beneath the shade
> By those embowering hollies made,
> The leaves in myriads jump and spring,

Title. whirl-blast: OED: 'Apparently a word of the Cumberland dialect, for which Wordsworth is the earliest literary authority'.

As if with pipes and music rare   20
Some Robin Goodfellow were there,
And all those leaves, that jump and spring,
Were each a joyous, living thing.

Oh! grant me Heaven a heart at ease,
That I may never cease to find,   25
Even in appearances like these,
Enough to nourish and to stir my mind!

20–1. Robin Goodfellow is here as diminutive as Shakespeare's Puck, but
not as mischievous; he is imagined playing pipes for the leaves to dance to.
Newlyn (1986: 107) comments that 'Robin Goodfellow may be seen as
Pan.'
20. rare: splendid.

Song for the Wandering Jew

Probably composed in 1800, completed by mid August, and considerably tinkered with in successive revisions. In 1827 new stanzas were added between verses 1 and 2, and 4 and 5; in 1836 verses 3 and 4 were put in the opposite order; and verses 2 and 3 were substantially revised between different editions. Nothing is known about the genesis of this poem, and it does not fit easily in the collection (and only one other poem in *LB*, 'To a Sexton', pp. 271–2, is trochaic). Behind the poem may lie *Matthew* 8:20. The Wandering Jew was the subject of popular ballads, as attested by Crabbe (*Parish Register*, 1807, I, 114). There is an example in Percy's *Reliques*.

Though the torrents from their fountains
Roar down many a craggy steep,
Yet they find among the mountains
Resting-places calm and deep.

Though almost with eagle pinion   5
O'er the rocks the chamois roam,
Yet he has some small dominion
Which, no doubt, he calls his home.

If on windy days the raven
Gambol like a dancing skiff,   10
Not the less he loves his haven
On the bosom of the cliff.

Though the sea-horse in the ocean
Own no dear domestic cave;
Yet he slumbers without motion   15
On the calm and silent wave.

Day and night my toils redouble!
Never nearer to the goal,
Night and day I feel the trouble
Of the wanderer in my soul.   20

Michael
A pastoral poem

Composed in early winter 1800. Revised with considerable freedom in various editions, with some tendency towards greater brevity, and some noteworthy changes of substance, as at l. 455 (see note). For fifteen lines on Michael's spiritual and imaginative life which Wordsworth contemplated adding in 1801 see *PW* II, 84. The process of composition and its close link with the site beside Greenhead Ghyll are interestingly recorded in Dorothy's journal (De Selincourt 1941: 65–72); Woof (1970) and Reed (1972) are important accompaniments to these entries. Also illuminating are the letters to Fox (pp. 42–4) and Poole (p. 48); for comment on the category of Lakeland 'statesmen' as it appears in this material, see note to l. 230 (there is also an important passage on the development of the characteristic local land tenure pattern in Wordsworth's *Guide*: Owen and Smyser 1974, II, 198–201). The implication in the Fenwick note (pp. 376–7), that the models for not only Luke and the house but also for the builder of the sheepfold were in real life quite discrete, is confirmed by an 1836 reminiscence of Wordsworth's: 'Michael was founded on the son of an old couple having become dissolute and run away from his parents; and on an old shepherd having been seven years in building up a sheepfold in a solitary valley' (*PW* II, 478). Other real individuals are known with more or less certainty to have contributed something: the family mentioned in the Fox letter, Thomas Poole himself, and the Ashburner family (who may in fact be intended by Wordsworth in his 1836 reminiscence rather than the previous owners of Dove Cottage mentioned to Isabella Fenwick; see De Selincourt 1941, I, 83 and *PW* III, 427). Some of the most emotionally charged portions of *Genesis* are tales of father/father-in-law and son relationships, involving the patriarch Abraham and his descendants. Elements from these are remembered at several points in the poem, and noted below. All these Biblical stories, it should be observed, have a happy outcome, as does the parable of the Prodigal Son (*Luke* 15:11–32), another Biblical prototype influencing 'Michael'.

Wordsworth's description of his hero in the Poole letter as a man of 'strong mind' and 'lively sensibility' puts its finger on some of the most moving effects in the poem, and perhaps on some part of its meaning. It is the contrast between the unbending and demanding (both of himself and others) in Michael ('mind' being also the poem's term for this aspect of him at ll. 44–5 and 166) and the whole-heartedness of his capacity for love that is the key to the power of episodes such as Michael nursing Luke (ll. 157–63 – here the 'mind' is not in abeyance but brought to bear on a deliberately 'female' action), and above all the 'covenant' and its sequel. Ll. 421–3 offer the spectacle of a great abasement transfigured into a great nobility as the stern, high-minded shepherd tells his son without shame or reservations that he will love him whatever happens to him in the world of prostitution and sharp practice. It is suggested in the notes that this moment has a religious bearing.

Michael does love as he promises and, in a beautiful paradox, this is said to sustain him in his tragedy (ll. 453–5). The nature of Michael's 'endurance' of Luke's loss nevertheless has a certain ambiguity which, though it should not be overstated, does in turn raise a question about authority in the poem. The narrator follows up the great statement of ll. 453–5 with evidence of Michael's continued capacity to work and even to find value in his life, but the celebrated ll. 470–1 give a glimpse of a man who *might* be paralysed by a sense of futility. The latter perception is enshrined particularly in the communal belief about Michael (' 'Tis not forgotten ... 'tis believed by all') and we are in some respects in 'The Thorn's' atmosphere of speculation about an enigmatic solitary with a tragic history (Michael *might* equally be sitting at the sheepfold remembering the boy Luke lovingly and feeling grateful for that love, even if he does no building; on this, see note to l. 17). It is true that the evidence of a 'comforted' Michael at ll. 459–67 also owes something to local reminiscence, but it echoes the words of the Preface on the Poet pleasurably contemplating a man himself balanced towards pleasure (ll. 538–46). Magnuson (1982) takes the unreliability of the community in the poem to some lengths, and even argues that l. 1 has a metaphorical significance here: 'If from the public way you turn your steps ...'. Wordsworth is certainly clear that the right audience for the poem will be narrow in quantity and quality ('a few natural hearts ... youthful poets', ll. 36–8), and it might be said that he states a test for membership of this group at ll. 62–79 ('grossly that man errs ...'). The climax of this passage is the enunciation of the principle of 'The pleasure which there is in life itself'. Hereafter one of the distinctive rhetorical features of the poem is the turn of phrase in which the reader's assent to particular psychological effects is assumed: 'what could they less?' (l. 76); 'The shepherd ... must needs / Have loved' (ll. 143–4); 'as you will divine' (l. 193); and – most emphatically – 'why should I relate ...?' (ll. 203–8). Dings (1973: 112–3) explores interestingly how the poem 'produces the feeling of resolution' for the reader, even though 'Michael's final state is ... as indeterminate as the sheepfold'.

> If from the public way you turn your steps
> Up the tumultuous brook of Green-head Gill,
> You will suppose that with an upright path
> Your feet must struggle; in such bold ascent
> The pastoral mountains front you, face to face.   5
> But, courage! for beside that boisterous brook
> The mountains have all opened out themselves,
> And made a hidden valley of their own.

1–17. Green (1977: 270–1) observes the affinity with the rhetoric of the picturesque guidebook (as does Barrell 1972: 183) and offers a 1776 parallel from the tourist literature: 'Wordsworth has completely absorbed the influence of the picturesque movement, and subordinated it to his own mature narrative style.' The whole passage may also be thought of as an adaptation of the wayside inscriptional exhortation to the traveller (see note to l. 1, p. 112).

5. pastoral: see note to 'Tintern Abbey', l. 17 (p. 208).

No habitation there is seen; but such
As journey thither find themselves alone   10
With a few sheep, with rocks and stones, and kites
That overhead are sailing in the sky.
It is in truth an utter solitude;
Nor should I have made mention of this dell
But for one object which you might pass by,   15
Might see and notice not. Beside the brook
There is a straggling heap of unhewn stones!
And to that place a story appertains,
Which, though it be ungarnished with events,
Is not unfit, I deem, for the fire-side,   20
Or for the summer shade. It was the first,
The earliest of those tales that spake to me
Of Shepherds, dwellers in the valleys, men
Whom I already loved, not verily
For their own sakes, but for the fields and hills   25
Where was their occupation and abode.
And hence this tale, while I was yet a boy
Careless of books, yet having felt the power
Of Nature, by the gentle agency
Of natural objects led me on to feel   30
For passions that were not my own, and think
(At random and imperfectly indeed)
On man, the heart of man, and human life.

17. The sheepfold in its present form (referred to as its 'remains' at l. 485) has deteriorated since Michael's day, for he definitely worked at the structure after Luke's departure (l. 447) and this cannot mean the collecting of stones, which has already been done (ll. 332–4), nor dressing them, since the drystone construction would have used 'unhewn' stones; moreover, at Michael's death the sheepfold seems to have been in sight of completion (l. 477). Hence this description of the vestiges of the sheepfold gives no clue as to the accuracy of the celebrated l. 471. For the use of an exclamation mark in connection with the apparently unremarkable, see note to l. 6, p. 245.

21–2. It was ... to me: 'Although "Michael" was one of the last poems added to the *Lyrical Ballads* (in 1800), Wordsworth here suggests that Michael's story is a kind of prototypical "lyrical ballad" ' (Heinzelman 1980: 216).

25. fields and hills: Maclean (1950: 92) explains the pattern of land use involved in 'Michael': 'The villages ... were, we may say, semi-enclosed, with walled-in arable and pasture but with very extensive commons waste on the mountains where all the sheep and cattle of a village grazed together.' The field/hill distinction occurs also at ll. 65–6, 74, 356–7. See also *Prelude*, 1805, VIII, 261–3.

33. heart: the first use of a word which occurs a score of times in the poem.

Therefore, although it be a history
Homely and rude, I will relate the same   35
For the delight of a few natural hearts,
And, with yet fonder feeling, for the sake
Of youthful Poets, who among these hills
Will be my second self when I am gone.

Upon the forest-side in Grasmere Vale   40
There dwelt a Shepherd, Michael was his name,
An old man, stout of heart, and strong of limb.
His bodily frame had been from youth to age
Of an unusual strength; his mind was keen,
Intense and frugal, apt for all affairs,   45
And in his Shepherd's calling he was prompt
And watchful more than ordinary men.
Hence he had learned the meaning of all winds,
Of blasts of every tone; and, oftentimes,
When others heeded not, he heard the south   50
Make subterraneous music, like the noise
Of bagpipers on distant Highland hills;
The Shepherd, at such warning, of his flock
Bethought him, and he to himself would say,
'The winds are now devising work for me!'   55
And, truly, at all times the storm, that drives
The traveller to a shelter, summoned him
Up to the mountains: he had been alone
Amid the heart of many thousand mists,
That came to him and left him on the heights.   60
So lived he till his eightieth year was past.

And grossly that man errs, who should suppose
That the green valleys, and the streams and rocks
Were things indifferent to the Shepherd's thoughts.

35. *rude*: unsophisticated.
36. *few*: perhaps, given the context, recalling Milton's well-known 'fit
audience ... though few', *Paradise Lost* VII, 31.
39. Many commentators have noted the parallel with Michael's relation-
ship to Luke.
40. *forest-side*: the forested (eastern) side of the valley.
61. The line sounds as if it is establishing Michael's age at the time of
some event about to be narrated, but in fact it is not picked up until the
'now' of l. 125, which in turn is picked up at l. 210. So the long-delayed
event is Luke's departure, which occurs when Michael is eighty-four
(l. 395).

Fields, where with cheerful spirits he had breathed 65
The common air; the hills, which he so oft
Had climbed with vigorous steps; which had impressed
So many incidents upon his mind
Of hardship, skill or courage, joy or fear;
Which like a book preserved the memory 70
Of the dumb animals, whom he had saved,
Had fed or sheltered, linking to such acts,
So grateful in themselves, the certainty
Of honourable gain; these fields, these hills,
Which were his living being, even more 75
Than his own blood – what could they less? – had laid
Strong hold on his affections, were to him
A pleasurable feeling of blind love,
The pleasure which there is in life itself.

He had not passed his days in singleness. 80
He had a wife, a comely matron, old –
Though younger than himself full twenty years.
She was a woman of a stirring life,
Whose heart was in her house; two wheels she had
Of antique form, this large for spinning wool, 85
That small for flax; and if one wheel had rest,
It was because the other was at work.
The pair had but one inmate in their house,
An only child, who had been born to them
When Michael telling o'er his years began 90
To deem that he was old – in Shepherd's phrase,
With one foot in the grave. This only Son,

65–79. Dings (1973: 130–1) observes that the syntax of this long sentence – of which 'fields' and 'hills' are the initially mentioned and then reiterated grammatical subject – 're-enacts the process of living the rooted life'.
73. grateful: pleasing.
84–7. two wheels . . . work: by the time of the 1835 *Guide* Wordsworth had come to understand the decline of the Cumbrian statesmen as due to the destructive impact of the factory system on cottage industry, but he was evidently not yet thinking in these terms in *LB*. However, the importance of spinning in the economy of the statesman household is well to the fore in 'Michael', as are its vulnerably small capital resources (see ll. 245–6, 257–61) which in 1835 Wordsworth said 'above all' prevented the statesmen from changing their activities in response to the new circumstances (Owen and Smyser 1974, II, 224). For Wordsworth's 1843 recollection of how common was Isabel's pattern of work in his youth, see *PW* III, 422.
90–2. When Michael . . . grave: Michael must have been about sixty-six (see ll. 210, 395).

With two brave sheep-dogs tried in many a storm,
The one of an inestimable worth,
Made all their household. I may truly say,   95
That they were as a proverb in the vale
For endless industry. When day was gone,
And from their occupations out of doors
The Son and Father were come home, even then
Their labour did not cease; unless when all   100
Turned to their cleanly supper-board, and there,
Each with a mess of pottage and skimmed milk,
Sat round their basket piled with oaten cakes,
And their plain home-made cheese. Yet when their
    meal
Was ended, LUKE (for so the Son was named)   105
And his old Father both betook themselves
To such convenient work as might employ
Their hands by the fire-side; perhaps to card
Wool for the Housewife's spindle, or repair
Some injury done to sickle, flail, or scythe,   110
Or other implement of house or field.

Down from the ceiling by the chimney's edge,
Which in our ancient uncouth country style
Did with a huge projection overbrow
Large space beneath, as duly as the light   115
Of day grew dim the Housewife hung a lamp,
An aged utensil, which had performed
Service beyond all others of its kind.
Early at evening did it burn and late,
Surviving comrade of uncounted hours,   120
Which going by from year to year had found
And left the couple neither gay perhaps
Nor cheerful, yet with objects and with hopes,
Living a life of eager industry.

97–111. Compare Virgil, *Georgics* I, 259–67. For an interesting account of the poem's debt to the *Georgics* and the Georgic tradition, see Green 1977: 244–54. Sambrook (1983: 126) compares 'Michael' to Greek pastoral verse, in particular the seventh idyll of Theocritus. Dispossession and forced departure from the land, endured by the shepherd characters, are themes in Virgil's First and Ninth Eclogues.

102. mess of pottage: not actually used in the Authorized Version's story of Jacob and Esau, but a customary formula appearing in the Genevan Bible's title to *Genesis* 25 and in other English Bible translations; a boiled dish, usually vegetable or oatmeal.

110. sickle, flail, or scythe: implements belonging to Michael's field-based activities (see note to l. 5).

And now, when LUKE was in his eighteenth year,   125
There by the light of this old lamp they sat,
Father and Son, while late into the night
The Housewife plied her own peculiar work,
Making the cottage through the silent hours
Murmur as with the sound of summer flies.   130
The light was famous in its neighbourhood,
And was a public symbol of the life
The thrifty pair had lived. For, as it chanced,
Their cottage on a plot of rising ground
Stood single, with large prospect, North and South,   135
High into Easedale, up to Dunmal-Raise,
And Westward to the village near the Lake;
And from this constant light, so regular
And so far seen, the house itself, by all
Who dwelt within the limits of the vale,   140
Both old and young, was named The EVENING STAR.

Thus living on through such a length of years,
The Shepherd, if he loved himself, must needs
Have loved his help-mate; but to Michael's heart
This Son of his old age was yet more dear –   145
Effect which might perhaps have been produced
By that instinctive tenderness, the same
Blind spirit, which is in the blood of all –
Or that a child, more than all other gifts,
Brings hope with it, and forward-looking thoughts,   150
And stirrings of inquietude, when they
By tendency of nature needs must fail.
From such, and other causes, to the thoughts
Of the Old Man his only Son was now
The dearest object that he knew on earth.   155
Exceeding was the love he bare to him,
His heart and his heart's joy! For oftentimes
Old Michael, while he was a babe in arms,
Had done him female service, not alone

145. *son of his old age*: compare *Genesis* 37:3 (and see generally Jacob's feelings for Joseph at this point).

151. *they*: hope, forward-looking thoughts, stirrings of inquietude (which tend to be less vigorous as life advances). 'Hope' (l. 150) is a much-used term in 'Michael', especially, somewhat ironically, in connection with Luke's expedition.

157. *heart*: the sense of 'loved one' was still current in Wordsworth's day but this usage, if relevant at all, is rather the occasion for a complex application of the word in Michael's case.

For dalliance and delight, as is the use 160
Of fathers, but with patient mind enforced
To acts of tenderness; and he had rocked
His cradle with a woman's gentle hand.

And, in a later time, ere yet the Boy
Had put on Boy's attire, did Michael love, 165
Albeit of a stern unbending mind,
To have the young one in his sight, when he
Had work by his own door, or when he sat
With sheep before him on his Shepherd's stool,
Beneath that large old oak, which near their door 170
Stood, and, from its enormous breadth of shade
Chosen for the shearer's covert from the sun,
Thence in our rustic dialect was called
The CLIPPING TREE, a name which yet it bears,
There, while they two were sitting in the shade, 175
With others round them, earnest all and blithe,
Would Michael exercise his heart with looks
Of fond correction and reproof bestowed
Upon the child, if he disturbed the sheep
By catching at their legs, or with his shouts 180
Scared them, while they lay still beneath the shears.

And when by Heaven's good grace the Boy grew up
A healthy lad, and carried in his cheek
Two steady roses that were five years old,
Then Michael from a winter coppice cut 185
With his own hand a sapling, which he hooped
With iron, making it throughout in all
Due requisites a perfect Shepherd's staff,
And gave it to the Boy; wherewith equipped
He as a watchman oftentimes was placed 190
At gate or gap, to stem or turn the flock;
And to his office prematurely called
There stood the urchin, as you will divine,
Something between a hindrance and a help;
And for this cause not always, I believe, 195
Receiving from his Father hire of praise,
Though nought was left undone which staff or voice,
Or looks, or threatening gestures could perform.
But soon as Luke, full ten years old, could stand
Against the mountain blasts, and to the heights, 200
Not fearing toil, nor length of weary ways,

174. CLIPPING TREE: 'Clipping is the word used in the North of England for shearing' (Wordsworth's note).

He with his Father daily went, and they
Were as companions, why should I relate
That objects which the Shepherd loved before
Were dearer now? that from the Boy there came   205
Feelings and emanations, things which were
Light to the sun and music to the wind;
And that the Old Man's heart seemed born again.
Thus in his Father's sight the Boy grew up:
And now when he had reached his eighteenth year,   210
He was his comfort and his daily hope.

While in the fashion which I have described
This simple household thus were living on
From day to day, to Michael's ear there came
Distressful tidings. Long before the time   215
Of which I speak, the Shepherd had been bound
In surety for his brother's son, a man
Of an industrious life, and ample means, –
But unforeseen misfortunes suddenly
Had pressed upon him – and old Michael now   220
Was summoned to discharge the forfeiture,
A grievous penalty, but little less
Than half his substance. This unlooked-for claim,
At the first hearing, for a moment took
More hope out of his life than he supposed   225
That any old man ever could have lost.
As soon as he had gathered so much strength
That he could look his trouble in the face,
It seemed that his sole refuge was to sell
A portion of his patrimonial fields.   230

---

203. why should I relate: on this and similar formulae, see headnote.
223–6. This unlooked-for ... host: 'In the sickening drop after "took" ...
and the dwindling away of impulse to that final "lost", the vital nature of his
tie to the land is manifest' (Guest 1978).
228. Interestingly, the line seems to have struck Wordsworth's brother
John as a 'vulgar' and 'low' idiom which should have been put into
Michael's own mouth (he found it similar in this respect to the imagery of
l. 281, though the latter was less objectionable because Michael's
utterance); see Ketcham 1969: 94, 101.
230. patrimonial fields: Wordsworth understands Michael's land to be his
property in the strongest sense, i.e. his freehold. This makes Michael
somewhat unusual in the system of statesmen, two-thirds of whom were in
the less independent position of copyholders (Maclean 1950: 101). The
point does not invalidate Wordsworth's references to the property of the
statesmen in the Fox and Poole letters; Maclean's eighteenth-century

Such was his first resolve; he thought again,
And his heart failed him. 'Isabel,' said he,
Two evenings after he had heard the news,
'I have been toiling more than seventy years,
And in the open sunshine of God's love   235
Have we all lived; yet if these fields of ours
Should pass into a stranger's hand, I think
That I could not lie quiet in my grave.
Our lot is a hard lot; the sun itself
Has scarcely been more diligent than I,   240
And I have lived to be a fool at last
To my own family. An evil man
That was, and made an evil choice, if he
Were false to us; and if he were not false,
There are ten thousand to whom loss like this   245
Had been no sorrow. I forgive him – but
'Twere better to be dumb than to talk thus.
When I began, my purpose was to speak
Of remedies and of a cheerful hope.
Our Luke shall leave us, Isabel; the land   250
Shall not go from us, and it shall be free;
He shall possess it, free as is the wind
That passes over it. We have, thou knowest,
Another kinsman – he will be our friend
In this distress. He is a prosperous man,   255
Thriving in trade – and Luke to him shall go,
And with his kinsman's help and his own thrift
He quickly will repair this loss, and then
May come again to us. If here he stay,
What can be done? Where everyone is poor   260
What can be gained?' At this the Old Man paused,
And Isabel sat silent, for her mind
Was busy, looking back into past times.

sources also speak of the copyholders as 'owners' of 'properties'. For a very
full list of relevant references on land tenure, see Douglas 1948.

251–3. it shall . . . over it: an important point is involved here: Michael
rejects the solution of taking out a mortgage on his land and thus burdening
Luke as he had been burdened in his youth (see ll. 380–2).
257–8. And with . . . this loss: a token of the meagreness of the family's
earning power: a sum which Michael can raise only by selling hard-won
property can be earned quickly and certainly by a young man in urban
commerce.
259–61. If here . . . gained: another solution is ruled out, that Luke should
work for someone locally.

There's Richard Bateman, thought she to herself,
He was a parish-boy – at the church-door   265
They made a gathering for him, shillings, pence,
And halfpennies, wherewith the neighbours bought
A basket, which they filled with pedlar's wares;
And with this basket on his arm the lad
Went up to London, found a master there,   270
Who out of many chose the trusty Boy
To go and overlook his merchandise
Beyond the seas; where he grew wondrous rich,
And left estates and moneys to the poor,
And at his birth-place built a chapel floored   275
With marble, which he sent from foreign lands.
These thoughts, and many others of like sort,
Passed quickly through the mind of Isabel,
And her face brightened. The Old Man was glad,
And thus resumed: – 'Well, Isabel! this scheme   280
These two days has been meat and drink to me.
Far more than we have lost is left us yet.
– We have enough – I wish indeed that I
Were younger – but this hope is a good hope.
– Make ready Luke's best garments, of the best   285
Buy for him more, and let us send him forth
Tomorrow, or the next day, or tonight:
– If he could go, the Boy should go tonight.'
Here Michael ceased, and to the fields went forth
With a light heart. The Housewife for five days   290
Was restless morn and night, and all day long
Wrought on with her best fingers to prepare
Things needful for the journey of her son.
But Isabel was glad when Sunday came
To stop her in her work, for, when she lay   295

264. *There's Richard Bateman*: 'The story alluded to here is well known in
the country. The chapel is called Ings Chapel; and is on the right-hand side
of the road leading from Kendal to Ambleside' (Wordsworth's note).
265. *parish-boy*: i.e. on poor relief.
270–3. Compare the accounts of Joseph's prosperity in Egypt (*Genesis*
39:1–4; 41:40–9).
275–6. *built . . . marble*: Dings (1973: 133) notes: 'the ironic counterpart of
the sheepfold'.
281. *meat and drink*: see note to l. 228.
282. Michael has paid the sum guaranteed on his nephew (see ll. 220–3);
for the problem of his economic survival without Luke's earnings see note
to l. 464.
285–7. Compare Jacob's behaviour when Benjamin departs (*Genesis*
43:11–14).

By Michael's side, she for the two last nights
Heard him, how he was troubled in his sleep:
And when they rose at morning she could see
That all his hopes were gone. That day at noon
She said to Luke, while they two by themselves   300
Were sitting at the door, 'Thou must not go:
We have no other child but thee to lose,
None to remember – do not go away,
For if thou leave thy Father he will die.'
The lad made answer with a jocund voice;   305
And Isabel, when she had told her fears,
Recovered heart. That evening her best fare
Did she bring forth, and all together sat
Like happy people round a Christmas fire.

Next morning Isabel resumed her work;   310
And all the ensuing week the house appeared
As cheerful as a grove in Spring: at length
The expected letter from their kinsman came,
With kind assurances that he would do
His utmost for the welfare of the Boy;   315
To which requests were added that forthwith
He might be sent to him. Ten times or more
The letter was read over; Isabel
Went forth to show it to the neighbours round;
Nor was there at that time on English land   320
A prouder heart than Luke's. When Isabel
Had to her house returned, the Old Man said,
'He shall depart tomorrow.' To this word
The Housewife answered, talking much of things
Which, if at such short notice he should go,   325
Would surely be forgotten. But at length
She gave consent, and Michael was at ease.

Near the tumultuous brook of Green-head Gill,
In that deep valley, Michael had designed
To build a sheep-fold; and, before he heard   330

---

299. all his hopes were gone: Michael's wildly ambivalent attitude to Luke's departure is in strong contrast to the powers of confident foresight described at ll. 46–55, but in the latter case it is his 'mind' which is operating (see headnote).
304. Compare *Genesis* 44:22.
330. 'It may be proper to inform some readers, that a sheep-fold in these mountains is an unroofed building of stone walls, with different divisions. It is generally placed by the side of a brook, for the convenience of washing

The tidings of his melancholy loss,
For this same purpose he had gathered up
A heap of stones, which close to the brook side
Lay thrown together, ready for the work.
With Luke that evening thitherward he walked;   335
And soon as they had reached the place he stopped,
And thus the Old Man spake to him: – 'My Son,
Tomorrow thou wilt leave me: with full heart
I look upon thee, for thou art the same
That wert a promise to me ere thy birth,   340
And all thy life hast been my daily joy.
I will relate to thee some little part
Of our two histories; 'twill do thee good
When thou art from me, even if I should speak
Of things thou canst not know of. – After thou   345
First cam'st into the world, as it befalls
To new-born infants, thou didst sleep away
Two days, and blessings from thy Father's tongue
Then fell upon thee. Day by day passed on,
And still I loved thee with increasing love.   350
Never to living ear came sweeter sounds
Than when I heard thee by our own fire-side
First uttering, without words, a natural tune;
When thou, a feeding babe, didst in thy joy
Sing at thy mother's breast. Month followed month,   355
And in the open fields my life was passed
And in the mountains, else I think that thou
Hadst been brought up upon thy Father's knees.
But we were playmates, Luke: among these hills,
As well thou know'st, in us the old and young   360
Have played together, nor with me didst thou
Lack any pleasure which a boy can know.'
Luke had a manly heart; but at these words
He sobbed aloud. The Old Man grasped his hand,
And said, 'Nay, do not take it so – I see   365
That these are things of which I need not speak. –

the sheep; but it is also useful as a shelter for them, and as a place to drive
them into, to enable the shepherds conveniently to single out one or more
for any particular purpose' (Wordsworth's note).

340. See the various promises of offspring made to the ageing Abraham in
Genesis 15 and 17.
348. blessings from thy Father's tongue: paternal blessings are of particular
importance in the story of Jacob and Esau.

Even to the utmost I have been to thee
A kind and a good Father; and herein
I but repay a gift which I myself
Received at others' hands; for, though now old   370
Beyond the common life of man, I still
Remember them who loved me in my youth.
Both of them sleep together; here they lived,
As all their forefathers had done; and when
At length their time was come, they were not loth   375
To give their bodies to the family mould.
I wished that thou shouldst live the life they lived.
But 'tis a long time to look back, my Son,
And see so little gain from sixty years.
These fields were burthened when they came to me;   380
Till I was forty years of age, not more
Than half of my inheritance was mine.
I toiled and toiled; God blessed me in my work,
And till these three weeks past the land was free.
– It looks as if it never could endure   385
Another master. Heaven forgive me, Luke,
If I judge ill for thee, but it seems good
That thou shouldst go.' At this the Old Man paused;
Then, pointing to the stones near which they stood,
Thus, after a short silence, he resumed: 390
'This was a work for us; and now, my Son,
It is a work for me. But, lay one stone –
Here, lay it for me, Luke, with thine own hands.
Nay, Boy, be of good hope – we both may live
To see a better day. At eighty-four   395
I still am strong and stout – do thou thy part,
I will do mine. – I will begin again
With many tasks that were resigned to thee;
Up to the heights, and in among the storms,
Will I without thee go again, and do   400
All works which I was wont to do alone,
Before I knew thy face. – Heaven bless thee, Boy!
Thy heart these two weeks has been beating fast

---

376. *family mould*: Chandler (1984: 165) detects in the phrase 'rich
Wordsworthian paronomasia', with senses of both 'earth' and 'pattern'.
385. This unexpected way of expressing what is in effect a decision about
his finances presumably indicates the extent to which the emotional side of
Michael's nature is operative here. Compare 'it seems', l. 387.
386. *Another master*: probably, in view of the train of thought in the
preceding lines, another mortgagee.

With many hopes – It should be so – Yes – yes –
I knew that thou couldst never have a wish   405
To leave me, Luke; thou hast been bound to me
Only by links of love; when thou art gone,
What will be left to us! – But, I forget
My purposes. Lay now the corner-stone,
As I requested; and hereafter, Luke,   410
When thou art gone away, should evil men
Be thy companions, think of me, my Son,
And of this moment; hither turn thy thoughts,
And God will strengthen thee; amid all fear
And all temptation, Luke, I pray that thou   415
Mayst bear in mind the life thy fathers lived,
Who, being innocent, did for that cause
Bestir them in good deeds. Now, fare thee well –
When thou return'st, thou in this place wilt see
A work which is not here; a covenant   420
'Twill be between us – But whatever fate
Befall thee, I shall love thee to the last,
And bear thy memory with me to the grave.'

The Shepherd ended here: and Luke stooped down,
And, as his Father had requested, laid   425
The first stone of the sheep-fold. At the sight
The Old Man's grief broke from him, to his heart
He pressed his Son, he kissed him and wept;
And to the house together they returned.

Next morning, as had been resolved, the Boy   430
Began his journey, and when he had reached
The public way, he put on a bold face;
And all the neighbours as he passed their doors
Came forth with wishes and with farewell prayers,
That followed him till he was out of sight.   435

420–1. a covenant ... us: the main Biblical prototype for this covenant at a heap of stones is *Genesis* 31:43–55 (the covenant of Jacob and his father-in-law Laban). The background researches of Helms (1977) have strengthened the link.

421–2. But whatever ... last: Michael's moving declaration of unstinting, unconditional love for Luke is offered by him over and above the reciprocal terms of their covenant ('But, whatever ...') rather in the manner of the New Testament dispensation transcending the covenant of the Old. Its truthfulness is tested to the hilt and proved at ll. 453–5. The parable of the Prodigal Son is a key Biblical image of the new moral calculus taught by Christ.

423. Compare Jacob's mourning for Joseph (*Genesis* 37:35).

A good report did from their kinsman come,
Of Luke and his well-doing: and the Boy
Wrote loving letters, full of wondrous news,
Which, as the Housewife phrased it, were throughout
The prettiest letters that were ever seen.   440
Both parents read them with rejoicing hearts.
So, many months passed on; and once again
The Shepherd went about his daily work
With confident and cheerful thoughts; and now
Sometimes when he could find a leisure hour   445
He to that valley took his way, and there
Wrought at the sheep-fold. Meantime Luke began
To slacken in his duty; and at length
He in the dissolute city gave himself
To evil courses; ignominy and shame   450
Fell on him, so that he was driven at last
To seek a hiding-place beyond the seas.

There is a comfort in the strength of love;
'Twill make a thing endurable, which else
Would break the heart: – Old Michael found it so.   455
I have conversed with more than one who well
Remember the Old Man, and what he was
Years after he had heard this heavy news.
His bodily frame had been from youth to age
Of an unusual strength. Among the rocks   460
He went, and still looked up upon the sun.
And listened to the wind; and as before
Performed all kinds of labour for his sheep,
And for the land his small inheritance.

450. ignominy and shame: compare *Troilus and Cressida* V, x, 33.
453. strength of love: primarily for Luke (as pledged at ll. 421–2), and the challenging psychological heart of the poem. Secondarily (in view of ll. 460–4) for the other objects which have called forth Michael's great capacities for attachment in the past.
455. In 1820 the line is changed to 'Would overset the brain, or break the heart'. While the idea of a paradoxical comfort from a strong love remains, it is not so explicitly claimed for Michael's experience by the narrator.
464. The question of what happens to Michael's finances has been oddly sidestepped by the commentators. Metzger (1976) and Levinson (1985) touch on the question, assuming that he loses the fields he has tried to save, but the present line implies the opposite, and is confirmed by ll. 479–80. Dings (1973: 110–11) sees the problem and believes that Wordsworth is inconsistent: 'the loss of Luke ought to bring on the loss of the property'. But it is made clear earlier that other means of raising money are available

And to that hollow dell from time to time 465
Did he repair, to build the fold of which
His flock had need. 'Tis not forgotten yet
The pity which was then in every heart
For the Old Man – and 'tis believed by all
That many and many a day he thither went, 470
And never lifted up a single stone.

There, by the sheep-fold, sometimes was he seen
Sitting alone, with that his faithful dog,
Then old, beside him, lying at his feet.
The length of full seven years from time to time 475
He at the building of this sheep-fold wrought,
And left the work unfinished when he died.
Three years, or little more, did Isabel
Survive her husband: at her death the estate
Was sold, and went into a stranger's hand. 480
The cottage which was named The EVENING STAR
Is gone – the ploughshare has been through the ground
On which it stood; great changes have been wrought
In all the neighbourhood: – yet the oak is left
That grew beside their door; and the remains 485
Of the unfinished sheep-fold may be seen
Beside the boisterous brook of Green-head Gill.

to Michael if he is not concerned to pass on a mortgage-free legacy.
Bushnell (1981) does go into detail on the question but seems to assume
(contrary to the clear evidence of l. 384) that the guarantee to Michael's
nephew took the form of a mortgage on his property (the threatened sale of
land then has to be explained as a means of raising money for interest, with
Michael's retention of the fields until his death appearing to be an
unsatisfactory obscurity).

469–71. 'tis believed ... stone: for the status of this belief, see headnote.

Arrangements and classifications

Here are set out the arrangements of the poems in the first and second editions of *Lyrical Ballads* (the edition of 1802 was identical in arrangement with 1805), and in Wordsworth's collected works from 1815. 1805 titles are used where there is more than one version.

Lyrical Ballads 1798

The Ancient Mariner
The Foster-mother's Tale
Lines (Left upon a Seat in a Yew-tree)
The Nightingale
The Female Vagrant
Goody Blake and Harry Gill
Lines (Written at a small distance from my house)
Simon Lee
Anecdote for Fathers
We are Seven
Lines Written in Early Spring
The Thorn
The Last of the Flock
[The Dungeon]
The Mad Mother
The Idiot Boy
Lines Written near Richmond
Expostulation and Reply
The Tables Turned
Animal Tranquillity and Decay
The Complaint of a Forsaken Indian Woman
[The Convict]
Lines (Written a few miles above Tintern Abbey)

Lyrical Ballads 1800

Expostulation and Reply
The Tables Turned
Animal Tranquillity and Decay
The Complaint of a Forsaken Indian Woman
The Last of the Flock
Lines (Left upon a Seat in a Yew-tree)
The Foster-mother's Tale
Goody Blake and Harry Gill
The Thorn
We are Seven
Anecdote for Fathers
Lines (Written at a small distance from my house)
The Female Vagrant
[The Dungeon]
Simon Lee
Lines Written in Early Spring
The Nightingale
Lines (Written when sailing)
Remembrance of Collins
The Idiot Boy
Love
The Mad Mother
The Ancient Mariner
Lines (Written a few miles above Tintern Abbey)
Hart-leap Well
'There was a Boy . . .'
The Brothers
Ellen Irwin
'Strange fits of passion I have known . . .'
'She dwelt among th'untrodden ways . . .'
'A slumber did my spirit seal . . .'
The Waterfall and the Eglantine
The Oak and the Broom
Lucy Gray
The Idle Shepherd-Boys
' 'Tis said, that some have died for love . . .'
Poor Susan
Inscription (for the Spot where the Hermitage stood)
Lines (Written with a pencil upon a stone)
To a Sexton
Andrew Jones
The Two Thieves
'A whirl-blast from behind the hill . . .'

Song for the Wandering Jew
Ruth
Lines (Written with a slate-pencil)
'If Nature . . .'
The Two April Mornings
The Fountain
Nutting
'Three years she grew . . .'
The Pet-Lamb
Written in Germany
The Childless Father
The Old Cumberland Beggar
Rural Architecture
A Poet's Epitaph
[A Character]
A Fragment
Poems on the Naming of Places
Michael

Wordsworth's classifications
Key to categories

Ins: Inscriptions; MP: Miscellaneous Poems; MTS: Memorials of a Tour in Scotland; PF: Poems of the Fancy; PFA: Poems Founded on the Affections; PI: Poems of the Imagination; PNP: Poems on the Naming of Places; PRPC: Poems Relating to the Period of Childhood; PRPOA: Poems Relating to the Period of Old Age; PSR: Poems of Sentiment and Reflection; PWY: Poems Written in Youth.

Anecdote for Fathers	PRPC
Animal Tranquillity and Decay	PRPOA
The Brothers	PFA
The Childless Father	PFA
The Complaint of a Forsaken Indian Woman	PFA
Ellen Irwin	PFA; to MTS 1827
Expostulation and Reply	PSR
The Female Vagrant	PWY
The Fountain	PSR
A Fragment	PF
Goody Blake and Harry Gill	PI; to MP 1845
Hart-leap Well	PI
The Idiot Boy	PFA
The Idle Shepherd-Boys	PRPC
'If Nature . . .'	PSR

Inscription (for the Spot where the Hermitage stood)	PRPOA; to Ins 1845
The Last of the Flock	PFA
Lines (Left upon a Seat in a Yew-tree)	PSR; to PWY 1845
Lines (Written a few miles above Tintern Abbey)	PI
Lines (Written at a small distance from my house)	PSR
Lines (Written when sailing)	PSR; to PWY 1845
Lines Written in Early Spring	PSR
Lines (Written with a pencil upon a stone)	Ins
Lines (Written with a slate-pencil)	Ins
Lucy Gray	PRPC
The Mad Mother	PFA
Michael	PFA
Nutting	PI
The Oak and the Broom	PF
The Old Cumberland Beggar	PRPOA
The Pet-Lamb	PRPC
Poems on the Naming of Places	PNP
A Poet's Epitaph	PSR
Poor Susan	PI
Remembrance of Collins	PSR; to PWY 1845
Rural Architecture	PRPC
Ruth	PFA; to PI 1827
'She dwelt among th'untrodden ways . . .'	PFA
Simon Lee	PSR
'A slumber did my spirit seal . . .'	PFA
Song for the Wandering Jew	PF
'Strange fits of passion I have known . . .'	PFA
The Tables Turned	PSR
'There was a Boy . . .'	PI
The Thorn	PI
'Three years she grew . . .'	PI
' 'Tis said, that some have died for love . . .'	PFA
To a Sexton	PF
The Two April Mornings	PSR
The Two Thieves	PRPOA
The Waterfall and the Eglantine	PF
We are Seven	PRPC
'A whirl-blast from behind the hill . . .'	PF
Written in Germany	PSR

Authors' later comment

In this section are brought together all the significant recorded comment and apparatus offered by the authors after 1805, except for a few brief pieces of material which are cited in the notes to individual poems. The heading 'Fenwick' indicates that the comment is one of those dictated by Wordsworth in 1843 to his friend Isabella Fenwick. The shortest Fenwick notes have been digested in the annotation, but those reproduced here have been given in virtually their full form. It seemed right to retain Wordsworth's responses intact, even though some of the matter is not directly relevant to the poetic texts.

The Ancient Mariner
1817 epigraph

Facile credo, plures esse Naturas invisibiles quam visibiles in rerum universitate. Sed horum omnium familiam quis nobis enarrabit? et gradus et cognationes et discrimina et singulorum munera? Quid agunt? quae loca habitant? Harum rerum notitiam semper ambivit ingenium humanum, nunquam attigit. Juvat, interea, non diffiteor, quandoque in animo, tanquam in tabula, majoris et melioris mundi imaginem contemplari: ne mens assuefacta hodiernae vitae minutiis se contrahat nimis, et tota subsidat in pusillas cogitationes. Sed veritati interea invigilandum est, modusque servandus, ut certa ab incertis, diem a nocte, distinguamus.

The source is Thomas Burnet, *Archaeologiae Philosophicae* (1692: 68). The sense is: 'I can easily believe that in the totality of things there are more invisible than visible beings. But who will describe the family of all these, their ranks, relations, differences, and distinctive functions? What do they do? Where do they live? Man's intelligence has always sought knowledge of these things, and has never achieved it. Meanwhile, I do not deny that it pleases me sometimes to contemplate in my mind, as in a picture, the image of a greater and better world: lest the mind, accustomed to the small matters of everyday life, narrows itself and sinks wholly into petty thoughts. But at the same time we must be watchful for truth, and keep within limits, so that we distinguish the certain from the uncertain, day from night.' (My translation)

1817 glosses

Line numbers indicate as clearly as possible, given some changes in the text, the part of the poem to which each marginal gloss was attached; which lines at this point they apply to must sometimes be deduced from the sense.

1–4. An ancient Mariner meeteth three gallants bidden to a wedding-feast, and detaineth one.

17–20. The wedding-guest is spellbound by the eye of the old seafaring man, and constrained to hear his tale.

29–34. The Mariner tells how the ship sailed southward with a good wind and fair weather, till it reached the line.

37–40. The wedding-guest heareth the bridal music; but the Mariner continueth his tale.

45–7. The ship driven by a storm towards the south pole.

53–6. The land of ice, and of fearful sounds where no living thing was to be seen.

61–6. Till a great sea-bird, called the Albatross, came through the snow-fog, and was received with great joy and hospitality.

69–76. And lo! the Albatross proveth a bird of good omen, and followeth the ship as it returned northward through fog and floating ice.

77–80. The ancient Mariner inhospitably killeth the pious bird of good omen.

89–92. His shipmates cry out against the ancient Mariner, for killing the bird of good luck.

93–8. But when the fog cleared off, they justify the same, and thus make themselves accomplices in the crime.

99–103. The fair breeze continues; the ship enters the Pacific Ocean, and sails northward, even till it reaches the line.

105–6. The ship hath been suddenly becalmed.

115–16. And the Albatross begins to be avenged.

127–30. A Spirit had followed them; one of the invisible inhabitants of this planet, neither departed souls nor angels; concerning whom the learned Jew Josephus, and the Platonic Constantinopolitan, Michael Psellus, may be consulted. They are very numerous, and there is no climate or element without one or more.

135–8. The shipmates, in their sore distress, would fain throw the whole guilt on the ancient Mariner: in sign whereof they hang the dead sea-bird round his neck.

141–3. The ancient Mariner beholdeth a sign in the element afar off.

151–5. At its nearer approach, it seemeth him to be a ship; and at a dear ransom he freeth his speech from the bonds of thirst.

158. A flash of joy;

161–4. And horror follows. For can it be a ship that comes onward without wind or tide?

171. It seemeth him but the skeleton of a ship.

179–82. And its ribs are seen as bars on the face of the setting sun. The Spectre-Woman and her Death-mate, and no other on board the skeleton ship.

188–9. Like vessel, like crew!

193–6. Death and Life-in-Death have diced for the ship's crew, and she (the latter) winneth the ancient Mariner.

203–4. At the rising of the Moon,

206–7. One after another,

210–11. His shipmates drop down dead.

214–17. But Life-in-Death begins her work on the ancient Mariner.

218–21. The wedding-guest feareth that a Spirit is talking to him;

224–9. But the ancient Mariner assureth him of his bodily life, and proceedeth to relate his horrible penance.

230–1. He despiseth the creatures of the calm.

234–7. And envieth that *they* should live, and so many lie dead.

247–50. But the curse liveth for him in the eye of the dead men.

257–60. In his loneliness and fixedness he yearneth towards the journeying Moon, and the stars that still sojourn, yet still move onward; and everywhere the blue sky belongs to them, and is their appointed rest, and their native country and their own natural homes, which they enter unannounced, as lords that are certainly expected and yet there is a silent joy at their arrival.

266–70. By the light of the Moon he beholdeth God's creatures of the great calm.

276–7. Their beauty and their happiness.

279–81. He blesseth them in his heart.

282–3. The spell begins to break.

291–4. By grace of the holy Mother, the ancient Mariner is refreshed with rain.

303–6. He heareth sounds and seeth strange sights and commotions in the sky and the element.

321–4. The bodies of the ship's crew are inspirited, and the ship moves on;

341–7. But not by the souls of the men, nor by daemons of earth or middle air, but by a blessed troop of angelic spirits, sent down by the invocation of the guardian saint.

371–6. The lonesome Spirit from the south pole carries on the ship as far as the line, in obedience to the angelic troop, but still requireth vengeance.

387–99. The Polar Spirit's fellow daemons, the invisible inhabitants of the element, take part in his wrong; and two of them relate, one to the other, that penance long and heavy for the ancient Mariner hath been accorded to the Polar Spirit, who returneth southward.

416–19. The Mariner hath been cast into a trance; for the angelic power causeth the vessel to drive northward faster than human life could endure.

424–7. The supernatural motion is retarded; the Mariner awakes, and his penance begins anew.

436–7. The curse is finally expiated.
458–61. And the ancient Mariner beholdeth his native country.
476–7. The angelic spirits leave the dead bodies.
478–9. And appear in their own forms of light.
508–9. The Hermit of the wood,
521–2. Approacheth the ship with wonder.
540–1. The ship suddenly sinketh.
544–7. The ancient Mariner is saved in the pilot's boat.
568–73. The ancient Mariner earnestly entreateth the Hermit to shrieve him; and the penance of life falls on him.
576–84. And ever and anon throughout his future life an agony constraineth him to travel from land to land;
604–7. And to teach, by his own example, love and reverence to all things that God made and loveth.

1817 note to ll. 220–1

For the last two lines of this stanza I am indebted to Mr Wordsworth. It was on a delightful walk from Nether Stowey to Dulverton with him and his sister, in the autumn of 1797, that this poem was planned and in part composed.

From Coleridge, *Biographia Literaria* (1817), Ch. 14

The thought suggested itself (to which of us I do not recollect) that a series of poems might be composed of two sorts. In the one, the incidents and agents were to be, in part at least, supernatural; and the excellence aimed at was to consist in the interesting of the affections by the dramatic truth of such emotions, as would naturally accompany such situations, supposing them real. And real in *this* sense they have been to every human being who, from whatever source of delusion, has at any time believed himself under supernatural agency. For the second class, subjects were to be chosen from ordinary life; the characters and incidents were to be such, as will be found in every village and its vicinity, where there is a meditative and feeling mind to seek after them, or to notice them, when they present themselves.

In this idea originated the plan of the *Lyrical Ballads*; in which it was agreed, that my endeavours should be directed to persons and characters supernatural, or at least romantic; yet so as to transfer from our inward nature a human interest and a semblance of truth sufficient to procure for these shadows of imagination that willing suspension of disbelief for the moment, which constitutes poetic faith. Mr Wordsworth, on the other hand, was to propose to himself as his object, to give the charm of novelty to things of every day, and to excite a feeling analogous to the supernatural, by awakening the mind's attention from the lethargy of custom, and directing it to the loveliness and the wonders of the world before us; an inexhaustible treasure, but for which, in consequence of the film of familiarity and selfish solicitude, we have eyes, yet see not, ears that hear not, and hearts that neither feel nor understand.

With this view I wrote 'The Ancient Mariner,' and was preparing among other poems, 'The Dark Ladie,' and the 'Christabel,' in which I should have more nearly realized my ideal, than I had done in my first attempt.

Remark, dated 31 May 1830, in Coleridge's *Table Talk*

Mrs Barbauld once told me that she admired *The Ancient Mariner* very much, but that there were two faults in it – it was improbable, and had no moral. As for the probability, I owned that that might admit some question; but as to the want of a moral, I told her that in my judgment the poem had too much; and that the only, or chief fault, if I might say so, was the obtrusion of the moral sentiment so openly on the reader as a principle or cause of action in a work of such pure imagination. It ought to have had no more moral than the *Arabian Nights'* tale of the merchant's sitting down to eat dates by the side of the well, and throwing the shells aside, and lo! a genie starts up, and says he *must* kill the aforesaid merchant, *because* one of the date shells had, it seems, put out the eye of the genie's son.

I took the thought of *grinning for joy*, in that poem, from my companion's remark to me, when we had climbed to the top of Plinlimmon, and were nearly dead with thirst. We could not speak from the constriction, till we found a little puddle under a stone. He said to me, 'You grinned like an idiot!' He had done the same.

From *The Poems of Samuel Taylor Coleridge*, ed. D. and S. Coleridge, 1852, pp. 383–4.

The following interesting notices concerning 'The Ancient Mariner' are contained in a letter of the Rev. Alexander Dyce, the well-known admirable editor of old plays, to the late H.N. Coleridge:–

'When my truly honoured friend Mr Wordsworth was last in London, soon after the appearance of De Quincey's papers in *Tait's Magazine*, he dined with me in Gray's Inn, and made the following statement, which, I am quite sure, I give you correctly: " 'The Ancient Mariner' was founded on a strange dream, which a friend of Coleridge had, who fancied he saw a skeleton ship, with figures in it. We had both determined to write some poetry for a monthly magazine, the profits of which were to defray the expenses of a little excursion we were to make together. 'The Ancient Mariner' was intended for this periodical, but was too long. I had very little share in the composition of it, for I soon found that the style of Coleridge and myself would not assimilate. Besides the lines (in the fourth part),

> 'And thou art long, and lank, and brown,
> As is the ribbed sea-sand,'

I wrote the stanza (in the first part),

> 'He holds him with his glittering eye –
> The wedding-guest stood still,
> And listens like a three-years' child:
> The Mariner hath his will,'

and four or five lines more in different parts of the poem, which I could not now point out. The idea of *'shooting an albatross' was mine; for I had been reading Shelvocke's Voyages, which probably Coleridge never saw*. I also suggested the reanimation of the dead bodies, to work the ship." '

(The episode must have taken place in the early 1840s.)

From Wordsworth's Fenwick note to 'We are Seven'

In the spring of the year 1798, he, my Sister, and myself, started from Alfoxden, pretty late in the afternoon, with a view to visit Linton and the Valley of Stones near it; and as our united funds were very small, we agreed to defray the expense of the tour by writing a poem, to be sent to the new Monthly Magazine set up by Phillips the bookseller, and edited by Dr Aikin. Accordingly we set off and proceeded along the Quantock Hills, towards Watchet, and in the course of this walk was planned the poem of 'The Ancient Mariner', founded on a dream, as Mr Coleridge said, of his friend, Mr Cruikshank. Much the greatest part of the story was Mr Coleridge's invention; but certain parts I myself suggested, for example, some crime was to be committed which should bring upon the Old Navigator, as Coleridge afterwards delighted to call him, the spectral persecution, as a consequence of that crime, and his own wanderings. I had been reading in Shelvocke's Voyages a day or two before that while doubling Cape Horn they frequently saw Albatrosses in that latitude, the largest sort of sea-fowl, some extending their wings 12 or 13 feet. 'Suppose,' said I, 'you represent him as having killed one of these birds on entering the South Sea, and that the tutelary Spirits of those regions take upon them to avenge the crime.' The incident was thought fit for the purpose and adopted accordingly. I also suggested the navigation of the ship by the dead men, but do not recollect that I had anything more to do with the scheme of the poem. The Gloss with which it was subsequently accompanied was not thought of by either of us at the time; at least, not a hint of it was given to me, and I have no doubt it was a gratuitous after-thought. We began the composition together on that, to me, memorable evening. I furnished two or three lines at the beginning of the poem, in particular:

> 'And listened like a three years' child;
> The Mariner had his will.'

These trifling contributions, all but one (which Mr C. has with unnecessary scrupulosity recorded) slipt out of his mind as they well might. As we endeavoured to proceed conjointly (I speak of the same evening) our respective manners proved so widely different that it would have been quite presumptuous in me to do anything but separate from an undertaking upon which I could only have been a clog. We returned after a few days from a delightful tour, of which I have many pleasant, and some of them droll enough, recollections. We returned by Dulverton to Alfoxden. 'The Ancient Mariner' grew and grew till it became too important for our first object, which was limited to our expectation of five pounds, and we began to talk of a Volume, which was to consist, as Mr Coleridge has told the world, of Poems chiefly on natural subjects taken from common life, but looked at, as much as might be, through an imaginative medium. Accordingly I wrote 'The Idiot Boy', 'Her eyes are wild, etc.', 'We are Seven', 'The Thorn', and some others.

Anecdote for Fathers
Fenwick

This was suggested in front of Alfoxden. The boy was a son of my friend Basil Montagu, who had been two or three years under our care. The name of Kilve is from a village on the Bristol Channel, about a mile from Alfoxden; and the name of Liswyn Farm was taken from a beautiful spot on the Wye. When Mr Coleridge, my Sister, and I, had been visiting the famous John Thelwall, who had taken refuge from politics, after a trial for high treason, with a view to bring up his family by the profits of agriculture, which proved as unfortunate a speculation as that he had fled from, Coleridge and he had both been public lecturers; Coleridge mingling, with his politics, theology, from which the other elocutionist abstained, unless it were for the sake of a sneer. This quondam community of public employment induced Thelwall to visit Coleridge at Nether Stowey, where he fell in my way. He really was a man of extraordinary talent, an affectionate husband, and a good father. Though brought up in the city on a tailor's board, he was truly sensible of the beauty of natural objects. I remember once, when Coleridge, he, and I were seated together upon the turf on the brink of a stream in the most beautiful part of the most beautiful glen of Alfoxden, Coleridge exclaimed, 'This is a place to reconcile one to all the jarrings and conflicts of the wide world.' – 'Nay,' said Thelwall, 'to make one forget them altogether.' The visit of this man to Coleridge was, as I believe Coleridge has related, the occasion of a spy being sent by Government to watch our proceedings, which were, I can say with truth, such as the world at large would have thought ludicrously harmless.

The Brothers
Fenwick

This poem was composed in a grove at the north-eastern end of Grasmere Lake, which grove was in a great measure destroyed by turning the high-road along the side of the water. The few trees that are left were spared at my intercession. The poem arose out of the fact, mentioned to me at Ennerdale, that a shepherd had fallen asleep upon the top of the rock called The Pillar, and perished as here described, his staff being left midway on the rock.

The Childless Father
Fenwick

When I was a child at Cockermouth, no funeral took place without a basin filled with sprigs of boxwood being placed upon a table covered with a white cloth in front of the house. The huntings on foot, in which the Old Man is supposed to join as here described, were of common, almost habitual, occurrence in our vales when I was a boy; and the people took much delight in them. They are now less frequent.

Ellen Irwin
Fenwick

It may be worthwhile to observe, that as there are Scotch poems on this subject, in the simple ballad strain, I thought it would be both presumptuous and superfluous to attempt treating it in the same way; and accordingly, I chose a construction of stanza quite new in our language; in fact, the same as that of Bürger's 'Leonora', except that the first and third lines do not, in my stanzas, rhyme. At the outset I threw out a classical image, to prepare the reader for the style in which I meant to treat the story, and to preclude all comparison.

The Female Vagrant
'Advertisement' to the first printing of 'Guilt and Sorrow', 1842

Not less than one-third of the following poem, though it has from time to time been altered in the expression, was published so far back as the year 1798, under the title of 'The Female Vagrant'. The extract is of such length that an apology seems to be required for reprinting it here: but it was necessary to restore it to its original position, or the rest would have been unintelligible. The whole was written before the close of the year 1794, and I will detail, rather as matter of literary biography than for any other reason, the circumstances under which it was produced.

During the latter part of the summer of 1793, having passed a month in the Isle of Wight, in view of the fleet which was then preparing for sea off Portsmouth at the commencement of the war, I left the place with melancholy forebodings. The American war was still fresh in memory. The struggle which was beginning, and which many thought would be brought to a speedy close by the irresistible arms of Great Britain being added to those of the Allies, I was assured in my own mind would be of long continuance, and productive of distress and misery beyond all possible calculation. This conviction was pressed upon me by having been a witness, during a long residence in revolutionary France, of the spirit which prevailed in that country. After leaving the Isle of Wight, I spent two days in wandering on foot over Salisbury Plain, which, though cultivation was then widely spread through parts of it, had upon the whole a still more impressive appearance than it now retains.

The monuments and traces of antiquity, scattered in abundance over that region, led me unavoidably to compare what we know or guess of those remote times with certain aspects of modern society, and with calamities, principally those consequent upon war, to which, more than other classes of men, the poor are subject. In those reflections, joined with particular facts that had come to my knowledge, the following stanzas originated.

In conclusion, to obviate some distraction in the minds of those who are well acquainted with Salisbury Plain, it may be proper to say that, of the features described as belonging to it, one or two are taken from other desolate parts of England.

Fenwick note for 'Guilt and Sorrow'

Unwilling to be unnecessarily particular, I have assigned this poem to the dates 1793 and 1794; but in fact much of the 'Female Vagrant's' story was composed at least two years before. All that relates to her sufferings as a sailor's wife in America, and her condition of mind during her voyage home, were faithfully taken from the report made to me of her own case by a friend who had been subjected to the same trials and affected in the same way. Mr Coleridge, when I first became acquainted with him, was so much impressed with this poem, that it would have encouraged me to publish the whole as it then stood; but the mariner's fate appeared to me so tragical as to require a treatment more subdued and yet more strictly applicable in expression than I had at first given to it. This fault was corrected nearly fifty years afterwards, when I determined to publish the whole. It may be worth while to remark, that, though the incidents of this attempt do only in a small degree produce each other, and it deviates accordingly from the general rule by which narrative pieces ought to be governed, it is not therefore wanting in continuous hold upon the mind, or in unity, which is effected by the identity of moral interest that places the two personages upon the same footing in the reader's sympathies. My rambles over many parts of Salisbury Plain put me, as mentioned in the preface, upon writing this poem, and left on my mind imaginative impressions the force of which I have felt to this day. From that district I proceeded to Bath, Bristol, and so on to the banks of the Wye, where I took again to travelling on foot. In remembrance of that part of my journey, which was in 1793, I began the verses – 'Five years have passed'.

The Foster-mother's Tale
Coleridge's note to *Remorse*, 1813, IV, ii

The following scene as unfit for the stage was taken from the tragedy in 1797, and published in the *Lyrical Ballads*. But this work having been long out of print, and it having been determined, that this with my other poems (the *Nightingale, Love,* and the *Ancient Mariner*) should be omitted in any future edition, I have been advised to reprint it as a note to the second scene of Act the Fourth.

A Fragment
1827 headnote

These stanzas were designed to introduce a Ballad upon the story of a
Danish Prince who had fled from battle, and, for the sake of the valuables
about him, was murdered by the inhabitant of a cottage in which he had
taken refuge. The house fell under a curse, and the Spirit of the Youth, it
was believed, haunted the valley where the crime had been committed.

Hart-leap Well
Fenwick

Town-End. 1800. *Grasmere.*
The first eight stanzas were composed extempore one winter evening in the
cottage; when, after having tired myself with labouring at an awkward
passage in 'The Brothers', I started with a sudden impulse to this to get rid
of the other, and finished it in a day or two. My sister and I had passed the
place a few weeks before in our wild winter journey from Sockburn on the
banks of the Tees to Grasmere. A peasant whom we met near the spot told
us the story so far as concerned the name of the well, and the hart, and
pointed out the stones. Both the stones and the well are objects that may
easily be. missed; the tradition by this time may be extinct in the
neighbourhood: the man who related it to us was very old.

The Idiot Boy
Fenwick

The last stanza – 'The Cocks did crow to-whoo, to-whoo, And the sun did
shine so cold' – was the foundation of the whole. The words were reported
to me by my dear friend, Thomas Poole; but I have since heard the same
repeated of other Idiots. Let me add that this long poem was composed in
the groves of Alfoxden, almost extempore; not a word, I believe, being
corrected, though one stanza was omitted. I mention this in gratitude to
those happy moments, for, in truth, I never wrote anything with so much
glee.

The Idle Shepherd-Boys
Fenwick

Grasmere Town-End, 1800.
I will only add a little monitory anecdote concerning this subject. When
Coleridge and Southey were walking together upon the Fells, Southey
observed that, if I wished to be considered a faithful painter of rural
manners, I ought not to have said that my Shepherd-boys trimmed their
rustic hats as described in the poem. Just as the words had passed his lips
two boys appeared with the very plant entwined round their hats. I have

often wondered that Southey, who rambled so much about the mountains, should have fallen into this mistake, and I record it as a warning for others who, with far less opportunity than my dear friend had of knowing what things are, and far less sagacity, give way to presumptuous criticism, from which he was free, though in this matter mistaken. In describing a tarn under Helvellyn, I say,

> There sometimes doth a leaping fish
> Send through the tarn a lonely cheer.

This was branded by a critic of these days, in a review ascribed to Mrs Barbauld, as unnatural and absurd. I admire the genius of Mrs Barbauld, and am certain that, had her education been favourable to imaginative influences, no female of her day would have been more likely to sympathise with that image, and to acknowledge the truth of the sentiment.

'If Nature . . .'
From Wordsworth's letter to Henry Reed, March 1843

The character of the School Master about whom you inquire, had like the Wanderer in the *Excursion* a solid foundation in fact and reality, but like him it was also in some degree a composition; I will not and need not call it an invention – it was no such thing. But were I to enter into details I fear it would impair the effect of the whole upon your mind, nor could I do it at all to my own satisfaction.

Fenwick

Such a Tablet as is here spoken of continued to be preserved in Hawkshead School, though the inscriptions were not brought down to our time. This and other poems connected with Matthew would not gain by a literal detail of facts. Like the Wanderer in *The Excursion*, this Schoolmaster was made up of several both of his class and men of other occupations. I do not ask pardon for what there is of untruth in such verses, considered strictly as matters of fact. It is enough if, being true and consistent in spirit, they move and teach in a manner not unworthy of a Poet's calling.

The Last of the Flock
From Wordsworth's letter to John Kenyon, September 1836

You ask how the Muses came to say, 'weep in the public roads *alone*.' Did you ever attend an execution? Funerals, alas! we have all attended, and most of us must have seen then weeping in the public roads on one or both of these occasions.

I was a witness to a sight of this kind the other day in the streets of Kendal, where male mourners were following a body to the grave in tears. But for my own part, notwithstanding what has here been said in verse, I never in my whole life saw a man weep *alone* in the roads; but a friend of mine *did* see this poor man weeping *alone*, with the Lamb, the last of his flock, in his arms. I hope you are satisfied, and willing that the verse should stand as I have written it.

Lines (Left upon a Seat in a Yew-tree)
Fenwick

Composed in part at school at Hawkshead. The tree has disappeared, and the slip of common on which it stood, that ran parallel to the lake, and lay open to it, has long been enclosed; so that the road has lost much of its attraction. This spot was my favourite walk in the evenings during the latter part of my school-time. The individual whose habits and character are here given, was a gentleman of the neighbourhood, a man of talent and learning, who had been educated at one of our Universities, and returned to pass his time in seclusion on his own estate. He died a bachelor in middle age. Induced by the beauty of the prospect, he built a small summer-house on the rocks above the peninsula on which the ferry-house stands. This property afterwards passed into the hands of the late Mr Curwen. The site was long ago pointed out by Mr West in his Guide, as the pride of the lakes, and now goes by the name of 'The Station.' So much used I to be delighted with the view from it, while a little boy, that some years before the first pleasure-house was built, I led thither from Hawkshead a youngster about my own age, an Irish boy, who was a servant to an itinerant conjurer. My motive was to witness the pleasure I expected the boy would receive from the prospect of the islands below and the intermingling water. I was not disappointed; and I hope the fact, insignificant as it may appear to some, may be thought worthy of note by others who may cast their eye over these notes.

Lines (Written a few miles above Tintern Abbey)
Fenwick

July 1798. No poem of mine was composed under circumstances more pleasant for me to remember than this. I began it upon leaving Tintern, after crossing the Wye, and concluded it just as I was entering Bristol in the evening, after a ramble of 4 or 5 days, with my sister. Not a line of it was altered, and not any part of it written down till I reached Bristol. It was published almost immediately after in the little volume of which so much has been said in these notes. (The *Lyrical Ballads*, as first published at Bristol by Cottle.)

Lines (Written at a small distance from my house)
Fenwick

Composed in front of Alfoxden House. My little boy-messenger on this occasion was the son of Basil Montagu. The larch mentioned in the first stanza was standing when I revisited the place in May, 1841, more than forty years after. I was disappointed that it had not improved in appearance as to size, nor had it acquired anything of the majesty of age, which, even though less perhaps than any other tree, the larch sometimes does. A few score yards from this tree grew, when we inhabited Alfoxden, one of the most remarkable beech-trees ever seen. The ground sloped both towards and from it. It was of immense size, and threw out arms that struck into the soil, like those of the banyan tree, and rose again from it. Two of the branches thus inserted themselves twice, which gave to each the appearance of a serpent moving along by gathering itself up in folds. One of the large boughs of this tree had been torn off by the wind before we left Alfoxden, but five remained. In 1841 we could barely find the spot where the tree had stood. So remarkable a production of nature could not have been wilfully destroyed.

Lines Written in Early Spring
Fenwick

Actually composed while I was sitting by the side of the brook that runs down from the Comb, in which stands the village of Alford, through the grounds of Alfoxden. It was a chosen resort of mine. The brook fell down a sloping rock so as to make a waterfall considerable for that country, and across the pool below had fallen a tree, an ash, if I rightly remember, from which rose perpendicularly boughs in search of the light intercepted by the deep shade above. The boughs bore leaves of green that for want of sunshine had faded into almost lily-white; and from the underside of this natural sylvan bridge depended long and beautiful tresses of ivy which waved gently in the breeze that might poetically speaking be called the breath of the waterfall. This motion varied of course in proportion to the power of water in the brook. When, with dear friends, I revisited this spot, after an interval of more than forty years, this interesting feature of the scene was gone. To the owner of the place I could not but regret that the beauty of this retired part of the grounds had not tempted him to make it more accessible by a path, not broad or obtrusive, but sufficient for persons who love such scenes to creep along without difficulty.

Lines (Written when sailing)
Fenwick

The title is scarcely correct. It was during a solitary walk on the banks of the Cam that I was first struck with this appearance, and applied it to my own feelings in the manner here expressed, changing the scene to the Thames near Windsor. This and the three stanzas of the following poem, *Remembrance of Collins*, formed one piece: but, upon the recommendation of Coleridge, the three last stanzas were separated from the other.

Lucy Gray
Fenwick

Written at Goslar in Germany in 1799. It was founded on a circumstance told me by my sister, of a little girl who, not far from Halifax in Yorkshire, was bewildered in a snowstorm. Her footsteps were traced by her parents to the middle of the lock of a canal, and no other vestige of her, backward or forward, could be traced. The body however was found in the canal. The way in which the incident was treated and the spiritualizing of the character might furnish hints for contrasting the imaginative influences which I have endeavoured to throw over common life with Crabbe's matter of fact style of treating subjects of the same kind. This is not spoken to his disparagement, far from it; but to direct the attention of thoughtful readers, into whose hands these notes may fall, to a comparison that may both enlarge the circle of their sensibilities, and tend to produce in them a catholic judgment.

The Mad Mother
From Wordsworth's letter to John Kenyon, September 1836

It was in the English tongue – you say 'is not this, in an English poem, superfluous?' Surely here is an oversight on your part; whether the poem were in English, or French, or Greek is a matter wholly indifferent as to the expression I have used. She came from afar . . . in the instance to which you object it was expedient to specify, that – though she came from far, English was her native tongue – which shows her either to be of these Islands, or a North American. On the latter supposition, while the distance removes her from us, the fact of her speaking our language brings us at once into close sympathy with her.

Michael
Fenwick

Written about the same time as *The Brothers*. The sheepfold, on which so much of the poem turns, remains, or rather the ruins of it. The character and circumstances of Luke were taken from a family to whom had belonged, many years before, the house we lived in at Town-End, along with some fields and woodlands on the eastern shore of Grasmere. The name of the Evening Star was not in fact given to this house but to another on the same side of the valley more to the north.

Nutting
Fenwick

Written in Germany: intended as part of a poem on my own life, but struck out as not being wanted there. Like most of my schoolfellows I was an impassioned nutter. For this pleasure, the vale of Esthwaite, abounding in coppice-wood, furnished a very wide range. These verses arose out of the remembrance of feelings I had often had when a boy, and particularly in the extensive woods that still stretch from the side of Esthwaite Lake towards Graythwaite, the seat of the ancient family of Sandys.

The Oak and the Broom
Fenwick

Suggested upon the mountain pathway that leads from Upper Rydal to Grasmere. The ponderous block of stone, which is mentioned in the poem, remains, I believe, to this day, a good way up Nab-Scar. Broom grows under it and in many places on the side of the precipice.

The Old Cumberland Beggar
Fenwick

Observed, and with great benefit to my own heart, when I was a child: written at Racedown and Alfoxden in my 28th year. The political economists were about that time beginning their war upon mendicity in all its forms, and by implication, if not directly, on almsgiving also. This heartless process has been carried as far as it can go by the AMENDED poor-law bill, though the inhumanity that prevails in this measure is somewhat disguised by the profession that one of its objects is to throw the poor upon the voluntary donations of their neighbours; that is, if rightly interpreted, to force them into a condition between relief in the Union poor-house, and alms robbed of their Christian grace and spirit, as being *forced* rather from the benevolent than given by them; while the avaricious and selfish, and all in fact but the humane and charitable, are at liberty to keep all they possess from their distressed brethren.

The Pet-Lamb
Fenwick

Barbara Lewthwaite, now living at Ambleside (1843), though much changed as to beauty, was one of two most lovely sisters. Almost the first words my poor brother John said, when he visited us for the first time at Grasmere, were, 'Were those two angels that I have just seen?' and from his description I have no doubt they were those two sisters. The mother died in childbed; and one of our neighbours at Grasmere told me that the loveliest sight she had ever seen was that mother as she lay in her coffin with her babe in her arm. I mention this to notice what I cannot but think a salutary custom once universal in these vales. Every attendant on a funeral made it a duty to look at the corpse in the coffin before the lid was closed, which was never done (nor I believe is now) till a minute or two before the corpse was removed. Barbara Lewthwaite was not in fact the child whom I had seen and overheard as engaged in the poem. I chose the name for reasons implied in the above; and will here add a caution against the use of names of living persons. Within a few months after the publication of this poem, I was much surprised, and more hurt, to find it in a child's schoolbook which, having been compiled by Lindley Murray, had come into use at Grasmere School where Barbara was a pupil. And, alas, I had the mortification of hearing that she was very vain of being thus distinguished; and, in after-life, she used to say that she remembered the incident and what I said to her upon the occasion.

Poems on the Naming of Places
I
Fenwick

This poem was suggested on the banks of the brook that runs through Easedale, which is, in some parts of its course, as wild and beautiful as brook can be. I have composed thousands of verses by the side of it.

II   To Joanna
Fenwick

The effect of her laugh is an extravagance; though the effect of the reverberation of voices in some parts of the mountains is very striking. There is, in the *Excursion*, an allusion to the bleat of a lamb thus re-echoed, and described without any exaggeration, as I heard it, on the side of Stickle Tarn, from the precipice that stretches on to Langdale Pikes.

III
Fenwick

It is not accurate that the Eminence here alluded to could be seen from our orchard-seat. It rises above the road by the side of Grasmere lake, towards Keswick, and its name is Stone-Arthur.

IV
Fenwick

The character of the eastern shore of Grasmere Lake is quite changed, since these verses were written, by the public road being carried along its side. The friends spoken of were Coleridge and my sister, and the fact occurred strictly as recorded.

Poor Susan
Fenwick

Written 1801 or 1802. This arose out of my observation of the affecting music of these birds hanging in this way in the London streets during the freshness and stillness of the spring morning.

Rural Architecture
Fenwick

These structures, as everyone knows, are common among our hills, being built by shepherds as conspicuous marks, occasionally by boys in sport. It was written at Town-end, in 1801.

Simon Lee
Fenwick

This old man had been huntsman to the Squires of Alfoxden, which, at the time we occupied it, belonged to a minor. The old man's cottage stood upon the common, a little way from the entrance to Alfoxden Park. But it had disappeared. Many other changes had taken place in the adjoining village, which I could not but notice with a regret more natural than well-considered. Improvements but rarely appear such to those who, after long intervals of time, revisit places they have had much pleasure in. It is unnecessary to add, the fact was as mentioned in the poem; and I have, after an interval of 45 years, the image of the old man as fresh before my eyes as if I had seen him yesterday. The expression when the hounds were out, 'I dearly love their voices' was word for word from his own lips.

'There was a Boy . . .'
From the Preface to the collected poems of 1815

In the series of poems placed under the head of Imagination, I have begun with one of the earliest processes of Nature in the development of this faculty. Guided by one of my own primary consciousnesses, I have presented a commutation and transfer of internal feelings, co-operating with external accidents, to plant, for immortality, images of sound and sight, in the celestial soil of the Imagination. The Boy, there introduced, is listening, with something of a feverish and restless anxiety, for the recurrence of those riotous sounds which he had previously excited; and, at the moment when the intenseness of his mind is beginning to remit, he is surprised into a perception of the solemn and tranquillizing images which the poem describes.

Fenwick

Written in Germany. This is an extract from the poem of my own poetical education. This practice of making an instrument of their own fingers is known to most boys, though some are more skilful at it than others. William Raincock of Rayrigg, a fine spirited lad, took the lead of all my schoolfellows in this art.

The Thorn
Fenwick

Arose out of my observing, on the ridge of Quantock Hills, on a stormy day, a thorn which I had often passed in calm and bright weather without noticing it. I said to myself, 'Cannot I by some invention do as much to make this Thorn permanently an impressive object as the storm has made it to my eyes at this moment?' I began the poem accordingly, and composed it with great rapidity. Sir George Beaumont painted a picture from it which Wilkie thought his best. He gave it to me; though, when he saw it several times at Rydal Mount afterwards, he said, 'I could make a better, and would like to paint the same subject over again.' The sky in this picture is nobly done, but it reminds one too much of Wilson. The only fault, however, of any consequence is the female figure, which is too old and decrepit for one likely to frequent an eminence on such a call.

The Two Thieves
Fenwick

This is described from the life as I was in the habit of observing when a boy at Hawkshead School. Daniel was more than 80 years older than myself when he was daily thus occupied, under my notice. No book could have so early taught me to think of the changes to which human life is subject, and while looking at him, I could not but say to myself – we may, any of us, I, or the happiest of my playmates, live to become still more the object of pity than this old man, this half-doating pilferer.

The Waterfall and the Eglantine
Fenwick

Suggested nearer to Grasmere [than 'The Oak and the Broom'] on the same mountain track. The eglantine remained many years afterwards, but is now gone.

We are Seven
Fenwick

The little girl who is the heroine I met within the area of Goodrich Castle in the year 1793.... I composed it while walking in the grove at Alfoxden. My friends will not deem it too trifling to relate that while walking to and fro I composed the last stanza first, having begun with the last line. When it was all but finished, I came in and recited it to Mr Coleridge and my sister, and said, 'A prefatory stanza must be added, and I should sit down to our little tea-meal with greater pleasure if my task were finished.' I mentioned in substance what I wished to be expressed, and Coleridge immediately threw off the stanza thus:

'A little child, dear brother Jem,' –

I objected to the rhyme, 'dear brother Jem,' as being ludicrous, but we all enjoyed the joke of hitching-in our friend, James Tobin's name, who was familiarly called Jem. He was the brother of the dramatist, and this reminds me of an anecdote which it may be worth while here to notice. The said Jem got a sight of the *Lyrical Ballads* as it was going through the press at Bristol, during which time I was residing in that city. One evening he came to me with a grave face, and said, 'Wordsworth, I have seen the volume that Coleridge and you are about to publish. There is one poem in it, which I earnestly entreat you will cancel, for, if published, it will make you everlastingly ridiculous.' I answered that I felt much obliged by the interest he took in my good name as a writer, and begged to know what was the unfortunate piece he alluded to. He said, 'It is called "We are seven." ' Nay! said I, that shall take its chance, however, and he left me in despair.

From the Fenwick note to 'Ode: Intimations of Immortality . . .'

Nothing was more difficult for me in childhood than to admit the notion of death as a state applicable to my own being. I have said elsewhere – 'A simple child ... know of death!' But it was not so much from feelings of animal vivacity that *my* difficulty came as from a sense of the indomitableness of the spirit within me. I used to brood over the stories of Enoch and Elijah, and almost to persuade myself that, whatever might become of others, I should be translated, in something of the same way, to heaven. With a feeling congenial to this, I was often unable to think of external things as having external existence, and I communed with all that I saw as something not apart from, but inherent in, my own immaterial nature. Many times while going to school have I grasped at a wall or tree to recall myself from this abyss of idealism to the reality. At that time I was afraid of such processes. In later periods of life I have deplored, as we all have reason to do, a subjugation of an opposite character.

Written in Germany
Fenwick

A bitter winter it was when these verses were composed by the side of my sister, in our lodgings at a draper's house in the romantic imperial town of Goslar, on the edge of the Hartz Forest. In this town the German emperors of the Franconian line were accustomed to keep their court, and it retains vestiges of ancient splendour. So severe was the cold of this winter, that when we passed out of the parlour warmed by the stove, our cheeks were struck by the air as by cold iron. I slept in a room over a passage which was not ceiled. The people of the house used to say, rather unfeelingly, that they expected I should be frozen to death some night; but, with the protection of a pelisse lined with fur, and a dog's-skin bonnet, such as was worn by the peasants, I walked daily on the ramparts, or in a sort of public ground or garden, in which was a pond. Here, I had no companion but a kingfisher, a beautiful creature, that used to glance by me. I consequently became much attached to it. During these walks I composed the poem that follows, *The Poet's Epitaph*.

Sources

The Ancient Mariner

The cold is certainly much more insupportable in these, than in the same latitudes to the *Northward*; for, although we were pretty much advanced in the summer season, and had the days very long, yet we had continual squalls of sleet, snow and rain, and the heavens were perpetually hid from us by gloomy dismal clouds. In short, one would think it impossible that any living thing could subsist in so rigid a climate; and, indeed, we all observed, that we had not had the sight of one fish of any kind, since we were come to the Southward of the streights of *le Mair*, nor one seabird, except a disconsolate black *Albitross*, who accompanied us for several days, hovering about us as if he had lost himself, till *Hatley* (my second captain) observing, in one of his melancholy fits, that this bird was always hovering near us, imagined, from his colour, that it might be some ill omen. That which, I suppose, induced him the more to encourage his superstition, was the continued series of contrary tempestuous winds, which had oppressed us ever since we had got into this sea. But be that as it would, he, after some fruitless attempts, at length shot the *Albitross*, not doubting (perhaps) that we should have a fair wind after it. I must own that this navigation was truly melancholy, and was the more so to us, who were by ourselves without a companion ... and as it were, separated from the rest of mankind to struggle with the dangers of a stormy climate.

(George Shelvocke, *A Voyage Round the World, by the way of the Great South Sea*, 1726, pp. 72–3)

A Wonderful Ballad of the Seafaring Men.

1. In Babylon lived a king of yore,
      – The seafaring men. –
    he had twenty sons and four.
      – The seafaring men,
    in the greenwood grew their oars. Oh!

2. Some would sail, and some would roam,
    none would stay with his father at home.

3. They went to the strand with bang and boast,
   they forgot God the Father, Son and Holy Ghost,

4. They laid out to sail so bold,
   they hoisted their sails with silk and gold.

5. 'Now we will sail, now we will fare,
   nothing less than seven year.'

6. They sailed and sailed the billows blue,
   till under a rock, where wind never blew.

7. All were of the same kin and blood,
   the old steersman was the only odd.

8. They lay down crying and weeping,
   no crumb was left for eating.

9. Quoth the old mate: 'Before you starve,
   rather ye may me kill and carve.'

10. They took and bound him to the mast,
    they slaughtered him as another beast.

11. They slaughtered him as calf or lamb,
    they cooked and carved him as veal or ham.

12. They cut out both liver and lung,
    and bore it for the king so young.

13. 'Keep it yourselves, and salt your meat;
    I will much rather die than eat.'

14. There came a dove from the heavens high
    it sat down on the sailing tree.

15. Quoth the young king to his boy so wee:
    'Shoot me that bird, and cook it for me.'

16. 'I am no bird to be shot for food,
    I am from heaven an angel good.'

17. 'If thou art a God's angel, as thou dost tell,
    in the name of Christ thou help us well.'

18. 'Lay yourselves down to sleep and rest;
    while I will sail the salt sea best.'

19. Up awoke sailor the airest:
    'Now we have the wind the fairest.'

20. Up and spoke another:
    'I see the land of my mother.'

21. There was mirth, and there was glee,
       – The seafaring men. –
    when father and sons each other did see.
       – The seafaring men,
    in the greenwood grew their oars. Oh!

(English translation of a seventeenth-century Danish original, *Folk-lore Record* III, 1881, pp. 255–7)

The Complaint of a Forsaken Indian Woman

One of the Indian's wives, who for some time had been in a consumption, had for a few days past become so weak as to be incapable of travelling, which, among those people, is the most deplorable state to which a human being can possibly be brought. Whether she had been given over by the doctors, or that it was for want of friends among them, I cannot tell, but certain it is, that no expedients were taken for her recovery; so that, without much ceremony, she was left unassisted, to perish above ground.

Though this was the first instance of the kind I had seen, it is the common, and indeed the constant practice of those Indians; for when a grown person is so ill, especially in the summer, as not to be able to walk, and too heavy to be carried, they say it is better to leave one who is past recovery, than for the whole family to sit down by them and starve to death, well knowing that they cannot be of any service to the afflicted. On those occasions, therefore, the friends or relations of the sick generally leave them some victuals and water; and, if the situation of the place will afford it, a little firing. When those articles are provided, the person to be left is acquainted with the road which the others intend to go; and then, after covering them well up with deer skins etc. they take their leave, and walk away crying.

Sometimes persons thus left, recover; and come up with their friends, or wander about till they meet with other Indians, whom they accompany till they again join their relations. Instances of this kind are seldom known. The poor woman above mentioned, however, came up with us three several times, after having been left in the manner described. At length, poor creature! she dropped behind, and no one attempted to go back in search of her.

A custom apparently so unnatural is perhaps not to be found among any other of the human race: if properly considered, however, it may with justice be ascribed to necessity and self-preservation, rather than to the want of humanity and social feeling, which ought to be the characteristic of men, as the noblest part of the creation. Necessity, added to national custom, contributes principally to make scenes of this kind less shocking to those people, than they must appear to the more civilized part of mankind.

(Samuel Hearne, *A Journey from Prince of Wales's Fort in Hudson's Bay to the Northern Ocean*, 1795, pp. 202–3)

Goody Blake and Harry Gill

I received good information of the truth of the following case, which was published a few years ago in the newspapers. A young farmer in Warwickshire, finding his hedges broke, and the sticks carried away during a frosty season, determined to watch for the thief. He lay many cold hours under a haystack, and at length an old woman, like a witch in a play, approached, and began to pull up the hedge; he waited till she had tied up her bottle of sticks, and was carrying them off, that he might convict her of the theft, and then springing from his concealment, he seized his prey with violent threats. After some altercation, in which her load was left upon the ground, she kneeled upon her bottle of sticks, and raising her arms to heaven beneath the bright moon then at the full, spoke to the farmer already shivering with cold, 'Heaven grant, that thou never mayest know again the blessing to be warm.' He complained of cold all the next day, and wore an upper coat, and in a few days another, and in a fortnight took to his bed, always saying nothing made him warm; he covered himself with very many blankets, and had a sieve over his face, as he lay; and from this one insane idea he kept his bed above twenty years for fear of the cold air, till at length he died.

(Erasmus Darwin, *Zoonomia*, 1794–6, II, 359)

The Mad Mother
Lady Anne Bothwell's Lament

Balow, my babe, lye still and sleipe!
It grieves me sair to see thee weipe:
If thoust be silent, Ise be glad,
Thy maining maks my heart ful sad.
Balow, my boy, thy mothers joy,
Thy father breides me great annoy.
  Balow, my babe, ly stil and sleipe,
  It grieves me sair to see thee weepe.

Whan he began to court my luve,
And with his sugred wordes to muve,
His faynings fals, and flattering cheire
To me that time did not appeire:
But now I see, most cruell hee
Cares neither for my babe nor mee.
  Balow, &c.

Lye still, my darling, sleipe a while,
And when thou wakest, sweitly smile:
But smile not, as thy father did,
To cozen maids: nay, God forbid!
Bot yett I feire, thou wilt gae neire
Thy fatheris hart, and face to beire.
  Balow, &c.

I cannae chuse, but ever will
Be luving to thy father still:
Whair-eir he gae, whair-eir he ryde,
My luve with him doth still abyde:
In weil or wae, whair-eir he gae,
Mine hart can neire depart him frae.
  Balow, &c.

But doe not, doe not, prettie mine,
To faynings fals thine hart incline;
Be loyal to thy luver trew,
And nevir change hir for a new:

If gude or faire, of hir have care,
For womens banning's wonderous sair.
 Balow, &c.

Bairne, sin thy cruel father is gane,
Thy winsome smiles maun eise my paine;
My babe and I'll together live,
He'll comfort me when cares doe grieve:
My baby and I right saft will ly,
And quite forgeit man's cruelty.
 Balow, &c.

Fareweil, fareweil, thou falsest youth,
That evir kist a womans mouth!
I wish all maides be warnd by mee
Nevir to trust mans curtesy;
For if we doe bot chance to bow,
They'le use us then they care not how.
 Balow, my babe, ly stil, and sleipe,
 It grives me sair to see thee weipe.

(Text from Percy's *Reliques*)

Ruth, ll. 49–60

Companies of young, innocent Cherokee virgins, some busy gathering the rich fragrant fruit, others having already filled their baskets, lay reclined under the shade of floriferous and fragrant native bowers of Magnolia, Azalea, Philadelphus, perfumed Calycanthus, sweet Yellow Jessamine and cerulean Glycine frutescens, disclosing their beauties to the fluttering breeze, and bathing their limbs in the cool fleeting streams; whilst other parties more gay and libertine, were yet collecting strawberries, or wantonly chasing their companions, tantalising them, staining their lips and cheeks with the rich fruit.

The sylvan scene of primitive innocence was enchanting, and perhaps too enticing for hearty young men long to continue idle spectators.

In fine, nature prevailing over reason, we wished at least to have a more active part in their delicious sports. Thus precipitately resolving, we cautiously made our approaches, yet undiscovered, almost to the joyous scene of action. Now, although we meant no other than an innocent frolic with this gay assembly of hamadryades, we shall leave it to the person of feeling and sensibility to form an idea to what lengths our passions might have hurried us, thus warmed and excited, had it not been for the vigilance and care of some envious matrons who lay in ambush, and espying us, gave the alarm, time enough for the nymphs to rally and assemble together. We however pursued and gained ground on a group of them, who had incautiously strolled to a greater distance from their guardians, and finding their retreat now like to be cut off, took shelter under cover of a little grove; but on perceiving themselves to be discovered by us, kept their station, peeping through the bushes; when observing our approaches, they confidently discovered themselves, and decently advanced to meet us, half unveiling their blooming faces, incarnated with the modest maiden blush, and with native innocence and cheerfulness, presented their little baskets, merrily telling us their fruit was ripe and sound.

We accepted a basket, sat down and regaled ourselves on the delicious fruit, encircled by the whole assembly of the innocent jocose sylvan nymphs.

(Bartram 1792: 355–6)

The tall aspiring Gordonia lasianthus, which now stood in my view in all its splendour, is every way deserving of our admiration. Its thick foliage, of a dark green colour, is flowered over with large milk-white peduncles, at the extremities of its numerous branches, from the bosom of the leaves, and renewed every morning; and that in such incredible profusion, that the tree appears silvered over with them, and the ground beneath covered with the fallen flowers. It at the same time continually pushes forth new twigs, with young buds on them; and in the winter and spring, the third year's leaves, now partly concealed by the new and perfect ones, are gradually changing colour, from green to golden yellow, from that to a scarlet, from scarlet to crimson; and lastly to a brownish purple, and then fall to the ground. So that the Gordonia lasianthus may be said to change and renew its garments every morning throughout the year; and every day appears with unfading lustre. And moreover, after the general flowering is past, there is a thin succession of scattering blossoms to be seen, on some parts of the tree, almost every day throughout the remaining months, until the floral season returns.

(*Ibid.*, pp. 159–60)

1798 Text of
'The Ancient Mariner'

THE RIME
OF THE
ANCYENT MARINERE,
IN SEVEN PARTS

I

It is an ancyent Marinere,
   And he stoppeth one of three:
'By thy long grey beard and thy glittering eye
   'Now wherefore stoppest me?

'The Bridegroom's doors are open'd wide
   'And I am next of kin;
'The Guests are met, the Feast is set, –
   'May'st hear the merry din.

But still he holds the wedding-guest –
   There was a Ship, quoth he –
'Nay, if thou'st got a laughsome tale,
   'Marinere! come with me.'

He holds him with his skinny hand,
   Quoth he, there was a Ship –
'Now get thee hence, thou grey-beard Loon!
   'Or my Staff shall make thee skip.

He holds him with his glittering eye –
   The wedding guest stood still
And listens like a three year's child;
   The Marinere hath his will.

The wedding-guest sate on a stone,
  He cannot chuse but hear:
And thus spake on that ancyent man,
  The bright-eyed Marinere.

The Ship was cheer'd, the Harbour clear'd –
  Merrily did we drop
Below the Kirk, below the Hill,
  Below the Light-house top.

The Sun came up upon the left,
  Out of the Sea came he:
And he shone bright, and on the right
  Went down into the Sea.

Higher and higher every day,
  Till over the mast at noon –
The wedding-guest here beat his breast,
  For he heard the loud bassoon.

The Bride hath pac'd into the Hall,
  Red as a rose is she;
Nodding their heads before her goes
  The merry Minstralsy.

The wedding-guest he beat his breast,
  Yet he cannot chuse but hear:
And thus spake on that ancyent Man,
  The bright-eyed Marinere.

Listen, Stranger! Storm and Wind,
  A Wind and Tempest strong!
For days and weeks it play'd us freaks –
  Like Chaff we drove along.

Listen, Stranger! Mist and Snow,
  And it grew wond'rous cauld:
And Ice mast-high came floating by
  As green as Emerauld.

And thro' the drifts the snowy clifts
  Did send a dismal sheen;
Ne shapes of men ne beasts we ken –
  The Ice was all between.

The Ice was here, the Ice was there,
  The Ice was all around:
It crack'd and growl'd, and roar'd and howl'd –
  Like noises of a swound.

At length did cross an Albatross,
   Thorough the Fog it came;
And an it were a Christian Soul,
   We hail'd it in God's name.

The Marineres gave it biscuit-worms,
   And round and round it flew:
The Ice did split with a Thunder-fit;
   The Helmsman steer'd us thro'.

And a good south wind sprung up behind,
   The Albatross did follow;
And every day for food or play
   Came to the Marinere's hollo!

In mist or cloud on mast or shroud
   It perch'd for vespers nine,
Whiles all the night thro' fog smoke-white
   Glimmer'd the white moon-shine.

'God save thee, ancyent Marinere!
   'From the fiends that plague thee thus –
'Why look'st thou so?' – with my cross bow
   I shot the Albatross.

II

The Sun came up upon the right,
   Out of the Sea came he;
And broad as a weft upon the left
   Went down into the Sea.

And the good south wind still blew behind,
   But no sweet Bird did follow
Ne any day for food or play
   Came to the Marinere's hollo!

And I had done an hellish thing
   And it would work 'em woe;
For all averr'd, I had kill'd the Bird
   That made the Breeze to blow.

Ne dim ne red, like God's own head,
   The glorious Sun uprist:
Then all averr'd, I had kill'd the Bird
   That brought the fog and mist.
'Twas right, said they, such birds to slay
   That bring the fog and mist.

The breezes blew, the white foam flew,
  The furrow follow'd free:
We were the first that ever burst
  Into that silent Sea.

Down dropt the breeze, the Sails dropt down,
  'Twas sad as sad could be
And we did speak only to break
  The silence of the Sea.

All in a hot and copper sky
  The bloody sun at noon,
Right up above the mast did stand,
  No bigger than the moon.

Day after day, day after day,
  We stuck, ne breath ne motion,
As idle as a painted Ship
  Upon a painted Ocean.

Water, water, every where
  And all the boards did shrink;
Water, water, every where,
  Ne any drop to drink.

The very deeps did rot: O Christ!
  That ever this should be!
Yea, slimy things did crawl with legs
  Upon the slimy Sea.

About, about, in reel and rout
  The Death-fires danc'd at night;
The water, like a witch's oils,
  Burnt green and blue and white.

And some in dreams assured were
  Of the Spirit that plagued us so:
Nine fathom deep he had follow'd us
  From the Land of Mist and Snow.

And every tongue thro' utter drouth
  Was wither'd at the root;
We could not speak no more than if
  We had been choked with soot.

Ah wel-a-day! what evil looks
  Had I from old and young;
Instead of the Cross the Albatross
  About my neck was hung.

CPW: The Complete Poetical Works of Samuel Taylor Coleridge, ed. Ernest Hartley Coleridge, Oxford, 1912.

Crawfurd, O. (1896) (ed.), *Lyrical Verse from Elizabeth to Victoria*, London, p. 434.

*Curran, S. (1986), *Poetic Form and British Romanticism*, Oxford.

*Danby, J.F. (1954), 'The "Nature" of Wordsworth', *Cambridge Journal* VII, pp. 387–407.

*Danby, J.F. (1960), *The Simple Wordsworth*, London.

Darlington, B. (1977) (ed.), *Home at Grasmere*, Ithaca and London.

Darwin, Erasmus (1791), *The Botanic Garden*, London.

Davenant, Sir William (1971), *Gondibert*, ed. David F. Gladish, Oxford.

De Selincourt, E. (1939) (ed.), *The Letters of William and Dorothy Wordsworth: the later years*, Oxford.

De Selincourt, E. (1941) (ed.), *Journals of Dorothy Wordsworth*, London.

De Selincourt, E. and Hill, A.G. (1978) (eds), *The Letters of William and Dorothy Wordsworth*, Oxford.

De Selincourt, E. and Shaver, C.L. (1967) (eds), *The Letters of William and Dorothy Wordsworth*, Oxford.

*Dings, J.G. (1973), *The Mind in its Place*, Salzburg.

Dings, J.G. (1974), 'Bostetter on Wordsworth', *Paunch* XXXVIII, pp. 32–9.

Douglas, W.W. (1948), 'The Problem of Wordsworth's Conservatism', *Science and Society* XII, pp. 387–99.

Durrant, G. (1963), 'The Idiot Boy', *Theoria* XX, pp. 1–6.

Durrant, G. (1969), 'Zeno's Arrow – Time and Motion in Two of Wordsworth's Lucy Poems', *Mosaic* II, iii, pp. 10–24.

*Durrant, G. (1970), *Wordsworth and the Great System*, Cambridge.

Empson, W. (1951), 'Sense in the Prelude', *Kenyon Review* XIII, pp. 285–302.

Empson, W. (1961), *Seven Types of Ambiguity*, Harmondsworth.

Empson, W. and Pirie, D. (1972) (eds), *Coleridge's Verse: a selection*, London.

Enfield, W. (1796), 'Is Verse Essential to Poetry?', *Monthly Magazine* II, pp. 453–6.

Ferguson, F. (1973), 'The Lucy Poems: Wordsworth's quest for a poetic object', *ELH* XL, pp. 532–48.

*Ferry, D. (1959), *The Limits of Mortality*, Connecticut.

Fruman, N. (1972), *The Damaged Archangel*, New York and London.

*Garber, F. (1971), *Wordsworth and the Poetry of Encounter*, Urbana.

Garrod, H.W. (1923), *Wordsworth*, Oxford.

*Gérard, A.S. (1964), 'Of Trees and Men: the unity of Wordsworth's *Thorn*', *Essays in Criticism* XIV, pp. 237–55.

*Gill, S. (1969), 'Wordsworth's Breeches Pocket: attitudes to the didactic poet', *Essays in Criticism* XIX, pp. 385–401.

Gill, S. (1975) (ed.), *The Salisbury Plain Poems*, Ithaca and Hassocks.

*Glen, H. (1983), *Vision and Disenchantment: Blake's Songs and Wordsworth's Lyrical Ballads*, Cambridge.

Goldsmith, O. (1812), *Miscellaneous Works*, London.

Grave, S.A. (1968), 'Some Eighteenth-century Attempts to Use the Notion of Happiness' in R.F. Brissenden (ed.), *Studies in the Eighteenth Century*, Canberra.

Graves, R. (1948), *The White Goddess*, London.

Gravil, R. (1982), '*Lyrical Ballads* (1798): Wordsworth as ironist', *Critical Quarterly* XXIV, no. 4, pp. 39–57.

Green, K.E. (1977), *Wordsworth's Michael: a Textual and Critical Study*, PhD Thesis, University of London.

Griggs, E.L. (1956), *Collected Letters of Samuel Taylor Coleridge 1785–1806*, Oxford.

Guest, J. (1978), 'Wordsworth and the Music of Humanity', *Critical Review* XX, pp. 15–30.

Hale White, W. (1897) (ed.), *A Description of the Wordsworth and Coleridge Manuscripts in the Possession of Mr T. Norton Longman*, London.

Harris, R. (1935), 'Wordsworth's Lucy', *After-Glow Essays* 8, London.

Hartley, D. (1749), *Observations on Man*, London.

*Hartman, G.H. (1965), 'Wordsworth, Inscriptions, and Romantic Nature Poetry' in F.W. Hilles and H. Bloom (eds), *From Sensibility to Romanticism*, New York.

Hartman, G.H. (1968), 'False Themes and Gentle Minds', *PQ* XLVII, pp. 55–68.

Hartman, G.H. (1975a), 'Wordsworth and Goethe in Literary History', *New Literary History* VI, pp. 393–413.

Hartman, G.H. (1975b), *The Fate of Reading*, Chicago.

Hartman, H.H. (1934), 'Wordsworth's Lucy Poems', *PMLA* XLIX, pp. 134–42.

Hearne, S. (1795), *A Journey from Prince of Wales's Fort in Hudson's Bay to the Northern Ocean*, London.

Heinzelman, K. (1980), *The Economics of the Imagination*, Amherst.

Helms, A. (1979), 'The Sense of Punctuation', *Yale Review* LXIX, pp. 177–96.

Helms, R. (1977), 'On the Genesis of Wordsworth's *Michael*', *English Language Notes* XV, pp. 38–43.

Heron, R. (1793), 'A Critical Essay on the Seasons' in *The Seasons, by James Thomson*, Perth.

Hill, A.G. (1974), 'New Light on *The Excursion*', *Ariel* V, pp. 37–47.

Hill, J.L. (1974), 'The Frame for the Mind', *Centennial Review* XVIII, pp. 29–48.

Hooker, E.N. (1939), *The Critical Works of John Dennis 1692–1711*, Vol. I, Baltimore.

Hopkins, R.H. (1968), 'Coleridge's Parody of Melancholy Poetry in "The Nightingale: a Conversation Poem, April 1798" ', *English Studies* XLIX, pp. 436–41.

House, H. (1953), *Coleridge: The Clark Lectures 1951–2*, London.

Howe, P.P. (1930–4) (ed.), *The Complete Works of William Hazlitt*, London and Toronto.

Huxley, A. (1932), *Texts and Pretexts*, London.

*Jacobus, M. (1976), *Tradition and Experiment in Wordsworth's Lyrical Ballads (1798)*, Oxford.

Johnson, L.M. (1982), *Wordsworth's Metaphysical Verse*, Toronto.

*Jordan, J.E. (1976), *Why the Lyrical Ballads?*, Berkeley.

Ker, W.P. (1961) (ed.), *Essays of John Dryden*, New York.

Ker, W.P. (1966), *Form and Style in Poetry*, New York.

Ketcham, C.H. (1969) (ed.), *The Letters of John Wordsworth*, Ithaca.

King-Hele, D. (1986), *Erasmus Darwin and the Romantic Poets*, London.

Lamb, J. (1982), 'Hartley and Wordsworth: philosophical language and figures of the sublime', *MLN* XCVII, pp. 1064–85.

Levinson, M. (1985), 'Spiritual Economics: a reading of Wordsworth's *Michael*', *ELH* LII, pp. 707–31.

Little, G. (1977), ' "Tintern Abbey" and Llyswen Farm', *The Wordsworth Circle* VIII, pp. 80–2.

Locke, J. (1690), *An Essay Concerning Human Understanding*, London.

*Lowes, J. (1927; new ed. 1951), *The Road to Xanadu*, London.

Lowth, R. (1787), *Lectures on the Sacred Poetry of the Hebrews*, London.

*Maclean, K. (1950), *Agrarian Age: a background for Wordsworth*, New Haven, Connecticut.

Magnuson, P. (1982), 'The Articulation of "Michael": or, could Michael talk?', *The Wordsworth Circle* XIII, pp. 72–9.

*Maniquis, R.M. (1969), 'Comparison, Intensity and Time in "Tintern Abbey" ', *Criticism* XI, pp. 358–82.

Manning, P.J. (1986), 'Placing Poor Susan: Wordsworth and the new historicism', *Studies in Romanticism* XXV, pp. 351–69.

Mason, W. (1775) (ed.), *The Poems of Mr Gray*, London.

Masson, D. (1889–90) (ed.), *The Collected Writings of Thomas De Quincey*, Edinburgh.

*Mayo, R. (1954), 'The contemporaneity of the *Lyrical Ballads*', *PMLA* LXIX, pp. 486–522.

McNulty, J.B. (1945), 'Wordsworth's Tour of the Wye, 1798',

MLN LX, pp. 291–5.

McNulty, J.B. (1981), 'Self-awareness in the Making of "Tintern Abbey" ', *The Wordsworth Circle* XII, pp. 97–100.

Mendilow, A.A. (1957), 'Robert Heron and Wordsworth's Critical Essays', *Modern Language Review* LII, pp. 329–38.

Metzger, L. (1976), 'Wordsworth's Pastoral Covenant', *Modern Language Quarterly* XXXVII, pp. 307–23.

Milton, M.L.T. (1981), *The Poetry of Samuel Taylor Coleridge: an annotated bibliography of criticism 1935–1970*, New York.

Mitchell, J. (1974), 'Wordsworth's Tail-rhyme "Lucy" Poem', *Studies in Medieval Culture* IV, pp. 561–8.

Moorman, M. (1957), *William Wordsworth: a biography – the early years*, Oxford.

Morley, E.J. (1927) (ed.), *The Correspondence of Henry Crabb Robinson with the Wordsworth Circle*, Oxford.

Morley, E.J. (1938) (ed.), *Henry Crabb Robinson on Books and their Writers*, London.

Murray, R.N. (1967), *Wordsworth's Style: figures and themes in the Lyrical Ballads of 1800*, Lincoln, Nebraska.

*Nabholtz, J.R. (1974), 'The Integrity of Wordsworth's Tintern Abbey', *JEGP* LXXIII, pp. 227–38.

Newlyn, L. (1986), *Coleridge, Wordsworth and the Language of Allusion*, Oxford.

Noyes, R. (1944), 'Wordsworth and Burns', *PMLA* LIX, pp. 813–32.

O'Donnell, B. (1989), *Numerous Verse*, *Studies in Philology* LXXXVI, No. 4.

Owen, W.J.B. (1956), 'The Major Theme of Wordsworth's 1800 Preface', *Essays in Criticism* VI, pp. 144–59.

Owen, W.J.B. (1957) (ed.), *Wordsworth's Preface to Lyrical Ballads*, *Anglistica* IX, Copenhagen.

Owen, W.J.B. (1982), 'Two Addenda', *The Wordsworth Circle* XIII, p. 98.

Owen, W.J.B. and Smyser, J.W. (1974) (eds), *The Prose Works of William Wordsworth*, Oxford.

Page, J.W. (1985), 'Wordsworth and the Psychology of Metre', *Papers on Language and Literature* XXI, pp. 275–94.

*Parrish, S.M. (1957), ' "The Thorn": Wordsworth's dramatic monologue', *ELH* XXIV, pp. 153–63.

*Parrish, S.M. (1960), 'Wordsworth and Coleridge on Metre', *JEGP* LIX, pp. 41–9.

*Parrish, S.M. (1973), *The Art of the Lyrical Ballads*, Cambridge, Massachusetts.

Payne, R. (1978), ' "The style and spirit of the elder poets": the *Ancient Mariner* and English literary tradition', *Modern Philology*, pp. 173–7.

Peacock, M., Jr (1946), 'Variants to the Preface to *Lyrical Ballads*', *MLN* LXI, pp. 175–7.

Percy, T. (1765) (ed.), *Reliques of Ancient English Poetry*, 1st edn, London, and many subsequent editions.

Piper, H.W. (1955), *Nature and the Supernatural in 'The Ancient Mariner'*, New South Wales.

Piper, H.W. (1962), *The Active Universe*, London.

*Pirie, D.B. (1982), *William Wordsworth: the poetry of grandeur and of tenderness*, New York and London.

Primeau, J.K. (1983), 'The Influence of Gottfried August Bürger on the "Lyrical Ballads" of William Wordsworth: the supernatural vs. the natural', *Germanic Review* LVIII, pp. 89–96.

PW: The Poetical Works of William Wordsworth, ed. E. de Selincourt, Oxford, 1940–9.

Raine, K. (1968), 'Thomas Taylor, Plato, and the English Romantic Movement', *Sewanee Review* LXXVI, pp. 230–57.

Randel, F.V. (1982), 'Coleridge and the Contentiousness of Romantic Nightingales', *Studies in Romanticism* XXI, pp. 33–55.

Reed, M.L. (1967), *Wordsworth: the chronology of the early years 1770–1799*, Cambridge.

Reed, M.L. (1972), 'On the Development of Wordsworth's *Michael*', *Ariel* III, no. 2, pp. 70–9.

*Ricks, C. (1984), *The Force of Poetry*, Oxford.

Roper, D. (1968) (ed.), *Lyrical Ballads 1805*, London.

Ruoff, G.W. (1966), 'Another New Poem by Wordsworth', *Essays in Criticism* XVI, pp. 359–60.

*Ryskamp, C. (1965), 'Wordsworth's *Lyrical Ballads* in their time' in F.W. Hilles and H. Bloom (eds), *From Sensibility to Romanticism*, New York.

Sambrook, J. (1983), *English Pastoral Poetry*, Boston, Mass.

Sampson, D. (1984), 'Wordsworth and the Poor: the Poetry of Survival', *Studies in Romanticism* XXIII, pp. 31–59.

*Sheats, P.D. (1973), *The Making of Wordsworth's Poetry 1785–1798*, Cambridge, Mass.

Stone, P.W.K. (1967), *The Art of Poetry 1750–1820*, London.

*Storch, R.F. (1971), 'Wordsworth's Experimental Ballads: the radical uses of intelligence and comedy', *Studies in English Literature* XI, pp. 621–39.

Sykes Davies, H. (1965), 'Another New Poem by Wordsworth', *Essays in Criticism*, XV, pp. 135–61.

Tave, K.B. (1983), *The Demon and the Poet*, Salzburg.

Thompson, T.W. (1970), *Wordsworth's Hawkshead*, ed. Robert Woof, London.

Toliver, H.E. (1971), *Pastoral Forms and Attitudes*, Berkeley.

*Trilling, L. (1963), 'The Fate of Pleasure: Wordsworth to Dostoevsky', *Partisan Review* XXX, pp. 167–91.

Bibliography and suggested reading

Ware, M. (1961), 'Coleridge's "Spectre-bark": a slave ship?', *Philological Quarterly* XL, pp. 589–93.

Watson, G. (1966), *Coleridge the Poet*, London.

*Wilkie, B. (1973), 'Wordsworth and the Tradition of the Avant-garde', *JEGP* LXXII, pp. 194–222.

Wilson, M. (1983), 'Bodies in Motion: Wordsworth's myths of natural philosophy' in Eleanor Cook *et al.* (eds), *Centre and Labyrinth*, Toronto.

Woof, R. (1970), 'John Stoddart, "Michael", and *Lyrical Ballads*', *Ariel* I, no. 2, pp. 7–22.

Zall, P.M. (1979), 'The Cool World of Samuel Taylor Coleridge: Vicesimus Knox, elegant activist', *The Wordsworth Circle* X, pp. 345–7.

Index of Titles and First Lines

Titles are given in italic type

III

I saw a something in the Sky
   No bigger than my fist;
At first it seem'd a little speck
   And then it seem'd a mist:
It mov'd and mov'd, and took at last
   A certain shape, I wist.

A speck, a mist, a shape, I wist!
   And still it ner'd and ner'd;
And, an it dodg'd a water-sprite,
   It plung'd and tack'd and veer'd.

With throat unslack'd, with black lips bak'd
   Ne could we laugh, ne wail:
Then while thro' drouth all dumb they stood
I bit my arm and suck'd the blood
   And cry'd, A sail! a sail!

With throat unslack'd, with black lips bak'd
   Agape they hear'd me call:
Gramercy! they for joy did grin
And all at once their breath drew in
   As they were drinking all.

She doth not tack from side to side –
   Hither to work us weal
Withouten wind, withouten tide
   She steddies with upright keel.

The western wave was all a flame,
   The day was well nigh done!
Almost upon the western wave
   Rested the broad bright Sun;
When that strange shape drove suddenly
   Betwixt us and the Sun.

And strait the Sun was fleck'd with bars
   (Heaven's mother send us grace)
As if thro' a dungeon grate he peer'd
   With broad and burning face.

Alas! (thought I, and my heart beat loud)
   How fast she neres and neres!
Are those *her* Sails that glance in the Sun
   Like restless gossameres?

Are those *her* naked ribs, which fleck'd
   The sun that did behind them peer?
And are those two all, all the crew,
   That woman and her fleshless Pheere?

His bones were black with many a crack,
   All black and bare, I ween;
Jet-black and bare, save where with rust
Of mouldy damps and charnel crust
   They're patch'd with purple and green.

Her lips are red, *her* looks are free,
   Her locks are yellow as gold:
Her skin is as white as leprosy,
And she is far liker Death than he;
   Her flesh makes the still air cold.

The naked Hulk alongside came
   And the Twain were playing dice;
'The Game is done! I've won, I've won!'
   Quoth she, and whistled thrice.

A gust of wind sterte up behind
   And whistled thro' his bones;
Thro' the holes of his eyes and the hole of his
    mouth
   Half-whistles and half-groans.

With never a whisper in the Sea
   Oft darts the Spectre-ship;
While clombe above the Eastern bar
The horned Moon, with one bright Star
   Almost atween the tips.

One after one by the horned Moon
   (Listen, O Stranger! to me)
Each turn'd his face with a ghastly pang
   And curs'd me with his ee.

Four times fifty living men,
   With never a sigh or groan,
With heavy thump, a lifeless lump
   They dropp'd down one by one.

Their souls did from their bodies fly, –
   They fled to bliss or woe;
And every soul it pass'd me by,
   Like the whiz of my Cross-bow.

IV

'I fear thee, ancyent Marinere!
   'I fear thy skinny hand;
'And thou art long and lank and brown
   'As is the ribb'd Sea-sand.

'I fear thee and thy glittering eye
  'And thy skinny hand so brown –
Fear not, fear not, thou wedding guest!
  This body dropt not down.

Alone, alone, all all alone
  Alone on the wide wide Sea;
And Christ would take no pity on
  My soul in agony.

The many men so beautiful,
  And they all dead did lie!
And a million million slimy things
  Liv'd on – and so did I.

I look'd upon the rotting Sea,
  And drew my eyes away;
I look'd upon the eldritch deck,
  And there the dead men lay.

I look'd to Heaven, and try'd to pray;
  But or ever a prayer had gusht,
A wicked whisper came and made
  My heart as dry as dust.

I clos'd my lids and kept them close,
  Till the balls like pulses beat;
For the sky and the sea, and the sea and the sky
Lay like a load on my weary eye,
  And the dead were at my feet.

The cold sweat melted from their limbs,
  Ne rot, ne reek did they;
The look with which they look'd on me,
  Had never pass'd away.

An orphan's curse would drag to Hell
  A spirit from on high:
But O! more horrible than that
  Is the curse in a dead man's eye!
Seven days, seven nights I saw that curse,
  And yet I could not die.

The moving Moon went up the sky
  And no where did abide:
Softly she was going up
  And a star or two beside –

Her beams bemock'd the sultry main
  Like morning frosts yspread;
But where the ship's huge shadow lay,
The charmed water burnt alway
  A still and awful red.

Beyond the shadow of the ship
  I watch'd the water-snakes:
They mov'd in tracks of shining white;
And when they rear'd, the elfish light
  Fell off in hoary flakes.

Within the shadow of the ship
  I watch'd their rich attire:
Blue, glossy green, and velvet black
They coil'd and swam; and every track
  Was a flash of golden fire.

O happy living things! no tongue
  Their beauty might declare:
A spring of love gusht from my heart,
  And I bless'd them unaware!
Sure my kind saint took pity on me,
  And I bless'd them unaware.

The self-same moment I could pray;
  And from my neck so free
The Albatross fell off, and sank
  Like lead into the sea.

V

O sleep, it is a gentle thing
  Belov'd from pole to pole!
To Mary-queen the praise be yeven
She sent the gentle sleep from heaven
  That slid into my soul.

The silly buckets on the deck
  That had so long remain'd,
I dreamt that they were fill'd with dew
  And when I awoke it rain'd.

My lips were wet, my throat was cold,
  My garments all were dank;
Sure I had drunken in my dreams
  And still my body drank.

I mov'd and could not feel my limbs,
   I was so light, almost
I thought that I had died in sleep,
   And was a blessed Ghost.

The roaring wind! it roar'd far off,
   It did not come anear;
But with its sound it shook the sails
   That were so thin and sere.

The upper air bursts into life,
   And a hundred fire-flags sheen
To and fro they are hurried about;
And to and fro, and in and out
   The stars dance on between.

The coming wind doth roar more loud;
   The sails do sigh, like sedge:
The rain pours down from one black cloud
   And the Moon is at its edge.

Hark! hark! the thick black cloud is cleft,
   And the Moon is at its side:
Like waters shot from some high crag,
The lightning falls with never a jag
   A river steep and wide.

The strong wind reach'd the ship: it roar'd
   And dropp'd down, like a stone!
Beneath the lightning and the moon
   The dead men gave a groan.

They groan'd, they stirr'd, they all uprose
   Ne spake, ne mov'd their eyes:
It had been strange, even in a dream
   To have seen those dead men rise.

The helmsman steerd, the ship mov'd on;
   Yet never a breeze up-blew;
The Marineres all 'gan work the ropes,
   Where they were wont to do:
They rais'd their limbs like lifeless tools–
   We were a ghastly crew.

The body of my brother's son
   Stood by me knee to knee:
The body and I pull'd at one rope,
   But he said nought to me –
And I quak'd to think of my own voice
   How frightful it would be!

The day-light dawn'd – they dropp'd their arms,
    And cluster'd round the mast:
Sweet sounds rose slowly thro' their mouths
    And from their bodies pass'd.

Around, around, flew each sweet sound,
    Then darted to the sun:
Slowly the sounds came back again
    Now mix'd, now one by one.

Sometimes a dropping from the sky
    I heard the Lavrock sing;
Sometimes all little birds that are
How they seem'd to fill the sea and air
    With their sweet jargoning,

And now 'twas like all instruments,
    Now like a lonely flute;
And now it is an angel's song
    That makes the heavens be mute.

It ceas'd: yet still the sails made on
    A pleasant noise till noon,
A noise like of a hidden brook
    In the leafy month of June,
That to the sleeping woods all night
    Singeth a quiet tune.

Listen, O listen, thou Wedding-guest!
    'Marinere! thou hast thy will:
'For that, which comes out of thine eye, doth make
    'My body and soul to be still.'

Never sadder tale was told
    To a man of woman born:
Sadder and wiser thou wedding-guest!
    Thou'lt rise to morrow morn.

Never sadder tale was heard
    By a man of woman born:
The Marineres all return'd to work
    As silent as beforne.

The Marineres all 'gan pull the ropes,
    But look at me they n'old:
Thought I, I am as thin as air –
    They cannot me behold.

Till noon we silently sail'd on
    Yet never a breeze did breathe:
Slowly and smoothly went the ship
    Mov'd onwards from beneath.

Under the keel nine fathom deep
  From the land of mist and snow
The spirit slid: and it was He
  That made the Ship to go.
The sails at noon left off their tune
  And the Ship stood still also.

The sun right up above the mast
  Had fix'd her to the ocean:
But in a minute she 'gan stir
  With a short uneasy motion –
Backwards and forwards half her length
  With a short uneasy motion.

Then, like a pawing horse let go,
  She made a sudden bound:
It flung the blood into my head,
  And I fell into a swound.

How long in that same fit I lay,
  I have not to declare;
But ere my living life return'd,
I heard and in my soul discern'd
  Two voices in the air,

'Is it he? quoth one, 'Is this the man?
  'By him who died on cross,
'With his cruel bow he lay'd full low
  'The harmless Albatross.

'The spirit who bideth by himself
  'In the land of mist and snow,
'He lov'd the bird that lov'd the man
  'Who shot him with his bow.'

The other was a softer voice,
  As soft as honey-dew:
Quoth he the man hath penance done,
  And penance more will do.

VI

First Voice
'But tell me, tell me! speak again,
  'Thy soft response renewing –
'What makes that ship drive on so fast?
  'What is the Ocean doing?

Second Voice
'Still as a Slave before his Lord,
  'The Ocean hath no blast:
'His great bright eye most silently
  'Up to the moon is cast –

'If he may know which way to go,
  'For she guides him smooth or grim,
'See, brother, see! how graciously
  'She looketh down on him.

First Voice
'But why drives on that ship so fast
  'Withouten wave or wind?

Second Voice
'The air is cut away before,
  'And closes from behind.

'Fly, brother, fly! more high, more high,
  'Or we shall be belated:
'For slow and slow that ship will go,
  'When the Marinere's trance is abated.'

I woke, and we were sailing on
  As in a gentle weather:
'Twas night, calm night, the moon was high;
  The dead men stood together.

All stood together on the deck,
  For a charnel-dungeon fitter:
All fix'd on me their stony eyes
  That in the moon did glitter.

The pang, the curse, with which they died,
  Had never pass'd away:
I could not draw my een from theirs
  Ne turn them up to pray.

And in its time the spell was snapt,
  And I could move my een:
I look'd far-forth, but little saw
  Of what might else be seen.

Like one, that on a lonely road
  Doth walk in fear and dread,
And having once turn'd round, walks on
  And turns no more his head:
Because he knows, a frightful fiend
  Doth close behind him tread.

But soon there breath'd a wind on me,
   Ne sound ne motion made:
Its path was not upon the sea
   In ripple or in shade.

It rais'd my hair, it fann'd my cheek,
   Like a meadow-gale of spring –
It mingled strangely with my fears,
   Yet it felt like a welcoming.

Swiftly, swiftly flew the ship,
   Yet she sail'd softly too:
Sweetly, sweetly blew the breeze –
   On me alone it blew.

O dream of joy! is this indeed
   The light-house top I see?
Is this the Hill? Is this the Kirk?
   Is this mine own countrée?

We drifted o'er the Harbour-bar,
   And I with sobs did pray –
'O let me be awake, my God!
   'Or let me sleep alway!'

The harbour-bay was clear as glass,
   So smoothly it was strewn!
And on the bay the moon light lay,
   And the shadow of the moon.

The moonlight bay was white all o'er,
   Till rising from the same,
Full many shapes, that shadows were,
   Like as of torches came.

A little distance from the prow
   Those dark-red shadows were;
But soon I saw that my own flesh
   Was red as in a glare.

I turn'd my head in fear and dread,
   And by the holy rood,
The bodies had advanc'd and now
   Before the mast they stood.

They lifted up their stiff right arms,
   They held them strait and tight;
And each right-arm burnt like a torch,
   A torch that's borne upright.
Their stony eye-balls glitter'd on
   In the red and smoky light.

I pray'd and turn'd my head away
    Forth looking as before.
There was no breeze upon the bay,
    No wave against the shore.

The rock shone bright, the kirk no less
    That stands above the rock:
The moonlight steep'd in silentness
    The steady weathercock.

And the bay was white with silent light,
    Till rising from the same
Full many shapes, that shadows were,
    In crimson colours came.

A little distance from the prow
    Those crimson shadows were:
I turn'd my eyes upon the deck —
    O Christ! what saw I there?

Each corse lay flat, lifeless and flat;
    And by the Holy rood
A man all light, a seraph-man,
    On every corse there stood.

This seraph-band, each wav'd his hand:
    It was a heavenly sight:
They stood as signals to the land,
    Each one a lovely light:

This seraph-band, each wav'd his hand,
    No voice did they impart —
No voice; but O! the silence sank,
    Like music on my heart.

Eftsones I heard the dash of oars,
    I heard the pilot's cheer:
My head was turn'd perforce away
    And I saw a boat appear.

Then vanish'd all the lovely lights;
    The bodies rose anew:
With silent pace, each to his place,
    Came back the ghastly crew.
The wind, that shade nor motion made,
    On me alone it blew.

The pilot, and the pilot's boy
    I heard them coming fast:
Dear Lord in Heaven! it was a joy,
    The dead men could not blast.

I saw a third – I heard his voice:
  It is the Hermit good!
He singeth loud his godly hymns
  That he makes in the wood.
He'll shrieve my soul, he'll wash away
  The Albatross's blood.

VII

This Hermit good lives in that wood
  Which slopes down to the Sea.
How loudly his sweet voice he rears!
He loves to talk with Marineres
  That come from a far Contrée.

He kneels at morn and noon and eve –
  He hath a cushion plump:
It is the moss, that wholly hides
  The rotted old Oak-stump.

The Skiff-boat ne'rd: I heard them talk,
  'Why, this is strange, I trow!
'Where are those lights so many and fair
  'That signal made but now?

'Strange, by my faith! the Hermit said –
  'And they answer'd not our cheer.
'The planks look warp'd, and see those sails
  'How thin they are and sere!
'I never saw aught like to them
  'Unless perchance it were

'The skeletons of leaves that lag
  'My forest brook along:
'When the Ivy-tod is heavy with snow,
'And the Owlet whoops to the wolf below
  'That eats the she-wolf's young.

'Dear Lord! it has a fiendish look –
  (The Pilot made reply)
'I am a-fear'd. – 'Push on, push on!
  'Said the Hermit cheerily.

The Boat came closer to the Ship,
  But I ne spake ne stirr'd!
The Boat came close beneath the Ship,
  And strait a sound was heard!

Under the water it rumbled on,
  Still louder and more dread:
It reach'd the Ship, it split the bay;
  The Ship went down like lead.

Stunn'd by that loud and dreadful sound,
   Which sky and ocean smote:
Like one that hath been seven days drown'd
   My body lay afloat:
But, swift as dreams, myself I found
   Within the Pilot's boat.

Upon the whirl, where sank the Ship,
   The boat spun round and round:
And all was still, save that the hill
   Was telling of the sound.

I mov'd my lips: the Pilot shriek'd
   And fell down in a fit.
The Holy Hermit rais'd his eyes
   And pray'd where he did sit.

I took the oars: the Pilot's boy,
   Who now doth crazy go,
Laugh'd loud and long, and all the while
   His eyes went to and fro,
'Ha! ha!' quoth he – 'full plain I see,
   'The devil knows how to row.'

And now all in mine own Countrée
   I stood on the firm land!
The Hermit stepp'd forth from the boat,
   And scarcely he could stand.

'O shrieve me, shrieve me, holy Man!
   The Hermit cross'd his brow –
'Say quick,' quoth he, 'I bid thee say
   'What manner man art thou?

Forthwith this frame of mine was wrench'd
   With a woeful agony,
Which forc'd me to begin my tale
   And then it left me free.

Since then at an uncertain hour,
   Now oftimes and now fewer,
That anguish comes and makes me tell
   My ghastly aventure.

I pass, like night, from land to land;
   I have strange power of speech;
The moment that his face I see
I know the man that must hear me;
   To him my tale I teach.

What loud uproar bursts from that door!
　　The Wedding-guests are there;
But in the Garden-bower the Bride
　　And Bride-maids singing are:
And hark the little Vesper-bell
　　Which biddeth me to prayer.

O Wedding-guest! this soul hath been
　　Alone on a wide wide sea:
So lonely 'twas, that God himself
　　Scarce seemed there to be.

O sweeter than the Marriage-feast,
　　'Tis sweeter far to me
To walk together to the Kirk
　　With a goodly company.

To walk together to the Kirk
　　And all together pray,
While each to his great father bends,
Old men, and babes, and loving friends,
　　And Youths, and Maidens gay.

Farewell, farewell! but this I tell
　　To thee, thou wedding-guest!
He prayeth well who loveth well,
　　Both man and bird and beast.

He prayeth best who loveth best,
　　All things both great and small:
For the dear God, who loveth us,
　　He made and loveth all.

The Marinere, whose eye is bright,
　　Whose beard with age is hoar,
Is gone; and now the wedding-guest
　　Turn'd from the bridegroom's door.

He went, like one that hath been stunn'd
　　And is of sense forlorn:
A sadder and a wiser man
　　He rose the morrow morn.

Bibliography and suggested reading

Items marked with an asterisk are recommended for further reading, as containing particularly worthwhile discussions of all or part of *Lyrical Ballads*.

Abrams, M.H. (1954), 'Wordsworth and Coleridge on Diction and Figures' in *English Institute Essays 1952*, New York.

Abrams, M.H. (1958), *The Mirror and the Lamp*, New York.

Ainsworth, E.G. (1934), 'Another source of the "lonesome road" stanza in the "Ancient Mariner" ', *MLN* XLIX, pp. 111–12.

*Alexander, J.H. (1987), *Reading Wordsworth*, London.

*Armstrong, I. (1978), ' "Tintern Abbey": from Augustan to Romantic' in *Augustan Worlds*, ed. J.C. Hilson *et al.*, Leicester.

*Averill, J.H. (1980), *Wordsworth and the Poetry of Human Suffering*, Ithaca.

*Barrell, J. (1972), *The Idea of Landscape and the Sense of Place 1730–1840*, Cambridge.

Barstow, M.L. (1917), *Wordsworth's Theory of Poetic Diction*, New Haven, Connecticut.

Bartram, W. (1792), *Travels through North and South Carolina, Georgia, East and West Florida . . .*, London.

Bateson, F.W. (1953), 'Rational Irrationality: "She dwelt among the untrodden ways" ', *Northern Miscellany of Literary Criticism* 1, pp. 41–6.

Bauer, N.S. (1978), 'Wordsworth's Poems in Contemporary Periodicals', *Victorian Periodicals Newsletter* XI, pp. 61–76.

Beattie, J. (1776), *Essays. On Poetry and Music . . .*, Edinburgh.

Bement, P. (1982), 'Simon Lee and Ivor Hall: a possible source', *The Wordsworth Circle* XIII, pp. 35–6.

*Benziger, J. (1950), '*Tintern Abbey* revisited', *PMLA* LXV, pp. 154–62.

*Bialostosky, D.H. (1978), 'Coleridge's Interpretation of Wordsworth's Preface to *Lyrical Ballads*', *PMLA* XCIII, pp. 912–24.

*Bialostosky, D.H. (1984), *Making Tales: the poetics of Wordsworth's narrative experiments*, Chicago.

Blackstone, B. (1981), 'A Koranic Echo in *The Ancient Mariner*', *Notes and Queries* XXVIII, p. 313.

Blair, H. (1785), *Lectures on Rhetoric and Belles Lettres*, 2nd edn, London.

*Bloom, H. (1961), *The Visionary Company*, New York.

Bohm, A. (1983), 'Georg Forster's *A Voyage round the World* as a Source for *The Rime of the Ancient Mariner*: a reconsideration', *ELH* L, pp. 363–77.

Brantley, R.E. (1975), *Wordsworth's 'Natural Methodism'*, New Haven, Connecticut.

Brett, R.L. and Jones, A.R. (1963) (ed.), *Lyrical Ballads*, London.

*Brooks, C. (1965), 'Wordsworth and Human Suffering: notes on two early poems' in *From Sensibility to Romanticism*, ed. F.W. Hilles and H. Bloom, New York.

Burgum, E.B. (1940), 'Wordsworth's Reform in Poetic Diction', *College English* II, pp. 207–16.

Burke, E. (1757), *A Philosophical Enquiry into our Ideas of the Sublime and the Beautiful*, London.

Bushnell, J.P. (1981), ' "Where is the lamb for the burnt offering?" Michael's Covenant and Sacrifice', *Wordsworth Circle* XII, pp. 246–52.

Camp, D. (1971), 'Wordsworth's *Lines Composed a few Miles above Tintern Abbey*, 22–4', *Explicator* XXIX, item 57.

Chandler, J.K. (1984), *Wordsworth's Second Nature*, Chicago.

Christie, W. (1983), 'Wordsworth and the Language of Nature', *Wordsworth Circle* XIV, pp. 40–7.

*Clarke, C.C. (1962), *Romantic Paradox*, London.

Coburn, K. (1957) (ed.), *The Notebooks of Samuel Taylor Coleridge, Volume I: 1794–1804*, London.

Cook, A.S. (1926) (ed.), *Addison, Criticisms on Paradise Lost*, New York.

Cottle, J. (1847), *Reminiscences of Samuel Taylor Coleridge and Robert Southey*, London.

Cox, C.B. (1963), 'A Seminar on Wordsworth', *Critical Survey* I, pp. 169–71.